UNDISCIPLINING KNOWLEDGE

Undisciplining Knowledge

Interdisciplinarity in the Twentieth Century

HARVEY J. GRAFF

Johns Hopkins University Press

Baltimore

© 2015 Harvey J. Graff
All rights reserved. Published 2015
Printed in the United States of America on acid-free paper
2   4   6   8   9   7   5   3   1

Johns Hopkins University Press
2715 North Charles Street
Baltimore, Maryland 21218-4363
www.press.jhu.edu

Library of Congress Cataloging-in-Publication Data
Graff, Harvey J.
Undisciplining knowledge : interdisciplinarity in the
twentieth century / Harvey J. Graff.
pages cm
Includes bibliographical references and index.
ISBN 978-1-4214-1745-5 (hardcover : alk. paper) — ISBN 978-1-4214-1746-2
(electronic) — ISBN 1-4214-1745-6 (hardcover : alk. paper) — ISBN 1-4214-1746-4
(electronic)   1. Interdisciplinary approach in education—United States—
History.   2. Education, Higher—Aims and objectives—United
States—History.   3. Universities and colleges—United
States—Departments—History.   I. Title.
LB2361.5.G73 2015
378.00973—dc23   2014041151

A catalog record for this book is available from the British Library.

*Special discounts are available for bulk purchases of this book. For more
information, please contact Special Sales at 410-516-6936 or
specialsales@press.jhu.edu.*

Johns Hopkins University Press uses environmentally friendly book materials,
including recycled text paper that is composed of at least 30 percent post-
consumer waste, whenever possible.

For Michael B. Katz,
teacher, colleague, and friend,
with appreciation for all that he taught me

Unlike its nearest rivals—borderlands, interdepartmental, cooperative, coordinated—"interdisciplinary" has something to please everyone. Its base, *discipline*, is hoary and antiseptic; its prefix, *inter*, is hairy and friendly. Unlike fields with their mud, cows, and corn, the Latinate *discipline* comes encased in stainless steel: it suggests something rigorous, aggressive, hazardous to master. *Inter* hints that knowledge is a warm, mutually developing, consultative thing. The prefix not only has the right feel, but like an unhinged magnet, draws to itself all other inters. And from the twenties on between-ness was where the action was: from interpersonal, intergroup, interreligious, interethnic, interracial, interregional and international relations to intertextuality, things coming together in the state known as inter encapsulated the greatest problems facing society in the twentieth century.

ROBERTA FRANK
" 'Interdisciplinarity': The First Half-Century" (1988)

CONTENTS

As a social and cultural historian, I have pursued interdisciplinary teaching, research, and program development in several different environments. Influenced by the heady atmosphere and strong currents of undergraduate education in the late 1960s and graduate education in the "new history" in the 1970s, I began my academic career in a newly established, nondepartmental, avowedly interdisciplinary public university and subsequently served briefly as director of an interdisciplinary division of behavioral and cultural studies at another public university. I have taught in programs of history, education, arts and humanities, interdisciplinary studies, social sciences, English, literacy and languages, urban and policy studies, and comparative studies.

I am now a historian of literacy in the largest English department in the United States, where I founded and developed LiteracyStudies@OSU as a university-wide interdisciplinary initiative at The Ohio State University. From seemingly formless but not particularly flexible institutional and intellectual environments, I discovered more spaces to build between and among the "silos" of what may well be the United States' most departmentalized public university. By that point, I had developed a much better idea of where to look and how to build. I have written about this process in "LiteracyStudies@OSU as Theory and Practice," in my *Literacy, Myths, Legacies, and Lessons: New Essays on Literacy* (New Brunswick, NJ: Transaction, 2011), 141–78.

More than three decades of teaching and building programs in new universities and, more recently, teaching in a department outside of my own discipline have taught me a great deal. It led me to questions that I am trying to answer both in my university life and in my scholarship. At the same time, I have worked in and helped to develop international scholarly fields in literacy studies; the history of children, adolescents, and families; and urban studies. The interests and stakes are personal, so I do not write at length about these endeavors in this book.

In order to understand the expectations, difficulties, and mixed outcomes of developing interdisciplinary research and programs, I explore the history of interdisciplinary initiatives across the academy. My goal in this book is to write a history of interdisciplinarity that reorients how we think and talk about and build interdisciplinarity, and with it, disciplinary organization in the production, dissemination, and use of knowledge. That is also critical to my work in developing LiteracyStudies@OSU as a university-wide interdisciplinary initiative at Ohio State.

A final prefatory note, needless to say but necessary: I cannot write one book that seeks to pass muster by specialists in a dozen very different fields. Although I have attended closely to and respected the words of specialists and tried to do justice in all cases, faults will inevitably be found. I ask for a fair hearing and judgment of the project as a whole.

For responding to questions about their scholarly organizations, I thank the executive directors and officers of the Social Science History Association, Cognitive Science Society, Materials Research Society, and Cultural Studies Association. I also thank a number of Ohio State University and other colleagues across many fields for answering queries.

For editorial advice, I am grateful to Greg Britton, editorial director of Johns Hopkins University Press; Douglas Mitchell, University of Chicago Press; and Grey Osterud, editor extraordinaire and intellectual advisor. Glenn Perkins proved a fine copyeditor and Becky Hornyak a skilled indexer. At Johns Hopkins University Press, I have benefited from the excellent work of Catherine Goldstead, Juliana McCarthy, Laura Ewen, Hilary S. Jacqmin, Courtney Bond, and others.

At The Ohio State University, I was aided over nearly a decade of research by an outstanding group of graduate assistants. This project benefited not only from their intellectual and physical labor but also from their comments, questions, and requests for clarification about the library work, photocopying, and tabulating that they were asked (and paid) to do. In chronological order, I thank Susan Hanson, Kelly Bradbury, Kate White, Lindsay DiCuirci, Michael Harker, Shawn Casey, Karin Hooks, Heather Thompson-Gillis, Seth Reno, Cate St. Pierre, Julia Voss, Cassie Patterson, Krista Bryson, and Nora McCook. Undergraduate work-study students also assisted with copying and library work. I thank Kate Curry, Richard Kingsly, Lillie Hoy, Windy Hawkins, Gabe Neff, and Lauren McCane.

Many friends and colleagues enriched this book by their interest, their questions, their learning, and their support. I extend my personal thanks to Andy Abbott, Dan Amsterdam, Deborah Brandt, Johanna Drucker, John Duffy, Shirley Brice Heath, Jerry Jacobs, Ira Katznelson, John Martin, Paul Mattingly, M. J. Maynes, Leslie Moch, Jan Reiff, Mike Rose, Myra Strober, Michael Wilson, and Jerry Zaslove. The Social Science History Association, where I met many of them annually, was a special learning and nurturing environment.

I am grateful to my colleagues at OSU, particularly Ed Adelson, Phil Binkley, Alan Farmer, Angus Fletcher, Susan Fisher, Jared Gardner, Bob Holub, Elizabeth Renker, Steve Rissing, Randy Roth, Peter Shane, and Chris Zacher.

At The Ohio State University, the College of Humanities, the College of Arts and Sciences, the Department of English, the Humanities Institute, and

LiteracyStudies@OSU and its Endowment Fund contributed to this project in a variety of ways over the years. I am grateful to Valerie Lee, Richard Dutton, and Mark Shanda for supporting my work. I benefitted from Grants-in-Aid, Special Research Assignments, Faculty Professional Leave, and an Extended Fellowship Subsidy, as well as my appointment as Ohio Eminent Scholar.

Friends and colleagues at Duke University and the University of North Carolina contributed by communicating their interest, offering support, and sharing good meals: Cathy Davidson, John Martin, Konrad Jarausch, and William Sturkey.

Both the National Humanities Center and the Center for Advanced Studies in the Behavioral Sciences generously offered to support the completion of this book. I declined the CASBS fellowship but am honored by their recognition. Most of this book was drafted while I was Birkelund Fellow at the National Humanities Center. In addition to acknowledging the center's financial support, I thank the excellent librarians, supportive staff, and fellow fellows who showed an interest in my work and asked stimulating questions. In ways that I did not anticipate, the environment of the center animated my passion for this project. I thank, in particular, Marie Brubaker, Joel Elliott, Brooke Andrade, Sarah Harris, Jean Houston, and Eliza Robertson.

I am grateful to Raphael Foshay for inviting me to participate in the 2008 symposium on the Scope of Interdisciplinarity at the University of Alberta sponsored by Athabasca University. For that conference, I wrote the first essay that formed part of this project: "Literacy Studies and Interdisciplinary Studies: Reflections on History and Theory," published in *The Valences of Interdisciplinarity: Theory, Practice, Pedagogy*, ed. Raphael Foshay, Cultural Dialectics Series (Edmonton, AB: Alberta University / Athabasca University Press, 2012), 273–307. Other aspects of this project have figured in many different ways in various invited lectures and conference presentation over the years.

Finally, I thank Michael Katz. In ways that neither of us could have known, this book, along with so much of my other scholarship, began in 1970 when he became my graduate supervisor at the University of Toronto.

My superb and supportive physicians, Tom Mauger, Janet Bay, Cynthia Kreger, and Peter Zafirides, keep me going.

At home, I have, and I thank, Al B. Tross, Tekno, and the incomparable Vicki Graff, for whom (once again) there are no appropriate words of gratitude.

UNDISCIPLINING KNOWLEDGE

The Problem of Interdisciplinarity in Theory and Practice over Time

The ubiquity of the term "interdisciplinary" in current academic and educational writing suggests that it is rapidly becoming the dominant form of scholarly work. Major newspapers and periodicals create the same impression, especially in discussing research on current issues ranging from health care to the environment and national security. Commentators disagree about whether this trend is positive or negative. They also disagree about what they mean by "interdisciplinary."[1]

Consider the wording of a spate of announcements from major universities. In 2008, the University of Michigan initiated searches for 25 junior faculty in the interdisciplinary fields of data mining, energy storage, global change, global HIV/AIDS, microbial ecology, and social science and energy, targeting "scholars whose work crosses boundaries and opens new pathways . . . to explore [collaboratively] significant questions or address complex problems."[2] At the same time, the University of Minnesota sought to hire 21 new faculty, plus graduate students and postdocs, "across a broad range of disciplines" in interdisciplinary informatics. Northeastern University advertised for 50 scholars "who aspire to create new areas of scholarship and new disciplines by combining their knowledge and mastery of different fields with others . . . combining fundamental and translational research to solve social problems."[3] Recognizing that interdisciplinary work demands a greater command of methodologies than individual scholars may possess, universities contend that the organization of learning, and of work, depends on and advances collaboration.[4] These statements reveal the discourse of interdisciplinarity, which asserts its transformative power and vital importance. They also suggest implicit tensions between applied research and fundamental problems of knowledge or theory, as well as between existing disciplines and emerging ones.

Ironically, a 2013 study from the Cornell Higher Education Research Institute, based on data from "all people who earned Ph.D.s in 2010," found that "those in the cohorts who did interdisciplinary dissertations" earned "on average

$1,700 less than those who completed dissertations in a single field. . . . The current value system in academia clearly imposes a cost on boundary spanning."[5] Relatedly, interdisciplinary research was reported to be "experiencing growing pains" because of countervailing institutional pressures. Conventional departmental hiring, review, tenure, and promotion practices can slow or block careers; developing new procedures to evaluate the work of interdisciplinary scholars represents a real challenge.[6]

These complications remind us that disciplinary and interdisciplinary work are inextricably linked, regardless of the assumptions of many proponents and opponents of interdisciplinarity.[7] That each usually depends on the other is not often recognized or appreciated. In a discourse sharply divided by dichotomies, some commentators see the recent rise of interdisciplinarity as primarily a reaction against overspecialization and fragmentation in the disciplines. They urge integration and synthesis. Others declare that critical problems demand collaboration among specialists from different fields and disciplines. A more complete appreciation of interdisciplinarity's historical development needs a longer look backward, at least to the late-nineteenth-century origins of modern disciplines in the developing research university and the relationships among them.

Philosopher of science Steve Fuller, a self-proclaimed "ideologue of interdisciplinarity," argues that "disciplines are artificial 'holding patterns' of inquiry whose metaphysical significance should not be overestimated." "Inquiry needs a social space where it can roam freely" and finds its "natural home" in the university. Yet, Fuller cautions, disciplinarity is "a necessary evil of knowledge production . . . and a function of institutionalization." "Universities restructure themselves to face an increasingly competitive market for both training and research services." Under the shadow of "the mindless repetition of old lectures and the artificial extension of exhausted research programs," "the ability to undertake interdisciplinary research is seen as a mark of 'flexibility' and 'adaptiveness,' which are highly valued in today's 'knowledge economy.'"[8] This pretense may be mere window dressing, however. The *Chronicle of Higher Education* repeats a common claim about the institutional uses—or, perhaps, abuses—of interdisciplinarity: "Universities . . . which have few individual disciplines at the top of the research food chain see the interdisciplinary route as a way to diversify and distinguish themselves."[9] Exaggerated and unrealistic expectations abound in the rhetoric, ideology, and political economy of interdisciplinarity. What sociologist Jerry Jacobs calls "interdisciplinary hype," particularly dreams of the financial payoffs from commercialization, patents, and licensing, dazzle with dollars but attract pointed criticism.[10]

"Interdisciplinary research may be hot, but it is hardly new," the *Chronicle* observed in 2002. "From the 1940s through the 1960s, scientists engaged in novel collaborations to make the atomic bomb, isolate the structure of DNA, and discern movement of continents on tectonic plates. That tradition continued into the 1990s with the effort to map the human genome, which linked geneticists and information-technology experts. Today, scientists are interested increasingly in problems so broad and complex that they are unlikely to be solved by researchers trained in one discipline, working alone."[11] This impressive genealogy supports the assumption that change is recent and concentrated in the sciences. "Integration" and "convergence" are the new mantras. But is there a tradition of interdisciplinarity? Can it bear the claims being made for it? Are the current problems being addressed broader and more complex than those in the past?

As studies by Julie Klein have demonstrated, the diversity in the definitions, organization, scope, and scale among interdisciplinary projects demands recognition.[12] Their approaches range from borrowing to problem solving, and ways of thinking about their internal relationships proliferate, from cross- to multi-, pluri-, inter-, trans-, and anti-disciplinary. Variations in the nature and scale of collaboration equally demand recognition. Despite the rhetoric, there is no one form of interdisciplinarity. We must adopt distinct approaches to interdisciplinarity in different fields or disciplinary clusters.

The Paradigm of "Big Science"

The traditional canon of "novel collaborations" centers on unusually grand and sweeping research findings whose consequences far exceed any reasonable expectations for most research, whether interdisciplinary or disciplinary. Significantly, these achievements include both fundamental theoretical advances, such as studies of genetics and the brain, and innovative approaches to major contemporary problems, such as poverty and cancer. To some observers, the coupling of interdisciplinarity with applied research is an advantage, although applied work often occupies a lower place in the hierarchies of research and prestige. Nonetheless, interdisciplinary research underlies a great deal of basic and theoretical work, as the great breakthroughs demonstrate.

Despite the diversity of interdisciplines, "big science" has become a normative model that shapes expectations for and evaluations of interdisciplinarity in nonscientific as well as scientific research.[13] Large-scale, team-driven, experimental science is hegemonic in current thinking about the scale and organization of research. With those expectations for costs go judgments of importance.

General education curricula, integrated media across the arts, digital humanities, or transdisciplinarity pale in comparison. So does the interdisciplinary work of individual scholars and small groups. Efforts to claim the trappings of big science multiply mimetically.[14] Many interdisciplines, including sociology, communications, social relations, and operations research, have at one time or another attempted to pass as sciences. Attesting to the power and lure of science as a cover or badge of identity, this effort has only confused questions about the wider applicability of the standard version and made it harder to identify alternative forms, locations, organization, and expectations. Recent notions of hybridity struggle with this complication.

Describing what I call the standard version of interdisciplinarity, the National Institutes of Health provides a succinct, conflict-free, and romanticized account of a "great transformation" neatly unconstrained by time, place, and historical context. New ways depend on changes in "academic research culture" and proudly, albeit ironically, claim their status as "unconventional" and distinctive. "As opposed to multidisciplinary research, which involves teams of scientists approaching a problem from their own discipline, interdisciplinary research integrates elements of a wide range of disciplines, often including basic research, clinical research, behavioral biology, and social sciences so that all of the scientists approach the problem in a new way. The members of interdisciplinary teams learn from each other to produce new approaches to a problem that would not be possible through any of the single disciplines. Typically, this process begins with team members first learning the language of each other's disciplines, as well as the assumptions, limits, and valid uses of those disciplines' theoretical and experimental approaches."[15] Significantly, this model draws together researchers to address a problem that transgresses the borders of their separate fields but does not rely on the invention of new methodologies.

How well, in fact, does this paradigm fit the most important research breakthroughs? Unusual wartime circumstances propelled the Manhattan Project, which invented the atomic bomb. Should credit be assigned to the roles of leading scientists or to military and civilian organizers? Watson and Crick's collaboration in identifying the structuring of DNA's double helix was relatively informal, as their exclusion of coworker Rosalind Franklin indicates. Close coordination among many laboratories in separate institutions contributed to mapping the human genome. How do we assess the crucial roles of external circumstances, nonscientific influences, institutional elements, leadership, and specific circumstances, as they interacted with intellectual breakthroughs and the marshaling of resources? Certain factors emerge as especially significant, chief among them the location, relationships, and organization of the interdisciplinary effort and its historical context. Preconditions, particularly research pointing the way to the critical moment and the social and political-economic context, matter enormously. These themes are explored in this book.

Alternative Approaches to Interdisciplinarity

Undisciplining Knowledge begins with the understanding that interdisciplinarity is part of the historical making and ongoing reshaping of modern disciplines. It is inseparable from them, not oppositional to them. The organization, production, and dissemination of knowledge around universities, disciplinary departments, and research institutes, especially in the United States and Europe, have long given rise to interdisciplinary efforts and movements. Over time, those endeavors have crossed disciplines and disciplinary clusters in different ways and with differing outcomes. The fields that provide the comparative case studies on which this study builds range from genetic biology and sociology in the late nineteenth and early twentieth centuries to molecular biology, nanotechnology, and cultural studies in the mid-to-late twentieth century.

In my view, interdisciplinarity is defined and constructed by questions and problems of theory or practice, knowledge or conditions of living, and the means developed to answer those questions in new and different ways. Interdisciplines are fashioned from elements of different disciplines to form distinct approaches, understandings, or contexts. Interdisciplines are themselves historical constructs. I emphasize questions and problems, not the number of disciplines that are supposedly "mastered," "integrated," or "transcended" or the claim that normative disciplinary practices are bypassed. While avoiding dichotomies that interfere with our understanding, I recognize key conflicts and underlying contradictions. In the making of interdisciplinarity, disciplinary elements are interactive, not additive. Similarly, interdisciplinarity derives from the selection of appropriate and relevant ideas, approaches, theories, concepts, methods, and comparisons from different fields or disciplines. Those choices, whether successful or not, influence central questions and problems. In no way does interdisciplinarity depend on knowledge of entire disciplines or on global notions of the unity of knowledge. There is no single path to interdisciplinarity, no single model, no single standard for successful development. The process and results vary across disciplines and clusters. Like disciplines, interdisciplines are diverse in paths, locations, relationships to disciplines, organization and institutionalization.

The Culture and Politics of Interdisciplinarity

The cause of interdisciplinarity is simultaneously advanced and retarded by the cultural and political associations of interdisciplinarity. After all, if a novel or rediscovered approach to a major problem in theory or practice draws from more than one basic discipline, it must be beyond the understanding of any one person—or so academe suggests! University and governmental promotion of interdisciplinarity for problem solving draws on and furthers both the attractions of interdisciplinarity and deep suspicions of its soundness. The dynamics of inclusion and exclusion interact, constituting one among the many contradictions that revolve around the ideals and practices of interdisciplinarity. We forget, at our peril, that interdisciplines, like disciplines, are historical constructs shaped by external and internal factors.

Oppositional dichotomies contribute to a sense of distance and disconnection between disciplines and interdisciplines, blurring their connections. How simply and easily do we assume differences between disciplines and interdisciplines rather than relationships and connections! Typically, the discourse and the expectations of interdisciplinarity weigh more heavily on the addition of disciplines than their interactions. Heinz Heckhausen is exceptional in incorporating this point in his definition of interdisciplinarity: "Interaction may range from simple communication of ideas to the mutual integration of organising concepts, methodology, procedures, epistemology, terminology, data, and organisation of research and education in a fairly large field."[16] Still, the sense of difference is usually stronger than that of dynamic relationships. In many hierarchical discursive constructions, interdisciplinarity marks an "end" to discipline rather than a view of relationships and interdisciplines as part of the disciplinary process itself. Here conceptualization and epistemology meet, and claims about the significance and contemporary relevance of interdisciplinary studies conflict with those of "pure" research.[17]

The emphasis on interdisciplinarity is often linked to contemporary concerns and to pressures and threats in the "real world." "Convergence" across life sciences, physical science, and engineering exemplifies this orientation.[18] Concerted responses to crucial matters of the moment, such as health and the environment, are central to interdisciplinarity designs, cooperation, and collaboration. These initiatives may serve as models for others or, in different eyes, represent the inferiority of applied as opposed to "pure" research. Forging interdisciplinary groups to save the world may seem hyperbolic, but it is sincere and often beneficial. The commercial potential of fields such as molecular biology, nanotechnology, or communication carries both intellectual and ethical complications.

Robert Frodeman, editor of the 2010 *Oxford Handbook of Interdisciplinarity*, reminds us of the "real world" emphases in recent initiatives. The problem, as he sees it, is that "disciplinary knowledge has tacitly functioned as an abdication. By focusing on standards of excellence internal to a discipline academics have been able to avoid larger responsibilities of how knowledge contributes to the creation of a good and just society."[19] This comment is more ideological than substantive, for it oversimplifies the positions of scholars across disciplines and clusters of disciplines in an effort to justify certain forms of cross-disciplinary and multidisciplinary work. The relationships between and among disciplines that are developed in the pursuit of approaches to specific problems of research, as well as their historical contexts, are slighted in rhetorical formulations that are often far from the conduct and results of research.[20]

Uses and Abuses

Given its associations with supposedly new and unconventional studies and its interest in revision and improvement, an alliance between interdisciplinarity and liberal or left politics is presumed by those who defend disciplines. This is often but not always the case. Revealing further contradictions, in recent years new conflicts have emerged. Contrasting disciplinary doctoral programs with interdisciplinary or transdisciplinary programs, sociologist Stanley Aronowitz articulates connections and counter trends. "As academic jobs have dried up in nearly all domains, since the late 1980s the pressure on faculty to forfeit or otherwise jettison experiments in transdisciplinary or interdisciplinary masters' and Ph.D. programs has become intense. As a result the student hoping to use graduate school . . . to explore intellectual options freely finds departments becoming more protective of their turf and their disciplinary boundaries and hardening into academic fortresses. . . . Graduate education today is once again the site of the learner's socialization and acculturation to conventional professional roles, even as the nature of higher education veers away from conventions, if not always for the better."[21]

That view is rejected by other critical voices on the left. In an exposé of the uses of interdisciplinarity in the transformation of universities and their institutional complicity in the growing dominance of neoliberalism, cultural studies professor Bill Readings writes, "One form of such market expansion is the development of interdisciplinary programs, which often appear as the point around which radicals and conservatives can make common cause."

> This is partly because interdisciplinarity has no inherent political orientation. . . . It is also because the increased flexibility they offer is often attractive to administrators as a way of overcoming entrenched practices of demarcation, ancient privileges, and fiefdoms in the structure of universities. The benefits of interdisciplinary openness are numerous . . . but they should not blind us to the institutional stakes that they involve. At present interdisciplinary programs tend to supplement existing disciplines; the time is not far off when they will be installed in order to replace clusters of disciplines. Indeed, this is a reason to be cautious in approaching the institutional claim to interdisciplinarity staked by Cultural Studies when it replaces the old order of disciplines in the humanities with a more general field that combines history, art history, literature, media studies, sociology, and so on.[22]

The growth in interdisciplinary studies programs and the great expansion of research centers claiming to be multi- or interdisciplinary pose a major dilemma for practitioners, promoters, and students.

Recent research identifies rising levels of interest and discussion on local, national, and sometimes international levels: financial support from federal agencies, foundations, institutional initiatives and seed money; hiring initiatives; and undergraduate and graduate program development. Jerry Jacobs and Scott Frickel found 2,366 centers at the 25 leading research universities. Some initiatives are bottom-up, beginning with faculty and students; others are top-down, from administrators and external sponsors. Academic writing about interdisciplinarity has grown steadily to 300–400 articles a year. There is much discussion of reducing barriers and creating incentives.[23]

But the uses—or, depending on the commentator's viewpoint, abuses—of interdisciplinarity are contradictory intellectually, politically, and economically. According to Steven Brint, "To a considerable degree, this remarkable interest in interdisciplinary work reflects a sense that the intellectual excitement lies at the boundaries of fields, rather than in the development of existing disciplinary specialties. . . . But budgetary exigencies may ultimately figure at least as prominently in the thinking of university administrators. . . . Interdisciplinarity may only make the case that humanities faculty are all interchangeable and hence that many are expendable. Interdisciplinarity has tended to weaken the argument for coverage . . . and might thereby facilitate downsizing."[24]

At the same time, interdisciplinarity itself has been the target of serious intellectual and even philosophical criticism. Jacobs has voiced profound skepticism about the theory, need for, and practice of interdisciplinarity. He and Frickel refer to the "relative absence of epistemic clarity" and warn about potential harm to the disciplines, including their further fragmentation. Other criticism comes from promoters of transdisciplinarity and hybridity. Critics of interdisciplinarity express concern about inadequate or absent evaluation of research. Some criticisms focus on the influence of factors external to universities and issues of objectivity and neutrality, while others question the extent of applied research and professional programs. Jacobs and Frickel conclude: "We do not believe that the case has been fully made, theoretically or empirically, for the general superiority of interdisciplinary over disciplinary knowledge."[25]

Regardless of the hopes and prayers of some inter- and transdisciplinary believers, the disciplines are not about to wither away. Studies regularly document their relative dominance and stability, sometimes to researchers' relief and sometimes to their chagrin. Andrew Abbott observes: "The established disciplines are not as static or as isolated as advocates of interdisciplinarity sometimes suggest. . . . Established academic disciplines remain dynamic centers of knowledge production that are open to external developments even while insisting on internal standards."[26] Underscoring the long history and stability of interdisciplinarity, as well as disciplinarity through the twentieth century, he emphasizes the role of academic labor markets and other institutional factors. Craig Calhoun agrees: "A crucial dimension of all this is the development of highly distinct academic disciplines. This is not just—or perhaps even crucially— a matter of intellectual distinctions. It is a matter of power and turf control."[27] This nightmarish scenario disturbs interdisciplinarity's proponents.

Just as the development and conceptions of interdisciplinarity are divided by conflicts and contradictions, so too is its present status. Muddying the situation further are conflicts and competition between new areas of undergraduate studies and more traditional majors in disciplinary departments, as well as tensions between research and teaching and between graduate versus undergraduate education. Fears of interdisciplinarity also play a role. Rather than challenging the myths of interdisciplinarity, such as its novelty or autonomy, these currents tend to reinforce them. The 2010 *Oxford Handbook of Interdisciplinarity* articulates the same mixed messages as Jacobs and Frickel's skeptical 2009 review.[28]

These are among the reasons why interdisciplinarity, especially in the abstract, generates such strong and conflicting responses and can be taken as reflecting the promise of a better future or a path destined to fail. Although the choices are sometimes expressed in that way, the pursuit of academic research and teaching is not a zero-sum game, but these challenging circumstances give rise to anxiety, ambivalence, conflict, and contradiction.

Explaining Interdisciplinarity

Efforts to explain interdisciplinarity exhibit problems of conflict and contradiction. The formulation of major explanations tends to reinforce myths of interdisciplinarity. From boundary making and maintenance to conflict, specialization, and unity, the list of explanations exemplifies this confusion, which is inseparable from the myths and dichotomies of interdisciplinarity.

The prevailing explanations reflect not only their influence on each other but also the influence of major myths of interdisciplinarity. At the same time, they clearly indicate the strong influence—dare we say bias?—of a smaller number of scholarly areas: science studies, especially the philosophy and sociology of science; organizational theories principally from sociology; labor market and more general market considerations; boundaries and regulation in sociology and economics. Not surprisingly, they follow academic fashions, and their limits, from boundary maintenance to social movements, competition, discourse, functionality, labor markets, power relations, and specialization. They are short on history and on social and political contexts. In various combinations and with different degrees of forcefulness, a relatively small subset of a larger list of factors dominates. While not searching for single-factor explanations, researchers aim to isolate a relatively few overriding factors. Ironically, disciplinary approaches appear to dominate efforts to understand interdisciplinarity, limiting our understanding. The relatively traditional set of issues also detracts from exploring complexity, similarities and differences among interdisciplines, interactions among disciplines and interdisciplines, and connections among internal and external elements.[29]

Jacobs and Frickel support approaches that probe the historical contingency of both interdisciplines and disciplines; the cultural production of knowledge; rhetoric and ideology; and social and political movements, including the commitments of researchers. But they point out the lack of studies that take historical context into account:

> Interdisciplines are shaped by social forces beyond disciplinary labor markets. . . .
> Research suggest[s] that the movements for civil rights, women's equality, and
> environmental protection contributed to student demand for programs. . . .
> Institutional instability . . . can provide conditions for the emergence of inter-
> disciplinary SIMs [scientific/intellectual movements]. Although the concentration

of new interdisciplinary fields in the 1970s in the social sciences and the humanities is related to that decade's signature social movements, the creation of area studies programs in previous decades is more likely an outcome of national security interests, whereas interdiscipline formation in the 1980s and 1990s in the life sciences was likely spurred by instabilities created by technological innovation and changes in the legal structures governing proprietary knowledge. . . . Researchers have yet to study in any detail the rise of interdisciplines comparatively or over broad historical periods.[30]

Moreover, studies of interdisciplinarity often reveal expectations of similarity among interdisciplines, which is yet another myth. Those assumptions tend to interfere with much-needed comparisons of interdisciplines from different disciplinary clusters, institutions, times, and places. They lead to incomplete examinations lacking in sufficient evidence to test their major hypotheses in meaningful contexts. Missing are case studies and comparative studies of interdisciplines that explore intellectual dimensions, internal and external elements, and patterns of similarity and difference: variability, complexity, comparison, contextual, and history. This book turns to the history of interdisciplinarity in order to probe these questions in new and different ways, focusing on history, comparison, and the location, relationships, and organization of interdisciplines.

Linking Disciplines with Interdisciplines

Interdisciplinarity can be better understood when it is situated within a longer chronological span of intellectual and sociocultural development and examined with a broader, more dynamic focus on its place among a wide array of disciplines and institutional locations. As Julie Stone Peters remarks, "interdisciplinarity . . . tended to exaggerate disciplinarity, caricaturing disciplinary difference through each discipline's longing for something it imagined the other to possess," and in the process it "exaggerated the very disciplinary boundaries it sought to dissolve."[31] Social, cultural, political, and economic factors and developments presumed to be external to the normal workings of a discipline or field, such as wartime needs, consequences of global cross-cultural contacts and colonialism, discovery of new social problems, economic downturns, and health or ecological fears, combine with shifting currents within and across disciplines. They may stimulate changing views that, in the context of universities and their organization of knowledge, lead to criticism, different assertions, and sometimes institutional articulations both within and outside the boundaries of departments or divisions that take the name of interdisciplinarity.

Abbott neatly captures this dynamic:

> Bodies of academic work are perpetually being redefined, reshaped and recast by the activities of disciplines trying to take work from one another or to dominate one another. These . . . intellectual moves of interdisciplinary deconstruction and reconstruction are the tactical engagements of interdisciplinary conflict. Indeed, new areas emerge not only through conflict, but also from the processes or fractal combination and recombination . . . that are in the first instance internal to disciplines. . . . It is common for new groups to emerge at disciplinary margins, as for example did biochemistry. In other cases, bordering disciplines stably coexist, physical chemistry and chemical physics being an example. Often this leads to effective merger.[32]

On the one hand, how we construe *both* disciplines and interdisciplines actively, relationally, and historically has implications for how we pursue knowledge and teaching. On the other hand, interdisciplinary development results in different locations—within a department or disciplinary cluster, or in a separate and distinct location—with differing relationships to related departments.

Abbott argues that "interdisciplinarism has generally been problem driven, and problems . . . have their own life cycle. There is ample evidence that problem-oriented empirical work does not create enduring, self-reproducing communities like disciplines, except in areas with stable and strongly institutionalized external clienteles like criminology." He points toward one perspective on paths toward interdisciplinarity. Others exist and demand identification. The field of play is potentially broad. Some interdisciplines are likely to be shorter-lived, not "enduring, self-reproducing communities."[33] That might be a very useful, potentially liberating path.

Likening interdisciplines to disciplines and to each other in search of similarities, our common, even reflexive, practice may mislead more than clarify. Interdisciplinary developments follow different paths toward a variety of institutional, intellectual, and societal ends, along timelines and lifetimes. They may prove influential without attaining the niche and continuity of disciplines. That is one of their strengths whose understanding may carry benefits.

Most stories of interdisciplinarity follow an accepted narrative of the development of fields of knowledge tied to the modern research university and the modern liberal arts college. Their trope is progressive; their ideals and models are scientific (or at least systematic), advanced, specialized, and sometimes synthetic. The humanities, human and social sciences, management, organization, and professional studies are accorded a lesser place. The lure of science leads to imitating that object of desire, though sometimes to marching in what is presumed to be an opposite direction. The narrative is linear, almost teleological in its expectations that in selected areas of study, when circumstances make it possible, recognizable interdisciplinarity evolves from earlier disciplinary developments and their perceived limitations in theory, practice, or data. Those circumstances include factors both internal and external to the field and universities, perceptions of research needs, resources, leadership, and sponsors, combined with a sense of the romance of discovery and brilliance of leading researchers who draw from two or more disciplines. The distinctive interdisciplines that develop represent an end to the process of disciplinary formation chronologically, conceptually, and discursively.

In the accepted view, the making of interdisciplines is more or less standard from one field to the next, especially in the sciences and often in the social sciences and technical fields. Expectations about the process shape judgments about an interdiscipline's success or failure, as does its location among disciplines and disciplinary clusters. Successful development leads to at least partial independence through research recognition and an institutional location separate from and beyond disciplines.

Focusing on World War II and the past few decades, principally in the sciences and technological fields, the standard version resembles a morality play between interdisciplinarity's proponents and critics, both of whom exaggerate the dangers if their views are not followed. There is one true interdisciplinarity. Failure to appreciate diversity, multiple paths, and different or mixed forms of success across interdisciplines stimulates endless dickering over multi-, pluri-, inter-, trans-disciplinarity, even anti- or a-disciplinarity and poses such derisive questions as "how many disciplines does it take to . . . ?" Oppositions and dichotomies stand in for critical definitions and in-depth, comparative research.

In this book I revise the standard version. The stirring story told in biology, medicine, or physics is an incomplete, misleading guide to interdisciplinarity. Beginning with the World War II era and science and technology, the standard version shortens the historical timespan of interdisciplinarity. It also reduces the means by which we may identify and understand the varied processes of interdisciplinary development. Broadening the scope chronologically, conceptually, and interpretively, this study ranges widely across the disciplines that constitute the modern university. As interdisciplinarity is historicized, disciplines and disciplinary clusters, their relationships, and their university bases are recognized as active elements.

When the sciences and fields such as cognitive studies and operations research are taken to be paradigmatic, efforts in the humanities, human sciences, and communication are sidelined or entirely overlooked. All interdisciplinary efforts reflect external factors, but those may be more diffuse outside the sciences and social sciences. Among the sciences, identification and institutionalization more often, but not always, lead to separate location and degree of independence. Centers, institutes, committees, schools, new departments, and joint sponsorship or locations are among the forms of organization and locations. That is not the only sign of success. Other indicators include identification and recognition, sponsors and funding, professional organization, communications, and reorganization of disciplines and disciplinary clusters.

In contrast with other tellings of interdisciplinary tales, this book reorients approaches to and understandings of interdisciplinarity. The primary moves are historical, contextual, and comparative; the trajectory nonlinear; the metaphors neither rising nor falling teleologically. In practice this means an expanded chronology of interdisciplinarity; attention to the varied roles that disciplines play, constructively and otherwise, in the development of interdisciplines (including cases of unsuccessful and partly successful development), including conception, incubation, and boundary maintenance; and recognition that beginnings of development are often crucial. In addition, I devote new attention to fundamental differences between interdisciplinarity, disciplinarity, and disciplinary clusters in the sciences, social sciences, and humanities. Differences in definitions, discourse, institutional locations, disciplinary relationships, sponsors and resources, traditions, and expectations combine in the formation of distinct patterns, scope and scale, and organization. Failure to recognize differences and similarities not only creates confusion and limits comparison but also neglects history. Comparisons need to be both diachronic and synchronic. Historicizing interdisciplinarity and its study helps to guard against the power of myth, dichotomy, and contradiction.

An exploration of interdisciplinarity's roles in changing universities and disciplines, this book is also a comparative study in the shifting organization of knowledge and its creation, production, circulation, and uses. Interdisciplinarity is neither a dream nor a nightmare; a romantic, nostalgic golden age of integrated, unified knowledge did not exist before the triumph of modern disciplines; there was no golden age of interdisciplinarity before the late nineteenth century.

What are the similarities and differences of interdisciplinarity across the disciplines and disciplinary clusters? What are the limits of interdisciplinarity? When and why does interdisciplinarity develop? What kinds of institutions promote or limit interdisciplinarity? What does it mean to develop from disciplinary to interdisciplinary? What are the internal and external understandings and myths associated with them? How important are external factors, such as war, economic decline, and health and environmental questions. Surveying many interdisciplines over many decades certain great themes stand out: life/collective/individual; security/national/personal; and democracy/advancement. How are success and failure defined and determined? How are differences understood and explained?

Case Studies and Methods

Undisciplining Knowledge's conceptualization, methodology, and narratives build on comparative case studies set in institutional and historical contexts. Considering genetic biology and sociology; humanities and communication; social relations and operations research; cognitive studies and "new" histories; materials science and cultural studies; and molecular biology and literacy studies, these case studies reflect diverse experiences across the major disciplinary clusters of the sciences, social sciences, humanities, management and organization, and engineering. They span the critical period from the late nineteenth century to the early twenty-first century, the life and times of the modern research university and the organization and production of knowledge of which it is a central part.

The chapters are ordered chronologically. Specific efforts to develop interdisciplinarily encountered different institutional, disciplinary, and external opportunities or constraints. Each chapter considers two more or less contemporaneous interdisciplinary initiatives whose origins lay in different disciplines or disciplinary clusters. The stories of each attempt, and comparisons among them, contribute to a larger, more diverse, and more complicated understanding of interdisciplinarity. Taken together, these fields represent distinct historical contexts; disciplinary clusters; states of both university and disciplinary development; opportunities and constraints; internal and external structures and influences; expectations and assumptions; and standards, outcomes, and patterns of success. They facilitate, in fact promote, historical and comparative investigation and understanding.

The discriminating factors in these comparisons include changing times and institutional contexts, the locations and configurations of interdisciplines within universities and disciplinary clusters, the relationships of interdisciplines to disciplines and disciplinary clusters organizationally and intellectually, and the organization of interdisciplinary research units. My conceptualization emphasizes three intersecting spheres: (1) interdisciplines in formation and operation, including individuals, ideas, and influences; (2) organizational and institutional contexts, including disciplines and departments, universities, research institutes, professional organizations, and sponsorship; and (3) wider social, cultural, and political economic influences and contexts. In all cases, I consider both internal and external elements. I also test previous explanations that emphasize structure and process, function, specialization, collective movements, boundary making and maintenance, markets, status, and conflict. The case studies include experiences of both relative success and failure.

All interdisciplinary efforts reflect external factors, but their influence may be more diffuse outside the sciences and social sciences. Among the sciences, identification and institutionalization more often, but not always, lead to at least partly separate location, apparent degree of autonomy, and aspects of collective research endeavor. The case studies made it clear that those dimensions are not the only signs or measures of success or limits. Other indicators include identification and recognition, leadership, sponsors and funding, connections outside disciplines of origin, professional organization and activity (regular meetings, journals, etc.), a critical mass of researchers and students, communications, and reorganization of disciplines and disciplinary clusters in terms of locations, relationships, and organization. Successfully or not, interdisciplines take different paths toward interdisciplinarity.

This study attends to and compares patterns of success, partial or limited success, and failure in various efforts to found and develop interdisciplines. This judgment is interpretive, not objective; it stands as a relative rather than an absolute conclusion. My efforts to move beyond the blinders of the science-dominated standard version and the contra-cases it has stimulated and to consider relationships between interdisciplines and disciplines lead to certain judgments that readers may not share but that are worthy of consideration even by those who dissent from them.

The narrative begins with the place of *genetic biology*—representations of life and its formative elements—in the construction of experimental science in the modern university, in contrast with *sociology*'s lineage and transformation in the institutionalization of the social sciences. In the process of professionalization and institutionalization, biology assimilated earlier disciplinary dimensions into a new interdisciplinary discipline. In contrast, as it took on the attributes of a discipline, sociology lost its potential to be an interdiscipline.

The early decades of the twentieth century saw the struggles of the newly reconstructed *humanities*—both as one field of study and as distinct disciplines, as integrative and specialized—for a central place among institutionalizing and modernizing intellectual and organizational pursuits. That process includes elevating culture, maintaining a common core of values and knowledge, and advancing democracy in the western world and beyond it. It also represents the humanities' search for an appropriate place in modern universities with a shifting international presence. By and large, inter- or multidisciplinary synthesis and integration failed, leaving a newly traditional liberal arts or general education curriculum, on the one hand, and separate departments of languages, literature, philosophy, the fine arts, and history, on the other hand.

Between the world wars, fears about the state and fate of democracy, the stresses of modern life, and need for communication and social organization also contributed to the formation and divergent histories of *communication* and *social relations*. Communication's supposedly foreign and theoretical origins, quest to be a science, entanglement with the new mass media of the early to mid-twentieth century, and close association with the new consumer and advertising industries limited its acceptance by the academy as either a discipline or an interdiscipline. While sometimes blurred, the lines between advancing consumer capitalism and its culture and advancing democracy socially, as well as politically, conflicted with and contradicted each other. Social relations, also seen as somewhat alien, highly abstract, and theoretical, proposed to reintegrate and synthesize the social sciences for a changing world. It sought to improve the quality of life, social and individual integration, advancement, and authority on the basis of a science of society. Yet despite the disciplinary and interdisciplinary issues it pressed, it failed to attract great professional institutional interest.

With World War II also came a new synthesis and basis for action in *operations research* (OR), another "science" of the future. Fresh from its wartime triumphs of organization and coordination, operations research joins a new search for unification, order, and control for progress, theory, and practice for war and peace. Within the limits of organization and management studies, OR is a model interdiscipline. In other spheres, its parts are known better than the whole, and it sits on the margins.

Another new science of the mind in society, *cognitive science* (for some, cognitive studies), in various forms from psychology to behavioral science and

organizational science to cybernetics and neuroscience, changed the landscape of knowledge. More than most interdisciplines, cognitive studies is distinguished by its many academic homes and attachments: a sign of both its potential
and its limits. Its quest to become an interdisciplinary discipline across disciplinary clusters conflicts with opportunities to develop and become established
as an interdiscipline.

A very different interdiscipline, the many *new histories* of the mid-twentieth
century, shares cognitive studies' concern with linking mind and mentality,
social theory, and new methods, often quantitative, to explain past behavior. They
include, for example, new social, political, economic, cultural, racial, ethnic, and
gender histories. Developing on the borders of the humanities and the social
sciences, new histories rarely found homes of their own, with partial exceptions
such as economic history. The hyphenated fields of racial, ethnic, and gender
studies raise still more questions. In some formulations, the new histories aimed
at the status of science. Most practitioners sought a novel synthesis of social sciences and humanities, with the goal of changing both. Sometimes they were
partly successful. Within the traditional domain of history, considerable interdisciplinarity, along with definite limits, was possible. Yet the threat to the discipline posed by these challenges stirred formidable opposition, which often
isolated these developments from "mainstream" history.

The narrative returns to a differently constituted and located *materials science*, including nanotechnology, in the second half of the twentieth century.
Deemed "revolutionary," new interdisciplinary sciences are a novel synthesis of
other traditions and disciplines within the natural sciences and engineering
with new theories, methods, and technologies. Materials science sits rather un-
comfortably between engineering and the natural sciences. Like bioscience or
molecular biology, of the double helix, the marketplace, and beyond, it has the
power to change, at least in part, the image of science in the university and society. In their unprecedented commercial possibilities, each represents both a triumph and a threat. Each negotiates its interdisciplinary location in relationship
to biology, other experimental sciences, and engineering. At least as important,
each has led to new levels of successful relationships to the realms of commercial production, marketing, and sales. They have also led to serious questions
about the effect on academic research and universities.

Earlier threads of the social sciences and the humanities, combined with
new interests, concerns, theories, and methods, returned with the advent of
cultural studies and *literacy studies*. Each of these interdisciplinary efforts represents a critical response, sometimes a rejection of dominant currents. This

includes the methods, theories, and claims made for a foundation, at least in part, in empirical science, and in critical theories, which are important to so much interdisciplinarity in the twentieth century. Both cultural studies and literacy studies struggle for homes of their own. They often fare better as interdisciplinary dimensions of other fields and disciplines than in their own right. Both intellectually and organizationally, their success is incomplete.

CHAPTER ONE

Sciences of Life and Society in the Making of the Research University

Genetic Biology and Sociology, 1890s–1920s

We begin when there were neither disciplines nor interdisciplines. These were constructed along with the modern research university, which is built on disciplinary departments and organized into colleges and schools comprising disciplines and fields that are formally organized in relation to one another. Disciplines and interdisciplines were created alongside each other. Despite the nostalgic or utopian appeal of an intellectual world before disciplinary divisions and an ahistorical narrative, chronology and context count. In both theory and practice, history matters. Origins are formative. They are central to the story of modern universities and the organization and uses of knowledge.

Consider these accounts of the founding of biology and sociology. Historian of science Garland Allen writes in his history of the life sciences:

> The giants of post-Darwinian biology, Ernst Haeckel and August Weismann, had dreamed of a unified approach to the study of life in which all biological phenomena would be seen as intricately related. . . . Their dream was premature, the only unified approach that Haeckel and Weismann could offer was based almost wholly on speculation. By the 1920s, however, that dream was more of a reality. . . . The convergence of disciplines witnessed in the 1920s and 1930s occurred primarily within two large areas. On the one hand, embryology, biochemistry, cytology, and genetics began to come together to form a unified, cellularly and physiologically oriented view of development. On the other, biometrics, Darwinian evolution, field natural history, and classical Mendelian genetics converged to provide a rigorous, quantitative, and, for the first time, logically consistent theory of the origin of species. . . . In the convergence of this later period, genetics, evolution, and embryonic developments began to remerge in a new, and less speculative theory of the living system.[1]

Compare this argument with intellectual historian Dorothy Ross's analysis of the process that led to the emergence of sociology. "For American social scientists, the problem of the interwar years was not the weakness of disciplinary structures but their strength. Disciplinary form and scientific aspiration created an expectation of disciplinary unity, but in terms of theory, internal practice, and public voice, the disciplines were fractured. At the same time, they divided the human/social subject into separate and often incompatible pieces. If sociologists in the United States had firmer authority over the 'social' than did their European counterparts, they gained it by abandoning large areas of the economic, political, and cultural world that might well have been within their purview."[2] In these narratives about the founding and early development of genetic biology and sociology, science is increasingly accepted as the most appropriate basis for judgments and as a model for emulation. These fields gain recognition, support, and institutionalization; specialization follows.

Despite their similar early histories, the development of biology and sociology followed distinct courses. Biology claimed to be *the* science of life. As it moved from the field into the laboratory, it sought to unify the many fields that it encompassed. A new discipline emerged from many disciplines, although separate departments of botany and zoology continued to exist. Different domains competed for dominance, scientifically, interpretively, organizationally, and professionally. Overall, the formation of biology can be understood as an interdisciplinary integration of preexisting fields. For its part, sociology sought recognition as *the* science of society. It had to shed the associations with social reform and political radicalism that marked many of its European (and some of its American) practitioners in order to gain academic legitimacy and philanthropic sponsorship. Although it sought the status of a science, its claims for unifying that endeavor were weaker, its science less persuasive, its appeal less imperative and less widespread. In fact, its acceptance as an organized academic discipline and the professionalization of its practitioners narrowed its scope and weakened its potential for interdisciplinarity. It also faced greater challenges from other emerging social sciences than biology did from comparable scientific fields, such as mathematics, physics, and chemistry.

Biology appeared under many disciplinary names, not only botany and zoology but also physiology, cytology, histology, systematics, plant physiology, entomology, and morphology. It gradually collected its many subfields under a single umbrella; at many universities, departments of botany and zoology persisted well into the 1920s.[3] Although this process was never entirely complete or linear, biology eventually prevailed. In comparison, there were many fewer sociology departments in the early decades of the twentieth century, as well as fewer sociologists in all departments. The number of subfields in the social sciences was also significantly fewer than in biology. Biology exhibited a greater connection

TABLE 1.1
Biology and sociology subfields, 1928

Biological sciences (biology, botany, and zoology): general and cellular physiology, general histology, cytology, physiology and pathology of plants, paleontology, comparative anatomy, entomology, limnology, cryptogamic botany, plant morphology, genetics, animal genetics, plant genetics, economic entomology, economic botany, plant physiology, dendrology, applied plant anatomy, systematic botany

Sociology: child welfare, community problems, criminology, delinquency, educational sociology, ethnology, family, penology, racial psychology, rural sociology, social ethics, social hygiene, social institutions, social pathology, social psychology, social statistics, social technology, social theory, surveys, urban sociology

TABLE 1.2
Department rankings of graduate programs, 1924

Botany: Chicago, Columbia, Harvard, Cornell, Wisconsin, Michigan, Johns Hopkins, Minnesota, Illinois, California, Ohio State, Stanford, Pennsylvania, Yale, Missouri, Nebraska

Zoology: Columbia, Chicago, Harvard, Yale, Johns Hopkins, Princeton, Illinois, Michigan, Wisconsin, California, Cornell, Stanford, Bryn Mawr, Ohio State, Missouri, Minnesota, Indiana, Texas

Sociology: Chicago, Columbia, Wisconsin, Michigan, Harvard, Missouri, Pennsylvania, North Carolina, Yale, Illinois, Ohio State, Cornell, Bryn Mawr

Source: R. M. Hughes, president of Miami University, Ohio, American Council on Education, *American Universities and Colleges*, ed. David Allan Robertson (New York: Charles Scribner's Sons, 1928), 161.
Note: Weighted rankings are from Miami faculty

between the parts and the whole, though that assertion risks exaggeration. As it institutionalized, biology replicated and emphasized distinctions among professional scientific, agricultural and animal, medical, and more popular domains, and those divisions have continued under many names (tables 1.1–1.3). At the same time, amateur and popular sociology had a less visible and weighty presence than biology or natural history.[4] While biology was practiced in departments with various names, sociology was sometimes based in economics, combined with anthropology, or subsumed by social work, criminology and penology, psychology, education, and other fields, rather than located in an autonomous disciplinary department.[5]

These university-based disciplines were founded at a time of great interest in and hope for science in Europe and the United States. Aspiring disciplines and interdisciplines from many areas of knowledge proclaimed their place among the sciences. Models came from Europe, Germany especially (but not exclusively), and from American universities as well. Many disciplines in the social and the natural sciences looked for recognition and support. Some fields found greater

TABLE 1.3A
Faculty in biology and sociology at three U.S. universities, 1910–1936

	N	P	I	N	P	I	N	P	I
Pennsylvania	1910			1920			1927		
Botany	8	3	2	17	7	6	29	9	3
Histology & Embryology	3	1	1	—	—	—	—	—	—
Zoology	11	2	4	20	6	6	24	6	5
Sociology	2	1	0	5	2	2	11	5	2
Johns Hopkins	1909–10			1919–20			1929–30		
Biology	1	0	—	0	0	—	12	4	—
Botany-Plant Science	3	2	—	2	2	—	2	2	—
Zoology	7	3	—	5	4	—	11	7	—
Medicine	101	77	—	166	69	—	300	116	—
Harvard College	1911–12			1918–19			1922–23		
Anatomy-Physiology	5	—	—	4	—	—	—	—	—
Botany	8	—	—	6	—	—	6	—	—
Horticulture-Forest	4	—	—	—	—	—	—	—	—
Zoology	4	—	—	4	—	—	5	—	—
All faculty	169	—	—	173	—	—	176	—	—

Sources: University catalogs, university registers, and annual reports, 1910–1936.
Note: N = total faculty; P = professors; I = instructors; — = not available.

success than others, generating distinctions among the clinical, theoretical, and experimental sciences, the social sciences, the arts and humanities, and the professions.[6]

Understanding the evolution of biology and sociology requires us to trace their passage from the ranks of amateurs to educationally certified and organized professionals; from a variety of informal and formal associations to universities and national professional organizations; from relative informality to institutionalization within formal structures; from collection, observation, and description to analytics and formal methods. We must also examine their struggles for the mantle of science and their explicit concerns over issues of precedence, priority, unity, and boundaries. Both their locations within universities and their relationships with other disciplines are important, as are consensus and contention about their boundaries, baselines and timelines, historical standing, and prominence. Historian of science David Allen calls this form of professionalization "academicization."[7]

Biology and sociology took their places as part of disciplinary clusters: genetic biology among the natural or experimental sciences in the grouping known as life sciences, sociology among the fields that took on the more ambiguous

TABLE 1.3B
Faculty in biology and sociology at ten U.S. universities and colleges,
1928, 1932, 1936

	1928		1932		1936	
	N	P	N	P	N	P
Chicago						
Bacteriology-Hygiene	5	1	7	4	5	2
Biochemistry	—	—	—	—	7	1
Botany	9	3	10	7	6	5
Sociology	6	2	7	5	8	6
Johns Hopkins						
Botany	1	1	1	1	—	—
Plant Physiology	1	1	1	1	1	1
Columbia						
Bacteriology	5	1	8	2	6	1
Biochemistry	2	1	9	2	12	2
Botany	5	5	7	3	7	3
Plant Physiology	1	1	—	—	—	—
Physiology	5	2	8	2	6	2
Zoology	13	9	15	10	13	9
Social Science	7	4	8	5	9	4
Wisconsin						
Bacteriology	6	3	10	6	6	3
Botany	3	1	7	3	9	4
Physiology	7	3	11	4	17	5
Social Science	16	6	24	14	43	20
Princeton						
Biology	6	5	11	6	10	4
Economics & Social Institutions	9	7	13	6	15	6
Michigan						
Physiology	—	—	—	—	4	1
Sociology	5	1	—	—	—	—
Berkeley						
Bacteriology-Hygiene	2	1	4	1	2	0
Biochemistry	—	—	4	1	—	—
Botany	6	2	6	3	5	2
Physiology	3	1	6	2	—	—
Experimental Biology	—	—	—	—	2	1
Social Institutions	1	1	3	2	2	1
Texas						
Botany and Bacteriology	—	—	—	—	6	4
Botany	3	2	3	3	—	—
Economics and Sociology	5	3	—	—	—	—
Sociology	—	—	2	1	2	1

TABLE 1.3B *(continued)*

	1928		1932		1936	
	N	P	N	P	N	P
Stanford						
Biology	4	3	4	3	14	9
Bacteriology	2	2	2	2	4	2
Botany	4	3	4	3	—	—
Physiology	—	—	6	1	5	2
Cornell						
Biology	30	22	20	16	22	17
Botany	—	—	9	8	—	—

Sources: American Council on Education, *American Universities and Colleges*, ed. David Allan Robertson (New York: Charles Scribner's Sons, 1928); *American Universities and Colleges*, 2nd ed., ed. John Henry MacCracken (Baltimore, MD: Williams & Wilkins, 1932); and *American Universities and Colleges*, 3rd ed., ed. Clarence Stephen Marsh (Washington, DC: American Council on Education, 1936).
Note: N = total faculty; P = professors; — = not available

rubric of social science. Locations within institutions and relationships among fields of knowledge and practice became basic and defining. Neither biology nor sociology was among the first disciplines to claim a continuing place in the work of research and teaching in the modern university. Nor were they latecomers, although sociology followed biology by one or two decades and spread more slowly. Their academic institutionalization in the formative era between the last decade of the nineteenth century and the first decades of the twentieth is roughly synchronous. Their paths to disciplinary status are characterized by similarities and differences.[8]

Biology sometimes claims to be an "old discipline" in ways that sociology cannot, but both disciplines had long held a secure place in liberal arts curricula. Biology previously appeared as part of natural history, while sociology was part of natural philosophy. Before and after their institutionalization, both stimulated divisions and debates. While these were often academic matters, sometimes they were public and attracted great interest from nonspecialists. Particularly contentious issues included evolution, eugenics, social reform, immigration control, labor rights, race, and the state's support of public or private social and economic interests. In their formative period, both were associated with controversies beyond the walls of universities, which helped as well as hindered their institutionalization. They bridged audiences, clientele, and communities: biology with medicine, agriculture, individual well-being, and public health; sociology with social institutions, charities and welfare, criminology and corrections, juvenile reform, women's education and rights, and the adaptation and assimilation of urban migrants and foreign immigrants (see table 1.1). By example and precedent, their histories influenced continuing relationships among disciplines and interdisciplines, sometimes through myths that accord power to their novelty.

Yet this is only part of the story. Counterintuitively, early relationships between disciplinarity and interdisciplinarity were seminal in biology and sociology, although in dissimilar ways. They were also nonlinear and nonsequential. The processes of disciplinary formation and interdiscipline-discipline interaction differed. In both cases, interdisciplinarity played an important early role and continued to affect the field throughout its history. Biology and sociology also reveal how context affects interdisciplinarity influences. Interdisciplinarity and its mythology are all but inseparable. Disciplinarity is the expectation, the historical product, and the norm in the modern university. Sometimes interdisciplinarity follows, philosophically, theoretically, temporally, and materially. Yet like so many of the many dichotomies that pervade the discourse of disciplinarity and interdisciplinarity, this consequence is neither universal nor inevitable. Received wisdom can mislead us. In emphasizing disciplines, the standard version leaves out an essential part of the story: the presence and the contribution of interdisciplinarity. Indeed, interdisciplinarity is the major missing element in the standard narrative of disciplinarity in history and theory. The standard version also misleads us about timing. If interdisciplinarity is expected to follow the development and indicate the maturation of a discipline, it appears relatively late, well after institutionalization. That means it may be seen as post-disciplinarity or even anti-disciplinarity. Comparing biology and sociology demonstrates that discipline and interdiscipline were at play from the beginning.

Recognizing the importance of these relationships helps us to understand the challenges and complications of disciplinary development, especially in social science in the United States, including what Mary Furner identifies as objectivity versus advocacy, Robert Bannister characterizes as a quest for scientism and objectivity, Dorothy Ross defines as the challenge of exceptionalism and socialism, and Thomas Haskell describes as the recognition of interdependence in social description and explanation.[9] Crossing all these elements, according to these historians, were crises of authority and professionalization in American social science and in society and the polity more generally during the late nineteenth century. Comprehending the story depends on seeing the similarities among and differences between biology and sociology simultaneously. Similar factors led to diverse patterns and relationships of institutionalization, disciplinarization, and professionalization for different disciplines, depending in part on the disciplines, the social and cultural context, and the nature of the intellectual issues and the challenges they raised.

Finally, understanding disciplinary formation demands the identification and comprehension of interdisciplinarity's contribution and its dynamic, ongoing interrelationship with disciplinarity. That recognition forces a major reconceptualization of both interdisciplinarity and disciplinarity.

Biology

The emergent discipline of biology had an almost limitless appeal. Tied to both science and religion, despite some disturbing contradictions between them, many in the public, well beyond academics and other biologists, regarded it as inseparable from progress. Biologists had long sought influence locally, nationally, and internationally. Many of their important contributions predated the formation of a university-centered discipline. Their quests for professionalization and institutionalization were fundamentally intertwined, sometimes supporting and sometimes contradicting each other.

That effort did not mandate academic institutionalization. Writing about late nineteenth-century Britain, historian David E. Allen observes that "the world of natural history" was "confident in what it was doing" and had "no expectation of changing its ways although its members were having to revise their convictions dramatically to accommodate evolutionary theory. Even those employed as professionals were content to continue as systematists, conscious of the magnitude of the task and expecting to carry on along essentially the same lines." But, in contrast to geology, where there was no great divide between professionals and amateurs, "the life sciences were about to be polarized by the emergence of the academic discipline of biology."[10]

As historian of biology Philip Pauly emphasizes in *Biology and the Promise of American Life*, the conviction "that biology provided a foundation for democracy by improving American life had long motivated American biologists and their supporters." Its most important projects included determining the extent and boundaries of the United States, exploiting the continent's resources in the interest of Euro-Americans, defining American identity, and creating "a sensibility among Americans appropriate to their position in the world." Moreover, "biologists' engagement with these problems was an important element in gaining support from national leaders in the development of biology, in shaping a national scientific network, and in orienting scientific work in particular directions."[11] In the last third of the nineteenth century, federal naturalists sought "to learn about North American organisms and to educate citizens about the range of potential uses these resources embodied" and "to compile a fund of reliable knowledge that the government and individual citizens could use."[12]

How this process took place varied from country to country and university to university. The costs of a shift toward laboratories and technology could cause opposition: "Resistance to the new disciplines was often as much for financial reasons as it was on intellectual grounds," Allen notes. He ascribes the leadership of German universities to their stronger state support when compared to other European nations and North America. But more than finance was at issue as German universities attracted foreign graduate students who acquired new ideals and forms of organization as part of their studies. Some initiatives were home grown. In American land-grant universities, strong interest in the practical applications of botany and zoology, especially for agriculture, combined with concerns about science education in primary and secondary schools. In addition, "economic needs in both the United States and Canada promoted the development of a market-oriented agriculture, which faced problems in combating insect infestations of crops grown on previously untilled land. This produced a flurry of posts for applied entomologists, with the result that entomology became rapidly professionalized and progressed at a faster rate than in Europe."[13]

The complications to managing these currents were conceptual and epistemological as well as disciplinary and institutional. In Pauly's view, academic leaders moved to organize biology under a rubric of life science "to coordinate . . . those working on organisms throughout the country." They pursued institutional professionalization "in ways that were largely independent of the longstanding partnership between naturalists and the state to inventory and manage the biotic contents of North America." These efforts "derived partly from convictions about the structure of the world and of knowledge. Life, for many scientists, was, in spite of its diverse manifestations, at root a single principle; they believed that their efforts to understand organisms ought to reflect this basic fact. In part, however, this search for order was also a desire to re-form scientific hierarchy." Instead of a "single peak in Washington, . . . organizers wanted a scientific terrain that was more pleasingly varied and that highlighted creativity on the part of the individual" subject.[14] Federal naturalists, in contrast, saw their purpose in their evolutionary work with biological species and the national organization of biological naturalists.

Disciplines Converging

How did the conception of biology evolve? " 'Biology' . . . was a single scientific term. By comparison with 'botany,' 'zoology,' or 'natural history,' it was a recent coinage, invented around 1800 simultaneously by scholars in both France and Germany. Its meaning and significance, however, remained uncertain throughout the century." An umbrella term for all life sciences to some, to others it referred to one "specialty, but one that was uniquely fundamental, an intellectual core around which all other inquiries stood as more applied, limited, or derived." Within that conceptualization, "there was uncertainty concerning the content of that core: was it chemical, cytological, historical, or ecological? A larger uncertainty was whether biology, by any definition, was an ordinary workaday scientific discipline, or whether it expressed as an a priori philosophical faith in the meaning of 'life.' A final problem was whether it was a science that already existed or an ideal that would be realized in the future with the development of new knowledge."[15]

Here, indeed, was a major complication for disciplinary and interdisciplinary formation, as well as for talking about biology itself. Pauley explains that the term " 'biology' gained concrete meaning only gradually in America. Prior to 1900 its denotations and implications varied so widely that a general definition, encompassing all significant usages, would be of minimal value." Among "the large number of intellectual and organizational developments" that "its establishment as a core discipline involved," Pauley highlights its

> emphasis on certain basic concepts such as protoplasm, the cell, and evolution[;] . . . ranking of research problems in order of importance and feasibility; development and spread of a set of instruments and techniques centered around the microscope; creation of institutions such as journals, graduate departments, and marine laboratories; development of college courses in "general biology" and promotion of a rationale for such elementary work; beliefs and plans regarding the coordination among the specialized disciplines within the general rubric of biology; mobilization of constituencies to provide financial and political support; and attacks upon, and when necessary compromises with, competing intellectual interests.

"Biologists convinced their university constituencies that their research problems were the most advanced and far-reaching of the life sciences" and, at the same time, "that their concepts and techniques were the best introduction to a large number of areas of more sophisticated study." As "universities at the turn of the century provided substantial support to a large number of scholars . . . pursuing highly technical studies," what many have called a " 'new' biology" developed around genetics and experimental laboratories.[16]

Universities were not easy places to create a more unified discipline. As Jonathan Harwood summarizes, " 'biology' has rarely been institutionalized as a single subject. Whenever the life sciences experienced growth, . . . they displayed a remarkable tendency to be institutionalized separately rather than to remain together as an internally differentiated whole. Just why this has occurred is not clear, but its historiographical implications is that 'biology' is best conceived as a collection of loosely connected areas of inquiry . . . sharing little more than their concerns with living organisms." The variations in the status, relationships, and locations of these fields or disciplines "defy description." According to Harwood, "Some of them (e.g., zoology or botany) were *disciplines* in the sense that they were central to the curriculum and were institutionalized in separate departments (or 'institutes'). But many fields," such as agriculture and medicine, "were established for long periods of time without ever acquiring disciplinary status."[17]

By the 1860s, Harvard, Yale, and Wisconsin had chairs in zoology. In 1876, as it deliberately defined itself as a research university, Johns Hopkins established a department it called "biology," with a physiologist and a morphologist its two faculty members. Positions in biology multiplied in the 1880s and 1890s, as Pennsylvania, Columbia, Texas, North Carolina, and Wisconsin, emulating Johns Hopkins, "assigned their life scientists to departments of 'biology.' . . . Significantly, however, in most cases these had split into separate departments for zoology and botany." Despite many differences, universities elsewhere imitated the new German departments and institutes in pursuit of laboratory and experimental studies in histology, embryology, physiology, and comparative anatomy, and later in experimental embryology, plant ecology, plant physiology, bacteriology, biochemistry, and genetics. "All of these fields soon had their own professional societies and journals," Harwood observes. "So stark was the scale and speed of these changes that by 1920 'specialization' had become a source of concern among a number of biologists." That concern may have been a sign of a growing sense of unity, as a discipline of biology had formed in the coming together of other disciplines and fields. At the same time, the division between medical schools and university science departments continued, severely complicating the development of biochemistry and then of molecular biology. The separation between botany and agricultural research, which received funding from the U.S. Department of Agriculture, was equally problematic. Plant pathology, ecology, bacteriology, and genetics became prominent at Berkeley, Minnesota, Wisconsin, and Cornell.[18] Industry and foundation interest and support paralleled specialization.

A distinctive discipline of biology had emerged by the turn of the twentieth century. As Pauly puts it, "At Hopkins, Chicago, Columbia, and Penn the administrative interest in scientific medicine produced the professional spaces for what eventually became biology. Where medicine did not in fact develop . . . biology became a core discipline; but . . . where medicine predominated, the school of biology was ephemeral. . . . The consequence of these events was the appearance of a substantial academic community that had the desire and the opportunity to concentrate on what appeared to them to be the fundamental questions in the life sciences."[19]

This development was one form of interdisciplinarity, as multiple disciplines came together to forge a unified discipline. This set of relationships and locations may seem counterintuitive, but it integrated preexisting disciplines in novel ways. Garland Allen captures the distinctive qualities of modern biology as interdiscipline when he emphasizes synthesis over summation; ideas from one area coming together to transform others; and a unified approach that was qualitatively more than the sum of its parts. Revealingly, in this case the result was disciplinary. Allen's use of "convergence" to describe the formation of biology as a discipline in the 1970s does not carry the rhetorical promotional weight of succeeding decades. As we will see, "convergence" has taken on a new, larger life in recent years. Allen's notion of a "new American biology," built on the basis of the emergence of a wider "new biology" after the mid-nineteenth century, is more than evocative of the intimate relationships between disciplines and interdisciplines.[20]

Later scholars describe a more gradual transformation, with a less sharp division between naturalists and experimentalists or between European influences and American developments. These critics demand closer attention to the institutional, intellectual, and social meanings and contexts of biology. Research relating to genetics and heredity that led to acceptance of T. H. Morgan's chromosome theory of heredity (CTH) depended on more than scientific accuracy or intellectual consensus. Changing questions and shifting angles of vision led to new perspectives that crossed and drew from different fields and disciplines.

Scientific agreement required the acceptance of fundamental theories, especially CTH, and the persuasiveness of the confirmation of novel predictions of change across experimental generations. Experimentation and measurement contributed to changing understanding but were not in themselves determinative. Stephen Brush points to "the chromosome theory of heredity's ability to . . . establish a firm connection between genetics and cytology. . . . It is remarkable that geneticists were willing to accept the CTH as applicable to *all* organisms at a time when it was been confirmed only for *Drosophilia*. The construction of maps showing the location on the chromosomes of genes for specific characters was especially convincing for non-geneticists."[21] Some researchers insist that such theoretical shifts involve not simply a search for scientific consensus but also a struggle for power and authority. Be that as it may, early twentieth-century genetic biology shows clearly the contributions of other biological disciplines and laboratory-based experimental science to changes in scientific understanding. The synthetic and distinctively interdisciplinary qualities that Allen's account of genetic biology evokes remain compelling. As historians tell the story of genetic biology, scientific and other contextual factors add to its complexity and reduce any sense of the power of autonomous intellectual idealism in the making of a discipline.

Convergent Developments

Universities were the principal sites of convergence. Information from the 1928 *American Universities and Colleges* (*AUC*) report illustrates the dimensions and the trappings of institutional development and organization at the universities highly ranked in the life sciences. (See tables 1.1. and 1.2 for fields of specialization and rankings.) Every department listed multiple laboratories, libraries, and botanical collections. Major private institutions, such as Columbia, Harvard, Stanford, Penn, Chicago, had exceptionally well-equipped facilities, as did a number of public universities (table 1.4). Each of these institutions also recorded multiple publications, which conveys the range and dynamism of the formative moment in the history of a converging discipline.

Consider, for example, the University of Chicago. "There was little sense of biology as a field before Whitman's activities in the early 1890s," recounts Pauly. Charles Otis Whitman's reshaping of the field "was possible because a number of young scientists had a decade of experience in unexpectedly open academic niches." It built on the growth of "a substantial academic community that had the desire and the opportunity to concentrate on what appeared to them to be the fundamental questions in the life sciences."[22] Whitman "consciously formulated a core discipline of biology and made a major effort from 1896 to 1898 to ground it in the university system." Once a zoology tutor to farm machinery magnate E. P. Allis, he dedicated himself "to developing a 'natural system' for organizing the various life sciences, by coordinating specialties and giving appropriate emphasis to research, graduate training, college education, and popularization." His emphasis shifted from animal morphology within an alliance with medicine to biology as an independent academic field. Critical of medicine's distorting impact on biology and rejecting the division of the field into botany and zoology,

TABLE 1.4
Biological laboratories, institutes, and their publications at major
U.S. universities, 1924

Columbia University
Torrey Botanical Club: *Bulletin, Memoirs, Torreya*
New York Botanical Garden: *Journal, Mycologia, Bulletin, Memoirs, Contributions, North
American Flora*

Harvard University
Contributions from the Grey Herbarium, Laboratories of Plant Morphology, Cryptogamic
Laboratories, and the Zoological Laboratory
Bulletin and *Memoirs* of the Museum of Comparative Zoology

Princeton University
Contributions from Biological Laboratories

Stanford University
Stanford University publications, University Series, Biological Sciences

University of California
Journals in botany and zoology

University of Chicago
The Botanical Gazette
Contributions from the Hull Botanical Lab
Miscellaneous publications of the Museum of Zoology

University of Michigan
Occasional Papers of the Museum of Zoology
Michigan *Handbook* series

University of Missouri
Bulletins, Missouri Agricultural Experiment Station
University of Missouri *Studies*

University of Nebraska
Botanical Survey of Nebraska
Flora of Nebraska

University of Pennsylvania
Contributions from the Botanical Department
Wistar Institute of Anatomy and Biology: *Journal of Morphology and Physiology, American
Journal of Anatomy, Anatomical Record, Journal of Comparative Neurology and Psychology,
Journal of Experimental Zoology, Contributions* of the Zoological Laboratory

Yale University
Contributions from the Osborn Botanical Laboratory
Collected Papers of the Osborn Zoological Laboratory

Sources: American Council on Education, *American Universities and Colleges*, ed. David Allan Robertson
(New York: Charles Scribner's Sons, 1928); *American Universities and Colleges*, 2nd ed., ed. John Henry
MacCracken (Baltimore, MD: Williams & Wilkins, 1932); and *American Universities and Colleges*, 3rd ed.,
ed. Clarence Stephen Marsh (Washington, DC: American Council on Education, 1936).

Whitman left Clark University to found an "independent school of biology" at W. R. Harper's new University of Chicago. In place of the existing specialties, Whitman aspired "to divide the field, as he said, 'according to the essential nature of the problems and methods, rather than according to the systematic or geographic relations to be studied'; this would mean elimination of 'zoology' and 'botany' and their replacement by finer functional divisions such as cytology, embryology, and taxonomy."[23] Programs like Chicago's produced a generation of graduates who saw the new organization of research and biological laboratories such as the Marine Biological Laboratory at Woods Hole, Massachusetts, as the proper environment for academic biology.

University registers and the *AUC* volumes for 1928, 1932, and 1936 document irregular change and a crazy-quilt quality of the names of biology departments and the organization of biological sciences in universities.[24] Although biology never became an integrated interdiscipline, its foundations are interdisciplinary.[25] What was new and distinctive in the making of modern biology was institutional, as well as disciplinary and interdisciplinary. The life sciences, as we recognize them, were constrained by, yet also influenced, the rules, requirements, structure, and culture of the modern research university. The formation of these departments also reflected the larger social context, the application of philosophical conceptions of experimentalism as a method of discovery and understanding, and mechanistic materialism and holism as an approach to the functioning body and the essence of life.[26]

Biology's interdisciplinary formation was a product of intersecting forces that shaped the convergence of disciplines. One essential cluster, academicization, involved the movement of biology from its practice in the fields, meeting rooms, and periodicals by amateur naturalists (unpaid, uncredentialed, or uncertified, but by no means ignorant) to demanding formal training in recognized institutions of higher learning and creating a profession with associations, meetings, and publications, as well as rewards. This process underlay both disciplinarity and interdisciplinarity. The location of education, training, and research changed most visibly. But the relationship of botanical, zoological, and other biological work to appropriate bodies of knowledge is also an inseparable part of the institutionalization and professionalization process. Disciplinization and departmentalization progressed together, albeit unevenly. This trend is inseparable from the more formal organization of research and teaching within departments or institutes and as part of a research university. Academicization reflected larger social, cultural, and political-economic changes, as well as disciplinary developments. In other words, both the micro and the macro dimensions mattered.[27]

In these complex processes we find some of the grounding for interdisciplinary organization. Here we see the relationships between the parts and the whole and the location and the organization of each element in new institutional settings, critical for disciplines such as embryology, cytology, genetics, physiology, evolutionary theory, and the new discipline of genetic biology. Fields, central questions, and syntheses shaped each other in a dynamic intellectual, as well as institutional and social, process. In terms of interdisciplinary potential, biology had many primary disciplinary connections, and conflicts, in its relationships to medicine, natural or experimental sciences, botany, and zoology and their location and organization.

The division of biology into related fields contributed to the need to bring aspects of certain fields or disciplines together in efforts to answer questions or solve problems beyond the boundaries of that field. Interdisciplinarity might be promoted in such instances. At times, in other words, the separation could be limiting, but not in all cases. Take, for example, the discovery that sex determinism can be understood through examination of chromosomes, a major advance in genetic biology during the early twentieth century. The story of Thomas Hunt Morgan at Columbia University, is easy to romanticize and to criticize.[28] But Morgan's famous "fly room" demonstrates how important it is that histories of science show how science is actually practiced, not how it is conceived after the fact and presented in textbooks and classrooms.

In Morgan's laboratory in Morningside Heights, observations of the genetic transmission of chromosomes in successive generations of *Drosophila* (fruit flies) contributed fundamentally to the acceptance of the theory of genes and their role in determination of the characteristics of living organisms. Although we can only hint at its dramas, this episode encapsulates much of the larger story about the convergence of biology as an interdiscipline. Biology took root at Columbia in close relationship with the university's College of Physicians and Surgeons. Under the leadership of H. F. Osborn and E. B. Wilson, it moved to the new main campus in the 1890s and developed closer connections to the sciences. At the same time, an emphasis partially shifted from biology to zoology.

In 1904, Johns Hopkins–trained T. H. Morgan moved from Bryn Mawr College to Columbia. His interest in evolution and Mendel's theories of inheritance shaped his research in morphology and embryology in Naples and at Woods Hole's Marine Biological Laboratory. His focus on chromosomes and

the determination of sex was stimulated by the discovery in cytological evidence that both males and female moths were heterozygous. This observation
led him to sex selection in *Drosophila* via tracking X and Y chromosomes that
transmitted dominant and recessive eye colors. Morgan's student A. H. Sturtevant, another famous biologist, recalls, "In 1909, for the one time during his
24 years at Columbia, Morgan gave the opening lectures in the beginning biology
class. . . . Nothing was said about genetics." But the next fall, Calvin "Bridges
and I got desks in his laboratory . . . where the three of us worked together for
the next 18 years. . . . Bridges and I practically lived in this room; we slept and ate
outside, but that was all. And we talked and talked and we argued, most of the
time. . . . Another important member of this team, H. J. Muller, . . . took his full
share in the general discussions and arguments and criticisms."[29]

Morgan's group of undergraduate, graduate, and postdoctoral students
proceeded to map the transmission of chromosomes. Neurophysiologist Eric
Kandel writes about the fundamental significance and far-reaching implications of this work: "The profound insight that genes are aligned on the chromosome like beads on a string with specific distances between them eventually produced a conceptual basis for hunting for disease genes through linkage
analysis and for mapping whole genomes, such as the human genome. All this
was accomplished by a nineteen-year-old Columbia third-year undergraduate
by simply skipping one night's homework! Morgan, who was not given to overstatement, later was to call the realization that genes could be precisely mapped
in relation to one another on the chromosome . . . 'one of the most amazing
developments in the history of biology.' "[30] Morgan, Sturtevant, Bridges, and
Muller, summarized their findings in *The Mechanism of Mendelian Heredity*
(1915). Morgan shared the 1933 Nobel Prize in Physiology with Sturtevant and
Bridges.

Morgan proposed and sought to institutionalize this vision of biology as
an integrative and interdisciplinary discipline in Pasadena when he accepted an
invitation from Robert Millikan and George Ellery Hale to establish a division
of biology at the California Institute of Technology. In 1927, Morgan wrote that
"the establishment of a Department of Biology" reflected "a desire to lay emphasis on the fundamental principles underlying the life processes in animals
and plants" and "an effort . . . to bring together, in a single group, men whose
common interests are in the discovery of the unity of the phenomena of living
organisms rather than in the investigation of their manifold diversities."[31] Historian Judith Goodstein concludes: "Biology at Caltech in the thirties was special because of its emphasis on genetics, *the* essential science for the future of

biology. . . . If [Morgan] had an ideology, it 'was that genetics was the root to finding out how life works.' "[32]

Sociology

Presenting the origins of sociology in a sweeping, romantic trope, Robert C. Bannister simplifies a complicated, contested process: "Sociology emerged in response to the problem of social order in modern society in the wake of the American and French Revolutions and the rise of industrialism and market capitalism. A precondition of the project was the recognition of a civil society apart from any particular political form. Combining skepticism and a faith in reason, sociologists insisted that society is not a reflection of a natural or divine order but is nonetheless subject to rational analysis. Whereas Enlightenment theorists had viewed society in terms of a 'social contract' and a convergence of individual interests, sociology explored the forms and structures that make 'society' possible."[33] While implying the challenges of disciplinarization and a potential for interdisciplinarity, Bannister's account only begins to suggest the problems of professionalization and the new interdisciplines' struggle for a place in the developing world of universities.

Taking sociality as its subject, sociology differed from anthropology, politics, economics, and other social sciences in claiming no specific area as its own. While the other social sciences took their subjects as given, the first academic sociologists expended vast energy arguing that there even *was* such a thing as "society" to be studied. As a result, the discipline developed a decade or more later than the leading social sciences. Strategies to legitimate the new discipline ranged from claims that it was the capstone of the social sciences to more limited proposals to study social relations.[34] Nonetheless, sociology made various alliances with biology, psychology, and a range of professions, as well as economics and anthropology. (See table 2.1 for the major social science subfields and table 2.2 for faculty numbers and, for some institutions, disciplinary combinations.)

On the one hand, sociology and biology shared critical elements as they confronted the changing demands and conceptions of professional expertise amid the processes of academicization and disciplinization that prevailed during the mid- to late nineteenth century. Both were influenced by perceptions of the urgent needs of the rapidly changing social, political, cultural, and economic worlds of which they were a part. Sociology was a response to the growth of cities, industry, population, inequality, immigration, and adaptation. Sociologists, like biologists, struggled to move from "amateur to professional" and from a variety of public and private positions into colleges and universities. Both engaged in conflicts over what fields and subfields to include and exclude in the negotiations between the parts and the whole that shaped and reshaped the field.

On the other hand, the challenges, strategies, circumstances, and opportunities were not the same. There is a great difference between a "science of life" and a "science of society," as they were perceived, accepted, practiced, and institutionalized. To paraphrase Philip Pauly, "biology and the promise of American life" was a more compelling sales appeal. The reasons go well beyond the boundaries of this book but, to put it bluntly, the science of "life" trumped that of "society." It appeared more scientific, more practical, more relevantly theoretical, and more directly and indirectly consequential. It attracted more interest and support; equally important, it stimulated less criticism and opposition. Biology has its politics and is allied to various ideologies, especially eugenics and evolution, which have been criticized on social, political, and religious grounds. Compared to the social sciences, however, what is problematic about biology is less obvious and has less often caused alarm. The questionable objectivity and scientism of biologists is rarely the main subject in histories of the discipline.

No less blunt, and easily misunderstood, is the so-called two cultures problem, which pits science against nonscience or, in many versions, an ambiguous notion of culture. Historian Guy Ortolano reminds us that C. P. Snow's 1959 polemic centering on the divide in knowledge and its organization into scientific and literary pursuits arose in a specific historical context. Yet sociology and other social sciences, especially economics, political science, psychology, and anthropology, have long been divided, with many practitioners leaning toward scientific, quantitative, and laboratory work while others focus on social observation and qualitative analysis. Both the conflict within disciplines and the failure to convince natural and mathematical scientists, public and private sponsors, and much of the general public of the field's value helped to determine sociology's definitions, relationships, and organization. With science came at least the expectation of truth and accuracy, the presumption of nonpartisanship, and a lesser imperative that most persons grasp its elements. Science also helped to mute the potentially divisive impact of disagreements over evolution and eugenics. The gulf between science and culture shaped sociology and limited its interdisciplinary possibilities.[35]

Despite the breadth of society and sociality to which Bannister appeals, sociology's scope was narrower than biology's, and the relationships between its parts became less clear as it developed into a recognized discipline. Its original potential for interdisciplinarity gradually diminished. Questions about relationships within and across fields and subfields and processes of inclusion and exclusion are critical to the processes of disciplinary institutionalization.

Making Sociology

One symptom and structural feature that powerfully influenced the founding and subsequent history of sociology was its rejection of an explicit historical orientation and method in its research, theory, and practice. This stance contrasted with biology's foundational historicity toward life forms and their remains. Sociologists as varied as Robert Nisbet and Philip Abrams have written brilliantly about this problem. Abrams comments that "logically ordered contrasts between structural types have been treated, quite naively for the most part, as though they effectively indicated chronologically ordered transitions. On this basis a sociological past has been worked up, a past which is linked to the present not by carefully observed and temporally located social interaction but by inferentially necessary connections between concepts."[36] Why did this occur? Abrams points to two main elements.

> First there was the intellectual ascendancy of evolutionism. Second one must recognize the apparent power of the analytical paradigm produced by the treatment of the past as a structural type. It did permit, as Marxism apart, nothing else did, a generalized account of the structure and tendency of industrialism. An exhaustive explanation would also have to consider the importance of some questions of academic convenience and convention. In establishing its own academic credentials, sociology had above all to differentiate itself from history. Since it, too, dealt in historical materials and problems, the differentiation virtually had to be in terms of sociology's special methodology. Once methodology became the hallway of the discipline at this level it was surprisingly easy for it to prove an obstacle to the adoption of new ways of dealing with the problems as well. . . . It was not historical action but objectified historical process that was of interest. The idea that process could be ascertained only through careful observational studies of action occurred to very few people.[37]

As sociology professionalized and institutionalized as an academic discipline, a complex and sometimes contradictory sense of what was necessary and possible developed. Science, objectivity, professionalism, disciplinary autonomy were overarching goals. Both historical specificity and grand theory were eschewed. So, too, were dangers of advocacy, partisanship, activism, and commitment to social reform, among many elements of nonscholarly involvement. A glance at sociology's subfields (see table 1.1) suggests the field's risky relationships and apparent lack of unity. That biology programs were divided across science, medicine, and agriculture and distinguished between pure and applied work mattered less than sociology's location across young professional areas (social work, criminology, juvenile justice, education); the often struggling, relatively new social sciences; and the realms of contemporary relevance. Those stand out among the forces that weighed on sociology to narrow and institutionalize in its path toward sounder disciplinary standing.

Dorothy Ross suggests the context for the rise of academic social science, describing its base in terms that parallel biology's. Although its economic underpinnings seem more urban and industrial, the economic work of biology in the nineteenth and early twentieth century, especially in agriculture, underlay urban and industrial capitalism's remaking of the Western world at that historical moment. In social science, she explains,

> Institutional support for disciplinary agendas came from the expanding university systems that provided centers of graduate education and research, but also from bases outside the universities—banks, trade unions, schools, prisons, hospitals, reform organizations, state bureaus, welfare agencies, museums, and colonial governments—that offered social scientists employment, markets for their expert services, and venues for research. This triangular base—the academy, the market, and political and social institutions—produced severe tensions between, in Mary Furner's phrase, "advocacy and objectivity." Yet these diverse locations also provided the disciplines with a degree of constrained autonomy within which to pursue scientific and practical activities.

Inseparable from the academic-institutional project in the social sciences were what Ross calls critical "constraints": "narrowed scientific and political vision and masculinization of the disciplines. Universities—whether state institutions, aristocratic corporations as in England, or private institutions funded by capitalists as in the United States—discouraged political, gender, and racial heterodoxy."[38]

> While many of the popular sites that pursued social science knowledge and practical investigation were well within the liberal fold, others, like the Fabian Society, were more radical, and many of them were also staffed by women. Hull House, a Chicago settlement house staffed by talented women social investigators, was central to the development of the social sciences at the University of Chicago, for example, though never fully utilized or acknowledged. Neither the politically

committed and participatory styles of work, nor the gender conventions that identified women with feeling, piety, and the arts, promised scientific authority. The
disciplinary project often involved colonizing these sites for academic social science. Practitioners were increasingly required to hold academic degrees, either in
the social science disciplines or in practice social science fields (social work, home
economics, clinical psychology, counseling) that themselves sought academic
legitimacy as sciences.[39]

Women and political radicals were excluded or subordinated as a result of selective university appointments and credentialing. The same obstacles limited the
participation of people from racial minority groups. These processes of exclusion and marginalization were inseparable from the professionalization and institutionalization of a discipline of sociology in the modern university. They
were instrumental in the narrowing of the field as it set its agenda.

As many of its historians and chroniclers have observed, sociology had special
problems of definition, relationships, location, organization, and institutionalization. Sociologist Craig Calhoun locates sociology's divisions at the field's
foundation and sees the tensions persisting. He reminds us of the "evolutionary"
and "organic" grounds and concerns about freedom and action that had allied
sociology with biology and, for a time, with economics. In his history of the American Sociological Society, Calhoun summarizes its origins:

> The founders did not have a clearly unified vision of the field, but they joined in
> a more or less cohesive debate framed by questions such as the extent to which
> evolution and broad patterns in historical change should be emphasized, ways
> to relate the organic wholeness of society to individual freedom and action, and
> the extent to which inequalities of power and economic position could be miti-
> gated by social reform. Many of the enduring lines of tension and division had
> already been established as well. The relation between science and social action,
> for example, has remained an enduring question for sociologists since the disci-
> pline's founding. But many sociologists truly desired to achieve both scientific
> authority and influence in social reform. Sociology has developed since in a
> recurrent interplay of visions of sociology's potential and divisions over how to
> pursue it.

Issues related to disciplinarity and interdisciplinarity, the relation of the parts
and the possible whole, the included and the excluded—all were central to the
complicated process. According to Calhoun, "both unity and boundaries were in
question as sociology overlapped a number of other more or less distinct fields:

social work, rural sociology, criminology, marriage and family studies, and anthropology. Indeed, many fields have been founded largely within sociology and then 'spun off.' For all the push toward a more scientific sociology, and the associations of science with quantification, sociologists remained committed to field research as well as quantification, especially survey methods."[40] Consider how many of sociology's subfields (see table 1.1) spun off and were institutionalized separately, including child welfare, criminology, delinquency, penology, rural sociology, social hygiene, and social psychology.[41]

In his exploration of explanation and causal attribution in early social science, historian Thomas Haskell probes the competing demands of an incipient science of society confronting the problem of studying a complex "interdependent" social order and desires to reform it. In his view, "sociology never really made good on its claims to be the interdisciplinary discipline, nor did it succeed in reuniting social theory with reform practice. Though it was at first a haven for reformers and came closer than any other academic discipline to proving [Daniel Coit] Gilman [president of Johns Hopkins University] wrong about the incompatibility of agitation and investigation, in the long run sociology has contributed far more to the analysis of society than to the practical solution of social problems."[42] In Haskell's view, the American Social Science Association (ASSA) was "an attractive forum for serious social thinkers. . . . Its orientation was strongly interdisciplinary. Its scheme of specialties (represented by the departments) ultimately proved too cumbersome to survive, but at least the Association was sensitive to the danger of specialization." As sociologists left the association in the 1890s, they "deprived the ASSA of its trump cards by promising an analysis of society that would be both interdisciplinary and voluntaristic—and, more than that, systematic. It is often forgotten today that the first professional sociologists initially advertised their discipline as the Queen of the Social Sciences. It was not just another branch of knowledge about man and society. . . . Sociologists not only admitted a degree of human freedom and therefore the possibility of social reform, *contra* [Herbert] Spencer, but they also promised—by recognizing remote causation—to be better reformers than the 'social scientists' of the Social Science Association."[43]

This portrayal demands internal and external contextualization. As Calhoun reminds us,

> Sociology developed in the context of dramatic social change and widespread debates over what constituted progress and how progress could be attained more surely and rapidly. . . . Nineteenth-century social science engaged intellectuals,

advocates, and administrators on the basis of a broadly shared concern with social problems and social change. . . . Theirs was not first and foremost an interest in research or knowledge for its own sake but instead for dealing with social (and sometimes personal) problems. Once the disciplinary project launched, however, advancing sociology became more often an end in itself. This did not go uncontested. The tension between achieving intellectual authority and being publicly engaged has been present throughout the discipline's history. Many academic sociologists articulated a commitment to science intended both to claim authority over and to secure independence from extra-academic reformers.[44]

Ross describes the historical project of social science as "paradoxical." Her perspective reflects the similarities and differences across disciplinizing fields of study, illuminating some of the central contradictions that were part of the remaking of the production and organization of knowledge in modern research universities and the relationships among disciplines, disciplinary clusters, and interdisciplines in the historical contexts of their institutionalization and professionalization. In theory and practice, "liberal goals were to be achieved through the intellectual authority of specialized scientific communities, organized increasingly into disciplines. Amid the clashing interests and growing irrationalism of industrial society, the social sciences would become authoritative sources of reason. We should note at once the paradoxical logic of this project. Disciplinary specialization promised to enhance the social scientists' combined scientific and political authority by narrowing their focus and distancing them from the pressures of politics."[45]

Disciplinary specialization worked against interdisciplinarity, as well as against political or social activism. It was also contradictory in terms and in practice. Narrowing carries a wide range of denotations and connotations. "But that strategy cut the taproot to the moral and political world that nourished their project, without insulating them from it, for disciplines are only relatively autonomous from the surrounding world and participate in the national cultures, political conflicts, and social divisions of their milieux. Institutionalized disciplines attenuated class connections, but created their own special class interests."[46]

In Ross's view, the social sciences were especially vulnerable to such conflicts. Indeed, these conflicts marked their individual and collective quests for a place among the disciplines in the modern research university. "Encouraging intellectual rigor and a measure of detachment, they also discouraged critical reflection on the moral and ideological dimensions that inevitably attached to their work. Although the social sciences were hardly alone in experiencing these tensions related to disciplinary specialization, their project exposed them more relentlessly to such hazards. . . . The new disciplines borrowed scientific authority from adjacent scholarly domains."[47]

One path toward legitimation and advancement lay in the use of statistics. Here, sociology joined other institutionalizing social sciences. Charles Camic and Yu Xie offer a comparative view across the social sciences. James McKeen Cattell in psychology, Franz Boas in anthropology, Franklin H. Giddings in sociology, and Henry L. Moore in economics "were doing boundary work to legitimize their disciplines in a competitive interdisciplinary field, where they confronted the 'newcomer's dilemma' of conformity versus differentiation in relation to other disciplines. All four innovators turned to statistical methods to demonstrate compliance with acceptable scientific models and at the same time carve out a distinctive mode of statistical analysis to differentiate their own discipline from the others."[48] Statistics signified science and larger claims to knowledge. As Ross observes, "functionalist approaches were also inspired by scientific ambition and began the move toward statistical techniques. After World War I, and particularly in the United States, they were reshaped by a more rigorous scientism. Historians have attributed this American desire to imitate the natural sciences to the quantitative inclinations bred by individualism and democracy and to the naturalistic bias of American exceptionalism." She stops short of "blanket national explanations" and points to a waxing and waning of scientism, depending in part on "heated ideological controversies, when science promised to overcome, or to avoid the appearance of, partisanship," especially after each world war. She also associates "the scientistic stringency that entered American social science during the 1920s" with "the adoption of what might be called an *engineering* conception of science. . . . The aim of direct social intervention placed social scientists in a more active role, and, in a culture that especially valued useful knowledge and that had invented pragmatism, practical intervention had been central to the professional and disciplinary aims of American social science from its inception." This approach included testing movements; the spread of national, state, and local statistical bureaus; and engineering tools to predict and control. Engineering social science proved less strong in Europe, where "social scientists occupied a wider philosophical and political range."[49]

Historians of sociology and social science disagree about the importance and extent of movement across disciplinary borders during the interwar period as new disciplines found their place, institutionalized, and organized professionally. Dorothy Ross argues that for American social scientists, the problem of the interwar years was not the weakness of disciplinary structures but their strength. . . . Disciplinary form and scientific aspiration created an expectation of disciplinary unity, but in terms of theory, internal practice, and public voice, the disciplines were fractured. At the same time, they divided the human/social subject into separate and often incompatible pieces. If sociologists in the United States had firmer authority over the "social" than did their European counterparts, they gained it by abandoning large areas of the economic, political, and cultural world that might well have been within their purview. . . . Theoretical approaches and statistical techniques developed in one discipline often crossed into others, but there took on different shapes. Each discipline asked different questions, framed by different assumptions, and these differences became traditions of discourse into which practitioners were socialized. The commonalities focused work inward, but could not produce fundamental agreement or halt the proliferation of subfields.[50]

Disciplinary definition, relationships, and organization reduced the potential for interdisciplinarity.

Divergent Developments

"Like all disciplines, sociology began small," Andrew Abbott quips. He reports that, as of 1894, one researcher found 29 colleges with courses in sociology, defined loosely and including charities and corrections, while 24 had "sociology proper," defined as the "study of society." Ten years later Frank Tolman discovered that 185 colleges had instruction of some kind in sociology, and 45 had three or more courses. "However, the reader should not be led to imagine sociology as a growing plant, unfolding inevitably toward its telos. These courses would be completely unrecognizable to the current sociology undergraduate; they included things like Anthropological Geography, History of English Cities and Towns, Modern Socialism, Organized Philanthropy, and Private Property Rights." The list embraced 96 courses in general sociology, 60 on "social economics," 56 on social reform, 40 on charities, 39 on social philosophy, 30 on criminology, 26 on social ethics, 22 on the state, and 20 or fewer on rural society, nationalities, social legislation, religion, education, art, democracy, comparative sociology, social history, primitive societies, social psychology, and history of social theory. These courses were rarely taught by PhDs in sociology, of whom there were probably not more than 100 in the United States by 1900.[51]

When the American Sociological Society (ASA) formed in 1905, although "the larger constituency of the new organization was composed of practical reformers, it was the professors who took the lead in founding it." Fifty people attended the first meeting. By the end of 1906, there were 115, climbing to 300 from 1909 to 1912, 800 from 1916 to 1920, and 1,100 from 1924 to 1928. Abbott underscored that "this was *not* a history of steady, slow growth, however; there was enormous turnover. . . . What this meant is that the inner core of founders was already in the organization by 1910 and was surrounded by a fast-changing penumbra that tried the organization and then quickly left." When L. L. Bernard surveyed the field in 1910, "the organization comprised all 55 full-time faculty, 50 to 100 part-time faculty, and 100 or so 'practical' workers."[52]

"Despite the coalescence implicit in the existence of a national society, the academic side of sociology was by no means fully organized in 1910." Bernard found sociology departments in only 20 of the 173 universities that responded to his survey. Sociology was taught in departments of "economics and sociology," economics, "history and political science," and in programs on "theology and economics" or "homiletics and applied Christianity." By 1928, 48 departments still combined economics and sociology, compared to 99 departments of sociology.[53] "University faculty thus initiated the institutionalization of the discipline, but they were by no means in a stable position in their home institutions, even by the 1920s."

Charles Camic's imaginative research on "three departments in search of a discipline" at Chicago, Columbia, and Harvard illustrates this point. Focusing on the development of disciplines and their relationships at individual universities, he discovers distinct visions of sociology, which corrects a historiography that emphasizes discipline-wide patterns. He finds basic divergences in their conceptions of the "tasks" and "methods" of sociology. The Columbia approach, for example, was more inductive and statistical. Chicago was marked by Albion Small's call for the "interpretation of the parts of life by the whole of life."[54] A Harvard approach developed only in the 1930s, with Talcott Parsons's distinctive goal of merging "abstraction" with empirical case studies.

To correct what he regarded as an overemphasis on disciplinary institutionalization across universities, Camic stresses the development of departments within universities. No doubt both sets of influences are formative. Camic's revision encourages a closer look at the specifics of disciplinization and disciplinary relationships in historical context. He sees early Chicago sociology as closer to other disciplines and notes that Small viewed sociology as similar to "general biology, which [provides] a synthetic view of the whole system . . . in vital phenomena."[55] Nonetheless, "scientific legitimacy for a new discipline involved not only conformity to other disciplines, but differentiation from them as well."[56] That led to a narrowing of foci, specializations, and relationships.

As early as the 1920s, sociology was marked by irregular patterns of departmentalization, the small size of its departments, and the nature and relationships of its principal subfields (see tables 1.1–1.3.) In contrast to biology, sociology searched for a university-based profession but not for disciplinary unity or interdisciplinary connections. Sociology exhibited no parallel to the convergence that characterized biology. Over time, the discipline's principal fields grew apart and were located, institutionalized, and organized separately. Some developed into professions or paraprofessions. The split between theory and practice that was present at the creation of the field continued and formalized. Social reform turned into social work, criminology, and child welfare.

The *American Universities and Colleges* reports underscore the inconsistent location and organization of sociology and the small size of departments. Department and program names are misleading. For example, Harvard was fifth ranked in sociology in *AUC*'s 1928 report but had no chair in sociology; its professor of sociology was in the department of economics. By the 1920s, Penn, Chicago, and Columbia, all among the highest ranked, had critical masses of faculty and noted graduate programs, as did Wisconsin, Michigan, and North Carolina. Major programs developed national journals and social laboratories. *Charities Review* at Catholic University; the *American Journal of Sociology* at the University of Chicago; *Studies in Child Welfare* at the University of Iowa; and *Social Forces* at the University of North Carolina were prominent. Chicago had its Social Science Library and Social Research Laboratory, while North Carolina developed its Institute for Research in Social Science. By the end of the 1920s, "sociology stood as an established component of the liberal arts program in an expanding number of universities and colleges, particularly in the Midwest (progress remained slowest in the older, East Coast institutions)."[57] Enrollments were rising, along with the number of undergraduate and graduate degrees.

Camic identifies major shifts "that served to bolster the discipline's stature." The first is "the reshaping of sociology as a science of culture rather than of nature."[58] Put simply, the discipline moved from a dominating influence of biology and conceptions that depended heavily on "natural science determinants, analogies, metaphors, and levels of explanation" that subordinated the study of social life to biological life, toward a more broadly social and anthropological foundation.[59] The second trend, potentially conflicting with the first, was the growing acceptance of scientism, "a combination of two methodological doctrines commonly referred to by other terms; positivism, the belief that the social sciences are modeled after the natural sciences and . . . aim principally to produce general statements of objective fact . . . ; and empiricism, the belief that objective statements of fact derive from systematic observations arrived at through research procedures that are impartial." Although Camic is adamant that "at no point . . . was scientism a retreatist movement, counselling the sociologist to turn inward and abandon issues on the public agenda," it did constitute a stepping back, a turn from "why" to "how" and from "ends" to "means": "Diffusion of this scientistic outlook was abetted by the growing separation of sociology from social work, the era's quintessential meliorative field."[60] In the process, research followed empirical data sources, empirical work supplanted abstract theoretical writing, and applied research focused increasingly on problems vetted by the discipline. The ASA turned to divisions to house its diverging parts. Eight sections were created by 1930: rural sociology, family, community, religion, education, statistics, social work, and psychiatry. "At the time, few sociologists expressed concern about this trend, although it accelerated tendencies in the discipline toward interstitiality—toward constituting fields of empirical research around the assorted leftovers of other social sciences . . . —and toward fragmentation into discrete topical subfields."[61]

Disciplinarity's rewards entailed real costs. Despite some claims to the contrary, authority did not necessarily follow from a narrowing of focus or a distancing from political pressures. The promise was powerful, though fallacious. Dorothy Ross is probably correct in concluding that those tendencies "cut the taproot to the moral and political world that nourished their project, without insulating them from it."[62] Indeed, disciplines are only "relatively autonomous," and the social sciences, particularly sociology, were more vulnerable, in theory as well as practice, than biology and other sciences. Only so much authority could be borrowed, even from the sciences, and interest rates could be high.

All of the disciplines and disciplinary clusters relinquished important elements of critical authority as they sought the status that accrued from narrowing and distancing. There was relatively limited development and little endorsement for interdisciplinarity. Yet sociology's ambiguity as a discipline had a greater impact on reducing the breadth of its appeal. Sociology was less attractive; its concepts and concerns were less compelling, its importance and utility less obvious and, in a word, more academic. As a social science, it lacked the presumed power and the utility of a natural science. Both the discipline of sociology and the disciplinary cluster of social science sought to develop their own locations, relationships, and authority. Sociology struggled over objectivity and appropriate theory and methods for research, its own scope and legitimacy. It also struggled to find or build an appropriate audience. That it sometimes shared a departmental home with economics and could be confused with social work and social reform all interfered with a broader recognition, appreciation, and influence.[63]

The political activism of some sociologists, such as Edward A. Ross, Richard T. Ely, and John R. Commons, led to a perception that the field itself leaned leftward and was associated with socialism. With respect to political ideology and certain strains of critical theory, it suffered from a taint of European approaches, discourse, and theory.[64] Ironically, sociology was more susceptible to accusations of bias than was biology, despite suspicion or criticism on the grounds of religious beliefs that conflicted with evolution or some biologists' espousal of eugenics. The political dangers of biology were more diffuse and less provoking of responses and criticisms than sociology. Biologists were accorded greater tolerance, in part because they were scientists and in part because the "science of life" was identified with convergence and unity.

Conclusion

Disciplinarity and interdisciplinarity intersected and interacted to shape both biology and sociology. While biology, initially a convergence of disciplines, expanded to encompass newly conceptualized dimensions of life, sociology narrowed as it became a social science discipline. That different disciplines shared some basic elements but differed in others reveals the open-ended nature and various possibilities of the discipline-formation process.[65] Although biology and sociology both set out to be sciences—of life and society, respectively—their intellectual, professional, institutional, and historical differences were fundamental. Intellectual relationships, institutional locations, and professional organizations were very influential.

Biology, especially genetic biology, originated as, and to a considerable extent has continued to be, a powerful integrative interdiscipline. Its intellectual foundations are built around the development of the organism; the evolution of species comprehended within a single, dynamic model of life. The discovery of genetics became the indissoluble link between the organismic and the evolutionary scales. The "queen" of the sciences flowered at a time of transformation in higher education and research as scientific discoveries interacted with public and private interests to create new ideals, images, and institutions.

Sociology, in contrast, was never able to establish itself as *the* science of society. It gained intellectual and institutional legitimacy not by promoting the intellectual synthesis of separate fields of social inquiry but rather by differentiating itself from a more dominant field of political economy (which was itself fragmenting into politics and economics) and from the study of culture. To a considerable extent, the study of culture drew from disparate fields and theories to form anthropology, a discipline that began much as biology did, by synthesizing the study of social order with a theory of social evolution, though that racist and imperialist model was soon discredited. In separating itself from history, moreover, sociology abandoned what might have served better as the parallel to evolution in biology. As we see in chapter 3, social relations later reattempted to create the missing synthesis.

Failing to become an integrative science of society, sociology was never able to capture the prestige of a science. Its claims to scientific status were mostly methodological, rather than theoretical or substantive. They were also discursive and metaphorical. Sociology continues to struggle over the centrality of quantification compared to alternative methodologies and epistemologies. Other social sciences' resistance to sociology is also part of the story. These are critical questions for conceptions of interdisciplinarity. Those concerns also beg the question: was any so-called social science able to make more sweeping claims convincingly? Economists might argue that their discipline became not only quantitative but also nomothetic and therefore predictive and amenable to being used as an instrument of control. It succeeded by narrowing. Political science, whose objectivity remained dubious, could not make large claims. Nor could history, which tended to emphasize its contrast with the general theoretical models that had prevailed in sociology.

Institutional locations intersected inseparably from disciplinary developments and relationships. In the United States in particular, biology was not enshrined in medical schools; instead, it established itself as the prerequisite foundation for clinical medicine. At the same time, it became a core science, competing and sometimes skirmishing with physics and chemistry. Perhaps necessarily, separate departments of biology and partly separate organizations of biologists expanded in colleges of arts and sciences, medicine and public health, and agriculture and veterinary science. Ohio State University, for instance, has nineteen departments of biology.

Sociology, too, became the foundation for a wide range of applied professional fields, such as criminology and social work. As part of its process of institutionalization, it separated itself from those specialties but maintained a significant degree of institutional and intellectual domination over them. In turn, they struggled for standing in the expanding realm of professions and professional education. Perhaps contradictorily, that success stands in contrast to sociology's inability to integrate the social sciences.

Is it ironic, or should it be expected, that biology continued to be confronted with the problem of the relationships among the parts and the wholes: the repeated challenge of convergence? Is that a mark of success? That complication is part of the political economy of disciplinarity and interdisciplinarity. As chapter 6 details, the story continues in the second decade of the twenty-first century.

CHAPTER TWO

Crossing and Remaking Boundaries

The Humanities and Communication, 1870s–1960s

In a misleading book entitled *The Three Cultures: Natural Sciences, Social Sciences, and the Humanities in the Twenty-first Century*, cognitive psychologist Jerome Kagan points to the hierarchical ranking of academic fields. Drawing on C. P. Snow's iconic metaphor of two cultures, but ignoring five decades of criticism,[1] Kagan argues that the natural sciences (naturally) are preeminent, followed by the social sciences and then the humanities.

While advocates of the humanities have on occasion sought the status enjoyed by practitioners of science and social science, proponents of the field of communication have vied for inclusion in each of the three clusters.[2] Among those clusters, the humanities occupy the lowest rank, and communication usually sits closer to the social sciences. Perhaps as a consequence, and certainly as a correlate, of this ranking, Kagan writes as if "the humanities" were a single entity.[3] The chronic proclamation of "crises" in the humanities by critics and proponents alike, despite their disagreements on causes and consequences, also impinges on issues of interdisciplinarity. Each of the three disciplinary clusters has claimed, often implicitly but sometimes explicitly, recognition as interdisciplinary. Both the differences and the similarities are instructive.

Kagan assumes a certain unity to the humanities that is absent from the other clusters of disciplines, but he regards that cohesiveness as problematic. His definition is marked by indistinctness: "Philosophers, scholars of literature, and historians differ from natural scientists and social scientists. . . . Most work alone, are not highly dependent on grant support from government agencies, and rely primarily on semantics as a form of evidence. . . . The humanists lost a great deal of the authority they enjoyed a few centuries earlier when professors of philosophy and theology commanded far more respect than the small cohort of natural philosophers."[4] The characteristics that the humanities supposedly lost are more typical of those associated with interdisciplinary domains today.

The humanities and communication have faced decline within the academy, but the problem is especially severe in the humanities. Contrary to current opinion, its loss of status has been recurrent over at least a century. Seen in social, historical, and institutional context, the peculiar relationships that each field holds with interdisciplinarity come more clearly into focus. Both fields boast striking achievements, including some that merit designation as interdisciplinary. But both have been presumed to be multi- or transdisciplinary by nature, definition, and history, which is another matter. Both have seized on interdisciplinarity in the quest for recognition and status. In that effort, both have asserted their interdisciplinarity without recognizing, admitting, or probing their relationships with disciplines, institutions, and the encompassing world. They have even neglected to pursue definitions seriously.

As an integrated cluster of disciplines, the humanities proclaim or imply their interdisciplinarity. Rather contradictorily, they simultaneously oppose themselves to science (or scientism) and seek to claim its status and advantages.[5] Yet the humanities are more often faulted as inferior in their quests and claims for knowledge when they are compared to the sciences. Communication has more often sought the mantle of science or social science but remains subject to the same fault lines between "hard" and "soft" research and modes of understanding. Relevance, applications, immediate value, and vocational preparation are often cited as hallmarks of interdisciplinarity, but so too are theoretical abstraction and merely "academic" significance.

In his critical review of the "two cultures controversy," historian Guy Ortolano argues that the issues underlying this division are ideological rather than disciplinary.[6] This is true, up to a point. In reinterpreting interdisciplinarity in historical, social, and institutional context, I emphasize its inseparability from disciplines and their ideology and political economics—that is, from society and culture. Tracing those connections is a major goal of this book. In this perspective, Kagan's stereotypical devaluation of the humanities in comparison to the sciences appears both inaccurate and ahistorical.

More helpful is literary historian Robin Valenza's *Literature, Language, and the Rise of the Intellectual Disciplines in Britain, 1680–1920*, which explores the relationship of the intellectual division of labor to the forms and uses of language in the early modern foundations of disciplines. Her perspective points to an omission or confusion Kagan shares with many scholars in the humanities and communication, an oversight that is a striking complication for interdisciplinarity and professional expertise more generally. The problem goes well beyond the contradictory discourse of interdisciplinarity.

Language poses special problems for both the humanities and communication. It is inseparable from the meanings, hierarchies, relationships, locations, and organization of disciplinarity and interdisciplinarity. The centrality of this problem is evident in communication scholars' contortions over the status and presumptive location of their field and the nature of its relationships with other fields; indeed, it is indivisible from communication itself. Moreover, Kagan's ordering of "cultures" has much to do with both his own language and his view of those fields' language.

Valenza argues that "a discipline's claim to systematic generation of knowledge often depends on a transformation of language. Although this transformation requires justification, disciplines that have squarely asserted that they have both special procedures and special means of representation are generally awarded a higher status in the modern university and in public culture." In her view, "a discipline or a profession constitutes itself by instituting and calling attention to the divide between itself and a broadly educated public. Some of these obstacles to lay participation might have been inevitable in the pursuit of specialized knowledge, but some were deliberately constructed and promulgated as such." For example, she points to "style" and its criticism across belles lettres, political theory, and literature.[7]

Historically and contemporarily, this separation has proven especially vexing to the humanities disciplines that aspire to reach citizens and educated publics. "The success of any discipline as being perceived as scientific seems to lie in the degree to which it can escape (and gain acceptance for this escape) from a thoroughgoing reliance on what Berkeley had called 'words . . . known to all.' Newton's intuition that he should rely on nonvernacular representation—even when it was possible to do otherwise—has proven over time to be an effective technique for arrogating to a field of study professional status and public respect." To be sure, she adds, "None of this is meant to reduce the difference between physics and philosophy simply to language. . . . The language a discipline uses affects how specialized it seems to those outside it."[8]

This issue divides humanities scholars, influences the course of the field's professionalization and institutionalization, and affects its sometimes contradictory turns toward interdisciplinarity. Valenza summarizes: "Those who have argued against the need for specialized languages in the humanities—in the eighteenth century and now—suggest that anyone who insists that research cannot be presented in broadly accessible language creates artificial linguistic barriers to public understanding, either 1. to create the illusion that the practitioner has knowledge that others do not have, or 2. to hide knowledge from the public. Both arguments may sometimes be true, and they need not only be true about the humanities."[9] Indeed, this stance is a legacy for the humanities and interdisciplinarity together and separately.

Analyses of communication's cultural and intellectual antecedents span centuries and multiple points of contact. The field's academic institutional origins lay in the disciplines of sociology, political science, and psychology, and the Institute for Social Research (Institut für Sozialforschung) founded in Frankfurt, Germany, in 1923, as well as schools of journalism.[10] In terms that range from personal influence and opinion to social action and political development, communication took shape near the center of several emerging social sciences.[11]

Nonetheless, the field has important points of connection with the humanities, particularly regarding matters of expression, representation, and reception in both subject matter and discourse. The two also may claim common origins in classical through Renaissance rhetoric and Enlightenment philosophy. Yet judgments of communication vary widely. Efforts to promote and advance the area have often focused on its interdisciplinarity, taking advantage of contemporary currents and institutional opportunities, from the status of the field to student enrollments and research funding. Unlike proponents of the humanities, however, communication scholars seldom presume their field's coherence, independence, or overarching value. Whether it is best seen as a discipline, a multidiscipline, an interdiscipline, or a professional field is not clear.

Combining relevance with interdisciplinarity, eminent political scientist and communication pioneer Harold Lasswell proclaimed in 1958: "No change in the academic world has been more characteristic of the age than the discovery of communication as a field of study. The university system of the United States is more flexible in adapting itself than corresponding institutions abroad. Hence it is not surprising that the arts and sciences of communication have been more actively cultivated here than elsewhere."[12] At the same time, however, Bernard Berelson pointed to the diversity of major lines of inquiry and their lack of fruitfulness. Although three dissenting responses accompanied Berelson's critique, none of them blunted the force of his comments.[13]

Writing fifty years later, Susan Herbst argues that "debates about the nature of our field have been extraordinarily productive. . . . A bit self-absorbed, perhaps, but it underscores our sensitivities as a relatively new discipline." Using words that demand careful scrutiny, she issues a rather conventional call for interdisciplinarity: "We need to keep building the field, proving our 'value added' on the scholarly scene but, at the same time, remain as broad and open to the offerings of other disciplines as possible. We need more coherence and more legitimacy if

we are to strengthen the field, yet not at the cost of isolation, an enticing temptation for us as we build our own house."[14]

Failing to inquire into communication's relations with the disciplines and
neglecting its own history, Herbst situates the field between the Scylla of coherence without scope and the Charybdis of breadth without legitimacy. She then
contradicts her own characterization of communication as a discipline: "The field
was stunningly interdisciplinary from the start. There were heavy hitters from
multiple established disciplines with interests in common. . . . The underlying
sensibilities of early media studies scholars were open and wide ranging. There
was a wonderful disrespect [for] (or disinterest [in]) disciplinary constraints."[15]
This definition of interdisciplinarity searches in vain for a place among the many
taxonomies of the fields of knowledge. It avoids critical matters of relationships,
institutionalization, and organization.

Herbst's essay opens an avowedly agenda-setting 2008 special issue of the
Journal of Communication, "Epistemological and Disciplinary Intersections,"
which attends primarily to the field's associations with particular disciplines.
Looking mostly toward the future, the issue neglects to consider communication's academic roots in political science, sociology, psychology, and the profession
of journalism. Herbst posits "postdisciplinarity," while those seeking "intersections" search for multidisciplinarity. Michael Pfau, the special issue editor, presumes communication's disciplinarity while aiming to enhance the extent to
which "our output is of interest and importance to scholars . . . in allied disciplines." In his view, the main problems are fragmentation and specialization;
he articulates an interplanetary view of disciplines "spiraling out."[16] Like many
commentators, both Herbst and Pfau conflate the benefits and risks of specialization and generalization. Neither direction constitutes movement toward disciplinarity or interdisciplinarity. Failing to explore the possibilities and limits of
connections, the authors offer contorted arguments about the status and presumptive location of their field, as well as its relationships with other fields and
epistemologies. Finally, given that language is indivisible from communication
itself, it is surprising and highly problematic that they slight the centrality of
language to the construction of different intellectual traditions.

Despite obvious appearances to the contrary, the humanities and communication share a great deal. Although communication is often designated a social
science or a profession linked to journalism, both fields claim the mantle of interdisciplines. Both have also struggled for an appropriate place in the university.
By "place," I refer to their intellectual position in the organization of knowledge
as well as the location of their programs, departments, divisions, schools, and

colleges. Both are largely twentieth-century constructions, too. Indeed, the academic humanities disciplines are younger than often presumed, emerging as formal units only quite recently, while communication is somewhat older than generally recognized, with a pre–World War II foundation and history. Still, traditions and the myths associated with them have significant legacies. Moreover, both fields suffer from unusually vague and imprecise definitions. Are they sui generis, as much discourse would suggest, or are they constructs, as recent commentary emphasizes?

Critical questions follow. Are the humanities singular or plural? Does the humanities comprise a set of disciplines, each with its own history and place, or is the humanities field a connected or integrated whole? Is communication a discipline, multidiscipline, or postdiscipline? Or is it better viewed as a nondiscipline, which is more popularly construed with regard to journalism and the mass transmission of information? Similarly, are interdisciplines better viewed as old or new? Do they have creation myths? Or can they be either old or new with respect to their particular circumstances and contexts? What is the place of interdisciplinary relationships in the formation and operation of both interdisciplinarity and disciplinarity? How do the humanities and hybrid fields such as communication compare to the dominant sciences? How much do location and relationships matter? In contrast to the humanities, communication never doubted its social relevance or practical value. It has incessantly reiterated its relations to democracy, rather than seeing such claims as demeaning or distracting. In part, that reflects its varied beginnings in the social sciences, in critical-theoretical-activist institutes, in public opinion and social research centers, and in politics and commerce. Its quest for recognition was always more explicit, consistent, and insistent than that for the humanities, whose legitimacy seemed embedded in the classical curriculum. While aspiring to prominence in both theory and practice, communication is acknowledged as an applied field—or, at least, as a way of understanding a powerful, concrete, and quite recent social phenomenon.

For the humanities, as for communication, the 1930s, 1940s, and 1950s were decades of assertion. Both fields were deeply affected by the postwar search to understand and promote the influence of capitalism and democracy and to oppose "ideology," especially in politics. Fears of totalitarianism stimulated by the rise of communist and then fascist regimes in Europe exploded. As historian Kenneth Cmiel sees that period "in western intellectual life, the 1940s threw everything up for grabs. The enormity of World War II, the revelation of the death camps, and the apocalyptic dawn of the nuclear age all contributed to the atmosphere." In that context, scholars agreed that "mass communication . . . was a critical glue for modern societies. It could foster a sense of belonging and bond strangers together in a national community," deterring the "more corrosive side effects" of modernity.[17] At the same time, it could also bind the populace to destructive ideologies, such as fascism, and blind them to those ideologies' social consequences. The challenges of mass society and mass communication were followed by those of diversity, multiculturalism, and new electronic media.

While the humanities field has been central to traditional and modern higher education its presence has diminished except in the first years of the undergraduate curriculum. The myth of the humanities alludes to historical roots reaching from classical antiquity through various renaissances and enlightenments to the special place of moral philosophy as the capstone of the liberal arts.

Anthony Grafton and Lisa Jardine have identified a transition "from humanism to the humanities" in early modern European education.[18] During the late nineteenth and twentieth centuries, humanities scholars sought in diverse and sometimes bewildering ways to combat their field's decline alongside the ascendency of science. Modern humanities advocates claim value and relevance in one sense or another of the field's interdisciplinarity. Paradoxically, interdisciplinarity has been used both to ward off the humanities' purported "decline" and to promote their novelty and relevance.[19]

Communication scholars also occasionally appeal to antiquity, the Renaissance, and the Enlightenment: to Aristotle, Cicero, and the rhetorical arts, or to the printing press and the emergence of public spheres. But mass communication, advertising and propaganda, and new information technologies hold pride of place. At least rhetorically, the field purports to contribute to maintaining and promoting democracy. Oscillating between liberalism and conservatism, the field's utility for building a better world, maintaining order, and advancing oneself is a sine qua non.[20]

Its interdisciplinarity, too, is more often presumed than examined. The presumption obscures communication's once prominent place within sociology, political science, and psychology and its eventual divergence from those disciplines. The quest for status as a distinctive field with a unique name and location—as a School of Communication, albeit primarily a vocational training ground—obstructs a deeper, more accurate, and more useful understanding of its intellectual and institutional development. The myths of communication can be instructive. If interdisciplinarity can succeed within disciplines, the drive for separation bears reconsideration. The question of how and why political scientists and sociologists lost interest in communication commands attention.

So too do the reasons for its proponents' push for its recognition as an interdisciplinary yet separate field.

The close fit between the growth of communication as a field and the dominant political-economic order has long troubled critics. Communication's commercial dimensions, whether for marketing political views or products, can clash with both academic integrity and support of democracy. Free enterprise is the religion of democracy for many, of course. But the deep and often compromising entanglements between capitalism and democracy play less well in the groves of academe than in the marketplace. To be sure, the Annenberg schools of communication at the University of Pennsylvania and the University of Southern California were built on the profits of *TV Guide*. Sponsored research that puts profit before knowledge raises serious questions, even though the phenomenon extends far beyond the field communication. So why do some commercialized or commerce-driven fields, such as bioscience and materials science, fare better in the academy than others?[21]

Proponents and field builders have long turned to interdisciplinarity to describe and promote the study of communication. Problems of location combine with challenges of justification. Communication's early relationships with political science and sociology and its significance in the Frankfurt School both helped and hindered the field. Its ties with schools of journalism have helped to maintain its academic presence and support but limited its autonomy. Asserting its intellectual credibility—demonstrating that it is free of commercial ties and not wholly associated with contemporary applications—has been a challenge.[22]

Both the humanities and communication are failed interdisciplines. While they share much, they differ greatly whether it is a matter of disciplinary location, institutional development, social context, or the uses of abuses of interdisciplinarity in conception, ideology, imitation, theory, and practice.

Humanities: Singular and Plural, Disciplinary and Interdisciplinary

The humanities, especially interdisciplinary humanities, are a cultural and historical construction that has emerged in response to changing social contexts and historical currents within and beyond the university. As with other academic efforts, the humanities' claims of contemporary social relevance have gone hand in hand with aspirations to interdisciplinarity. Amoeba-like, the humanities have changed shape in rather startling ways, and those aspirations to interdisciplinarity took different forms during the late nineteenth century, the World War I era, the period from the Great Depression through World War II, the postwar expansion of colleges and universities, and the more recent curricular reforms. Institutional changes in universities, including increasingly complex organizational structures, rising costs, new disciplinary specializations and clusters, and recurrent reforms and specters of decline, are active forces in a context of economic globalization.[23] The humanities claimed pride of place in the global struggle against fascism and totalitarianism and in preparing students and the nation for freedom and democracy, leadership and citizenship. Yet, Janus-faced, the humanities look both forward and backward. For academic and cultural reasons, humanities scholars often hesitated to promote their contemporary relevance and opted for academic conservatism.

Periodic proclamations of interdisciplinarity punctuated this procession, though they were just as often undercut. Interdisciplinarity has a complicated history of continuities and reconstructions, strivings for culture and cultivation, status and inclusion, and location and place, as well as appeals to the best of traditional values. But it is also a story of self-promotion and questionable claims and tactics.[24] Akin to the conflicts between the myth of the humanities' long history and their recent creation and multiplicity, these key contradictions underscore questions that remain unanswered because they are seldom asked.

The humanities plural have a problematic relationship with the humanities together, the parts versus the sum of the parts. The tale told in this chapter traces the persistence of separate disciplines and the recurrent promise of an interdiscipline. The story is marked by an incessant search for holism and unity and the repeated discovery of divisions. Is there more than one whole: the disciplines together and the disciplines reintegrated? What is greater, the humanities as a collection of disciplines that sometimes speak to each other or the humanities as an integrated system or structure of thought, knowledge, concepts, and ideals that, taken together, are distinct from other groups of disciplines?

Among the ambiguities and sources of confusion is the gap between interdisciplinarity as encompassing the various disciplines that constitute the humanities—history, literature, philosophy, art history, and languages—and interdisciplinary humanities.

Defining the humanities has proved all but impossible, which is simultaneously the cause and the effect of the singular-plural problem. For most of the twentieth century, a list of disciplines has substituted for a rigorous definition, whether inadequately or adequately, deceptively or usefully, depending on one's point of view. The National Endowment for the Humanities, created by U.S. government action in 1965, maintains its own definition. "The term 'humanities' includes, but is not limited to, the study and interpretation of the following:

language, both modern and classical; linguistics; literature; history; jurisprudence; philosophy; archeology; comparative religion; ethics; the history, criticism, and theory of the arts; those aspects of the social sciences which have humanistic content and employ humanistic methods; and the study and application of the humanities to the human environment with particular attention to reflecting our diverse heritage, traditions, and history and to the relevance of the humanities to the current conditions of national life." Definition by list-making generates many parts but no whole.[25]

Origins and Evasions

Some rationales and histories emphasize the antiquity and the classical roots of the humanities, while others stress the Renaissance and Enlightenment. Writing in *Inside Higher Education* on January 4, 2013, W. Robert Connor tries to have it both ways. "First, the good news. It is true that the familiar triadic American curricular structure of liberal education (natural science, social science and the humanities) is relatively recent. Hence, the form of humanistic studies is not chiseled in ancient marble, but has changed and can and should continue to change in response to circumstances." Assuming the unity of each triad, he continues, "The bad news is that recent history is only a small part of the story. The foreshortening perspective on the humanities comes at a price. . . . We risk losing sight of what motivated the great era of humanism."

Blurring the important distinction between humanism and the humanities, Connor repeats the accepted view that this "motivation" lay in training "learned, eloquent, and morally responsible leaders of society" by introducing them to "the great authors and texts of ancient Greece and Rome" and concludes that "leaders of colleges and universities in the early 20th century consciously and deliberatively evoked the tradition of Renaissance humanism in an effort to develop some equivalent amid mass education in the modern world." His defense is ahistorical, inaccurate, and misleading, but it nonetheless reveals notions of foundations and usefulness embedded in the dominant myths of the humanities.

These myths were under active construction by the last decades of the nineteenth century.[26] In a revealingly rare argument, Anthony Grafton and Lisa Jardine revise the accepted view of the humanities from a historical, rather than a contemporary cultural or political, perspective. In explicating the transition "from humanism to the humanities," they refuse to conflate distinct historical contexts, as scholars such as Connor often do. "The suggestion that it suited the ruling elites of fifteenth- and sixteenth-century Europe to support the new humanism as an educational movement is, we believe, an important one for modern professors of the humanities. . . . The decline in prosperity of the individual nations has brought with it a crisis of confidence in arts education as a 'profitable' undertaking. Where, it is asked, is the marketplace end-product in the non-vocational liberal arts faculties that justifies the investment of public money?"[27]

They argue that a "long history of evasiveness" of the humanities' conflicting social roles and ideologies has left the humanities "vulnerable to the charge of non-productiveness, irrelevance to modern industrial society, without those teachers themselves having deviated from their commitment to the liberal arts as a 'training for life.' "[28] Their charge delineates multiple myths of the humanities and their implicit interdisciplinarity. First is the historical context and social-political relationships of the origin myth. Second is the privileged place of the humanities as "an empire and a language with a unique destiny." Third is the common assumption that the humanities "are intrinsically supportive of 'civilisation'—that is, of the Establishment." Fourth is the fundamental and debilitating confusion between humanism as a "zealous faith" and the humanities as a curriculum.

Neglecting the humanities' interrelatedness and their debts to other sources of knowledge is itself a form of evasiveness, one that figures in the humanities' tangled relationships with interdisciplinarity. In the modern university, the notion of liberal arts carries conflicting meanings in different disciplines and disciplinary clusters, in different kinds of institutions, and at undergraduate and graduate levels. It becomes a form of justification and takes on elements of an ideology.

Novelty, Disciplinarity, and Interdisciplinarity

An opposing version of the humanities' origin myth emphases their recency. Writing in *Daedalus*, Steven Marcus dramatically shortens the historical life of the humanities in part by designating "the humanities" as an interdisciplinary field. Although he is aware that interdisciplinarity can develop only in relation to disciplines, he confuses and misdates the humanities' interdisciplinary connections. The humanities were never *one* discipline; rather, they form a disciplinary cluster.

Marcus emphasizes that specialization was the order of the day in late nineteenth-century universities. At that time, "some senior classicists began to think of themselves as members of an embattled cultural patriciate—which they in fact were. Distrustful of democracy, resentful of scientific methods, made anxious by the secular spirit of a crescent modernity, indifferent or hostile to the immigrant millions . . . they conceived of themselves as the custodians of a civilization under siege. . . . In the name of Culture, these older classicists promoted the humanist tradition of an educational ideal of gentlemanliness, a rather genial spirituality and anti-materialism." Yet these scholars had limited influence. "Younger philologists, and most students of philosophy, literature, and art, pledged allegiance, not to a bygone ideal of cultivation, but rather to the eminently modern ideals of science and systematic research." Marcus then asks, "How did 'the humanities' lose its association with the conservatism of old-fashioned classicists, and become instead a comprehensive term that described a group of academic disciplines distinguished in content and method from the physical, biological, and social sciences?"[29]

In the early twentieth century, he argues, younger scholars "began to use the word *humanities* as a general term to refer to what bound their inquiries loosely together." Until 1930, this use of the term was "intermittent and inconsistent. Sometimes it applied to everything that was *not* a science (but that understanding would exclude a good deal of important humanistic scholarship itself), and sometimes it meant any study that has no immediate *utility*. Only gradually did it take on the sense that we accept and assume today." The signal turning point in this telling is, perhaps fittingly, semiotic: "Only in the 1930s and 1940s does the idea of, as well as the term, 'the humanities' begin to be deployed with regular frequency and with the relative specificity of reference to the disciplines that we apply it to today."[30]

The available evidence does not support this argument. The largely untapped data on admission and graduation requirements and on college curricula published by the American Council on Education from 1928 to 1936 make clear the recognition of the humanities. The humanities were prominent in colleges of arts, literature, and sciences, much as they are today.[31] The volumes list departments, divisions, and growing numbers of faculty under the humanities and disciplinary departments. In addition, searching through major universities' histories and organization charts finds the presence of "humanities" wherever we might now expect that term. For example, *The Daily Princetonian* reported that "Classics Demand Place in Present-Day World" in 1919. In 1931, it reported the founding of the Council on Humanities. Five years later, it announced that " 'a Divisional Program in Humanistic Studies' will be added to the University curriculum," marking "a significant step in adjusting Princeton's educational policy to one of its most apparent needs." (Following Professor Theodore Green, the students confused the humanities with humanism.)

Marcus's misreading of the sources fails to address the presence or absence of disciplinarity, multidisciplinarity, or interdisciplinarity. Only that omission allows Marcus to argue, in contrast to commentators as diverse as Connor and Grafton and Jardine, "that the humanities are essentially a modern invention, not the legacy of a longstanding tradition. Thus, when the authors of *General Education in a Free Society*, a Harvard Red Book published in 1945, confidently claimed, 'Tradition points to a separation of learning into the three areas of natural science, social studies, and the humanities,' they were talking nonsense, for they were summoning forth a tradition that did not exist before the 1930s." Ignoring the humanistic defense of freedom in the prewar period, Marcus insists on this reading for ideological reasons. He adopts a narrative trope of a rise and fall, for "the tradition thus conjured up" was short lived. Although the war "brought an influx of European refugee scholars, . . . the experience of the war years underlined the fragility of the humanist ideal . . . understood now as an imperiled but essential bulwark against barbarism."[32]

Marcus then makes another leap in pursuit of his revision of the traditions of the humanities, confusing multidisciplinarity with interdisciplinarity—a common misstep in the history of interdisciplinarity. He contends that in the postwar period "the organizational model customarily pursued was that of the interdisciplinary programs of American studies, many of which had gotten underway in the late 1940s and 1950s. Such innovations began frequently as movements within disciplines and departments. They then typically branched out into interdepartmental explorations, faculty seminars, interdisciplinary team-taught seminars, and then largely undergraduate courses of study." Among the programs he casts in this mold are African American and African studies; cultural studies; comparative studies; women's, gender, and sexuality studies; ethnic studies of various kinds, including Latino/a and Asian American; postcolonial studies; New Historical studies; and gay and lesbian studies. "They are, as the saying goes, where the action has been, and it isn't difficult to see why—they are doing something intrinsically right, however much one may want to hold concretely and specifically in reserve."[33] The conclusion that "something intrinsically right" somehow follows from successive rises and falls of the humanities is an astounding inference.[34] Hurtling to identify the interdisciplinary humanities, Marcus all but erases the humanities as more than individual disciplines and departments. In these terms, in fact, the humanities are dead.

All too often, unsympathetic critics take aim at the humanities, citing cultural and other so-called hyphenated studies as grounds for dismissing interdisciplinarity. These attacks, which come from left, right, and center, are based not only on intellectual, epistemological, methodological, and evidential grounds but also on political, ideological, and economic ones.

Despite its contemporary appeal at several private universities and endorsement in some quarters, Marcus's message is neither correct nor the only narrative of interdisciplinarity in the humanities. Beyond the contradictory myths are revealing historical complexities.

Language and Culture among and across the Disciplines

The usual narrative of the development of the modern university—and of the humanities and social sciences within it—emphasizes secularization, the rise of science, and the specialization and professionalization of research.[35] Historians Jon Roberts and James Turner fundamentally recast this account: "No one in 1850 could have predicted the shapes into which academic knowledge would shift by 1900. In probably the least likely turn, a congeries of studies almost unknown to earlier American colleges rapidly gained prominence in the liberal arts curriculum. These usurpers, dethroning the Greek and Latin regnant for centuries, were 'the humanities.'" Despite the dominant image of the "age of science," Roberts and Turner conclude that "it was not the natural or social sciences that provided the great novelty of academe, but the new humanities. . . . By 1900 the 'humanities' meant a wide range of 'cultural studies,' most new to the curriculum: literature, philosophy, art history, often general history as well." They emphasize that knowledge was transformed along with its academic organization. In a partial approach to interdisciplinarity, they see the humanities field as more than the sum of its parts.[36]

Interdisciplinarity is too often seen as opposed to specialization. But interdisciplinarity can be built on specialization, and even in the humanities it has sometimes has been viewed as essentially scientific. Interdisciplinarity can be specialized or nonspecialized. This quality varies by time period, by disciplines and disciplinary clusters, and by what we look for. The history of interdisciplinarity is a story of many misses, myths, and misconceptions, beginning with notions of the humanities as general and science as specialized.

Generalizing broadly about nineteenth-century America, Roberts and Turner argue that "disciplinary specialists . . . declared, though still uncertainly and confusedly, two revolutionary dogmata: that knowledge does *not* form a whole but, on the contrary, properly divides itself into distinct compartments, and that unique methodological principles and scholarly traditions govern life within each of these boxes."[37] At the same time, these specialists adopted a "variety of strategies for subduing the threat of disciplinary specialization and of intellectual secularization more broadly," reflecting prevailing concerns for civilization and cultivation as well as constituting an effort to restore coherence to knowledge.

As scholars navigated between the old and the new, they sought to fill perceived needs. "Compared to the old classical curriculum, subjects like English and history sported a tough-minded air of practicality."[38]

Yet the new or revised disciplines of the humanities differed from the natural sciences and social sciences. In part, this divergence revolved around the question of the general and the specialized within the developing orientation of scholarship and questions about the curriculum. They often pertained to perceptions of a gap between the undergraduate and graduate curricula. Notions of unity and coherence cut across emerging opinions among disciplinary clusters, hand in hand with greater acceptance of specialization and, quite likely, the equation of specialization with disciplinarity among the sciences, especially when compared with the humanities. The sciences and new social sciences made fewer gestures toward coherence and unity, while the humanities laid the groundwork for what later would be called interdisciplinary. Herein lay the foundations for many constructions and contradictions.

In effect, the humanities sought to have it both ways—to be general and to be specialized—which planted the seeds for conflicting conceptions of the field's interdisciplinarity and disciplinarity. Roberts and Turner write, "For their teachers, the humanities' highest merit seemed to lie in their capacity to restore coherence to knowledge and to sustain its religious character." Although many faculty approved of specialized graduate courses and "increasingly pursued their own research along disciplinary lines," they held to a different "ideal of undergraduate instruction." The construction was problematic on many levels. "That literature and art possess peerless power to ward off specialization and promote 'spiritual exchanges' is not intuitively obvious," and "they deployed these commonplaces with greater éclat and effect than colleagues in geology and sociology."[39]

Presented as a source of the humanities' uniqueness and strength, these evasions also stimulated criticism and opposition. This formulation of a unitary canon of "Culture" lent itself to marketing in the form of Great Books, classics, and encyclopedias. General education curricula often bill themselves as interdisciplinary, but in my view none carries that mantle deservedly. No less important, the idea of the humanities was repeatedly repackaged and represented in the form of core curricula, liberal arts, interdisciplinary humanities, contemporary civilization or its foundations, civics, and vocational preparation.[40]

Roberts and Turner problematically explain this split between the sciences and the humanities by arguing that they "derived from two different approaches to knowledge. European education had since antiquity encompassed two more or less distinct wings: rhetoric (roughly, the art of persuasion) and philosophy (roughly, the science of demonstration)." By the nineteenth century, they claim, the distinction evolved into one between "law-seeking natural science" and "an interpretive kind of knowledge" embodied in the humanities. In contrast to most dichotomized views, they point to the appeal of science and scientism throughout the humanities. Thus, "disciplinary specialization grew from the physical sciences. Their much-admired practitioners, as the nineteenth century moved toward the twentieth, increasingly communicated with each other in arcane dialects, more and more mathematical or otherwise formalized, more and more inaccessible to outsiders."[41]

For Roberts and Turner, the origins of "disciplines" in the humanities "lay in philology—in its fascination with texts and contexts, in its interpretive animus." Philology "provide[d] a tolerable substitute for the old unifying frame of knowledge embodied in moral philosophy." This foundation was based on two closely related assumptions: the principle that cultural context shaped every text; and the second historicism, the context of historical change.[42]

Roberts and Turner emphasize the integrating spirit of "textual philology" and argue that it "inspired" scholars and teachers of the humanities to believe "that the proper approach to a text was to treat it as illuminating, and as being illuminated by, its culture (in the historian's sense of that last word)." Making a certain leap, they maintain that "the integrative impulse imbued . . . in philology by its historicist practices was decisive," although "this integrative urge" was "often eclipsed by the dust of scholarship."[43] Reasserted regularly in the form of integrative liberal arts education, this "philological" tradition was presented as multi- or interdisciplinary. As Grafton and Jardine take pains to remind us, however, it was not connected with the history of humanism despite recurrent appeals to that image.

The new liberal education, Roberts and Turner assert, had two major elements: beauty and continuity. "The first was to acquaint students with beauty, especially as manifest in 'poetry' broadly conceived. Because the point was to cultivate wide human sympathies, it made no sense to subdivide the humanities into bins divided by disciplinary specialization. . . . But simple breadth . . . did not actually make knowledge more coherent; indeed, it might diffuse it." The second element was "a stress on continuities linking the 'poetry' of one era to that of succeeding periods and ultimately to our own. . . . Thus the notion of a continuous European civilization gained pedagogical importance. The concept descended from a common earlier idea of 'universal civilization.'" The second theme, in contrast, stressed cultural distinctiveness and continuity. In this way, the humanities aimed to "counteract the new specialized college studies that narrowed 'intellectual vision.'" For proponents of this view, "the cultural and cultivating agenda of the humanities exerted special appeal, for it had both resonance with the regnant ideal of 'liberal culture' and program specificity. . . . The 'unity and independence of culture studies' was widely assumed."[44]

Roberts and Turner make an unusually strong historical argument for the humanities' claims for its place in the formation of the modern world and its centrality to the modern disciplinary university. Although it is not their purpose, they also help us to understand its quest for interdisciplinarity. At the same time, they suggest some of the contradictions and continuing challenges for the humanities as a field, its interdisciplinarity initiatives, and interdisciplinarity more generally. "The knowledge offered around 1900 in the humanities had a hard time qualifying as 'real' knowledge, for it looked very different from the more disciplinary knowledge that 'serious' scholars pursued. Even professors of literature or classics usually took a different, more disciplinary tack when they left the classroom for research. The cobbling together of general education programs—typically around the humanities, as in the Western Civilization curricula of the 1950s—has ever since proved both awkward and remarkably remote from the hard-core research concerns of the American university."[45]

In their conclusion, Roberts and Turner add to Grafton and Jardine's story of the humanities' evasiveness. Insofar as that evasiveness influenced what has come to be presented as interdisciplinary humanities, whether as liberal or general education, civilization, "humanities education," or, more recently, cultural studies, it is contradictory at its core. The humanities' axiomatic *"philological historicism* militated against any cogent epistemological holism," they write. "'Civilization' gave breadth and meaning to college studies, but it did so at the implicit cost of denying the possibility of a single unified knowledge."[46]

If proponents of the revolution in the humanities such as Roberts and Turner come to such conclusions, are Kagan's and Marcus's views, however inaccurate, so surprising? Two major problems remain. First, this integrative, illuminating impulse constitutes one narrative of the humanities, but it is not the only one. Second, "replac[ing] disciplinary knowledges with knowledges that were in the end equally incommensurable" is hardly interdisciplinary. Nondisciplinarity and adisciplinarity have long substituted falsely for interdisciplinarity or even multidisciplinarity. This confusion, I suggest, is inseparably related to the putative and real decline of the humanities.[47]

Philology, Science, and Interdisciplinarity

In contrast to Roberts and Turner, other commentators emphasize the quest for professionalization and specialization in the humanities. Although this impulse was never dominant, the humanities have sought currency, acceptance, and authority in science by imitating science's methods and truth claims. This more specialized, alternative approach to interdisciplinarity has surfaced periodically in initiatives in "new" histories, literary and language studies, cognitive science, neurology, and evolution. But its sources run much deeper and reach back much farther.

Writing in the inaugural volume of the *Transactions of the Modern Language Association of America* in 1884–1885, H. C. G. Brandt, professor of French and German at Hamilton College, asked:, "How far should our teaching and textbooks have a scientific basis?" While cautioning against "going too fast and too far" in adopting the "new facts and new laws of language," Brandt declared that "in the department of Modern Languages as in many other departments the danger lies in the other direction, not merely in ultra-conservatism in appropriating and digesting the new results, not merely in ignoring them, but in unpremeditated, unconscious, downright ignorance of them." Many professors of language adamantly deny that "our department *is* a science."[48]

Brandt's reasons reveal his assumptions. "By basing our instruction and textbooks upon a scientific ground-work, our department and our profession gain dignity and weight." Science would allow teachers to remedy the fact that the "still prevailing method of teaching Latin and Greek is old-fashioned, stale and stereotyped. . . . Our teaching of modern languages is loose, random, unsystematic." The profession should recognize that "the teacher must be as specially and as scientifically trained for his work in our department as well as in any other." The benefits would be significant. "A scientific basis affords a valuable discipline, otherwise not attained from the study of a living language. There is a great deal of prejudice still on this score against our department, strongest, perhaps, against the study of English."[49] Language and literature departments should take their place among the disciplines, which confers status and dignity. Other humanities professors agreed with Brandt, evincing what some have called "discipline envy" promoting the *discipline* of their discipline.[50]

John Guillory accords greater emphasis to what he terms "scientificity" in the humanities, especially in language and literature. Tracing the origins of these fields to rhetoric and belles lettres, he stresses that as "discourses of knowledge were increasingly subject to norms of scientificity," the linguistic norms and tastes embedded in them failed to achieve full disciplinary status, yet "criticism" thrived. "Criticism became a capacious and indefinitely inclusive discourse, taking as its object not only poems or plays, but also social and political policies, and, finally, society itself." Guillory then generalizes to the humanities in familiar terms. "The constitution of a hierarchy of rationalities—scientific, moral, aesthetic—determined the formation of disciplines in the late nineteenth century, and in particular the modern character of the humanities. The humanistic disciplines were able to maintain their status among the disciplines only to the extent that they continued to make empirical claims. Over the long term, such empirical claims were hard to sustain, and this fact condemned the humanities to their familiar insecurity in the modern constellation of disciplines." As disciplines and disciplinary clusters took shape, Guillory observes, "the bipartite distinction of moral and natural philosophy somehow gave rise to the tripartite distinction of the humanities, social sciences, and natural sciences, . . . with the humanities now defined in opposition to all of the scientific disciplines."[51]

Concerned with experiences that "philosophy had come to call 'aesthetic'" but seemed to escape empirical study, belles lettres declined. It also failed as a disciplinary ideal because a concept of *bildung* and national culture was not institutionalized in the nineteenth-century Anglo-American university, while the translation of the ideals of science and research from German to English and American universities led to "a much more powerful ideal to its Anglo-American counterparts: *research*," writes Guillory. "The ideal of culture was linked from the beginning to the production of new knowledge, and not merely with the cultivation of taste."[52]

In Germany, and on the European continent more generally, science was constructed differently. "The scholarly discourses that developed into what we now call the 'humanities' were just as likely as the natural sciences to consider themselves 'empirical.' . . . All of these disciplines . . . were still comprised within the faculty of 'philosophy.'" Moreover, teaching and research remained united, even for the most distinguished scholars.[53] Because these disciplines were less closely connected in American universities, interdisciplinarity in the humanities was associated with undergraduate general education. This tradition, which persists, often distinguished specialized from general versions of interdisciplinarity.

Research in the humanities, and especially in languages, meant philology, the new, more historically oriented science of language that developed in the eighteenth century. Stating the centrality of this discipline even more strongly than Roberts and Turner, Guillory argues that philology was "one of the proto-humanistic empirical sciences."[54] "It translated the Idealist program of culture into an empirical discourse" and "strongly affected research protocols in the other disciplines that we now call the 'humanities'—classics, history, philosophy." It "brought these disciplines into a close relation to the current standards of scientificity at the same time that it unified scholarly enterprises within a total view of the history of civilization or culture."[55] As historian of linguistics Hans Aarsleff observes, philology was "'the' model humanistic discipline" that was "factual, descriptive, classificatory, empirical, and comparative."[56] Guillory elaborates: "Its identity as an empirical discipline was never perceived as incompatible with its reliance on archival or textual evidence. On the contrary, philology and related historical discourses arguably advanced a more plausible claim to empirical standards of verification than earlier arguments in moral philosophy, which often seemed deductive or speculative by comparison."[57]

Despite its role in launching the research university with the humanities at the core of the production of new knowledge, philology's status as empirical and allied to science did not last. It declined because of "rapid advances in the natural sciences and in technological applications that threw into relief the difference between the natural sciences and the humanistic disciplines."[58] It also declined because the concept of Kultur, while powerful, was in the end unstable. Newer scientific methods weakened philology's epistemological claims.

In the context of the division of knowledge into natural and social science, on the one hand, and the humanities, on the other, philologists dominated the new literature and language departments in the United States. "If the growing prestige of science enhanced the position of the philologists, this advantage was really the effect of a conjuncture, the coincidence of bureaucratic organization with a moment of heightened prestige for science." Yet what were soon called English departments remained divided between the teaching and study of language and of literature, the "distinction between them, that is, on the difference between the science of philology and the nonscientific, bellelettristic study of literature."[59] Ultimately, this disciplinary reorganization left philology at a disadvantage. "It attempted first to claim language as its scientific object; and then, in the form of a positivistic literary history, it claimed literature as well, the object that seemed to resist science by its very nature. . . . In the end, the failure of philology to establish the study of literature on scientific grounds weakened its claim to scientificity, and perhaps cleared the way for a new science of language—linguistics."[60]

General Education as Interdisciplinarity

Origins matter. The history of the humanities writ large—and of interdisciplinarity in the humanities—is a story of proclaimed continuities and revolutionary transformations. Underlying these continuities and transformations is a repeating pattern of recovery and rediscovery, sometimes with awareness but sometimes not, which carry powerful implications for disciplinarity and interdisciplinarity. Significantly, in this history, a chronicle of philosophy and other disciplines substituted for any systematic or critical account of them. Consequently, humanities courses were placed at the beginning as introductory, rather than the end, of undergraduate education. William Riley Parker, former secretary of the Modern Language Association and editor of its flagship journal, *PMLA*, observed in 1967: "Thanks first to its academic origins, and then to the spirit of competition and aggressiveness engendered by departmentalization, *'English' has never really defined itself as a discipline.*"[61]

Waldo G. Leland of the American Council of Learned Societies ignored the entire question of disciplinarity in "Recent Trends in the Humanities" in *Science* in 1934. Rehearsing a familiar analysis, Leland declared that knowledge "assumed the form of a triangle" with the sciences occupying one side, the social sciences the second, and the humanities the third. "The humanities concern themselves with the manifestations of spiritual existence . . . through the ages of human history and throughout the entire scene of human activity, and to interpret this experience for the enrichment of life as it must be lived in the present." The "data" of the humanities are "all the manifestations of the spiritual life of man"; the methods are "historical and descriptive; whether they are true sciences or whether they are something less and the same time more does not greatly matter." Much like NEH today, Leland defined the humanities by listing disciplines. "The collective term, humanities, refers, therefore, to a vast and complex group of studies, many of which are highly specialized, but all of which are related by a common ultimate objective—to contribute to the recovery and interpretation of the spiritual experience of mankind."[62]

After pointing briefly to "an increasing awareness of the close relation of the humanities to the sciences," Leland emphasized the irreducible unity of the field. The "most significant trend is the growing realization on the part of most scholars in the humanities that their respective disciplines or fields of study can not be shut off from each other as though in compartments. . . . The barriers due to the exigencies of university departmentalization, or to the technical dif-

ficulties of the disciplines, are artificial and must be done away with if the humanities are to advance upon a common front." Proclaiming the urgent need
for the humanities, he continued: "The scholars whose work lies in the fields
of the humanities have not shut themselves up in an ivory tower. . . . They are
aware of the acuteness of the problems that beset humanity to-day, and desire to
contribute to their solution. They believe that they have, in troublous times, a
special duty to minister to the needs to the world, but they believe that, foremost
among those needs, are a true knowledge and a clear understanding of the spiritual experience of mankind."[63] Herein the field's ultimate expansiveness was
inseparably intertwined with its ultimate limitations.

An instructive work published four years later, *The Meaning of the Humanities: Five Essays by Ralph Barton Perry, August Charles Krey, Erwin Panofsky, Robert
Lowry Calhoun, and Gilbert Chinard*, not only reveals the perception of a recurrent threat to the humanities earlier in the twentieth century but also confirms
Grafton and Jardine's argument by unproblematically presuming the unity and
universality of the humanities. Writing in the shadow of the Great Depression,
fascism, and the Third Reich, editor Theodore Greene discusses "humanists"
rather than "the humanities" and proffers a deeply conservative mix of the timeless and the timely. "The whole world is drifting or being driven with ever greater
acceleration into a state profoundly antagonistic to the values which the humanist most sincerely cherishes. Social mechanization, whether industrial, political,
or militaristic, threatens increasingly that freedom of thought and responsible
action which is the very condition of human dignity. . . . Both individually and
collectively we are in many ways the helpless victims of forces that still defy successful control." Failing to appreciate "unity amid diversity" and the humanities'
defense of it, anti-humanistic forces "have succeeded in arousing in their supporters a passionate and uncritical devotion to a 'common' cause."[64]

The problem, according to Greene, is that the humanist necessarily is out
of step with society. Opposing whatever is "common," he proudly proclaims his
elitism and idealism. "He is by definition an individualist; and the uncoordinated
activities of individuals are notoriously ineffective in a regimented society. He is
a natural aristocrat in taste and in sensitiveness to the finer values; and in every
society, truly imaginative individuals unhappily constitute a minority. He is
committed to reflective scrutiny and criticism. . . . The life of humanistic wisdom
and enjoyment demands, in short, both security and leisure, and where, today,
are security and leisure to be found in common?" Greene defends humanism against charges of irrelevance by challenging "the ultimate realism of the

self-styled 'realist.'" The humanist defends "the whole set of moral, aesthetic, and religious values which modern dictators misinterpret and twist to their own ends."[65]

Also in pursuit of *The Meaning of the Humanities*, Ralph Barton Perry, professor of philosophy at Harvard, sought to offer a definition of "the humanities" (putting the phrase in quotation marks to acknowledge their ambiguity). He implies that the humanities field "transcend[s] the sum of its parts and its temporal relations." His discourse slides alarmingly from university studies to humanism and humaneness. While advancing a strong defense, he concedes that the field found itself with less and less of a hearing within and outside the academy. The contradiction between claiming a superordinate place and feeling its ground shrinking reveals his anxiety. "I define 'the humanities,' then, to embrace whatever influences conduce to freedom. 'The humanities' is not to be employed as a mere class name for certain divisions of knowledge or parts of a scholastic curriculum, or for certain human institutions, activities and relationships, but to signify a certain condition which these may serve to create." Perry's concerns and goals lay in the realm of values, metaphysics, and ideology, but they are programmatic. "By freedom I mean enlightened choice. I mean the action in which habit, reflex or suggestion are superseded by an individual's fundamental judgments of good and evil; the action whose premises are explicit; the action which proceeds from personal reflection and integration. This, I take it, is liberal education. . . . The principle of freedom argues for breadth rather than concentration of knowledge, and for subject-matter rather than method."[66]

The problem in the United States, in his view, is the disciplinary specialization of higher education. Perry takes aim at liberal arts colleges, which had recently grouped their departments into divisions of "physical science, biological science, social science—*and* 'the humanities.' Now this is a most extraordinary arrangement. In an institution which professes to exist for the purpose of inculcating it, liberal culture is only one-quarter of the whole; and a nondescript quarter, occupying the place of a sort of rearguard appointed to pick up the stragglers and misfits which have no place higher up in the procession!" Organizing departments into divisions had "one merit," however; "it signifies the groping for a unity that shall counteract the pulverizing effect of specialized research and administrative decentralization."[67]

The resolute enemy of splitting within subjects and across knowledge, Perry ended up with a meaningless holism. In his ringing denial of the "humanistic possibilities" of "all studies," does he "define" the humanities as all but out of business or as a new business of distillation?

All studies are humanities, when ... their humanistic possibilities are realized in intercourse between the seasoned humanity of the teacher and the innocent humanity of the student. But these auspicious conditions cannot be guaranteed. Hence the importance of giving prominence in a curriculum of liberal education to those studies which are so stubbornly humanistic that they can scarcely fail to distil some humanism even between uninspired teachers and unreceptive students. Hence the indispensable role of "*the* humanities," the humanities *par excellence*, such as history, literature, art, and philosophy. These studies afford the highest probability in the long run that students, even if they do not want it, will obtain from teachers, even though these do not have it, some slight trace of that freedom, of that learning, imagination, and sympathy, of that dignity and demeanor proper to a man, which I have here called "humanity."[68]

Need we wonder about negative judgments of the value and usefulness of the humanities, charges of elitism, or the conflict between the disciplines of the humanities and the humanities as whole?[69]

We are left with a quandary. During the making of the humanities within the modern university, prominent humanities scholars rejected academic disciplines, and their implicit stance in favor of nondisciplines became inseparable from what was later deemed "interdisciplinary" humanities. That process of claiming or constructing the field was both retrospective and prospective and simultaneously competed with and imitated the sciences and social sciences.

Curricular Innovations

Humanities courses and programs in Western civilization were launched in the wake of the First World War, almost twenty years before the programs at Princeton, Columbia, Harvard, Yale, and Chicago that Steven Marcus emphasizes. These innovations were conceived in much the same spirit as *The Meaning of the Humanities*. They also followed Harvard president Charles William Eliot's Harvard Classics books, which were emulated by other great books curricula, reading programs, and promotions. Class, culture, commercialism, and modes of cross-disciplinarity combined, with potent consequences for the present and the future.

In 1922, John Erskine celebrated the General Honors program at Columbia College.[70] "When America entered the war, the Faculty ... had just adopted a plan to offset" the "centrifugal tendency" of disciplinary curricula. The two-year, optional program was "built on a list of fifty to sixty great books on which the faculty agreed," which included "masterpieces in all fields." Immediately after the war, the faculty added a required course in Contemporary Civilization, "which serves as a remarkable way to give the students a common intellectual world. The course was a natural outgrowth of the studies in the Causes of the War. . . . It was inevitable that similar enquiries should be made, though with no sinister prejudice, into the causes of contemporary civilization in the wake of global threats to the world as known." A few years later, Columbia revised the curriculum again. Different groups of disciplines took divergent paths, generating diverse forms of disciplinarity, inter- and cross-disciplinarity, and general education that have given rise to myriad misunderstandings, confusions, and debates. The departments of economics, government, history, philosophy, psychology, and sociology "reached such a degree of mutual understanding that they are able to envisage their problems not in terms of the vested interests of the several departments, but in terms of the education of young men. In fact, members of the staff of the college in these departments are pooling their interests to such an extent that one scarcely realizes that they are representing this or that department." Thus the required course was extended to two years "to simultaneously serve both the interests of the prospective scholar who would specialize in some one of these departments and also the general student." The sciences offered new general courses along with "more intensive and thorough courses."[71]

These changes planted the seeds for subsequent developments that were sometimes seen as interdisciplinary. At Columbia, they included the widely imitated University Seminars and, on a much larger scale, what has been called the general education movement. These curricular and research changes may be considered as a social and intellectual movement along the lines suggested by Scott Frickel and Neil Gross in 2005.[72] The programs' mixed reviews stemmed from their contradictory objectives, which ranged from common foundations to acculturation, civilization, and civics and promised a better distribution of credits and workloads as well as cost effectiveness. Interdisciplinarity played many parts.[73]

The University Seminar movement at Columbia, which was stimulated by World War II, built on cross-disciplinary mandates but aimed at greater specificity and specialization than earlier humanities efforts. Writing in 1953, Frank Tannenbaum quoted Professor Edgar G. Miller's 1950 report: "In the winter of 1940–1941, the world was in as much a mess as now, and the University was terribly worried. President Butler asked Jessop to ask the University to get conscious. The point of view on which that original thinking started was that the university scholars were contributing heavily to the world. Here on Morningside Heights our concentration of special knowledge, and adding New York City, was pretty hot. Was there any way of bringing this specialized knowledge, apart from individual efforts, into focus on problems presented to the University and to the world?" In Miller's view, the faculty "flunked the project completely." But about four years later, the faculty of political science "dreamed up this seminar thing—the best answer available. The problem that originally sparked the whole thing—the ability to focus on a problem—is really the reason for the seminar." He conceived of the seminars "as being, in effect, permanent, independent organisms . . . cutting across all departments and calling for cooperative participation from scholars in various fields." They would be "devoted to the study of some of the basic institutions continuous in human society, such, for instance, as the state, war, the organization of labor including the history of slavery, crime, or such ever-present issues as conflict between church and state, friction between urban and rural areas, or the human family." Defined by subject, seminars "would achieve one of the things long sought for—cooperation between the departments in the University. It would, for the purpose of those seminars, obliterate the departmental lines and throw the emphasis from a 'subject' to a 'going concern.' "[74]

Eight years after the founding of the Columbia Seminars, Tannenbaum expounded on the rationale for interdisciplinarity. The theory he posited draws explicitly from the relationship between the university and the disciplines. "Unconsciously, perhaps, the University Seminar movement has a theory of the integration of human experience, as well as its own notion of the structure of knowledge that is different from that which underlies the organization of the University. Our Faculties of Political Science, Philosophy, and Pure Science, and our professional schools as well, are compounded of departments which rest upon the assumed existence of 'disciplines.' The discipline is conceived of as some unique body of knowledge—practical and theoretical—which is sufficiently self-contained, pure, isolated and independent, so that it can be studied meaningfully by itself." "In contrast, the University Seminar movement sees society organized in many continuing institutions, enriched by experiences peculiar to themselves, and possessed of knowledge and wisdom derived from their own associated existence." Focusing on institutions "as constituent bodies of our society," the seminars "aim to encompass all of these elements by building an academic fellowship in which they are represented. The University Seminar, therefore, reaches for membership into all disciplines and activities pertinent to the object."[75]

Growing out of the general education movement, the University Seminars looked toward specialized cross- or multidisciplinary organization. Yet they stopped short of becoming research enterprises. A seminar "is an intellectual fellowship which deals with ideas rather than facts. . . . It is concerned with meaning, direction, drift, purpose, value. The facts are plentiful; their many-sided significance is often hidden." Its goal was not integration or the development of a common methodology. Regardless of its limitations, the practice of bringing several distinct disciplines to bear on a common problem was touted as one form of interdisciplinarity.[76] As the University Seminars proliferated, their leadership shifted to the School of General Studies, which emphasized addressing public policy questions.

In 1982, education writer Ronald Gross observed a miscellany of programs and asked whether "the time is now riper for replication of the seminar idea" in order to employ "the unprecedented number of researchers in many fields who have advanced academic training but for whom there are no jobs as professors."[77] Gross failed to notice that multi- or interdisciplinarity has long been proposed as a solution for broad problems. The pressing issue, then and now, is whether such programs are best seen as occasioned by particular moments, and thereby have a short half-life, or serve as an oasis for a reserve army of academic laborers.[78]

The general education movement, which has often been described as or claimed to be interdisciplinary, developed from the same current as interdisciplinarity. General education is, however, more contradictory. Writing in the *Journal of General Education*'s inaugural issue in 1946, Earl James McGrath, a dean at the University of Iowa and future U.S. commissioner of education, declared without qualification that *"general education is not concerned with the esoteric and highly specialized knowledge of the scholar."* Rather, it

> *prepares the young for the common life of their time and their kind.* Hence it includes that fund of knowledge and beliefs and those habits of language and thought which characterize and give stability to a particular social group. It is the unifying element of a culture. It embraces the great moral truths, the scientific generalizations, the aesthetic conceptions, and the spiritual values of the race, ignorance of which makes men incapable of understanding themselves and the world in which they live. General education prepares the individual for a full and satisfying life as a member of a family, as a worker, as a citizen, and as an integrated and purposeful human being. . . . To this end general education provides youth with a knowledge of the origins and meaning of the customs and political traditions which govern the life of their time. It cultivates habits of effective writing and speaking of the modern tongue. It develops the faculty of critical thinking and the capacity

for intellectual workmanship. It introduces the student to the moral problems which have perplexed men through the ages and acquaints him with the solutions they have devised.[79]

The "salient features of this movement," McGrath said, are *"a revolt against specialism"* and a *"reaction against vocationalism."* They come together in *"an effort to integrate the subject matter of related disciplines."* In stating his case for what many came to see as interdisciplinarity, McGrath exaggerated the balkanization of the academy and its social implications: "The borders between even closely related departments are more carefully guarded than the frontiers of hostile nations. No academic sin is visited with more immediate and general disapprobation than that of speaking 'out of one's own field.' Subject matter is systematically organized in ladder-like units, up the rungs of which the student climbs to the empyrean of learning sublimely unaware of other areas of knowledge or of the teeming world of real life. . . . This intellectual isolationism is no less stultifying to the life of the mind than its political counterpart is to the life of the nation." For him, the route to integration lay in curricular reorganization, especially in survey and core courses: "A survey of the social sciences, for example, frequently contains elements of sociology, political science, psychology, and history. An alternative scheme for integration attempts an organization of appropriate materials from several fields around certain social problems such as crime and poverty."[80] McGrath was remarkably unconcerned about the specific interrelationships that constitute interdisciplinarity.

In "Changing Humanities," a survey of the postwar period, Julie Thompson Klein makes sweeping generalizations under the banner of interdisciplinarity. Like her predecessors, she fails to reflect on the sources of the strong and continuing backlash against the humanities. Instead, she proclaims that by the end of the century a "host of developments" had made interdisciplinarity a new mantra in the humanities.[81] This profusion of developments, however, engenders profound confusion, especially in the absence of systematic definitions. Although I am a strong supporter of sound general education and of interdisciplinarity, I am astonished by the claims, counterclaims, confusions, and so-called innovations of the postwar period. The history of general education is not an inspiring story.

One of the more prominent general education programs is that associated with Robert Maynard Hutchins, who served as president of the University of Chicago from 1929 to 1950. The common core curriculum he instituted, which constituted one-half of undergraduate degree requirements, became inseparable from the image of the university and the experience of its students. A cry of protest resounded when President Hugo Sonnenschein announced its reduction in February 1999. In her critical examination of the Chicago program, Anne H. Stevens finds contradictions in its philosophy of general education and concludes that its mythical "golden age" is belied by its rigid divisional structure and Great Books curriculum. The classic general education program was founded by elite liberal arts colleges. At St. John's College, for example, all four years centered on a list of one hundred great books discussed in seminars and complemented by lectures, laboratory experiments, and language tutorials. McGrath and Hutchins advocated popular higher education as a means of advancing democracy. But, Stevens points out, "the general education movement promoted democratic values within exclusionary institutions."[82] Moreover, although the curriculum was not interdisciplinary, general education was increasingly identified as multidisciplinary or even interdisciplinary.

John Guillory quips that general education's "curricular aim of giving Americans a crash course in the classics is the institutional analogue of the guilty cultural conscience that finds its expressive realization in the artifacts of middlebrow culture." More seriously, he argues that "the history of general education is marked by a recurrent failure to produce in its subjects the level of culture for which it reaches."[83] In his view, general education, which is uniquely American, was a response to the rapid growth of the university system and the elective curriculum in the late nineteenth and twentieth centuries. The demand for specialized credentials clashed with the desire to connect students to a "minimally 'common'" cultural tradition. Guillory is struck by general education's "consistent expression . . . of a desire to redress a perceived social ill—a great deficit in 'general' knowledge, in the most important knowledge a human being or citizen needs in life." Yet, paradoxically, the university devotes ever less time and space to meeting that need. Moreover, along the way, Guillory observes, general education was confused with liberal education, a point others have not emphasized. Both have been conflated with interdisciplinarity or multidisciplinarity. "Still more problematically, with the recession of liberal education as the governing ideal of the university, general education came to be elided with the humanities disciplines, understood as the field concerned chiefly with the preservation of traditional high cultural works of literature and philosophy."[84]

Integration, especially in the natural and social sciences, has often been abandoned in favor of distribution requirements. Although the humanities faculty has carried the burden of providing general education, the humanities "were themselves evolving rapidly into modern disciplines, organized along thoroughly professional lines and with modern research agendas," which "vitiated the conservative construction of their purpose in general education." While general education's "exalted claims" are undercut by their remedial function, "the need for these programs to annex claims for American democracy to the tradition of Western culture is an obvious sign of their innate weakness as ideological instruments."[85] No wonder interdisciplinarity was more pretense than presence.

Daniel Bell concluded his 1966 classic, *The Reforming of General Education*, with a familiar complaint:

> The interdisciplinary aim has suffered the most and has indeed all but disappeared from many educational curriculums. Institutional factors in part account for this failure: in many colleges the departments preferred to concentrate on the disciplinary sequences and directed their students to the specific research problems of their subject, instead of attempting the more difficult task of searching out a conceptual language common to several fields. . . . Even more telling were the intellectual difficulties inherent in interdisciplinary studies. To some scholars such studies meant a new holistic approach that would fuse disciplines. . . . To others it meant the study of policy problems, bringing the resources of different disciplines to bear on specific issues. . . . But students were often asked to consider complicated topics when they had no training in any of the disciplines necessary for intelligent judgments about the dispute. Criticism of such topics was airily dismissed with argument that these topics were primarily "value problems" or "moral issues," as if a discussion of goals required no technical knowledge at all.

"My objection to interdisciplinary courses is not to the idea itself, but to the place they occupied in the general education sequence," Bell declared.[86] In contrast to many other proponents of general education, he proposed multidisciplinarity applications to common problems, along with historical and philosophical understanding of the foundations of a field and comparative study for the final year. This is a rare specificity. We would do well to institute it anew.

Remaking the Interdisciplinary Humanities

That the landscape of interdisciplinary humanities is, at best, uneven should come as no surprise. Postwar exhortations on the benefits of integrative education extend earlier themes without clarification and confuse interdisciplinarity with general education. The general and the specialized, as well as lower- and upper-division undergraduate and graduate education, continue to compete in the views of scholars, the evaluation of administrators, the choices of students graduate and undergraduate, and the minds of outside publics, blurring their critical distinctions. Lists and elaborate taxonomies take the place of definition. The battles over terms and their seemingly endless proliferation exceed the rhetorical skills of even the best academic satirical novels. Reflecting its search for identity and recognition, the Association for Integrative Studies, which formed in 1979, changed its name to the Association for Interdisciplinary Studies in 2013. Perusing *Interdisciplinarity: Essays from the Literature*, edited by William Newell; *Interdisciplinarity and Higher Education*, edited by Joseph Kockelmans; and the mix of program descriptions and syllabi posted on the AIS's website reveals a miscellany of additive and multiplicative disciplinarities that cannot substitute for problems, questions, and intellectual relationships of knowledge, theory, method, and practice. AIS fosters diversity, multidisciplinarity, and nondisciplinarity, not interdisciplinarity.[87] That does not advance the case for the humanities in and of themselves in the university and other houses of knowledge.[88]

Julie Klein's list of disciplines and multidisciplines in the guise of interdisciplines testifies to this problem. In her 2005 compilation on the humanities, she enthuses:

> The rise of interdisciplinary fields is a major episode in the history of knowledge. They constitute one of the frontiers of innovation in higher education and have been a primary locus for new scholarship and teaching. Their emergence is often dated to the 1960s and 1970s. Their history began earlier, though, in the 1930s and 1940s, with the development of area studies, American studies, and the expansion of comparative literature. By the early twenty-first century, a host of examples populated the academic landscape: from molecular biology, cognitive science, and materials science to criminology, gerontology, and policy studies to gender studies, media studies, and cultural studies.[89]

Without inquiring into differences or definitions, Klein extends this list with labor studies, future studies, and fields that she supposes are based on "life experience"—black studies, women's studies, and ethnic studies. "The rise of new disciplines, interdisciplines, and paradisciplines is no longer regarded as an unusual event. In the wake of anti, cross-, and interdisciplinary studies, Marjorie Garber comments acidly, some traditional disciplines have been renamed, becoming English studies, literary studies, and romance studies." Her conclusion that "interdisciplinary studies serve a need that is not going away" does not follow, however. She is forced to concede that, as Ken "Wissocker reminds us, it is easier to produce disciplinary visions of purportedly interdisciplinary spaces such as literary cultural studies and sociological cultural studies than to construct and maintain full-fledged interdisciplinary spaces."[90]

The remainder of *Humanities, Culture, and Interdisciplinary* is an accounting of "Inter/disciplining Humanities"—cleverly divided into "Rewriting the Literary," "Refiguring the Visual," and "Retuning the Aural"—and "Interdisciplining 'America'"—comprising "Reconstructing American Studies" and "Defining Other Americas." Interdisciplinarity itself is neither (re)constructed nor defined. Interests and emphases within disciplines change. Presence and status rise and fall. The new and the old clash and compete. But neither encyclopedism nor holism equals interdisciplinarity. If relationships are key, interdisciplinarity may in fact lay closer to their antithesis. This may be the constructive critical lesson imparted by the new histories, and cultural studies, and the so-called hyphenated studies, including American studies.[91]

Communication: Discipline or Interdiscipline?

If interdisciplinarity within or across a field of study addresses gaps, disconnections, separations, or differences and is devoted to exploring and furthering relationships, pursuing questions, and resolving problems both old and new, then communication presents a curious case. First, the field is unusually marked by its foundations in distinct disciplines and the continuation of disciplinary research; its commercial applications in advertising; its political traditions in opinion surveys and polling (as well as persuasion and propaganda); and its persistent connections to the promotion of democracy and political-economic modernization. It has valuable professional dimensions, ranging from journalism, broadcasting, and public relations to digital communications, and it claims authority over writing that spans new and old media, mass and interpersonal communication, and academic and empirical research. Although diversity can be construed as a strength, it is not in itself a path to successful interdisciplinary relationships. The whole is lost in the parts.

Second, the organization and location of the field reflect these complications. Despite the stereotypically low opinion held by other faculty members of the field's intellectual stature, communication programs typically enroll many students and do relatively well in soliciting research funding and contracts. There are turf wars with sociology, psychology, political science, cultural studies, and English departments and with colleges of business and education. An online search of undergraduate and graduate programs in the humanities uncovered information on 180 universities, including 178 undergraduate degree programs,

113 master's, and 42 PhD programs. Forty programs awarded master's and doctoral degrees. Journalism, speech, and professional programs are among the oldest. The names and locations of programs illustrate the incoherence of this field.[92] This bewildering array highlights the myriad connections communication has with other fields but reveals that it has no core of its own. Similarly, numerous professional organizations reflect all these distinctions and blur scholarly, professional, and corporate lines.[93]

Third, communication scholars are unusually concerned with discovering, rediscovering (after presumably forgetting), or inventing its traditions. Its practitioners also admit imitating other popular trends, such as "paradigms" or "genealogies." The many bibliographies or anthologies show how deeply this preoccupation has shaped the literature. Much discussion in these volumes focuses on an absent or rediscovered "critical" tradition. Such an incessant search for traditions betrays a profound insecurity.[94]

Finally, the field seems preoccupied with hagiography, telling its story through the biographies of its "great men."[95] Identifying a genealogy that extends from John Dewey (or even Aristotle) through centuries of rhetoricians to Paul Lazarsfeld, Wilbur Schramm, and Marshall McLuhan (or even Michel Foucault and Jürgen Habermas) is a sign of its unstable institutional and intellectual location and its confusion about disciplinarity and interdisciplinarity.

On occasion, surveys of the field awkwardly summarize its traditions as historiographical. A dozen years before Susan Herbst, for example, Gertrude Robinson wrote: "Since the 1980s, we have been bombarded with numerous articles and books debating our field's theoretical foundations. . . . In addition, there seems to have been a sudden proliferation of theoretical approaches and vigorous debate and promotion of the so-called critical approach to communication studies by a group of young scholars. What does all of this . . . signify?" Despite her mistaken dating and failure to look to other fields, she proposed that a "proper historiography of our field . . . provides evidence for the genealogy of U.S. communication studies and their intersection with the disciplinary developments of sociology and psychology. Historiographical accounts also enable us to circumscribe periods where intellectual schemas changed and predominant concerns in communication studies were redefined."[96] But historiography is not history. Nor is a useful history of communication studies found in a series of "paradigms" arranged chronologically. Robinson fails to go beyond claiming that "some scholars reject this theoretical plurality as fragmentation, whereas others view it as an enrichment of the enlarged agenda of communication studies."[97] In the same volume, Ellen Wartella observes: "Students of the sociology of knowledge report that when there are challenges to the dominant research perspectives of a field, it is common for a preoccupation with history to follow."[98] But these short-lived endeavors serve the cause of legitimation more than they promote critical understanding.

Communication, like the humanities, has failed to achieve interdisciplinarity in significant part because it failed to understand and learn critically and constructively from its history. This is one theme in writing about the field by both Karin Wahl-Jorgensen and Jefferson Pooley. But those who seek mainly to promote the field have neglected the work of these authors, which helps to explain communication's simultaneous but contradictory claims for disciplinarity, interdisciplinarity, and postdisciplinarity.

In his innovative *Theorizing Communication: A History*, Dan Schiller essays a critical and integrated history, with some attention to sociocultural and political contexts. He also suggests ways communication might be developed in more interdisciplinary directions and orientations. Schiller begins after World War II, pointedly observing that "communication was institutionalized as a scholarly discipline during this period of brutal intellectual constraint. . . . In a process combining opportunism with Cold War allegiance, critical concerns about the far-flung implications of mass persuasion in America were driven to the margins. . . . Leading academic communication researchers made indispensable, if often covert[,] contributions to the Cold War propaganda effort. Battening on a stream of military and quasi-military contracts, and drawing on the personal and scientific networks they had found during the war, their practical study of propaganda flourished."[99]

As economic boom followed postwar recovery,

> communication study was recruited as a prime instrument of a ubiquitous corporate marketing and promotion apparatus. Dispassionate analysis of mass persuasion in such a world required a daunting critical engagement with the very institutions which, while depending increasingly routinely on propaganda's practical exercise, had also come to be staffed and serviced by social scientists themselves. University-based social scientists now found themselves within a thickening web of philanthropic foundations, government agencies, corporate sponsors, and, of course, the media industries, willing and able to contribute individual research grants, program endowments, student recruitment prospects, and even access to attractive research sites. Small wonder that many in the new crop of scholarly communication experts became positively committed to dispelling popular criticisms of dominant communication media.

"Far-reaching shifts were signaled in the tone and content of social study," including a focus on the centrality of science and an assertion of American exceptionalism. In Schiller's view, communication was reinvented as a formal and theoretically restricted social science. This development underlay the study of opinion, persuasion, and propaganda under conditions of "monopolized" mass media.[100]

As the communication field grew, "discussions of media effects domestically began to generate ever-thicker hedgerows of qualifications, caveats, abridgements." As a result, the social psychology of communication "developed at a distance from a second, concurrent conceptual tradition, known as 'information theory.'" While reinforcing "the field's newfound detachment from the study of social relations," information theory "helped . . . to accredit an academic communication study as a Cold War science."[101] Schiller also notes the eclipse of the earlier critique of mass culture. Again, we must ask: is this a story of disciplinarity, interdisciplinarity, or postdisciplinarity?

Schiller, along with other recent scholars, begins his inquiries too late. The field's roots are found in the disciplinarization of the social and human sciences during the first decades of the twentieth century.[102] He acknowledges disciplinary origins in sociology, political science, and psychology but does not consider how these relationships shaped the field's development, particularly the struggles between its parts and the whole. The critical personal reflections offered by Harold Lasswell, Bernard Berelson, and Elihu Katz on disciplinary relationships and their complications tell us as much about the field's development as the "dominant paradigm" of its institutional creation by a handful of leaders. While reminding us of the field's long history and its firm place and impressive record of achievements in established disciplinary departments, together they raise important questions about its relative decline or disappearance from those departments and its piecemeal movement into a wide range of institutional units. The stories of these transitions from multiple disciplines to a non-, multi-, or interdiscipline are strikingly diverse both intellectually and institutionally.

In "How Not to Found a Field: New Evidence on the Origins of Mass Communication Research," Karin Wahl-Jorgensen describes what she sees as the University of Chicago's failure to develop an interdisciplinary program in communication. Her account is telling but ultimately mistaken, in part because she confounds multidisciplinarity with interdisciplinarity.[103] Wahl-Jorgensen argues that Wilbur Schramm was correct when in 1959 he argued for mass communication research as an academic discipline in its own right. In 1958, however, Harold Lasswell observed that "political science, in particular, happened to play an important role at a certain time in the promotion of interdisciplinary research in communication. Since that time the initiative has moved elsewhere, although professional students of government and law continue to devote more and more attention to communication. . . . The largest body of work of immediate significance has been done by scholars whose major conventional identification is with sociology, social psychology, and, to a lesser extent, social anthropology."[104] Lasswell also points to sociologist Lazarsfeld's Bureau of Applied Social Research, statistics, and social laboratory and to the "cross-disciplinary" research of engineers and neurologists "who exploited their ties with mathematics and physics." In concluding, he stated the need for collaboration and communication across the university, not for institutionalizing it as a discipline.

Bernard Berelson identified four principal lines of inquiry: from Lasswell, propaganda, language of politics, and power; from Lazarsfeld, voting, market research, audience, and effects; from Kurt Lewin, social communications and personal relations in small groups; and from Carl Hovland, persuasion and its effects. David Riesman and Raymond A. Bauer agree in part with Berelson. What Wahl-Jorgensen and other communication advocates lack is a critical, comparative, and historical framework for the organization and development of knowledge.

Second-generation communication scholar Elihu Katz raises similar questions in "Why Sociology Abandoned Communication." He begins: "Sociologists once occupied a prominent place in the study of communication—both in pioneering departments of sociology and as founding members of the interdisciplinary team that constituted Departments and Schools of Communication. In the intervening years, I daresay that communication has attracted rather little attention in mainstream sociology and, as for Departments of Communication, a generation of scholars brought up on interdisciplinarity has lost touch with the disciplines from which their teachers were recruited."[105] By way of explanation, Katz points to but partially discounts presumptions of the "limited effects" theory of communication, disagreements about "mass society," and approaches to "media events." Admittedly, he does not begin to explain, or even demonstrate, his term "abandonment." Nor does he account for the continuing research of sociologists on communication. What does it mean "to abandon" a discipline? Where does abandonment lead? What are the consequences?[106] Even after this supposed schism, polling research (a practice claimed by communication) closely allied to university departments of sociology and political science has continued at Princeton, Columbia, Michigan, Iowa, and elsewhere.

In his critique of several "critical" histories of communication research, Jefferson Pooley observes that this "new history" fails to place the study of communication in the context of public opinion research from 1936, the 1950s debates over "mass culture," or the field's history as an "institutionalized 'discipline.'" "In a field with little in common save a label, selective memory and forgetting play outsized roles in holding the discipline together. . . . Communication research, as a field, badly needs the glue of tradition, however invented. This is true because of the field's peculiar (and intellectually retarding) institutionalization—in journalism schools, speech departments, and other sites scattered across the university. Faculty who work under the 'communication' label are normally expected to produce scholarship and, at the same time, impart career skills to industry-bound students. In practice, this means polarized departments or else schizophrenic faculty." Noting problems of location and academic responsibilities, he is silent on questions of disciplinary relationships and organization. But is communication as distinct as Pooley presumes? Adding that "much rests . . . on the field's self-narration of its past," he cautions that "the rigorous scrutiny of communication's past might fray the discipline's fragile bonds."[107] That fear constitutes powerful evidence of the field's nondisciplinarity rather than its interdisciplinarity.

Conclusion

As interdisciplines, both the humanities and communication have failed. Communication is best understood as part of other established and institutionalized disciplines, as multiple fields of study that are loosely connected, or as a nondiscipline. As a single entity, whether a discipline, multidiscipline, or interdiscipline, the humanities has always been problematic, often being re-created and making grand promises. We are left with the questions of why these fields have striven to be identified and legitimated as interdisciplinary and with what benefits and costs. These questions are inseparable from the relationships between disciplinarity and interdisciplinarity and the relationships among disciplines and disciplinary clusters.

Although the humanities and communication share significant elements and histories, they differ in important ways, including the reasons for their relative lack of success. To be sure, this is not a question of their contributions. In my view, the story of communication is simpler. Despite its centuries-old rhetorical, historical, and philosophical roots, communication as an academic and commercial endeavor always has been shaped by its close connections with the mass media, especially such means of persuasion as advertising. While the founders of the field and their successors attempted to elevate it by stressing both its relationships with accepted academic disciplines, such as linguistics, rhetoric, and social psychology, and its novelty, those in better established disciplines refused to relinquish their intellectual property rights to these questions, perhaps because they wanted to keep their distance from communication's crasser applications. By default and positively, communication's practitioners had more influence over its development than in most other fields, within important university-institutional limits where it has struggled to find an appropriate home. In terms of its academic establishment, communication can be precarious. In this respect, it resembles sociology except that it is even closer historically and in institutional location to its practitioners. Theory lends academic legitimacy to a field that properly belongs in the business schools, where its component parts have often found their institutional home. In none of this does it achieve either interdisciplinarity or disciplinarity.

The humanities' stories are more complicated, for historical and ideological reasons as well as intellectual and institutional ones. Creation and other myths, riddled with contradictions both implicit and explicit, permeate the humanities past and present, singular and plural, disciplinary and interdisciplinary. The major works of Grafton and Jardine, Roberts and Turner, and Guillory address them for different times and places. But all these works characterize the humanities field in terms of strong dichotomies: its separation from other disciplinary clusters; its stance in opposition to science; its fractured quest for foundational syntheses as opposed to specialization; and, indeed, the humanities disciplines' separation and even opposition from each other. Too often, the interdisciplinary humanities want to have it both ways, turning one side of the dichotomy against the other, with respect, for example, to the specialized and advanced as opposed to the general and basic. Often the opposition marks a contest over domination or subordination.

The interdisciplinary humanities are animated by aspirations to reconstitute themselves *at* and *as* the pinnacle of knowledge in a position similar to that previously occupied by natural philosophy. Yet, given the post-Renaissance shift from humanism to the humanities, and the post-Enlightenment shift from a unified epistemology to a plethora of discipline-specific methodologies, that aspiration has proven futile. It also neglects the ways the organization and production of knowledge have changed over recent centuries. Proclamations of interdisciplinarity in the humanities seldom attend to the relationships among the disciplines themselves or their distinct developments. In other words, synchronicity between the parts and the whole is presumed but not examined. In contrast to other possible relationships between and among the disciplines, the inroads that the interdisciplinary humanities has made are mainly curricular and, tellingly, in courses that are more often foundational than capstone. That is itself one major contradiction.

Ironically, humanities courses serve more often to fulfill distribution requirements for students in fields outside the humanities than they do as steps toward synthesis for students in various humanities disciplines. This development raises serious concerns about teaching positions for doctoral graduates and sets departments in competition with each other for enrollments.

The specter of "crisis" haunts the humanities more than other clusters of disciplines.[108] We have noted its frequency and shrillness. It is a driving force in recent movements for interdisciplinarity in the humanities. At the same time, the interdisciplinary humanities may exacerbate some of the problems that it seeks to resolve, another contradiction. The response to critical theory or the often misunderstood rejection of universalisms, both inside and outside the humanities, is a case in point, as is the quest for the new in defense of the old.

The disciplines that constitute the humanities compete for recognition, reward, majors, and enrollments, often under their own banners of interdisciplinarity and novelty. Required and elective general education courses prove a battleground for cross-disciplinary "theory" courses once taught by philosophy faculty who now face heady competition from literary postmodernists. The fact that faculty who teach humanities courses come from specific disciplines is probably related to that continual contest for intellectual dominance among and within departments. And it clashes with notions of interdisciplinary integration.

In opposing itself to science and social science in its quest for distinctive interdisciplinarity, the humanities engage in other conflicts. At the same time, interdisciplinary humanities has a longstanding tendency to imitate and borrow from the sciences in the hope of sharing their prestige. An alternative interdisciplinary humanities might seek to lead the sciences without setting itself directly in opposition to them.

CHAPTER THREE

In Search of Unification for War and Peace

Social Relations and Operations Research, 1930s–1960s

In *Working Knowledge: Making the Human Sciences from Parsons to Kuhn*, Joel Isaac summarizes the standard version of the history of the social sciences that he seeks to revise. The end of World War II ushered in a phase "of millennial expectations." At the height of the Cold War, "many commentators believed . . . that the sciences of society, politics, and mind were finally joining the experimental and mathematical sciences as value-neutral, technical disciplines. . . . These grand expectations . . . were intertwined with the emergence of the assertive, ecumenical liberalism in the postwar United States," which "rested on, and in turn reinforced notions of a liberal consensus in American history and a faith in the importance of professional elites in managing democratic regimes. . . . A neologism captured the mood: behavioral science."

> World War II had been the crucible of the behavioral vision, [as] the premium placed on technical problem-solving and discipline-blind collaboration by those engaged in war work banished talk of metaphysical differences between the social and human sciences. . . . A web of family resemblances between different methods and research orientations ensnared a certain comity of spirit among such diverse enterprises as rational choice theory, structural-functional sociology, information theory, behavioralism, operations research, systems engineering, modernization theory, and cognitive science. Explanations in each of these fields dealt with causal chains, or at any rate with "systems" of variables whose interrelations could be formally stated. The fundamental unit of explanation, meanwhile, was the individual, conceived as a culturally programmed human agent.[1]

Although the assumptions of behavioral science eventually came under attack and the distinct disciplines and methodologies that had been temporarily rejected were reasserted, the model of behavioral science has had an enduring influence.

Both Social Relations (Soc Rel) and Operations Research (OR) were forged in this crucible of war and peace. But Isaac's account of that era is insufficiently historical and pays too little attention to interdisciplinarity. Consider the conjunction implicit in "behavioral science." The two concepts, which originated in the late eighteenth century or even earlier, have commonly been coupled since the mid-nineteenth century.[2] Today, behavioral science is threatened with eclipse by the rise of cognitive science, reminding us that the age-old dualism between mind and action remains active. It also drives alternative, often competing, visions and practices of interdisciplinarity. In theory at least, Soc Rel and OR sought to cross that divide.

The roots of these intellectual and institutional developments are much older than is generally recognized. Rather than beginning with the post–World War II era, the urge toward interdisciplinarity is inseparable from the creation of the modern university and the formation of the disciplines. These developments are part of the battles for recognition and growth among the disciplines, especially but not only the social sciences, in the face of the lure and challenges of science. The origins of both Soc Rel and OR lie in the 1930s, with some significant precedents established even earlier.

Behavioral, human, and cognitive science, in particular their interactions and conflicts, constitute critical sites for presumptions and versions of interdisciplinarity. All of these terms are problematic. Especially revealing are the appeals of developing disciplines and interdisciplines to and uses of science, typically positively but sometimes negatively. In this chapter, we examine Social Relations, an instructive but generally forgotten development in the history of sociology and the social sciences. While Soc Rel is associated principally with Harvard University and Talcott Parsons, "it was part of the quest for a unified science of behavior"; in Isaac's reconstruction, it was a "human science."[3] In 1946, Gordon Allport and Edwin Boring proclaimed that "while departmental lines have remained rigid there has been developing, especially during the last decade, a synthesis of socio-cultural and psychological sciences which is widely recognized within the academic world in spite of the fact that there is no commonly accepted name to designate the synthesis."[4] Their name for this emergent field was Social Relations. In effect, Soc Rel took up the failed project of sociology to integrate the disciplines by incorporating social psychology and social anthropology along with sociology itself. Talcott Parsons's encompassing agenda was even broader.

A contemporary of Soc Rel was Operations Research, "a discipline that deals with the application of advanced analytical methods to help make better decisions," a powerful and influential field that is little known outside management and strategic circles but flourished during World War II.[5] It successfully moved from the military's emergency priorities to institutionalization in universities and corporations. Drawing from cybernetics, cognitive science and psychology, and organizational theory and decision science, it was typically housed in new schools of business management and engineering.[6]

Soc Rel is usually presented as an errant phase in the institutional and intellectual history of social science, but it illuminates the sources and stimuli for interdisciplinarity and the prospects and promises of new approaches to the organization and location of the production of knowledge. In contrast, OR remains a vigorous and widely institutionalized field. Despite being invisible outside circles of specialists, it has achieved notable success in applied science and commercial contexts. Indeed, it is one of interdisciplinarity's success stories.[7]

Although Soc Rel and OR share critical moments, motivations, and grounds of emergence, as well as certain key presumptions, they differ in important ways. In contrast to the problems of diffuseness and disorganization exemplified by the humanities and communication, both Soc Rel and OR highlight issues of location, relationship, organization and leadership, and theory and practice. To the extent that Soc Rel is a major example of a failed interdiscipline and OR of a successful one, their experience expands our understanding. In the next chapter, we follow closely related themes in the histories of cognitive science and the new histories of the 1960s and 1970s. Individually and together, these chapters in the long history of the behavioral sciences tell us a great deal about the successes and limits of interdisciplinarity.

Soc Rel and OR offer a special opportunity to identify the intersections that stimulated and constrained efforts at interdisciplinarity, including the social and political climate, shifting intellectual and cultural currents, and the grounds on which disciplinary, university, departmental, and other institutional elements came together or failed to do so. In the 1930s and 1940s, the Unity of Science Movement, the war and postwar recovery, and the status of disciplines in universities were especially consequential.

Most accounts of the developments of the behavioral sciences, whether intellectual or institutional, place a superordinate emphasis on World War II. So, too, do most accounts of interdisciplinarity. The war's importance is indisputable. It influenced the practice of research, through imperative demands to confront new problems and frame new solutions by working in groups that crossed many of the lines that delimited specializations and separated theory from practical applications. It provided unprecedented levels of external interest and funding. Scientific fields profited, and changed, the most. But the social sciences and the humanities were also affected, sometimes in transformative ways. Yet the weight of this exogenous factor is too often exaggerated. The war influenced developments that were already under way for other reasons.[8]

Social Relations

Isaac attempts to shift the grounds for understanding Social Relations away from the usual theoretical dichotomies and conflicting personalities in order to challenge the field's frequent dismissal. He offers a broad and revisionist intellectual context that derives from his "rediscovery" of a tradition of scientific philosophy that he identifies with the human sciences. "This alternative, post-Kantian tradition of epistemology was shaped not only by grand ideologies and epic narratives about knowledge, but by the very practices and analytical toolkit of scientists and mathematicians. It construed epistemology as a technical, instrumental, even worldly enterprise." He asserts, "Many research programs that are today thought to be straightforwardly either 'behavioralist' or 'interpretivist' are more accurately seen as part of the intellectual culture . . . of scientific philosophy." Without paying much attention to disciplinary formation in sociology, psychology, and anthropology, he describes the emergence of Soc Rel as part of "the uptake and transformation of scientific philosophy by thinkers operating within the 'interstitial academy' that Harvard nurtured within its walls."[9] Isaac's concept of an "interstitial academy" combines with the singularity of Soc Rel's development at Harvard to highlight the centrality of location, relationships, and organization, along with the balance of ideas and individuals, in the development of interdisciplinarity.[10] As it attracted and shaped scholars with similar interests, orientations, and questions, Soc Rel served as a location for efforts at interdisciplinarity in the social sciences at Harvard, albeit temporarily and incompletely. Both the success and the limits of these beginnings are important. They bear comparison with the histories of the humanities and communication, which sought a prominent presence at many universities but failed to develop central locations and organization.

According to Isaac, "the principal vehicles for the Harvard faculty's and student body's repeated engagements with scientific philosophy were a cluster of clubs, societies, seminars, and inchoate disciplinary ventures in the human sciences."[11] These organizations, which he characterizes as "extra-disciplinary, pre-professional, or avocational academic structures" were at the forefront of promoting "the culture of scientific philosophy" because they "cut across the prevailing institutional model of the American research university." Isaac argues that "what emerged from this Harvard complex forms a key part of the heritage of the mid-twentieth century human sciences": the Pareto circle's systems theory; the operationist theories of science of Percy Williams Bridgman, B. F Skinner, and S. S. Stevens; endorsement of logical empiricism and analytic philosophy; Talcott Parsons's general theory of action; and the history and sociology of science developed by Robert Merton and Thomas Kuhn.[12] To be sure, one university does not an interdiscipline or a discipline make. Both the larger and the local contexts demand attention. Constituting what we might construe as a critical mass is a necessary but not sufficient condition for the development of multi- and interdisciplinarity.

While Isaac's perspective helps us understand both Soc Rel and OR, it also enables us to distinguish them. Isaac lumps the disciplines and fields that he claims constitute scientific philosophy but neglects to split them when he should. In his efforts to explain the rise and growth of scientific philosophy, including Soc Rel, he conflates claims of disciplines and claims of scientific philosophy, failing to distinguish the Soc Rel program from that more encompassing project. The significance of this issue goes well beyond Soc Rel. The differences and relationships between the general and the specific, the holistic and the specialized, and boundaries and crossings plague conceptions of interdisciplinarity. Voicing common complaints about universities and the organization of knowledge, Soc Rel reflects persisting themes in the history of interdisciplinarity. As we see, they are present in the development of OR.

Uniting the Social Sciences?

In the midst of the seemingly inexorable press toward academic specialization that was the simultaneous cause and consequence of modernity, an alternative emerged that has too often been forgotten: the Unity of Science Movement. Through its focus on the logic and philosophy of science, the movement sought to integrate the natural, social, and human sciences, as well as philosophy. Significantly, it did not succumb to the dichotomy of the general versus the specialized, the collective versus the individual, which proved so destructive to the humanities.[13] Announcing the Fifth International Congress for the Unity of Science at Harvard in 1939, the first assembly held in the United States, Charles Morris declared: "The interest of the Congress will focus upon the relation of the concepts, laws, and methods of the various sciences. Attention will be devoted to general problems connected with the systematization of science." Guided by an organizing committee composed of experts from a wide range of disciplines, the program would "attempt . . . to discuss the relation of studies dealing with man and his activities to the natural sciences, and thus to bring the socio-humanistic studies within the scope of the unity of science movements."[14]

Explicitly as well as implicitly, both Soc Rel and OR were part of efforts to bring general theory to the social sciences. The quest to become more scientific took various forms, as the comparison between Soc Rel and OR demonstrates. Closely connected to Isaac's notions of human science and scientific philosophy, both were confident of science's ability to solve the problems of the modern world and of the disciplines in the developing universities. This faith survived World War I, the worldwide depression, and the rise of fascism, while it was spread by the international intellectual migration that occurred before and after World War II.[15] Both fields also reflect the state of disciplinary development and university growth. During the 1930s and 1940s, the social sciences were still establishing themselves; they came into conflict not only with the sciences and humanities but also among themselves. At Harvard, sociology, social psychology, and social anthropology struggled to find a firm place alongside economics, experimental psychology, and archeology.

Studying the development of the Social Relations department risks exaggerating its significance, although it is a valuable case study of the one important failure of interdisciplinarity.[16] Much too often, the idiosyncrasies of Harvard and the persona of Parsons distort the picture.[17] So, too, do ideological critiques that are short on historical context. Adam Kuper, for example, writes: "Parsons established an interdisciplinary Department of Social Relations"; "what he had in mind was a shake-up of the social sciences"; and he "set out the central features of this new theory of action"—all as if Parsons were acting alone.[18] Even noted sociologist Arthur Vidich, who published a highly critical reminiscence about his years as a graduate student from 1946 to 1950, stated that "the Social Relations Department was created in 1946 as an administrative mechanism to support Parsons's main intellectual project—framing a theory for a democratic social system."[19]

Missing is an account of the development of the social sciences as disciplines and their search for a firm place in the modern university between the sciences and the humanities. Concentrating too closely on Parsons risks the loss of context. Although it gives short shrift to Soc Rel, the landmark collection *Sociology in America: A History*, edited by Craig Calhoun, offers a fundamentally historical and developmental understanding that emphasizes the diversity and instability of the relatively new discipline through the mid-twentieth century.

Especially valuable are Charles Camic's and George Steinmetz's accounts of the variability of sociology as a discipline and department at major universities, including Chicago, Columbia, Michigan, Wisconsin, Berkeley, and Harvard. Camic stresses "localism and interdisciplinary interaction" in the institutionalization of sociology at Chicago, Columbia, and Harvard. "Aspiring social-scientific disciplines" competed for legitimacy and "experienced continual pressure to jus-tify themselves under the banner of 'science.'"[20] The struggle went on for decades, differing by disciplines and disciplinary clusters in particular universities.

Camic emphasizes "the pattern of relations obtaining among different disciplines at this or that particular university." Harvard began to teach sociology in the early 1890s, at the same time as Chicago and Columbia, but its develop-ment met serious opposition. A chair in the subject was created in the Depart-ment of Economics in 1930. A separate department came only in 1931, and "it was only in the mid-1930s, with the work of Talcott Parsons, that the University produced a distinctive vision of the sociological enterprise." Camic explains that "behind these developments were decades of local resistance to sociology, espe-cially by economists, and even when the Harvard sociology department was finally established, it was staffed mainly by giving extra part-time appointments to economists, political scientists," and those in other fields, "whose full-time voting rights in sociology meant that 'sociologists were outnumbered in their own department.' . . . Organizationally, sociology was located in the division of Economics, Government, and History, alongside three large and strong depart-ments, with no particular traditions of interdisciplinary cooperation."[21]

In Camic's view, following other Harvard social scientists who confronted the natural sciences, "Parsons accepted the search for 'uniform laws' as the measure of science." He attempted to "legitimate" sociology by "establishing its conformity with, but differentiation from, the other social sciences, above all economics." Parsons's foundational work, *The Structure of Social Action* (1937), like the program it aimed to "charter," was "less a dispassionate dialogue with the masters of sociol-ogy over the timeless questions of social theory than a deeply felt tract for the times."[22] Going beyond economics but marching to the beat of science, influenced by Harvard's "interstitial academy," scientific philosophy, and the Unity of Science Movement, Parsons moved from sociology to Social Relations.

The formation and location of the new department was announced in *The American Psychologist* in 1946. Incorporating the small department of sociology, social and clinical psychology, and social anthropology, the "emerging discipline" dealt "not only with the body of the fact and theory traditionally recognized as the subject-matter of sociology, but also with that portion of psychological science that treats the individual within the social system, and that portion of anthropo-logical science that is particularly relevant to the social and cultural patterns of literate societies. . . . The recent war greatly accelerated the fusion of research activities in this common territory. Work on wartime projects virtually obliterated distinctions that were already breaking down between social scientists engaged the fundamental problems of social relations." The theory of "culture and personality" was the first unifying perspective to emerge, but the "other topics of joint concern" that represented the "cooperative trend among the basic social sciences" resembles a laundry list: "community analysis, attitude assessment, the process of socialization in childhood and youth, the study of group conflict and prejudice, factors in national and international morale, the nature of institutional behavior, aspects of communication and propaganda, ethnic and national differences and similarities, [and] problems of social and mental adjustment of the individual in his social situation." The "common skills and tools" used in the "laboratory" of Social Relations included "statistical sampling, interviewing, participant observation, group experiments, coding and machine sorting, community mapping, [and] life-history analysis." Finally, drawing attention to the "urgent and increasing demands [that] will be laid upon the University for the study of the 'human factor' in a technological and atomic age," the statement projected that financial support would "come [in part] from the federal government, in part from the local community, and in part from the social conscience of the University itself."[23]

The charter for Social Relations' path to interdisciplinarity at Harvard is a textbook case of promises, practices, and problems. Its design was premature and incomplete. The university "acceded to the foundation of the new Department before a consensus" had "been reached either on the nature of 'basic social science' or the means by which that prospective science should be taught."[24] Departmentalization and degree-granting status were not the best vehicles for the development of interdisciplinarity. Moreover, its research questions and problems for study were not well formulated. Coming largely from the pen of one person, this blueprint was never truly shared. The questions began with how was Soc Rel conceptualized, especially in the Parsonian mode, and to what extent was the Department of Social Relations (DSR) in effect a slightly camouflaged department of sociology.

While Camic emphasizes the predicaments that Parsons and Harvard Sociology shared with sociologists and their emerging discipline at other universities, George Steinmetz highlights Harvard's differences. The program ranked first or second among sociology departments, attracted hundreds of applicants each year, and awarded 80 PhDs between 1946 and 1956. Steinmetz rejects the presumption of a deep divide between theory and positivism or empiricism, remarking that "the division of labor . . . was superimposed on deeper agreements about basic principles and goals." Moreover, Parsons was the only theorist.

"Most of the Harvard sociology PhD's from this period who went on to illustrious careers pursued Mertonian 'middle-range' topics and theories." Perhaps most important, "the interdisciplinarity of the social relations department bore little resemblance to some current versions of interdisciplinarity as a playground of epistemic diversity and experimentation. Parsons's vision of a convergence of theory in the various social sciences rather recalled the logical positivist dream of the unity of science. As Parsons wrote in his preface to the programmatic book *Toward a General Theory of Action*, 'these many streams of thought are in the process of flowing together.'"[25]

Parsons's program was unified and explicitly "interdisciplinary." He aimed to "defend" and "redeem the fledgling science in the face of powerful intellectual and institutional forces" that were "either content with the 'pariah' status" or mounted "an assault against its field of study, the sociological realm of subjective purposes, attitudes, and values."[26] With a hubris characteristic not only of his own personality but also of other interdisciplinary ventures, Parsons declared that the emergence of basic social science "is one of the really great moments of modern scientific thought, comparable, for instance, to the development of biology in the last third of the 19th century."[27]

Harvard agreed to the creation of a new department for a variety of reasons that had little to do with this agenda. Provost Paul Buck wished to keep a group of junior faculty members in the social sciences, which had long been marginalized. An umbrella department was a practical solution. Isaac points out that "the rise of problem-based 'interdisciplines' during the war was at the forefront of his mind in this regard." In his report on the 1945–46 academic year, he remarked that "a new Department of Engineering and Applied Physics has been formed in acknowledgement of the fact that the 'most useful man in our laboratories in solving engineering problems under war pressure was the man who was thoroughly grounded in all the basic sciences.'" Buck "went on to observe that many saw a parallel with the synthesis of specialisms in the foundations of the DSR."[28]

The Straightjacket of Theory

Soc Rel was flawed from the beginning, however. Intellectual visions are never sufficient in themselves; their development requires openness to cooperation and collaboration. The department was marked by a signal failure to develop common problems, protocols, or practices for research.

Both celebrants and critics call attention to the tension between the interdisciplinary aura of the department and the imperatives of graduate training.

The first-year proseminar in Social Relations was described as a pedagogical circus: "exciting, sometimes confusing, and for many a little frightening." Although graduate students were granted considerable freedom to roam around the disciplines, they had to take their degree in one of the department's constituent fields, not in Social Relations.[29] Despite funding from the Carnegie Corporation, "the Laboratory of Social Relations was never forced . . . to agree on an official program of research or single methodological training regime for graduate students" and "did little to advance or clarify the case for a fundamental behavioral science."[30] Neither its distinguished students nor its landmark studies promoted integration.[31] Instead, disparate research programs and fractured teaching agendas fomented clashes among faculty. Some of these conflicts, such as that between Parsons and George Homans, are legendary. Isaac remarks that "this fragmentation had a physical dimension: the Department had no single building of its own and consequently its staff was scattered across the Harvard campus."[32] Even more fructuous was the area of ideology, where "fissures were opened both among the founding members of the Department and between senior and junior faculty. . . . Battle was joined over . . . the conceptual primacy of 'culture' (i.e. anthropology) versus 'social systems' (sociology). [Samuel] Stouffer, meanwhile, 'tended to want statistics to explain everything.'" Anthropologist David Schneider found these differences to be "attractions"; to Clifford Geertz, they represented a "maze of grand possibilities, only loosely related, and even in serious tensions with one another."[33]

But these possibilities also stood as limits, contradicting the grand goals of the enterprise and frustrating all efforts to generate departmental unity. Institutional recognition and location, even when pursued at all costs, are not in themselves sufficient to sustain an interdisciplinary endeavor. The great leap from a band of "Levellers" in the "interstitial academy" to a department was far too ambitious. The founders' missteps were both organizational and intellectual. They "failed utterly to win over the next generation of DSR faculty to their way of thinking. . . . During the 1950s, when the youngest tranche of Social Relations faculty should have been rising through the ranks, a major proportion of junior staff resigned their posts for positions elsewhere."[34] In addition to personality clashes, Homans cited substantive differences. Despite a seminar on methodology, "we all kept on using the methods we felt comfortable with. It was soon abandoned." A signature "effort to integrate the department theoretically" was even more ambitious. Yet Talcott Parsons "dominated the discussion," and "no one could argue with him."[35]

Homans enjoyed joking about the number of "boxes (categories)" that proliferated weekly in Parsons's theoretical schemes. More seriously, he observed:
"Much research can be effectively carried out by teams, but I do not believe that
theories, good or bad, can be developed so. . . . When the final report of the
senior committee came out in 1951 in the form of a small paperback entitled
Toward a General Theory of Action and popularly referred to as the 'yellow book,'
it turned out to be largely the work of Parsons and Shils and represented their
views. They gave little more than lip service to the views of other participants,
who must by then have been too exhausted to argue further."[36] The collective or
integrative dimension of developing and practicing interdisciplinarity was
never present. The question of the practicality and usefulness of theoretical and
other approaches was seldom posed, let alone answered.

Homans continued: "I too thought little of the 'Yellow Book,' because I was
beginning to suspect that the authors' view of what constituted a theory was
bound to lead their 'approach' up a dead-end-street: it would not even begin to
move toward a theory of action. . . . Parsons himself laid the 'Yellow Book' before
a meeting of the whole department, including both tenured and nontenured
members, urging us all to read it and implying, though without quite saying as
much, that it ought to be adopted as they official doctrine of the department to
guide future teaching and research." Bringing to mind Albert Hirschmann's conception of "voice, exit, or loyalty," a notion that features in current conceptualizations and explanations of interdisciplinarity, Homans underscored the meaning
of unity, consensus, and cooperation—and of difference. "I was going to have
none of that, if I could help it. Accordingly, as soon as I really was satisfied that
Parsons had finished, I spoke up and said in effect: 'There must be no implication
that this document is to be taken as representing the official doctrine of the department and no member shall be put under any pressure to read it.' Indeed there
can be no official theoretical doctrines in science. A dreadful silence followed my
attack. . . . But finally Sam Stouffer . . . spoke up. . . . Somewhat reluctantly, he declared that the 'Yellow Book' ought not to be treated as department doctrine." Yet,
according to Homans, "for some years the structural-functionalism of Parsons
was the dominant school of thought among our graduate students in sociology."[37]

Arthur Vidich agreed with Homans that "Parsons dominated the seminar. . . .
The purpose of the proseminar was to lay out the distinctive intellectual line
that Parsons was then formulating for his version of sociology." Describing the
seminar in which he participated in 1948–49, Vidich described how *not* to build
an interdisciplinary program.

Exposure to a multiplicity of vocabularies did not lead inevitably to cross-fertilization or to an interdisciplinary perspective. Adding to the centrifugality of disciplinary vocabularies, each of the lecturers recommended the works of authors whom they regarded as significant figures in their fields. The names of Max and Alfred Weber, Émile Durkheim, Sigmund Freud, Alfred Kroeber, Franz Boas, Gregory Bateson, Susanne Langer, G. H. Mead, Leslie White, McDougall, Watson, Jung and many others were added as crucial authors. Notably absent from the lists were the works of Karl Marx, Thorstein Veblen, and Weber's *Protestant Ethic and the Spirit of Capitalism.* It soon became evident to us that no one could grasp the substance of the vocabularies of all the disciplines or read all the books in a semester or even a year.

The result was "interdisciplinary schizophrenia." Facing anxieties over examinations, students formed "study groups . . . to provide digests of books and summaries of lecture notes," called "hamburgers." Each report's main point was clear: "*The Structure of Social Action* was to be taken as a standard. Other books were to be evaluated from the point of view of Parsonian truths."[38]

Social Relations achieved high departmental rankings and student numbers, as well as broad recognition among anthropologists and social psychologists interested in "culture and personality." But the integrative dimension of interdisciplinarity was entirely absent, and as the department grew, its wings became increasingly disconnected. For Homans, the precipitating cause of dissolution was the period of student rebellions of the late 1960s. For others, its dissolution was present at the creation or clear from the early 1950s. "Over the years the Department of Social Relations gradually disintegrated as a department, though not for disreputable reasons, until in 1970, it formally dissolved into something like its original components." Rhetorically, but presciently, Homans asked: "After the formal efforts to integrate the methodology and theory of the department had failed, what was left to hold us together? The founding fathers had died or retired, and with them had gone the shared personal interests and antagonisms toward outsiders that had originally driven them together. Harvard had built a building to hold all of us. . . . But William James Hall, with its many floors, slow elevators, and dreary corridors, tended rather to divide than to unite us."[39] Entrenched antagonisms disrupted all efforts to nurture and institutionalize either interdisciplinary integration or collaborative relationships.

Moreover, Homans reflected, "a key challenge remained unmet." How could theorizing be elevated to "a legitimate and discrete professional activity" on a par "with the small group studies and macroscopic data collection projects also sponsored by the philanthropic foundations? How, in other words, could theory unite the practices of the postwar human sciences? . . . The theorist's importance in principle still had to be demonstrated in practice." As many scholars have shown, Parsons's structural functionalism of patterned variables—"abstract representations and cross-categorizations . . . to display the symmetries and transformations inherent in the systems of categories that underpinned the general theory of action as a whole"—was circular, at best reifying both culture and action and at worst self-contradictory.[40] As the department limped toward dissolution, Parsons observed with rare modesty that Soc Rel "had been nothing more than an 'experiment.'" Isaac concludes that "it had been much more. . . . The Project on Theory was designed to project an enduring synthesis in the study of human behavior. But . . . the Harvard complex was not conducive to interdisciplinary synthesis." Equally important, it proved hostile to interdisciplinary research in the social sciences.[41]

Operations Research

Operations Research languishes as the unloved orphan of the history of science, although some of those close to the events that marked its emergence argued that it "was one of the chief scientific features of the war." According to Philip Mirowski, "at first glance it looks suspiciously like a social science, but the history of economics has been written as though it were absent, or at best, irrelevant. . . . It is obvious that the practitioners themselves have suffered identity crises veering on neuroses, struggling again and again to define themselves."[42]

It is hardly coincidental that one of the more successful examples of interdisciplinarity is also one of the least well known among academics and the educated public. Familiar to specialists and certain industry, military, and government planners and strategists, OR typically resides in schools or colleges of business and administration.[43] It is identified by a long roster of synonyms, including management science, numerical control, strategic decision-making, information science, organizational theory, artificial intelligence, and optimization. Joel Isaac subsumes OR under an umbrella woven of behavioral science and systems analysis. Hunter Crowther-Heyck calls it a "bounded rationality of choice under control"; Philip Mirowski, a "cyborg science of machine dreams."[44] Stephen Waring stresses its Taylorist control of labor; Yehouda Shenhav, the "engineering foundations of organization theory."[45] Others emphasize its mathematical, economic, organizational, psychological, and cognitive dimensions.

The unavoidable and extensive overlap is central to OR's history and undermines all single-factor explanations.[46]

The field suffers from a recognition crisis, though not necessarily an identity crisis. OR often is accorded a subordinate position thanks to the longstanding academic divide between theory and application. The conflict over the orientation toward science of university-affiliated scientists as opposed to the problem-solving emphases of its military and corporate sponsors only complicates things more. Internally, its development is marked by conflicts over what roles different fields should play in it, from physics to mathematics and statistics, economics to cybernetics. Its pluralism can be a strength as well as a limitation.

OR is obsessed with its history, unlike most interdisciplines examined in this book. While a major, unified history has yet to be written, there are timelines of great moments, series of articles on OR during World War II, a "History in the Making," and "issue-oriented history."[47] Beginning in the 1980s, historians of science and technology began to discover the field, albeit in bits and pieces. This fragmentary rediscovery is a symptom of the nature of OR, a revealing thread that unravels between theory and practice, identity and uncertainty, and maturity and insecurity. Never a discipline, it is marked by deep divisions. Nonetheless, it succeeded, to an impressive degree, as an interdiscipline.

Operations Research is less marked than other fields by debates over "great questions" concerning the modern university and the production and division of knowledge. Although such questions are present, they have had little influence on the development of the field. The issues that matter more concern synthesis and integration, the meaning of science, theory versus application, the ideology and politics of OR (including the "need" for a "critical approach"), a brief tussle over "materialism," recurrent anxiety about "the future of OR," and especially its relationship to the state and capitalism. Similarities with the history of communication call out for study. As Isaac and Crowther-Heyck point out, OR overlapped with other efforts to develop a unified behavioral science. Its goals and methods connected with "big science" and medicine, on the one hand, and corporate expansion, on the other. In the end, however, OR was and remained more a methodological and applied field than a theoretical one.[48]

These divides, while constraining, did not prevent the field's growth, organization, and institutionalization; indeed, they may even have facilitated its development. Despite their complications and frustrations, its limits may have been beneficial and at least some of the conflicts productive. Especially important is the contribution of these divides to resolving the key conundrums of location, relationships, identity, expansion, and reproduction, at a practical level though not a theoretical level. That OR was *never* a discipline benefited its path to interdisciplinarity.[49]

War and Peace

Even more than for Soc Rel, histories of OR emphasize the crucibles of World War II and the Cold War. Historian Stephen Waring writes: "The Cold War shaped few intellectual disciplines more than operations research. The British and American militaries created the field to improve decision-making during World War II and continued using it throughout the Cold War. By the same token, few disciplines shaped the Cold War era more than operations research, which influenced the world view, rhetoric, and policy of military and civilian leaders throughout the period." Confusing and reifying disciplines with inter-disciplines, Waring defines the field by listing its components. "Operations research is an interdisciplinary field, comprised of mathematics, economics, engineering, and management, in which practitioners use formal analytic tech-niques to study and offer solutions to complex problems. In many ways the field represented a culmination of Western conceptions of rationality, and leaders in the field claimed that they could think about the unthinkable and solve the unsolvable. In other ways, however, operations research was an example of the Cold War's crazy rationality that the sociologist C. Wright Mills called 'crackpot realism.' "[50]

Isaac also situates these developments in relation to the wartime emergence of behavioral science and systems theory. " 'The actions and interactions of individual agents' were viewed as the product of motivations that were formed in the social environment and could be quantified, analysed, and thereby subjected to prediction and control once the key variables had been identified. . . . Systems analysts promised similar gains, but with somewhat different tools. Their disci-pline had coalesced among scientists and engineers charged during the Second World War with solving the problem of gunfire control. Systems theory was taken over into the human sciences after the war by a dedicated group of mathemati-cians and social scientists at RAND." A systems approach to logistical problems in complex organizations aimed at optimizing resources and making decisions by using mathematical and computer models. Management scientists and econ-omists used game theory, linear and dynamic programming, and social choice theory to analyze questions of allocating resources and operating efficiently. "The proponents of behavioural science and systems theory promised that social reform was a matter of the correct application of scientific expertise, deployed with the same dispassionate regard for efficiency that guided research in engineering."[51]

Emphasizing the limiting, reductionist focus of behavioral science and systems analysis as ideology, Isaac slights prewar developments in Operations Research. He is correct in arguing that "determining what 'behavioural science' or 'systems theory' meant was much harder than acknowledging their power as slogans for an equally indeterminate, yet all-encompassing, war effort. They provided an assurance of social control whilst avoiding the connotations of 'social planning,' associated with the left."[52] Yet this valuable beginning begs questions about their differences, development, and institutionalization and, especially, the interrelations between theory and practice in those processes.

Mirowski moves in the right direction when he suggests that OR should not be framed "as the harbinger of the practice of 'boundary work' and the attendant 'interdisciplinarity' that has come to be the hallmark of the military-induced organization of so many fin-de-siècle sciences." At the same time, he oversimplifies, confuses key connections, and conflates cause and effect when he writes, "OR should . . . be located by a process of triangulation between the natural sciences, economics, and the nascent field of policy science; furthermore, the computer was the tapis upon which the moves were carried out, which is the single most important fact rendering these developments so central to the inception of the cyborg sciences." Not only does Mirowski fail to conceptualize the "attendant 'interdisciplinarity' " but his own effort to subsume OR under economics and cybernetics does the opposite.[53]

Before its identification and institutionalization across the boundaries of universities, governments and the military, and private research centers and think tanks, OR had many precedents. Despite, or perhaps because of, its obsessions, OR's history is marked by exaggeration to the point of caricature. The standard histories present it as a story of success and beneficence. But critics offer it as a tale of the evils wrought by corporate capitalism, hierarchical control, or triumphant militarism.[54]

With his emphasis on calculation and computation, Mirowski notes that Charles Babbage "anticipated" OR in the first half of the nineteenth century; so did John von Neumann in his work on military ballistics in the late 1930s and early 1940s.[55] On its fiftieth anniversary, *OR/MS Today* (the journal of the Institute for Operations Research and the Management Sciences, INFORMS) published *Great Moments in HistORy*, compiled by Saul I. Gass. This catch-all begins in 1654 with "B. Pascal's Expected value" and 1655 with "Newton's Method for finding a minimum solution of a function." It includes high points in mathematics, statistics and probability, economics, gaming, engineering, management, and cybernetics, as well as organizational and institutional developments in OR.[56] The book-length *Annotated Timeline of Operations Research* by Saul Gass and Arjang Assad opens memorably: "What were the beginnings of OR? Decision making started with Adam and Eve. There are apocryphal legends that claim OR stems from biblical times—how Joseph aided Pharaoh and the Egyptians to live through seven fat years followed by seven learn years by the application of 'lean-year' programming."[57] The *Annotated Timeline* continues in this celebratory, often indiscriminate, vein to show the progress of "OR, *the science that aids in the resolution of human decision-making problems.*" Herein lies one origin myth.

Its "prehistory" is composed of "a collection of events, people, ideas, and methods that contributed to the study of decision-making before the official birth of OR. . . . Many of the early operations researchers were trained as mathematicians, statisticians and physicists; some came from quite unrelated fields such as chemistry, law, history, and psychology. The early successes of embryonic OR prior to and during World War II illustrate the essential feature that helped to establish OR: bright, well-trained, curious, motivated people, assigned to unfamiliar and difficult problem settings, most often produce improved solutions."[58]

Gass's origin myth has its own history. No less teleological, it mixes adventure with melodrama and features heroism in the face of adversity: "A corollary is that a new look, a new analysis, using methods foreign to the original problem environment can often lead to new insights and new solutions. We were fortunate to have leaders who recognized this fact; scientists such as Patrick M. S. Blackett and Philip M. Morse and their military coworkers. They were not afraid to challenge the well-intentioned in-place bureaucracy in their search to improve both old and new military operations. The urgency of World War II allowed this novel approach to prove itself. And, the foresight of these early researchers led to the successful transfer of OR to post-war commerce and industry." Although the narrative path is paved with pluralism, the hallmark of science remains OR's distinguishing crown.

OR's science is thoroughly contemporary: it is theoretical, it uses modeling, and it is holistic. Gass's formulation is simplistic. "Blackett and Morse brought the scientific method to the study of operational problems in a manner much different from the earlier scientific management studies of Fredrick Taylor and Frank and Lillian Gilbreth. . . . From today's perspective, what was missing from their work was (1) the OR emphasis on developing theories about the process under study, that is modeling, with the model(s) being the scientist's experimental laboratory where alternative solutions are evaluated against single or multiple measures of effectiveness, combined with (2) the OR philosophy of trying to take an holistic view of the system under study." The real story, according to Gass, is

> how OR moved from the classified confines of its military origins into being a new science. . . . The initial impetus was due to a few of the civilian and military OR veterans of World War II who believed that OR had value beyond the military. Post World War II we find: OR being enriched by new disciples from the academic and business communities; OR being broadened by new mathematical, statistical, and econometric ideas, as well as being influenced by other fields of human and industrial activities; OR techniques developed and extended by researchers and research centers; OR made doable and increasingly powerful through the advent of the digital computer; OR being formalized and modified by new academic programs; OR going world-wide by the formation of country-based and international professional organizations; OR being supported by research journals established by both professional organizations and scientific publishers; and OR being sustained by a world-wide community of concerned practitioners and academics who volunteer to serve professional organizations, work in editorial capacities for journals, and organize meetings that help to announce new technical advances and applications.[59]

Happily, OR typically respects its limits more than this list indicates and only on special occasions proclaims itself the Emperor's New Science.

From the same history, Philip Mirowski distills an equally whiggish and oversimplified origin myth.

> First and foremost, it was natural scientists, and primarily physicists, who were responsible for the creation, conduct, and codification of OR in World War II. . . . Second, . . . it would be imprudent to claim that the military "wanted" or actively sought out civilian advice on how to conduct the war; the same could probably be said for the captains of industry with their cadre of research scientists. It was not incidental that the application of OR was all bound up with struggles over the modality of the funding of scientific research and the ability of the paymasters to dictate the type of research pursued. . . . Third, the very idea that there was a generic "scientific method" to be deployed in advising clients, while certainly a popular notion in the era after the bomb, was repeatedly challenged by the fact that

there was no obvious unity or quiddity to what an operations researcher seemed to do. . . . Perhaps, then, it was all just a matter of possession of rare mathematical expertise in which everyone else was deficient—namely, the ability to make arguments *rigorous* through the instrumentality of formal expression.[60]

After setting up these straw men, he proceeds to knock them down. He delights in caricature. "Nevertheless, this definition of OR as a branch of mathematics founders on the inconvenient fact that mathematicians would rarely, if ever, deign to accord it that honorific status. There was nothing particularly novel or even erudite about the sorts of mathematics being used by the original OR cadres."[61]

Mirowski offers an alternative teleology to the OR establishment's. His less dramatic and more institutionalist version of the making of OR downplays prehistory and science but emphasizes the sinister influence of corporations and the military. Physicists active during the war

somehow had to innovate new roles balancing this delicate combination of engagement and aloofness from the chain of command. OR turned the humble role of consultant into a fully fledged "discipline," with everything that implies. The reason that OR became so important after the war was not due to any particular technical innovation or bit of mathematical wizardry; rather, it was the workshop where the postwar relationship between the natural scientists and the state was forged, and inadvertently, the site where neoclassical economics became integrated into the newfound scientific approach to government, corporate management, and the very conceptualization of society as a cybernetic entity.

Not only does Mirowski shoehorn OR into his cybernetic box, but he may get the story exactly backward when he writes, "The fact that OR could boast no uniform roster of practices did not mean that it was incapable of having profound effect upon the intellectual content of academic disciplines such as economics, psychology, and even computer science."[62] OR's achievements, and its interdisciplinarity, were founded in large part on its successful integration, selectively *and* with respect to solving specific problems that frequently spanned and connected theoretical matters and practical problems in those disciplines. Mirowski's OR emerges as a leaner and meaner cybernetic economics.[63]

Understanding OR in historical and developmental context requires an appreciation of its earlier history, including mathematics, physics, and computation; currents in industrial organization and psychology from the late nineteenth century to the 1920s; and what Joseph F. McCloskey calls "the beginnings of operations research, 1934–1941. . . . Operations research was born of radar on the

eve of World War II. But its advent was forecast before and during World War I
in connection with three technologies introduced during that war: the dread-
nought, the aeroplane and the submarine."[64] Strategic bombing and defending
against it by using radar to direct and control antiaircraft operations was central.
The Tizard Committee for the Scientific Study of Air Defence, created in England
in 1934, is recognized prominently in this history.[65] The division of labor between
an academic scientist and an industrial engineer foreshadowed the development
of the field. OR soon crossed the Atlantic to the United States. McCloskey quotes
a key participant's statement that this crossing signified "a notable milestone in
the progress of idea of operational research," a reassertion of the term and its
increasing use in the discourse and organization of the war.[66] The conception,
practice, and, to some extent, the language of OR gained currency, providing some
basis for the 1947 entry on Gass's timeline: "the definition of OR."[67]

William Thomas usefully redirects our attention by studying both British and
American efforts and by refusing to dichotomize scientists and military leaders.

> My own approach to OR places an understanding of its methodology and heu-
> ristics before the question of its importance to the scientific-political or scientific-
> military relationship. While scientists' pre-war work was important to their
> wartime contributions, . . . these contributions should not be seen as the Pro-
> methean introduction of scientific methods into an otherwise non-scientific or
> irrational context. . . . They were rooted in the creative yet disciplined skills that
> were honed in the construction and defense of scientists' own scientific arguments,
> and adapted to scrutinize and augment existing military heuristic practices.
> Although these skills were certainly associated with science, they were not unique
> to scientific activity.[68]

Accepting professional ideology and promoting the dominant origin myth,
Thomas focuses on careers and methods. Exploring the relationship between
the prewar and wartime OR work of two notable early practitioners, he argues that
its "identification as an activity allowed OR to escape its original wartime and
military contexts and continue to exist until the present by becoming a profession and, according to many of its proponents, a science unto itself." Eliding the
difference between escaping from and building on those foundations, Thomas
attempts to define the field through its practices. As he puts it, "The question of
whether OR was a scientific activity or an activity performed by scientists has
importance far beyond semantics." The answer, I suggest, is both, which would
prevent the reification of "science" and "scientists." In his view, "OR scientists
did not set out to replace existing military practices with their own scientific

methods. Instead they became scholars of them. Once they understood how military heuristics produced knowledge and supported mission-planning, they could scrutinize and critique these practices with the authority of a military expert. Ultimately, they became so adept at making arguments within the rational framework of military operations that OR became recognizable to them as a scientific activity in and of itself. For its own part, the military recognized scientists' investigative talent and found it valuable to retain their services."[69] Herein lay the foundations of OR's interdisciplinarity. This perspective helpfully shifts the focus to questions of conception and execution, organization, and institutionalization.[70]

Problem Solving in Theory and Practice

OR's success as an interdiscipline lies in its integration of many previously distinct factors without embarking on an unattainable quest to become yesterday's "newest" science. Despite the common tendency to list the many disciplines, methods, and tools on which it drew, OR's achievement lies much more in its attempts to answer questions and address problems in theory and in practice. That it did not integrate distinct disciplines and was never itself a distinct discipline formed the foundation of its interdisciplinarity.

Although Crowther-Heyck misses the dialectics between disciplinary departments and other forms of organization and institutionalization, his description is apt:

> Despite—or rather, because of—the pressures toward specialization created by the rapid growth in the postwar social sciences, there were strong countercurrents supporting interdisciplinary work, so much so that "interdisciplinary" became a word to conjure with. Specifically, support for interdisciplinary work came from a network of powerful new patrons, most notably the Ford Foundation and the military research agencies. These new patrons were interested in transforming social science into behavioral science and thus supported mathematical behavioral-functional analysis whatever the topic of study. In addition, they deliberately defined their goals in terms of solving problems, *not* building disciplines, in sharp contrast to the agenda of many leaders of the prewar social sciences, who desired above all to create intellectually sound, institutionally stable disciplines.[71]

The contrast with Soc Rel, with its quest for theoretical integration and disciplinary autonomy, is clear. So, too, is the relative success of OR in comparison with Soc Rel.

Examining the intersections and interactions of factors often treated as

determinative—whether World War II, "behavioral revolutions," or cybernetics—
is more useful to a sound understanding. First, OR's prehistory needs to become
part of its history, without sinking into an infinite regress. Developments that
predate World War II laid its foundation, including normal distributions, Bayes
rules, least squares, linear equations and their solutions, scientific management,
Pareto optimal curves, Markov chains, probability theory, econometrics, quality
control charts, and other forms of operations control. "Time Zero," signaling
the first use of the term, came with British military applications of operational
research for use in radar, and L. V. Kantorovich's "Mathematical Methods of
Organization and Planning" appeared in Russian in 1939. Charles Babbage's
and Frank and Lillian Gilbreth's fundamental contributions to numerical procedures and calculation were more than "cyborg anticipations." John von Neumann's
involvement with questions of turbulence and fluid flows in the mid-1930s led
to his participation in military boards, government committees, and research
units. "He was instrumental in blurring the lines between technical weapons
consultant and military strategist and, in the process, spreading the new gospel
of 'operations research,' conducting research in the area from at least 1942,"
Mirowski observes.[72] This account emphasizes continuities as well as formative
interdisciplinarity in the development of OR. By the end of World War II, its practitioners turned to the question of how to build a future. As William Thomas
describes the process, "the shift in O.R. from exclusive military patronage to
university and industrial affiliation" made it "necessary to actually define O.R. as
a set of techniques that could be written down and taught to others so they could
be hired as operations researchers" (table 3.1).[73]

In Britain and the United States, leaders of the field immediately grasped
the problems and the opportunity. In 1946, Philip Morse published a manifesto
with the evocative and hopeful title "Of Men and Machines: Airplane Attacks
on Submarines Have Little in Common with Better Automobile Traffic Systems.
Yet Their Common Element Promises Clearer Insight into Man's Behavior."
Charles Goodeve and Charles Kittel joined his call to build a new and better world
through partnerships between "government or industrial administrators and
operations analysts."[74]

> There is no reason why operations research should not be as fruitful in aiding in
> the solution of peacetime problems as it was in helping to solve military problems.
> As with problems of war, some operations will be much more fruitful to study
> than others. Traffic problems, for instance, are highly amenable, for data are easy
> to obtain. On the other hand, the design of city housing and facilities requires data

TABLE 3.1
Institutionalization of Operations Research (OR), 1936–1962

1936	British military applications and the first use of the term "operational research"
1942	UK Naval Operational Research, directed by P. Blackett
1942	U.S. Navy Antisubmarine Warfare Operations Research Group
1942	U.S. Air Force Operations Research
1945	U.S. Navy Operations Evaluation Group
1946	"Methods of Operations Research," classified OEG report by P. M. Morse and G. E. Kimball
1948	The RAND Corporation
1948	Johns Hopkins–U.S. Army Operations Research Office (ORO)
1948	First courses in OR at MIT
1948	Operational Research Club of Great Britain
1950	First OR journal, *Operational Research Quarterly*
1950	OR in industrial sector: British Iron and Steel Industry Research Association
1951	Unclassified version of "Methods of Operations Research," by P. M. Blackett and G. E. Kimball
1951	Naval Post Graduate School OR Program
1952	*Operations Research*, first U.S. OR journal
1952	Operations Research Society of America (ORSA) founded
1952	First MA and Ph.D program, Case Institute of Technology
1953	The Institute of Management Sciences (TIMS)
1953	Operational Research Society (UK)
1954	*Naval Research Logistics Quarterly*
1955	Operations Research Center at MIT, directed by P. Morse
1959	International Federation of Operational Research Societies (IFORS)
1961	Research Analysis Corporation (RAC)
1962	Center for Naval Analyses

which are difficult to obtain. . . . It does not necessarily follow, however, that difficulty of effecting the recommendations of operations research is a valid reason for failure to apply scientific study to important problems of society. . . . Wartime experiences give every expectation that peacetime extension of operations analysis will make its fair contribution toward the better, more rational, life which so universally desired.[75]

Under the Labour Party government in Britain, OR moved quickly into the industrial sector, especially in coal and steel. Corporate and industrial OR came later in the United States. But what came to be known as research and development (R&D) flourished. Famously or infamously, this trend was typified by the RAND Corporation. This prototypical think tank served as a model "for a method of organizing and financing research, development and technical evaluation that would be done at the behest of government agencies but carried out by privately run nonprofit research centers." It also spun off competitors and prompted other military branches to create their own units. Hybrid groups such as "the Mitre Corporation, the Systems Development Corporation, Analytic Services, the Center for Naval Analyses[,] have given military planners routine and sustained access to researchers with advanced scientific and technical skills."[76]

Think tanks crossed the lines between public and private; between governments, corporations, and universities; and between disciplines. They were apparently a natural home of an interdisciplinary OR. RAND, which grew out of Douglas Aircraft, celebrated its quasi-academic "organizational culture that prized intellectual curiosity and independence."[77] As Hounshell puts it, "This independence no doubt stemmed from the immediate postwar environment in which scientists, engineers, and mathematicians leveraged their wartime successes to assert the wisdom of abundant, unfettered research. The image that appears again and again in RAND's self-characterizations during its first fifteen years is 'a university without students.'"[78] Location and the institutionalization of relationships mattered. OR worked best as an approach to the solution of well-specified, soluble problems. The field moved in that direction, sometimes losing its luster but becoming better grounded in the process.[79]

Universities were also critical sites for OR. Field builders organized and institutionalized at major campuses. Philip Morse, professor of physics at MIT, one of the American "fathers" of OR, was

> acutely aware of the necessity of teaching O.R. at the university. He knew that because O.R. was a growing field, it would prove disruptive if new O.R. groups were formed by removing members from established ones. Accordingly, he took the lead in shaping MIT's fledgling O.R. curriculum from a single mathematics course taught by George P. Wadsworth into an interdisciplinary graduate degree program overseen by the Committee on Operations Research, which soon became the Operations Research Center. . . . Under this system, students studied problems at MIT, such as library circulation, but their dissertation work was supposed to be an active study for an actual operational authority. The overriding goal was to give students true-to-life experience while still under the tutelage of those who had successfully done O.R. in the past.[80]

Pioneering programs also developed at Case Western, Carnegie Tech, Penn's Wharton School, Columbia, Cornell, and Johns Hopkins, and at Birmingham and Imperial College in England, which had strengths in engineering.[81] Morse coauthored the landmark text *Methods of Operations Research* (published in 1951 but prepared for military use during the war as a classified document), which became the foundation of the field. "Though Morse's primary goal was expanding the pool of O.R. practitioners to meet demand, he was also committed to expanding the marketplace for O.R. . . . As many interested employers as there were at that time, it was not always easy to convince potential ones. Some were skeptical about scientific approaches in general, and others were uncertain that O.R. was anything new."[82]

The histories of businesses Booz, Allen & Hamilton and Arthur D. Little show OR's path to corporate acceptance. J. W. Pocock, a management consultant with Booz, Allen, urged that OR practitioners "demonstrate O.R.'s utility by seeking out small problems first as a bridge to managers' confidence." According to Thomas, "Although Pocock had problems convincing managers to adopt O.R. using technical explanations, the approach was not without merit. One method Morse used to expand the field's market was the establishment of an O.R. summer course at MIT designed primarily for people in industry, government and consulting. . . . Although ostensibly a primer in methods, Morse valued the course as much as a propaganda as a pedagogical tool."[83] Morse recalled that "it needed only one or two companies to take up the idea to convert an entire industry."[84]

OR professionalized, organized, and institutionalized interdisciplinarily. Perhaps contrary to expectations of both interdisciplinarity's starry-eyed proponents and its dark-browed deniers, splits and conflicts marked the field from the onset, underscoring the fact that even relatively successful interdisciplinary development is never seamless. There are central contradictions, perhaps necessary ones. This development process embraced the inception and incorporation of OR into business and industry, professional organizations, and universities. Conflicts over theory versus practice, cooperative professional consulting versus scientific expertise (especially in mathematics), academics versus practitioners, professional autonomy, the nature of practice, and the profession itself continue today, as debates in both colleges of business and management and professional journals immediately illustrate. Complicated relationships and matters of location thread their way through the efforts to institutionalize OR in universities and professional organizations.

We can tell the tale of professional organization briefly and simply. As Peter Horner relates in his capsule history of ORSA and INFORMS, the Operations Research Society of America formed on May 26, 1952, with 73 individuals from universities, the military, and corporate America.[85] "The early ORSA meetings were attended by a couple of hundred people, almost all of them employed by industry, government or the military," recalls longtime member Sid Hess. "The best parts of the meetings were late night bull sessions in the cocktail lounge."

"But all was not cozy in the OR community," Horner observes. Some members felt "that ORSA was too strongly oriented toward mathematics, that its leaders were just interested in military applications," remembered Andrew Vazsonyi. "ORSA was dominated by the Phil Morse and George Kimball crowd, people who were always talking about the things they did for the military during World War II. Many of us thought that ORSA needed another approach, something oriented toward management, but we didn't think we could get the Morse crowd to change. It turns out we were right." These perceptions were partly correct, but the caricatures and exaggerations are equally revealing. "ORSA's early focus on military matters at the expense of management, combined with its restrictive, layered membership policies, prompted several disenfranchised [sic] members to consider establishing a new society that catered to their needs." One member recalled, "Just 18 months after ORSA was founded[,] a room full of economists, engineers, mathematicians, statisticians, astronomers, philosophers, attorneys, and, yes, erstwhile operations researchers met on a cold winter's day at Columbia University to ponder the possibility of joining forces under another banner, this one called 'management science.' "[86]

A professional split developed between those who "were looking, in a scientific sense, for laws and regularities that [they] believed governed management" and those who "thought management science meant developing methodology, improving the way we do things." Another debate arose over the issue of ethics. "I'm a philosopher. When they said optimize, I thought they meant optimize in an ethical sense," recollected C. West Churchman. "You can optimize the decision-making function in linear programming and find out that it is only optimal in terms of what management perceives to be the monetary benefits minus cost. LP's only constraints are physical or purely financial, not ethical."[87] The Institute of Management Sciences (TIMS) was founded in 1953, and ORSA and TIMS went different ways. By the end of the 1950s, their membership was almost equal: ORSA had about 3,000, TIMS more than 2,600. The balance of interdisciplinarities weighed differently from different vantage points.

A gradual move toward reunion began in the 1970s. In 1994, ORSA and TIMS recombined into INFORMS (Institute for OR and the Management Sciences). Celebratory accounts of the reunion do not make the connections clear. Teleologically, the list of great moments culminates with the fiftieth anniversaries of the *Journal of Operations Research* (2000), the OR program of the Naval Post Graduate School (2002), and ORSA (2002), as well as the fortieth anniversary of TIMS in 1995 and publication of the *Encyclopedia of Operations Research and Management* in 1996.

Yet a divide remained, as John R. Hall Jr. showed in "An Issue-Oriented History of TIMS": "TIMS was created to synthesize *all* the management science disciplines—hence the 's' at the end of our name—so our field has always been defined primarily by its parts. Thus, it probably is not surprising that, after 30 years and millions of words in print, we still spend so much time wrestling with the definition of our field and worrying about the dangers of factional conflict and fragmentation. The evolution of TIMS has been a history of trying to find ways to accommodate its many interests within a framework of healthy pluralism." In his view, "we need to get back to the original goal of management science as a synthesis of all the sciences applicable to management, not just mathematical representation of management decisions. One step in this direction may be the recent creation of an operational science unit in the National Science Foundation. . . . It provides opportunities for multidisciplinary projects and interaction with other parts of the scientific community." Recognizing that the question was not closed, Hall asked: "Should our field still be seen as a synthesis of all the management sciences?"[88] Happily, almost no one made the attempt.

The history of OR in postwar universities illustrates the complicated process of interdisciplinary formation. William Thomas shows persuasively that the "transformation in OR" from wartime practice to professional practice and academic subject

> happened for different reasons in different places. To paint events in broad strokes: at the Case Institute of Technology, the philosophers of science West Churchman and Russell Ackoff taught OR as part of an attempt to reduce their "experimentalist" philosophy of science to practice; they fostered mathematical OR as a refinement of their ideas, but felt that the subject should never be confined to a mathematical canon. At the new Graduate School of Business Administration of the Carnegie Institute of Technology, theoreticians such as Herbert Simon regarded OR as part of a more general attempt to develop abstract, largely academic theories of managerial decision-making and economics. However, at the Johns Hopkins University, systems engineers led by Robert H. Roy regarded mathematical OR primarily as a set of practical techniques that were appropriate for specified tasks in industrial engineering.[89]

The history of OR in the postwar university is inseparable from the stories of professional education in business and management, the social sciences, and the sciences, especially mathematics and physics. Augier and March represent the grand narrative:

The emergence of the modern model of business education was embedded in this climate of policy research and of the rise of the idea of interdisciplinary collaboration among the behavioral and social sciences and between them and the natural sciences and engineering. The postwar culture of business schools was a culture in which traditional historical, institutional, and qualitative academicians were challenged by younger scholars with new research tools developed or highlighted during the Second World War and with enthusiasm for quantitative analysis and theory; for perspectives drawn from economic theory, decision theory, systems theory, and game theory; for developing more mathematical, analytical, and rigorous behavioral and social sciences; and for the enlistment of those sciences in the interdisciplinary solution of social and economic problems.

As they admit but do not elaborate, "Many of the modern tensions of academic institutions stem from the complications of engaging problems that cut across disciplines within an organization that is organized by disciplines, but such an interdisciplinary vision was a part of the postwar rhetoric of business schools and management education."[90]

Augier and March treat OR as a major example of "fundamental research in a business school." A leading example is the Graduate School of Industrial Administration (GSIA) at Carnegie Tech. Its faculty members were "defensive about accusations that they pursued knowledge 'only for knowledge's sake.' "[91] Marrying problem-solving with decision theory and mathematical tools made the GSIA the "poster child" of reform in business education. For fifteen or twenty years, the GSIA was "an extraordinary place for research." Compared to disciplinary departments, interdisciplinary and multidisciplinary programs have a short half-life.

What made GSIA such a special place to learn how organizations learn and make decisions? First and foremost, Crowther-Heyck cites "the interdisciplinary spirit of the school." Other factors include "the extent to which collegial interaction occurred without distinctions of labels or status"; a lack of concern for "relevance," which was based on the assumption that "any good idea would ultimately find its own usefulness"; and "its small size, lack of history or a sense of it, and a Protestant work ethic that encouraged innovation."[92] Ironically, when distinguished faculty left the GSIA and Carnegie Tech, many went to disciplinary departments rather than to business schools.

These observations lead us to appreciate how different the GSIA was from the Department of Social Relations at Harvard. In retrospect, however, it seems less so. Augier and March argue that "the postwar business school reformers had endorsed the twin virtues of fundamental research and interdisciplinarity. In practice, the two proved to be largely incompatible." But their explanation gives us pause.

> The clear auditors of fundamental research were found in the disciplines, and schools that sought to maintain a presence in fundamental research that gained approval from the disciplines were driven to become more explicitly linked to the disciplines, especially economics. In a standard feedback way, interdisciplinary programs grew to attract groups of scholars with lower means and higher variances of talent than found in disciplinary programs. Moreover, insofar as the theoretical, ideology, and political views of the new (Chicago) economics became the dogma of the economics discipline . . . a commitment to fundamental disciplinary knowledge in economics precluded most efforts toward interdisciplinary collaboration with other social science disciplines.[93]

They end by undercutting the value of interdisciplinarity by judging it against established disciplines and imputing too much power to one discipline. They do not ask about the potential for alternative relationships.

William Thomas tells a more nuanced tale in his comparison of OR as conceived and practiced by the Arthur D. Little consulting firm and as conceptualized at MIT. While both practices were presumed to be interdisciplinary, they were very different. Thomas deliberately adopts a different premise than other students of OR. "Prior accounts of OR's turn to mathematical specialization have not confronted the variety of visions that came to surround OR in the postwar period," he argues. "They have instead assumed that the development of a mathematical canon represented a sort of pathology of professionalization, which detached it from the generalist investigations touted by its wartime practitioners."[94] At MIT, OR had to find a home at the same time the university established a new School of Industrial Management. In contrast, "the start-up OR group established at Arthur D. Little in 1949 had to define its work in a way that capitalized on the firm's history of technical consulting to gain entry into the established field of management consulting, while not restricting the scope of their work by anchoring it to OR's increasingly technical content."[95] Contexts, interrelationships, and influences are central to the construction, conceptualizations, and practices of interdisciplines. Institutional locations, leaders and entrepreneurs, alternative visions of knowledge and its uses, notions of professionalization, and supply and demand all count.

For Arthur D. Little, the challenge was "to convince managers that OR was novel, but also compatible with existing managerial methods." Company consultants writing in the *Harvard Business Review* "did not presume that the idea of 'science' conveyed any inherent authority in the business world. They understood business and management expertise to be based on experience with specialized markets and on organizing effective teams, and they understood that scientists were imagined, by contrast, to embrace quantitatively dehumanized approaches to problems. . . . Expanding OR's intellectual interests to parallel managerial work allowed them to make a claim to working easily with managers, just as consultants did; restricting OR's *definition* to a technical jurisdiction avoided damaging claims that they sought to subsume managerial knowledge within their new profession." They also recognized that problems and their solutions were continuously "evolving."[96]

At MIT, interest in OR programs began before the end of the war. The first initiative was an "experimental" graduate course taught by mathematician George Wadsworth and researchers from the Navy's Operations Evaluation Group (OEG). They sought to balance instruction in "certain basic principles and viewpoints of operations research"—that is, mathematical methods—with "a more general ability to frame and investigate problems in parallel with managers' own deliberations," recognizing that "real problems do not fall neatly into one or another of the usual categories of knowledge, but cut widely across boundaries." Successful OR sought to ensure that the "wholeness of the problem" was "not artificially suppressed."[97]

Despite its "moderate" success, the course encountered problems. Economics and business administration students interested in research in OR topics lacked "an adequate mathematical background. . . . It also proved difficult to arouse student interest in the subject in the absence of a broader pedagogical program."[98] Institutional pressures to create an OR program at MIT mounted as Arthur D. Little set up an OR group and both Case Institute of Technology and the Naval Postgraduate School moved to establish programs. Philip Morse returned from service at the Weapons Systems Evaluation Group in the Department of Defense at the same time that Alfred Sloan of General Motors donated funds to build a School of Industrial Management. OR was viewed as a way to combine a new approach to industrial management with MIT's scientific leadership.

A revealing clash about the legitimacy, relevance, and utility of OR for management followed. In the face of strong skepticism about OR that ranged from its foundations to its pretensions and its value to management, which was shared by the dean of the Sloan School, Morse set up a committee to coordinate research and supervise graduate work. According to Thomas:

> Morse's committee . . . comprised members of several departments, including physics, mathematics, the management school, mechanical engineering, electrical engineering, and economics, and its members encouraged students to undertake diverse coursework. In a 1953 survey he filled out for ORSA's education committee, Morse mentioned, in addition to the mathematics department's continuing OR course, Machine Computation, Communication Theory, Social Psychology of Industry, Human Communication Networks, Group Organization, Econometrics, Technology of Industrial Control, and Probability and Statistics as relevant to OR. The committee maintained a relation with the Navy's OEG, and students were assigned local problems at MIT to work on. . . . Sometimes they also worked on the projects with the consultants at Arthur D. Little. . . . PhD dissertations done under the committee were supposed to be undertaken on behalf of outside organizations to give students practical experience.

With the help of Arthur D. Little and the OEG, a series of summer courses encouraged outreach to industry. Ironically, when the School of Industrial Management (SIM) became more receptive to OR and proposed incorporating Morse's interdepartmental OR committee, he and his OR colleagues chose to continue their separate cross-disciplinary status. "Convinced of the power of interdisciplinary work in OR," Morse thought "'that the effort should never be entirely within S.I.M.' It never was. When the MIT Operations Research Center was established soon thereafter, it remained an independent interdisciplinary organ of the institute that attracted participation from SIM."[99]

Thomas reflects: "The only way the OR profession could have retained an identification with the generalized investigatory role its proponents originally envisioned would have been to try to subsume general managerial knowledge as well as a number of business-related specialties within the rubric of OR. Such a maneuver likely would have been quixotic and reputation damaging. . . . Too often, though, this lament has come to define the history of OR, because it takes for granted the claim that OR *should* have been identified with the wider field of managerial expertise" (or, for that matter, with science, which Thomas surprisingly does not mention). "Rather than simply suppose that the ascendancy of technical OR represented an intellectual pathology, it seems more reasonable to examine the history of OR in terms of both the intellectual content that defined the profession and the less visible institutional networks that granted legitimacy to its practitioners' work."[100]

Conclusion

Perhaps this is how it should be. A separate location with variable cooperative and competitive relationships and open and perhaps unresolvable conflicts over theory and practice, science and application, and professional ideologies; "traditional academic disciplines and professional program"; and institutes and centers are all among the paths to interdisciplinarity.[101] Consider, finally, the similarities, differences, and contradictions between Social Relations and Operations Research.

Taking up the failed project of sociology, Soc Rel overly ambitiously sought to unify the social sciences. In its single institutional home and only established endeavor at Harvard University (where a department of sociology was startlingly absent), it encompassed sociology, social psychology, and social anthropology. None of these fields had found room to develop within its own disciplinary department. Despite unfurling a banner of unification portraying Soc Rel as a bold, integrative science of society, premature and unbalanced institutionalization seems to have been a fatal factor in its decline. One theoretical system maintained hegemony at the cost of other models that might have emerged collaboratively. Before long, social psychology and social anthropology went their separate ways, and a department of sociology replaced the department of Social Relations.

By contrast, OR is an exemplary showcase for the fusion of scientific methodologies, practical questions, and systematic inquiry. That conjunction was accelerated by the demands of war, but it was rooted in ongoing collaborations between theoretical scientists and industrial engineers. Among its prototypical practitioners were professionals, not applied scientists, especially in research and development. Academic leaders, such as Herbert Simon and Philip Morse, moved back and forth between academia, government, and public and private think tanks. In addition, the most vital translational work was done by teams. The development of OR as an academic field did not lead to the supersession of that characteristic structure.

While Soc Rel bears comparison with sociology, OR calls for comparison with communication. The narratives of their development slide confusingly between disciplinarity and interdisciplinarity, approaching a parody of history. They are similar in their inception and their ongoing ties to corporations, as well as claims for their importance and originality. At the same time, OR differs in its focus on innovation rather than on explaining and justifying existing practices. That revealing difference arises in part from the fact that OR theorists came more often from the sciences than the social sciences, which stems, also in part, from their differing origins and the problems they set out to solve. OR's notions of needs and solutions were more specific and focused. OR's founders were also more successful in promoting the field both publicly and privately, to governments, corporations, and universities. OR's disciplinary relationships in the sciences and social sciences are closely connected to its university and corporate locations. Although problematic and full of conflicts, as is its organizational history, Operations Research has succeeded to a much greater degree than communication.

CHAPTER FOUR

Between Mind and Mentality

Cognitive Science and New Histories, 1940s–1980s

Moving forward a decade, we turn from social relations and operations research to cognitive science and the "new" histories. A bit facetiously, I describe the former as an octopus and the latter as a bat. These are meant as complimentary rather than derisive terms. Cognitive science (Cog Sci) is everywhere, reaching out its intelligent arms to encompass many fields. Does it matter if it is called cognitive studies, dropping the declaration of science? The new histories are generally located within disciplines, making fugitive appearances here and there outside as well as inside of history. Like bats, they are difficult to see and often erroneously regarded as dangerous.

Both fields present themselves as interdisciplinary; many scholars have identified them as interdisciplines. Indeed, they have stood as representations and signatures of interdisciplinarity. Both have international organizations, journals, and annual meetings. They spawn subfields. Both have pretentions to interdisciplinarity and promote themselves as encompassing broad knowledge, although aspirations for cognitive science are unusually boundless. "Cognition . . . was said to be 'involved in *everything a human being might possibly do*', so that '*every* psychological phenomenon is a cognitive phenomenon.'"[1] In contrast to the ubiquity of Cog Sci, the new histories are sometimes hard to find. Moreover, both have sown sharp divisions and been met with vocal dissent, inside as well as outside their home bases. For example, cognitive science "does not have a clearly agreed upon sense of direction and a large number of researchers constituting a community, as is the case with, say, atomic physics or molecular biology. Rather, it is really more a loose affiliation of disciplines than a discipline of its own," write Francisco Varela, Evan Thompson, and Eleanor Rosch.[2] The new histories proudly proclaim their pluralism.

Cognitive science is the most challenging case study in this book. Seeking recognition as the apotheosis of interdisciplinarity, its spokesmen are distinguished by their hubris. Claiming to be all things for all purposes and to solve all problems with a science of human cognition as its putative core, it resembles a giant octopus camouflaging itself as a forest of seaweed. It is everywhere, but is it anywhere?[3]

Consider this typical definition:

> Cognitive science is the interdisciplinary scientific study of the mind and its processes. It examines what cognition is, what it does and how it works. It includes research on intelligence and behavior, especially focusing on how information is represented, processed, and transformed (in faculties such as perception, language, memory, reasoning, and emotion) within nervous systems (human or other animal) and machines (e.g. computers). Cognitive science consists of multiple research disciplines, including psychology, artificial intelligence, philosophy, neuroscience, linguistics, and anthropology. It spans many levels of analysis, from low-level learning and decision mechanisms to high-level logic and planning; from neural circuitry to modular brain organization. The fundamental concept of cognitive science is "that thinking can best be understood in terms of representational structures in the mind and computational procedures that operate on those structures."[4]

The *Stanford Encyclopedia of Philosophy* dates the field's intellectual origins to the mid-1950s and its organization to the mid-1970s with the formation of the Cognitive Science Society and the launch of its journal, *Cognitive Science*. This entry's 2010 revision refers to cognitive science programs in more than 70 universities worldwide.[5]

In contrast, cognitive scientist, linguist, and philosopher Jerry Fodor comments that "the history of cognitive science, insofar as it's been any sort of success, has consisted largely of . . . 'throwing some light on how much dark there is.' . . . For example, we don't know what makes some cognitive states conscious[,] . . . how cognitive states and processes are implemented by neural states and processes[, or] . . . how cognition develops (if it does) or how it evolved (if it did)." Indeed, "there is quite possibly something deeply wrong with the cognitive psychology that we currently have available." Fodor concludes that nobody actually knows how the mind works.[6] In a nutshell, the question of how the brain "represents" thinking and how cognitive scientists themselves identify and represent cognition, on the one hand, and the relationship between representation and computation, on the other hand, remain unresolved and problematic. Even the standard histories by Howard Gardner and Margaret Boden admit to doubts and some ambivalence.

In the introduction to his 2001 edited collection *New Perspectives on Historical Writing*, historian Peter Burke points to history's fragmentation. "In the last generation or so the universe of historians has been expanding at a dizzying rate. National history, which was dominant in the nineteenth century, now has to compete for attention with world history and with local history (once left to antiquarians and amateurs). There are many new fields, often supported by specialized journals. Social history, for example, became independent of economic history only to fragment, like some new nation, into historical demography, labour history, urban history, rural history, and so on."[7] By the 1990s, these subfields were joined by histories of women, children, and families and of ethnic and racial groups, as well as by "new" cultural and intellectual histories, the history of mentalities and deep structures, material and environment histories, and more. These new histories faced criticisms large and small, both immediately and later. Wave after wave of yet newer histories have followed. We need not return to early new histories associated with Vico or even Herodotus to grasp this fact. Our focus falls on the second half of the twentieth century.

Despite many differences, both superficial and major, the new histories share certain qualities with cognitive science, including problems of definition, coherence, and diffuseness. Although both fields have important precedents that qualify their incessant and excessive claims of novelty, their recent rises have similar chronologies. Both emerged and claimed a place in universities and research centers after World War II, especially in the 1960s and 1970s. Both have origins in their opposition to the reigning, albeit declining, orthodoxies: behaviorism in the case of Cog Sci, and conventional political and intellectual history in the case of new histories. There were generational and territorial issues as well as intellectual and disciplinary questions involving theory and methods. In both cases, issues of location and (inter)disciplinary relationships were critical. So, too, were matters of organization and institutionalization.

Context made an enormous difference. Both fields arose in the social, cultural, political economic, and intellectual climate sketched in the preceding chapter. The *longue durée* of interdisciplinary initiatives is seldom sufficiently appreciated. The specter and lure of science, the quest for the new, the concern with "mind" and its influences, and the thrust for relevance and recognition, as well as for funding, were driving forces. Both fields have been shaped by the disciplines in which they developed and against which they struggled; those disciplines—whether psychology or history—changed through these encounters. Both reflect theoretical, conceptual, and empirical advances in and influences from Europe, ranging from philosophy of mind and cybernetics to *histoire totale*. Although the latest new histories have only recently discovered cognitive science, they have long been fascinated by the history of *mentalités* and its relationship to and undergirding of behavior. Mind and behavior, the brain in the body, are central concerns even when they are not explicit. While the new histories are by definition historical and cultural,[8] cognitive science expressly denies the relevance and importance of history and culture, or at least its ability to study them scientifically.

The most dramatic differences, which are most pregnant with lessons for interdisciplinarity, have to do with how these fields have developed. Superficially and intramurally, cognitive science is one of the great success stories of interdisciplinarity. On closer examination, however, the foundations and the construction of that success appear less solid and more suspect. Most importantly, Cog Sci's case for interdisciplinarity is particular and problematic, as well as provocative. We need to ask: here, there, and anywhere? An answer lies, at least in part, as much in the disciplines and their relationships as in presumptions of *inter*disciplinarity. In this respect, neuroscience and artificial intelligence take on special importance. A list of disciplines does not constitute an interdiscipline.

New histories, in contrast, constitute a very interesting and heuristic example of interdisciplinarity mainly *within* disciplines. Some new historians had visions of founding new disciplines and departments. In the 1960s and 1970s, some proclaimed that *they* were scientists and their histories would be scientific, while more declared that they were social scientists or aspired to that recognition. The Social Science History Association, one of the major homes to new historians, was formed in 1976. Overwhelmingly, however, the practice of new history took place within history departments. Departments of history are sometimes located in colleges or divisions of the humanities and sometimes in the social or behavioral sciences. But that placement seldom influences the nature of the history and historiography found in them.[9]

Cognitive science presents itself as interdisciplinary by listing the disciplines with which it intersects. This Chinese menu approach not only skirts questions of the specific relationships and problems involved, but it does *not* constitute interdisciplinarity as defined in this book. On the other hand, most new historians do their research and teaching within departments of history, within social science (economics, political science, sociology, anthropology) departments, in women's or gender studies programs, or in hyphenated race or ethnic studies units. The new histories often constitute "turns" from one new history to another. Interdisciplinarity within a disciplinary location: though uncommon, it carries important implications.

Cognitive Science(s)

George Miller reminisced: "By 1960 it was clear that something interdisciplinary was happening. At Harvard we called it cognitive studies, at Carnegie-Mellon they called it information-processing psychology, and at La Jolla they called it cognitive science. What you called it didn't really matter until 1976, when the Alfred P. Sloan Foundation became interested."[10]

Cognitive science shares several features with other leading claimants to interdisciplinarity. It began with a declared mission: to understand cognition, the mind, and the brain. Exploring the field, its literature, and its discourse, we encounter "the cognitive revolution" at every turn. With irony, Miller refers to a cognitive counterrevolution in the face of a dominant behaviorism. On my desk is a stack of books with the "mind as machine" in their titles. Mechanical metaphors proliferate; much mention is made of mental "hardware" and "software," a distinction that neuroscientists are blurring, sometimes intentionally, sometimes not. The field is so heavily dependent on metaphors that debate has ensued over what George Lakoff and Mark Johnson have called "the metaphorical structure of the human conceptual system." Simply, the problem is that when unexamined and used repetitively and uncritically as familiar discourse, metaphors substitute for concreteness, concepts, connections, and questions. "*Metaphorical concepts* are those which are understood and structured not merely on their own terms, but rather in terms of other concepts. This involves conceptualizing *one kind* of object or experience in terms of *different kind* of object or experience."[11] With respect to cognition, this is especially complicated and dangerous.

Among the qualities that cognitive science shares with operations research, in addition to its association with behavioral science, is an anxious concern with provenance and pedigree. More curious and more blatant than for any other interdiscipline is the presence of lists of luminaries. In the Wikipedia entry for "cognitive science," which represents a consensus among published works, we find a section listing "Notable researchers" and "See also: list of cognitive scientists." The roster of "leading thinkers" is lengthy and rather indiscriminate, ranging from philosophers to anthropologists. "Some of the most recognized names in cognitive science are usually . . . the most controversial," it begins. But listings by disciplines include persons who are not associated with those disciplines. "Prominence" is mixed with "popular"; neither term is defined.[12] Venturing farther into the Internet, we encounter "Celebrities in Cognitive Science."[13] This list of more than 50 "writings by and about leading thinkers in cognitive science, and critics and observers of the philosophy of mind" runs from David Hume to Marvin Minsky with George Miller, Herbert Simon, and Noam Chomsky in between. Without splitting hairs (or, perhaps, neurons), we can ask about the absence of Descartes and the presence of John Dewey and Jack Goody. Those included among the "critics and observers of the philosophy of mind" are even more perplexing. But I want to raise a more basic question: why a list of "celebrities"? It suggests a field with a need for legitimation and road mapping, as well as serious questions about its legibility and coherence. This multiplication of authorities is part and parcel of defining the field by listing its contributory disciplines, a feature that cognitive science shares with the humanities.

Mapping Cognitive Sciences

Cognitive science occupies a distinctive place in the history of interdisciplines in part because it represents a particular pattern: defining interdisciplinarity by listing disciplines and not attending to their interrelationships (beyond "overlap") or to specific questions that might stimulate the emergence of a field. Depending on the source, Cog Sci is constituted by six or seven disciplines, which are often represented graphically. These representations are repeated endlessly. The six-sided hexagon includes philosophy, psychology, linguistics, computer science, anthropology, and neuroscience (figure 4.1). The original diagram appeared in the highly influential 1978 Sloan Foundation report, which legitimated and justified funding for an enterprise that was already well under way.[14]

In its original version (conveniently reproduced in Miller's 2003 volume, without the updating that others include), the diagram is highly symbolic rather than operational. Nevertheless, it raises basic questions. It does not link every one of the six disciplines with each of the others. For example, philosophy at the top of the hexagon and neuroscience at the bottom are not directly connected; nor are computer science and anthropology. Philosophy is not connected directly with computer science or anthropology. Interestingly, psychology and linguistics are linked by an unbroken line. This asymmetry is curious in a field in which forms and representations are held to be central and interdisciplinarity across all these disciplines is asserted. In fact, the connections of philosophy and anthropology with the other components of cognitive science are uneasy at best, despite their historical centrality. Longstanding and persisting problems begin with "mind-body" and "brain-mind" divides and continue with reductionism, materialism, and "artificial" intelligence. Both the status and the relationships of the disciplines in cognitive science are problematic, and the question of its location, organization, and institutionalization follows from these.

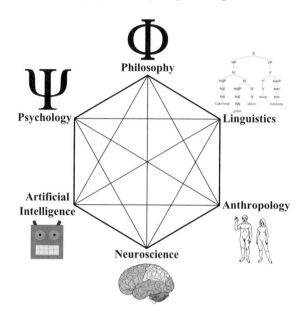

Figure 4.1 Cognitive science hexagon, adapted from George A. Miller. Cognitive science is often depicted as a hexagon, with the integrated disciplines connected (or unconnected) in a variety of ways. This graphic, displayed on Wikipedia, is adapted from one that originated in the Sloan report of 1976 and was later revised. "Cognitive science hexagon," by Charles Lowe, http://commons.wikimedia.org/wiki/File:Cognitive_Science _Hexagon.svg, CC BY-SA 3.0; originally adapted from George A. Miller, "The Cognitive Revolution: A Historical Perspective," *TRENDS in Cognitive Sciences* 7 (2003)

George Miller, whose vision guided the Sloan Foundation, remembers how neuroscience became cognitive science in an effort to "bridge the gap between brain and mind." He pronounced this arrangement of fields "institutionally convenient but intellectually awkward." Speaking of the hexagon, he said that "each line in the figure represented an area of interdisciplinary inquiry that . . . involved the tools of the two disciplines it linked together. Thus, cybernetics used concepts developed by computer science to model brain functions, elucidated in neuroscience. Similarly, computer science and linguistics were already linked through computational linguistics. Linguistics and psychology are linked by psycholinguistics, anthropology and neuroscience were linked by studies of the evolution of the brain, and so on."[15] The vagueness about common tools, shared concepts, and especially links between fields is telling.[16]

When Howard Gardner included the diagram in his acclaimed *The Mind's New Science: A History of the Cognitive Revolution*, he added "broken lines" between philosophy and neuroscience, artificial intelligence, and anthropology, which contrasted with the "unbroken lines" between the other disciplines. Following, at least metaphorically, the discourse of some social theorists and some writers on interdisciplinarity, he distinguished between the former's "strong interdisciplinary ties" and the latter's "weak interdisciplinary ties." But Gardner did not explain his usage, or the meanings of "strong" and "weak."[17] How seriously do cognitive scientists take representations? What are the relationships between disciplines in cognitive science? Where is the field located?

When cognitive science diagram came to Wikipedia, today's bridge between popular and more scholarly statements, strong and weak ties had been replaced without comment by bolder lines along the outline of the hexagon and lighter lines inside the figure (as updated July 23, 2013). Other than that, no distinctions are evident among the connections. Earlier efforts to distinguish differences in disciplinary contributions and inter- or multidisciplinary connections had disappeared. The legend for the diagram, originally adapted from George Miller, includes this statement: "This revised adaptation more accurately reflects the image as presented by Miller."[18] The Institute of Cognitive and Brain Research (ICBR) at Berkeley uses a more stylized and dynamic rendering of the hexagon (figure 4.2), adding a touch of mathematical set theory and a space-age quality. Is this the result of normalization, repetition, or obfuscation? At the risk of over-interpretation (if that is possible in the land of Cog Sci), such questions must be asked.

In contrast to the Sloan report's picture of the field, the Cognitive Science Society, the major multidisciplinary professional society, adds education to the list of disciplines. Curiously, it represents their interrelationships with an octagon; the eighth side is unmentioned and nameless (figure 4.3). Here we have *applied* Cog Sci in the most direct sense. According to its website, "The Cognitive Science Society, Inc. brings together researchers from many fields who hold a common goal: understanding the nature of the human mind. The Society promotes scientific interchange among researchers in disciplines comprising the field of Cognitive Science, including Artificial Intelligence, Linguistics, Anthropology, Psychology, Neuroscience, Philosophy, and Education." Around the octagon, in the form of a circle, the disciplines are arrayed alphabetically, beginning at the bottom. Interestingly, the connective lines of the original graphic are replaced by a maze, which seems to devolve into four quadrants. Or is a stylized brain's neural circuits, converging on a symbolic center? Is that cognitive science?

We again confront questions of disciplinary relationships, on the one hand, and, on the other, the challenge of representations in a field to which they are

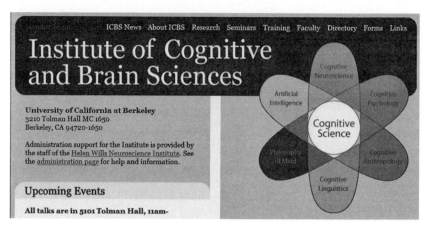

Institute of Cognitive and Brain Sciences

University of California at Berkeley
3210 Tolman Hall MC 1650
Berkeley, CA 94720-1650

Administration support for the Institute is provided by the staff of the Helen Wills Neuroscience Institute. See the administration page for help and information.

Upcoming Events

All talks are in 5101 Tolman Hall, 11am-

Figure 4.2 Cognitive science hexagon, from the Institute of Cognitive and Brain Sciences. This version, appearing on the webpage of the University of California–Berkeley ICBS, adds a touch of mathematical set theory and contemporary graphics quality to the diagram. From http://icbs/berkeley.edu/

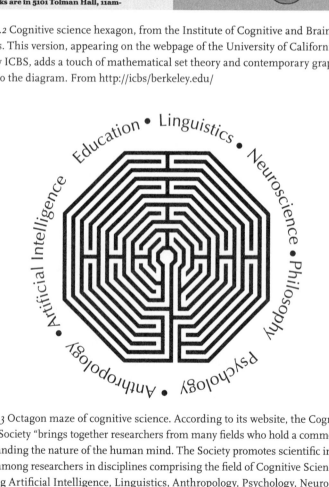

Figure 4.3 Octagon maze of cognitive science. According to its website, the Cognitive Science Society "brings together researchers from many fields who hold a common goal: understanding the nature of the human mind. The Society promotes scientific interchange among researchers in disciplines comprising the field of Cognitive Science, including Artificial Intelligence, Linguistics, Anthropology, Psychology, Neuroscience, Philosophy, and Education," Instead of a hexagon, it employs a hybrid octagon and maze to show disciplinary interrelationships, leading to one side with no name. From http://cognitivesciencesociety.org/index.html, © Cognitive Science Society, Inc.

explicitly central. In a typical statement, Gardner declares: "Cognitive science is predicated on the belief that it is legitimate—in fact, necessary—to posit a separate level of analysis which can be called the 'level of representation.' When working at this level, a scientist traffics in such representational entities as symbols, rules, images . . . and in addition, explores the ways in which these representational entities are joined, transformed, or contrasted with one another."[19] Should a field that claims its interdisciplinary stature and importance be open to such challenges over its own representation? Or might they be explicitly problematized and turned into an agenda for interdisciplinary research?

Multiple Paths toward a Multidisciplinary Project

A critical analysis of the numerous histories and manifestoes of cognitive science demonstrates that, despite its repeated assertions of its interdisciplinarity, this field has remained, at most, multidisciplinary, a congeries of discipline-based efforts to address a set of questions whose center is strangely undefined. The contrast with its less well-known cousin, operations research, is striking: OR has drawn together theorists and practitioners from a wide range of fields and addressed a bounded set of problems with great effectiveness. The differences are intellectual, institutional and organizational, aspirational, and rhetorical. Especially striking are the relationships among the often conflicting constituent disciplines and fields and the confusing locations of cognitive science.

George Miller, one of the founders of modern Cog Sci, presents the heroic version of the field's launching: "Cognitive science is a child of the 1950s, . . . when psychology, anthropology and linguistics were redefining themselves and computer science and neuroscience as disciplines were coming into existence. Psychology could not participate in the cognitive revolution until it had freed itself from behaviorism, thus restoring cognition to scientific respectability. By then, it was becoming clear in several disciplines that the solution to some of their problems depended crucially on solving problems traditionally allocated to other disciplines. Collaboration was called for."[20] For cognitive psychologist George Mandler, by contrast, "the well documented cognitive 'revolution' was, to a large extent, an evolving return to attitudes and trends that were present prior to the advent of behaviorism and that were alive and well outside of the United States." Rather than seeing this shift as revolutionary, he characterizes it as "slow and piecemeal."[21] As with all such "revolutions," we must tread lightly and try to recognize just what was revolutionized and to what effect.

At the other end of the timeline, linguistics scholar Geoffrey Pullum asked, "Is the cognitive revolution here yet?" at a 2013 British Academy conference,

"The Cognitive Revolution 60 Years On." "Some people at this conference think that it hasn't actually happened yet," he remarked. He concluded agnostically, "Maybe revolution is not quite the right metaphor."[22] Relatedly, a persistent but not very instructive debate swirls around the question of whether this development should be termed a cognitive revolution or a Kuhnian "paradigm shift."[23] This controversy suggests the embarrassing limits of supposed interdisciplinarity: although the commentators may have read Thomas Kuhn, they are unaware of Kuhn's own revisions and clarifications of his model and of the continuing debates over it in the history of science. If we use "revolution" carefully, we can see how a Cog Sci "movement" has affected psychology, the social sciences, and the humanities.

Significantly, another standard history, Robert M. Harnish's *Minds, Brains, Computers: An Historical Introduction to the Foundations of Cognitive Science,* dates the emergence of the field later than Miller does and points to a different mix of disciplines and formative questions. "Cognitive science . . . emerged in the mid-1970s" to explore "central questions in the domain of thought: how is knowledge acquired? how is it represented in the mind? how is knowledge then utilized in thought and action?" In this endeavor, "the problems and methods of researchers in various fields, such as psychology, neuroscience, computer science, linguistics, anthropology, and philosophy began to overlap" and "a remarkable convergence appeared among researchers concerned with understanding cognition." In his view, "cognitive science" became "established as a discipline."[24]

Harnish ignores not only developments before the 1970s but also such signal moments as the establishment of programs at Harvard and Carnegie Tech, as well as the Sloan Foundation initiative. No less importantly, his notions of "overlap" and "convergence" demand explication. Having asserted that cognitive science has formed into a discipline, Harnish immediately contradicts himself: "It has since become plausible that this is a 'natural' domain of investigation, and it has become clear that researchers will profit from being in systematic contact with others also interested in understanding cognition from their own point of view."[25] For Harnish and many others in this field, the approach to interdisciplinarity— as model and metaphor—is at best additive, not interactive. If this account fairly represents Cog Sci, it is not an interdiscipline.

Other views recognize cognitive science's historical context, both far and near. In contrast to Harnish, Howard Gardner embraces the old and the new: "Cognitive scientists, . . . as did the Greeks, conjecture about the various vehicles of knowledge: what is a form, an image, a concept, a word; and how do these 'modes of representations' relate to one another? They wonder about the priorities of specific sense organs as against a central 'general understanding' or 'common sense.' They reflect on language, noting the power and traps entailed in the use of words and their possible predominant influence over thoughts and beliefs. And they speculate at length on the nature of the very activity of knowing, and what are the limits of scientific knowledge about human knowing?" Unlike the Greeks, cognitive scientists proceed not through philosophical speculation but through "empirical methods" that pass muster as science. Equally important, they ask questions that were impossible to pose in classical antiquity or the Enlightenment: "New disciplines, like artificial intelligence, have arisen, and new questions, like the potential of man-made devices to think, stimulate research. Moreover, cognitive scientists embrace the most recent technological break-throughs in a variety of disciplines. Most central to their undertaking is the computer—that creation of the mid-twentieth century that holds promise for changing our conceptions of the world in which we live and our picture of the human mind."[26] Technological developments not only offered new tools for the solution of old problems but also generated new ones.

In both material and metaphorical senses, the computer is central to modern mechanistic computational cognitive science. The concreteness of the computer typically obscures the power of the metaphoric uses of this term. Hunter Crowther-Heyck captures part of the story when he argues that "psychologists interpreted the computer metaphor as antibehaviorist for three main reasons. . . . First, the computer metaphor was intimately connected to an approach to language—Noam Chomsky's mathematical linguistics—that saw mind as necessary to human language. Second, the computer metaphor was associated with an interdisci-plinary approach to psychology, an approach that stood in sharp contrast to the behaviorist effort to establish psychology's independence. Third, the adoption of the computer metaphor of mind entailed the adoption of a new research pro-gram for experimental psychology, one that sought to replace the laboratory rat with the human-computer system as the chief source of psychological data."[27] Unfortunately, Crowther-Heyck does not take "the computer metaphor" seriously as a metaphor. Similarly, many cognitive scientists fail to attend to the mecha-nistic and materialistic dimensions of "the mind as machine."

Margaret Boden, like Howard Gardner, takes a long view of the development of cognitive science and regards it as an interdisciplinary field. According to her, Cog Sci did not "come together" until the 1950s, although it had deep roots in classical philosophy and enlightenment science. This history establishes criti-cal traditions and poses fundamental questions. Considering epistemologies stretching from Plato to Descartes and from ancient to early modern automata

and thinking machines, she points to the emergence of "mind" as a complicated, seemingly intractable, problem that pervaded almost all philosophical,
theological, and scientific traditions. Boden shows that the behaviorist and cognitive revolutions were built on traditions founded by Descartes, Kant, and the
discourse that they stimulated. Cybernetics tended to adopt a Kantian model of
" 'organisms' as systems following *internal* laws, order, or organization," while
biology helped to create the undergirding for the "neurophysiological machine."
Behaviorism and cognitivism clashed and commingled, creating what Boden
describes in one of her chapter titles as "Psychology as Mechanism—But Not as
Machine."[28]

Yet mechanism and machine were inseparably intertwined. The impact of
Charles Babbage and his Difference Engine and then his Analytical Engine, the
first generally accepted digital computer, shows this connection with particular
clarity. The quest for thinking machines and the simulation of human cognition accelerated, while the confusion between them deepened. This trend cul-
minated in artificial intelligence (AI) within computer science and underlay
major aspects of neuroscience. John von Neumann's work was one major bridging point.

In addition to their differing periodizations, major accounts of the field's development disagree about what disciplines came together in its formation. Significantly, however, all accounts share a model in which two distinct disciplines
remain in tension even after their supposed convergence. For example, another
"overlapping" path shows the convergence of linguistics and computation via
philosophy, language, and mathematics, with Alan Turing in Great Britain in the
1930s and 1940s and Noam Chomsky in the United States in the 1950s and
1960s taking its penultimate steps. To paraphrase Gideon Siegfried, "mechanization," in the form of the electronic computer and its metaphors, "took command." Language and computers came together, raising the stakes of the debate
over the relationship between language and cognition. Philosophical disputation
followed, though not always happily,[29] as relationships among animals, machines,
and humans are highly problematic.

Here, the seeds of neuroscience took root. Metaphorically, the move was
from speculation and observation to the technologically enhanced study of neurons and neural connections. In practice, however, speculative extrapolations
from highly specific, localized examinations via increasingly complex technologies provide proximate and indirect bases for understanding cognition. Trained
in philosophy, psychology, neurology, and physiological psychology, Warren

McCulloch turned from psychiatric practice to MIT's Electronics Laboratory to focus on the circuit theory of brains. With Walter Pitts, he pushed conceptions of the mind as a logic machine. McCulloch's legacy includes his notion of his work as "experimental epistemology," about which Boden quips, "This may sound like a contradiction in terms, but it's not." It has also been called "meta-epistemology," neither neuroscience nor mathematics.[30]

In partial contrast, cybernetics gave rise to AI with the effort first to model this version of cognition and then to replicate it in computational simulations. Both neuroscience and cybernetics are computational. Boden calls the bringing together of cybernetics and computation under the banner of cognition a form of "infant interdisciplinarity." Paralleling these currents are the intersections of the biological with the neurological. "Neurophysiology . . . was prominent in cybernetics from the start." The social, environmental, human interactive, and cultural dimensions increasingly disappeared; they were difficult to control and distracted from the pursuit of science. Neurology also took a more physiological direction, with a focus on chemicals and cells, their possible roles in the structure and action of neurons, and their networks in the body and the brain. Working by analogy, influenced both by psychology and neurophysiology, Kenneth Craik imagined the brain as a modeling machine, a system that "constructs models representing the world (and possible worlds)." As Boden and others remind us, Craik was a psychologist, not a neuroscientist. The models of mind as representation he proposed are hypothetical and candidates for computation and simulation.[31] In this line of development, cybernetics and neuroscience converged on cognitive psychology as an object of inquiry.

"By the end of the 1940s," according to Boden, "there were two ways of thinking about mind as machine. One was symbolic-computational, the other cybernetic-dynamical. . . . One might even say that the former focused on *computer and mind*, the latter on *computer and brain*. . . . The cyberneticists—besides being more interested in the brain than the committed symbolists were—had little or nothing to say about specific mental contents. Adaptation, self-organization, feedback, purpose, reverberating circuits . . . took precedence over (for instance) doing logic or using natural language." By the 1960s, formal computationists and cyberneticists formed two distinct groups. "For many years afterwards, there was little love lost between them. . . . This splitting was due partly to the availability of two methodologies, involving different types of skill: 'logical' programming, and building or simulating dynamical or probabilistic systems."[32] A focus on adaptation or meaning reinforced the dividing lines.

Boden declares that "the 1950s saw the emergence of a self-consciously inter-disciplinary cognitive science—though not yet under that name. Both the in-terdisciplinarity and the ideas had been prefigured in the cybernetics move-ment of the 1940s." She makes the case for interdisciplinarity by listing the disciplines that were combined in the emerging field. After behaviorism in psychology had been overthrown, "computational accounts of perception, con-cepts, and human decision making appeared on both sides of the Atlantic." In greater detail than other accounts, Boden tells "how the various disciplines"—psychology, linguistics, neurophysiology, and finally AI—"came together . . . and how that led to the establishment of the first official research groups." She "high-lights the cooperation that's needed for science in general and interdisciplinarity in particular," which was stimulated by landmark conferences.[33] "The more inter-disciplinary a new field is, the more important face-to-face gatherings are likely to be. The different specialists need to enthuse each other, to convince each other that their particular field *is* potentially relevant even though this may not be immediately obvious. Only then can substantive interdisciplinary research be done. When this works well, the interchange quickly ratchets up to an intellec-tually provocative, and mutually enjoyable level." Boden's list includes the Macy seminars on cybernetics from 1946 to 1953; the 1956 Dartmouth College Sum-mer Research Project on AI; the MIT IEEE Symposium on Information Theory for researchers in psychology and linguistics, also held in 1956; and the 1958 National Physical Laboratory's London conference on the work of Alan Turing, AI, psychology, and neurophysiology. "At that point, cognitive science was truly on its way."[34]

Even the briefest of glances at the organization and institutionalization of cognitive science today demonstrates that, despite its varying incarnations and its relative domination by specific disciplines, programs are nearly ubiquitous at research-oriented universities in the United States. The website of the Cognitive Science Society (CSS) lists 40 undergraduate and graduate programs, some in disciplinary departments and others in multidisciplinary units, programs, or centers. On this mixed roster are programs and centers in psychology, neurosci-ence, cognitive science, linguistics, computer science and artificial intelligence, education, and even a master's program in philosophy of science, though these may well represent overreaching on the part of the professional society. To my surprise, given the scope of the field and its contributing disciplines and institu-tions, the CSS's membership in the fall of 2013 was only 1,918.[35]

The pattern of degree programs offered in cognitive sciences at all levels is dizzying. An Internet search conducted in 2012–13 found 77 U.S. institutions with programs under that rubric, of which 36 were at the bachelor's, 17 at the master's, and 33 at the doctoral level. Eight programs offered both master's and doctoral degrees; 24 offered graduate certificates, minors, or concentrations in other departments; and 31 offered undergraduate minors, certificates, and concentrations. The names of these programs run the gamut: Cognitive Systems and Behavioral Neuroscience; Cognition, Action, and Perception; Neuroscience, Mind, and Behavior; Neural Computation; Intelligent Systems; Human Factors / Applied Cognition; Mind/Brain/Behavior/Interfaculty Initiative; Symbolic Systems; and the expected disciplinary departments and their combinations. Some call themselves interdisciplinary, although most do not state that explicitly.[36] Some no doubt fit almost any definition of interdisciplinarity. But this plethora of programs does not suggest the existence of a unified whole.

Disparate Institutional Locations

Did cognitive science "come together"? I do not mean to slight Boden's magnum opus in turning her chapter title on its head. To an important extent, she is correct: what we know as cognitive science emerged at that time. Yet her subsequent chapters demonstrate that its subfields remained largely separate after this "coming together." Befitting a supposed interdiscipline that is defined by a list of disciplines, chapters take up (in order): computational psychology, the "missing discipline" of anthropology, linguistics, artificial intelligence old and new, neuroscience from neurophysiology to neurobiology and computational neuroscience. Certain themes—or, rather, metaphors, such as connectionism and philosophies of mind as machine—merit separate chapters. Missing throughout, however, is a clear focus on relationships between and among disciplines and on specific problems and questions amenable to research that cross disciplinary lines and lead to the integration of diverse approaches and perspectives.

As Howard Gardner observes, "since the term *cognitive science* first began to be bandied about in the early 1970s, dozens of scientists have attempted to define the nature and scope of the field." Gardner offers a descriptive approach to cognitive science that is useful for an appraisal of its interdisciplinarity and of its status as science in the normative American sense of the term. He identifies five elements as "symptomatic of the cognitive-scientific enterprise": "First of all, there is the belief that, in talking about human cognitive activities, it is necessary to speak about mental representations and to position a level of analysis wholly separate from the biological or neurological, on the one hand, and the sociological or cultural, on the other. Second, there is the faith that central to any understanding of the human mind is the electronic computer. Not only are computers indispensable for carrying out studies of various sorts, but, more crucially, the computer also serves as the most viable model of how the human mind functions."[37]

While these two elements define the "central beliefs of current cognitive science, the latter three concern methodological or strategic characteristics." The third is "the deliberate decision to de-emphasize certain factors which may be important for cognitive functioning but whose inclusion at this point would unnecessarily complicate the cognitive-scientific enterprise. These factors include the influence of historical and cultural factors, and the role of the background context in which particular actions or thoughts occur." Even if it is necessary for the advancement of a science, this exclusion is a powerful limitation. The fourth element is a "faith in interdisciplinarity," which Gardner recognizes as a goal that has not yet been achieved. At present, a group of disciplines, identified "severally as the 'cognitive sciences,'" constitute the field. Today "most cognitive scientists are drawn from the ranks of specific disciplines—in particular, philosophy, psychology, artificial intelligence, linguistics, anthropology, and neuroscience. . . . The hope is that some day the boundaries between these disciplines may become attenuated or perhaps disappear altogether, yielding a single, unified cognitive science." The fifth and final element is presented as "controversial": the recognition "that a key ingredient in contemporary cognitive science is the agenda of issues, and the set of concerns, which have long exercised epistemologists in the Western philosophical tradition."[38] We must inquire into the connections among Gardner's historical awareness, his recognition of the limits of interdisciplinarity, and the field's exclusion of cultural and historical factors that shape cognition.

Where most commentators, including Gardner, see cognitive science as progressively advancing toward interdisciplinarity, historian Jamie Cohen-Cole sees slippage. His fascinating essay "Instituting the Science of Mind" dances around the question of interdisciplinarity. "When the psychologists Jerome Bruner and George Miller founded the Center for Cognitive Studies in Harvard in 1960, they conceived of it as an interdisciplinary institution" and attracted scholars from a wide range of disciplines to "the cross-disciplinary field of cognitive science." This account shifts silently from interdisciplinary to cross-disciplinary research and from cognitive studies to cognitive science. Bruner and Miller wrote to Harvard's president Nathan Pusey: "It was an essential feature of the Center, as originally conceived, that it would be broadly interdepartmental. The slogan, only half in jest, was that the cognitive processes are far too complex and important to be left to psychologists." But bringing faculty together across departmental lines faculty does not guarantee that their work will be interdisciplinary. While Cohen-Cole claims that over its ten-year duration the center declined from its interdisciplinary foundation to cross-disciplinary or multidisciplinary research, we must wonder whether it was ever interdisciplinary at all. Nowhere does Cohen-Cole define interdisciplinarity, although he seems certain that the center's "research culture" rapidly lost that quality.[39] Sadly, this rhetoric adds to the mythology of interdisciplinarity, first by romanticizing it and then by imposing a trope of its rise and fall.

Cohen-Cole's research opens important questions that warrant serious investigation. Institutional and physical locations are enormously important, as are the relationships that take place within them. He explains that the founders' aspirations centered not so much on collaborative work on common problems as on "setting up a particular research economy and pattern of intellectual exchange" whereby researchers in different disciplines would "learn from one another by trading tools" and methodologies and participating in a "social culture characterized by negotiation and argument."[40] All too soon, however, as affiliated faculty developed a sense of solidarity, the center became less welcoming to outsiders.

These are important lessons about what interdisciplinarity is *not*. As with other forms of listing, repetitive mention of current synonyms for such aspects of research as culture, tools, knowledge production, intellectual economies, and environmental architecture and design, without evidence of relationships and connective arguments, fails to make the case. What were the relationships between scholars from different fields? What were their questions and problems? How did they use these methods and tools to answer them collectively and individually? Interested readers fare better with George Miller's own reminiscences.

Although Cohen-Cole lists several factors that produced a shift toward multidisciplinarity, including changing research priorities and funding patterns, he emphasizes the center's physical relocation from an older building on Kirkland Street to the 11th and 12th floors of the new William James Hall. In a curiously romantic form of environmental or spatial determinism, he asserts: "The Center's home at 61 Kirkland Street had played an important role in generating its collegial atmosphere. . . . While the Center's morale depended on an intimate setting, its communal sense was similarly derived from its geographic distance from both the Social Relations and the Psychology Departments."[41] All those qualities were lost in the move. Yet this change in the center's relationships with the other social and behavioral sciences suggest that the interdisciplinary foundations for cognitive studies at Harvard were not strong. If it ever existed, the "golden age" was brief. But perhaps that is what we should expect and plan. Anticipating the possibility of a much shorter "half-life" than, say, a discipline would lead to a different model of interdisciplinarity.

The history of cognitive science at the Carnegie Institute of Technology helps to articulate the place of interdisciplinarity and multidisciplinarity in cognitive science; indeed, it strongly suggests that the lens of interdisciplinarity may not be the best vantage point from which to view cognitive science. Like Cohen-Cole, Crowther-Heyck uses "interdisciplinarity" and "multidisciplinarity" interchangeably without defining either term. Focusing on what he calls "the informal, interdisciplinary community of social scientists devoted to creating a mathematical behavioral social science" in Carnegie Tech's Graduate School of Industrial Administration, he treats interdisciplinarity and specialization as if they were opposites.[42] He occasionally signals the complications by putting interdisciplinary in quotation marks or referring to "informal interdisciplinarity." The problem becomes more serious when questions of the location of new efforts join those involving relationships among disciplines.

The newly founded Graduate School of Industrial Administration initially provided Herbert Simon with a hospitable environment at Carnegie Tech. "Systems science" was his game. He hired young, talented, and "like-minded faculty," mostly social psychologists and organization theorists, and placed himself integrally in major team projects. This common route to beginning interdisciplinarity can create problems for its institutionalization. His entrepreneurial success with the Ford Foundation and RAND brought difficulties along with resources. Crowther-Heyck mentions Simon's concern about the dangers of isolation from other researchers and centers in interdisciplinary work. A greater danger lay in relationships with others on the faculty at the GSIA, especially neoclassical economists whose vision differed from his. As noted with respect to OR, "economics and, to a lesser extent, experimental psychology were the two social sciences most difficult to integrate into interdisciplinary research programs, primarily due to their higher status, access to distinct funding streams, and disciplinary self-confidence."[43] How this trouble with integration relates to transitions from experimental psychology to cognitive psychology and cognitive science is not clear, however. Nor is Crowther-Heyck's understanding of interdisciplinary research.

As occurred with cognitive studies and social relations at Harvard, intellectual changes mandated institutional relocation. Certain forms of multidisciplinarity and cross-disciplinarity have a short half-life, unlike disciplines whose departmentalization is assumed to be a sign of permanence. Simon's "research agenda shifted strongly after 1955 toward using computers to study cognition. As his interests changed, he withdrew from the GSIA's other research programs. . . . As the GSIA began to look less like the embodiment of Simon's vision of the ideal research center, the prospect of undertaking interdisciplinary research with a new set of partners became more appealing." He responded by redefining "his project from the mathematical modeling of decision making to the computer simulation of problem solving. This subtle but significant move enabled Simon to find a new set of patrons—ones interested in computing and simulation—and to establish a new interdisciplinary program."[44] How common this path may be bears investigation.

Ironically, "one of the most important factors" in his shifting to psychology "was Simon's intense dissatisfaction with the inherent problems with maintaining proper experimental control in social field experiments." On the basis of his RAND experience, he "used computers to help simulate the environment for the experimental subjects." In 1955–56, Simon and his colleague Allen Newell developed a program called the Logic Theorist. "Its success in simulating the problem-solving behavior of humans convinced them that the future of behavioral science lay in the study of such simulated systems." The Ford Foundation, RAND, and the Carnegie Corporation agreed, and their support helped to firm up the foundation for the "cognitive revolution." At Carnegie Tech, an interdepartmental program in Systems and Communications Sciences was designed as "a new interdisciplinary program covering the whole area of the behavioral analysis of complex systems . . . , thus bringing a unified method and instrumental practice to a wide range of fields."[45]

With additional funding from the Department of Defense's Advanced Research Projects Agency (ARPA) and the National Institute of Mental Health (NIMH), the program grew rapidly and became a leader in the emerging field. But Simon himself moved to computer science. He ended his career as the R. K. Mellon Professor of Computer Science and Psychology, as Crowther-Heyck puts it without irony, "trading his interdisciplinary affiliation for a bidisciplinary one." Here again, we find twists and turns on the roads to and from interdisciplinarity. But what were the ongoing and the changing relationships between the disciplinary and the interdisciplinary in these developments? Crowther-Heyck characterizes this familiar pattern as a successful multidisciplinary research community of centers, supported by military and foundation funding, which sooner or later devolves into its component disciplines or spins off new ones. The trope, like Cohen-Cole's, descends from triumph to incorporation of one kind of another. In this view, multi- or interdisciplinary initiatives follow funding streams, entrepreneurial leadership, and changing perceptions of fads and fancies in problem solving and technology.[46]

As these authors' own evidence often shows, this linear model is much too simple to account for the historical development of cognitive science. Such a cautionary tale of a brilliant beginning followed, seemingly inevitably, by a rapid decline clashes not only with the myths of interdisciplinarity but also with the standard narratives of OR. It obscures our understanding of the variable locations and patterns of organization, as well as the differing half-lives, of distinct kinds of entrepreneurial intellectual projects. The stories of cognitive science and Herbert Simon at Carnegie Tech and his movement from the GSIA to psychology and computer science point to the importance of disciplinary relationships, on the one hand, and organization and institutionalization, on the other.[47]

The Myriad of Sciences in Cognitive Science

Many cognitive scientists have commented that interdisciplinarity is a mark of their field. Accordingly, the question of interdisciplinarity as a signpost was on the script that Peter Baumgartner and Sabine Payr presented in preparing their interesting compilation, *Speaking Minds: Interviews with Twenty Eminent Cognitive Scientists*. Apparently oblivious to the contradiction involved, they also asked: "Which sciences do you think play an important role in cognitive science?" Significantly, the collection is dominated by philosophers followed by cognitive psychologists and includes relatively few linguists or neuroscientists, although AI is prominent.[48]

The editors' claims are predictable, but their observations are tentative and paradoxical. Cognitive science "is almost by definition interdisciplinary," they assert. Among the scholars themselves, however, "the range of views is very broad on this point." Some "found it necessary actually to learn the methods and problems of another field, and there are others who choose only occasionally to use the results of other fields to build their own work on, while continuing in the sort of research work in which they were trained. The notion of 'interdisciplinarity' itself is at once vague enough to describe this range of attitudes and too vague to differentiate among them." In sum, the editors conclude, cognitive science is more interdisciplinary in theory than in practice.[49]

Even more problematic are matters of the field's organization and institutionalization. The editors' muddled discussion supports a critical view of the uses and abuses of interdisciplinarity and testifies to the field's many locations and incarnations. They begin quite reasonably: "The institutional setting in which cognitive scientists work seems to play an important role in the development of practical interdisciplinarity." But they find no clear confirmation for their conjecture that institutionalization in a separate department or program promotes not merely cross-disciplinary dialogue but genuinely interdisciplinary development. While they point hopefully to the possibility that "cognitive scientists trained 'from scratch' could well redefine the field," they recognize that "the exact opposite is also possible": "cognitive science might disappear as a field, giving way to very specialized but possibly still interdisciplinary fields of research, perhaps centered around a certain specific aspect of today's cognitive sciences—such as vision, or language acquisition."[50]

The eminent researchers they interviewed are even less sanguine. Patricia Churchland remarks that philosophers "badly need to synthesize and theorize and ask the questions everyone else is either too embarrassed or too focused or too busy to ask." Paul Churchland, also a philosopher, agrees: "Our job is a synoptic job, a unifying job." But he also suggests that the "fundamental problems" inherent in AI also plague many philosophers working in inductive logic, epistemology, and philosophy of science. The limitations shared by AI and philosophy point to the need for "new theories of epistemology, new theories of perception, new theories of the nature of mind." Philosopher Hubert Dreyfus has been even more critical of cognitive science and AI for adopting philosophical models of the mind that had already been discredited by philosophers themselves. Worse still, they have turned "the empiricist, associationist tradition in philosophy, which goes from Hume to the behaviorists, into a research program." Dreyfus's target, he takes pains to make clear, is cognitivism, not cognitive science.[51] But uncritically adopting flawed theoretical frameworks from other disciplines because they can be readily operationalized with existing technologies does not constitute interdisciplinarity.

Other researchers express different criticisms of Cog Sci that reflect on the question of its interdisciplinarity. Cognitive psychologist Aaron Cicourel is nearly alone in calling attention to the field's striking limitations. "Cognitive scientists ignore the environment and social structure or interaction"—or, more precisely, they assume that these are universals rather than taking their specificity into account. The consequences can be costly: "When you take for granted culture and the way it is reflected in a local social ecology," he cautions, "you eliminate the contexts within which the development of human reasoning occurs. When culture, language use, and local interaction are part of cognitive studies, subjects are asked to imagine a sequence of events that have not been studied independently for their cultural basis or variation except for the self-evident variation assumed by the experimenter. But in everyday life, cognition and culture include local contingent, emergent properties while exhibiting invariant patterns or regularities whose systematic study remains uneven."[52]

Philosopher John R. Searle is even more skeptical, declaring: "I am not sure that there is such a thing as cognitive science." While acknowledging that its "official ideology" claims that "cognitive science ... succeeds or tries to succeed where behaviorism failed, in that it tries to study inner contents of mental processes," he argues that "many cognitive scientists repeat the same mistake of behaviorism. They continue to think that cognition is not a matter of subjective mental processes but a matter of objective, third-person computational operations. And, I think that cognitive science suffers from its obsession with the computer metaphor. Instead of looking at the brain on its own terms, many people tend to look at the brain as essentially a computer."[53] In this analysis, too, a flawed model from one field has been adopted wholesale, seriously limiting the thinking of cognitive scientists.

Philosopher Jerry Fodor, also a well-known critic, maintains that cognitive science is not a synthesis of several disciplines. "My own view is that cognitive science is basically just cognitive psychology, only done with more methodological and theoretical sophistication than cognitive psychologists have been traditionally trained to do. If you are a cognitive psychologist and know a little bit about philosophy of mind, linguistics, and computer theory, that makes you a cognitive scientist."[54] (Others would add, "a little bit about neurology.") Too many self-identified interdisciplinarians are looking at the basic issues the wrong way through the telescope, leaving the more fundamental question about the field's interdisciplinarity unanswered.

Similarly, artificial intelligence researcher Robert Wilensky, a professor of electrical engineering and computer science, accords his field a leading position within Cog Sci. "The idea of looking at things in terms of how we describe information processes has got to be central." Other disciplines have "strengths," but he found them lacking. "Linguists know a tremendous amount about language phenomena, but they are not very good at telling you about the mechanisms. . . . They are even misleading and controversial in how they describe their data. In computer science, we know about certain kinds of machines, but there tends to be a bias toward truly algorithmic solutions. . . . The mind is probably not going to be like that, and in some sense we all have to undo some of the prejudices of our fields in order to make progress." That may be a modified call for some form of interdisciplinarity. But, when asked to address the issue directly, he responds: "Is there too much that one needs to know in order to do cognitive science? I think this is right, but if you look at these disciplines, the answer is yes and no."[55]

When asked about "cooperation in groups" of researchers and the "intellectual atmosphere," cognitive psychologist James L. McClelland replies formulaically: "My feeling is that each individual researcher is a limited 'device' for incorporating expertise. What we have to do is create environments that bring together just the right combinations of things to allow people to make progress. . . . I think it is basically intellectual synergy between individuals, and maybe also a matter of fertility of the environment."[56] Here we return to the metaphors of interdisciplinarity. While powerful and important, they are not matters of practice.

Herbert Simon, reflecting on his own experiences and his movements from one home base to another, takes an in-between or "convenience" view of cognitive science's location and organization. Importantly, this is a (de)limiting approach to interdisciplinarity. "The reason why the term *cognitive science* exists over here [compared to Germany] and why we have a society is that people found it convenient to have conversations across disciplinary boundaries. . . . It does not matter whether it is a discipline. It is not really a discipline—yet. Whether cognitive science departments survive or whether people want to get their degrees in psychology and computer science remains to be seen. Here (at Carnegie-Mellon University) we decided that we will still give degrees in computer science and cognitive psychology, not in cognitive science. These are just labels for the fact that there is a lot of conversation across disciplines."[57] Simon's and McClelland's emphasis on cross-disciplinary conversations and their frank admission that these contacts do not constitute interdisciplinarity are refreshing. They did not pursue separate departments or programs. And they recognized, in Simon's case explicitly, that their initiatives did not have the seeming permanence of departments.

Stephen Palmer, a cognitive psychologist at the University of California, Berkeley, addresses the location and organization of cognitive science with greater hesitation than the many who rush to form programs at all degree levels, separate departments, centers, and organizations. His university chose to move slowly toward a cognitive science program. "The problem is . . . that the methods of the different disciplines are quite different. . . . The initial phase has to be educational to learn the vocabulary of the other fields and to obtain what I would call an 'outsider's view' of what those fields are like. But to do cognitive science, you have to be grounded in the methods of at least one discipline. My own view is that, at Berkeley, we are currently in the zeroth order of approximation to cognitive science, that is, where you start out with a bunch of people who are each in their own discipline and who learn about what the other people in other fields are doing." Like the editors of *Speaking Minds*, Palmer looked toward a future in which graduate programs in Cog Sci will be designed "from the ground up"; "from that will emerge the first generation of *real* cognitive scientists."[58] But interdisciplinarity does not necessarily follow from institutionalization. What are the common problems and questions? Where are the relationships between the fields and disciplines?

The University of California at San Diego is often cited as having of the best autonomous programs. Paul Churchland comments that his home institution's focus on neuroscience was "partly a coincidence, and partly . . . design. . . . There were good people here before they realized they had something in common. And as soon as they realized it, they brought in more good people."[59] The UCSD program developed later than the foundational and more entrepreneurial programs at Harvard and Carnegie Tech. Less dependent on external funding and institutional sponsorship and with a more established field to draw from, they could build selectively and strategically. That situation—more than their institutional autonomy—enabled them to establish core concerns and maintain a focus on questions and problems that contributed to sustained interdisciplinarity, while developing beyond defining their endeavor as interdisciplinary by listing disciplines and claiming that their conception of cognitive science embraced all elements in the cognitive domain.

The proud name cognitive science (or sciences or studies) covers myriad complications, contradictions, and outright failings. Profound problems of relationships among the disciplines and their parts, of locations, and of institutionalization and organization remain unresolved and, indeed, are seldom addressed.

Howard Gardner has made the most careful effort to deal with the problem of relationships among disciplines in Cog Sci. After considering each contributing discipline separately, he points to the "conversations" between them, to their shared immersion in the zeitgeist, and to the possibility that, in Michel Foucault's terms, "a common *episteme* has been imposed on disparate disciplines." He then leaps to a premise whose shaky foundations are all too clear in his language: "I shall briefly sketch the history of cognitive science as if it were a single coherent field." After shifting between disciplinarity and interdisciplinarity, Gardner observes:

> In the late 1950s and early 1960s, there was excitement in the already established disciplines and euphoria in the new, quintessentially cognitive discipline of artificial intelligence. But the promise of the cognitive sciences would not be so readily realized. There ensued serious debates about how best to approach the discipline: whether by top-down or bottom-up techniques; by general problem solving or expert systems; by programmatic long-term experimental work, highly selected demonstrations, or detailed case studies. And when it became clear that early predictions would not be confirmed, a reaction set in, during the early 1970s: perhaps a cognitive science was not to be, at least during the lifetime of its most fervent enthusiasts.

What follows mixes a description of recent developments with a recommendation for a new, more interdisciplinary approach.

> Perhaps the individual cognitive sciences have gone as far as they can within each of their disciplinary constraints and paradigms. What were once merely polite and brief conversations among them need to be converted into full-scale cooperative research efforts on problems central to several of them. Stemming both from a realization that many scientific problems are simply too complex to be handled by a single discipline, and from a genuine attraction to the methods and concepts worked out in neighboring disciplines, a growing number of scientists—many of them raised in the post-1950s environment—are switching allegiance from single disciplines to the broader practice of cognitive science and are engaging primarily interdisciplinary pursuits.[60]

In his vision of a "more promising" interdisciplinary future that recedes into the distance, Gardner resembles Baumgartner and Payr.

Gardner then lays out his agenda for a more problem-centered or question-driven interdisciplinarity. Identifying "lines of research that involve the central questions in cognitive science and that are considered by the cognitive-scientific community to be of high quality," he lists artificial intelligence, not alone but in association with neuroscience and psychology, to explain perception of forms and objects; with visual imagery in representations of knowledge in psychology and artificial intelligence; with classification of objects and elements in their work, in philosophy, linguistics, cross-cultural psychology, and linguistic anthropology; and with human rationality and criticism of its models, in psychology, linguistics, and artificial intelligence. "A survey of the best work, and the sharpest critiques of that work, is one way to evaluate current cognitive science," he suggests. "But, in the end, the way that the field presents itself—the overall charter— provides an equally important test."[61]

At that point, significantly, Gardner returns to philosophy. Although many working cognitive scientists do not agree, in his view cognitive science begins and ends explicitly with philosophy. "Central to my view of cognitive science is the claim that the field entails an empirical effort to answer long-standing epistemological questions. Classical philosophy has indeed supplied much of the intellectual agenda of the contemporary field. . . . Even those issues that could not have been formulated by the classical philosophers—such as the extent to which human thought is computational—have routinely been put forth in phil- osophical terms. Perhaps most notably, contemporary cognitive science has pro- vided reasonable answers to selected philosophical questions, even as it has re- jected certain issues and radically transformed others." But the question of the relationships among the disciplines remains. What is the status of the represen- tations in the iconic hexagon and the octagon, one with philosophy at the top and the other with philosophy on the bottom? His answer is neither convincing nor heartening. "In a sense, philosophy can be seen as standing outside of main- stream empirical cognitive science. On one bank of the mainstream, philosophy supplies many of the issues to be investigated. On the other, it examines the answers that are forthcoming, helps to interpret and integrate them, and pro- vides critiques of the overall enterprise. . . . Yet as members of a discipline that stands external to empirical science, philosophers concerned with cognitive sci- ence may seem in jeopardy. For, as philosophical questions are answered by empirical science, philosophers may ultimately recede from the science—as has, in fact, happened in vast areas of physics and biology."[62] What implications does the marginalization of philosophy have for the other disciplines that form the hexagon and the octagon in cognitive science?

Gardner retreats into a dichotomous conception of two "visions" of cognitive science. In contrast to the interdisciplinary but perhaps imperialistic agenda he has laid out, a "less ambitious" version "calls for cooperation among the six member disciplines, each still retaining its primary questions, methods, and goals. . . . On such an account, philosophy supplies the principal issues and helps to judge the extent to which they have been successfully handled. Neuroscience and anthropology remain as border disciplines, psychology and artificial intel- ligence are the core disciplines, and linguistics offers an account of that ability which is most central in the human cognitive armamentarium. When collaborating, these researchers are 'practicing cognitive scientists'; otherwise, they are simply doing their own thing." This "weak" version (the norm, in his view, when he is writing in 1987), "scarcely warrants the label of an important new science."[63]

He does not surrender his vision of an interdisciplinary future, however. In a proposal that constitutes a devastating critique of the status quo in the field, Gardner calls for "a stronger, more gritty version of cognitive science" in which "there will be gradual attenuation of disciplinary boundaries and loyalties. These will be replaced by a concerted effort by scientists committed to a representational account to model and explain the crucial human cognitive functions. . . . Organization around the traditional disciplines would be appropriate if the actual domains of cognition did not make a central difference; so long as the same processes are believed to occur irrespective of the content of the domain . . . , the conventional disciplinary division of labor makes sense." But, Gardner argues, these processes do not occur independently.[64] This shift would be an important step toward new approaches that cross and might integrate different disciplines.

Nonetheless, Gardner remains troubled: "The question of disciplines or, more broadly, of levels of explanation cannot be bypassed entirely—and here we confront the major challenge to contemporary cognitive studies. . . . Cognitive workers must trace out the ways in which [the level of representation] maps onto the other legitimate (and legitimized) ways in which human activities can be construed." The "splendid isolation" from culture and history in which cognitive science had proceeded "must be shattered," he declares. "We must come to understand how culture is mapped onto brains—and the royal road toward such understanding will be the representational level." Failure to do so

threatens the future of cognitive science (especially when compared to developments in the natural sciences). . . . But, paradoxically, much of the best work in cognitive science has been carried out as if only the level of mental representation existed. In the case of language . . . (more specifically, grammar), for example, the brilliant work of Chomsky and his followers makes no reference to, and could be maintained irrespective of, the actual conditions in the brain and in the surrounding culture. If computer science is to mature, however, the ultimate representational account of language must relate, at one extreme, to knowledge about neural architecture of certain regions of the left hemisphere of the brain; and, on the other, to knowledge about the structure and function of language in different cultural groups.[65]

A survey of recent literature suggests that this connection has yet to be made. Cognitive science has been interdisciplinary only to a very limited degree. It is better seen as a selective form of multidisciplinarity or cross-disciplinarity within which such fields as AI and neuroscience—and a vague conception of cognitive psychology—strive for supremacy. The octopus's arms entangle awkwardly.

Critiques and Conflicts

The deliberate exclusion of social, cultural, and historical context and mechanistic reductionism are debilitating to relationships across disciplines and to the emergence and development of interdisciplines. Has significant progress been made in the search for an interdisciplinary science of mind? In his 2012 polemic, *Psychology's Ghosts: The Crisis in the Profession and the Way Back*, developmental psychologist Jerome Kagan suggests not. Comparing psychologists to physicists or biologists, he points to "psychology's missing contexts," which include theories and concepts but also center on the sources of evidence and the context of the research itself. Sophisticated electronic measurements of physiological and brain responses to stimuli tell us little about cause and effect. Major gaps remain between machine and mind, as well as between animal and human studies, rendering these studies' conclusions quite dubious. Although to many researchers the experimental context is the "missing" link, there is an increasing outcry over the ethics and reporting of such studies. Even more fatally, most research fails to take biological and cultural differences into account. Experimental context and striving for the status of a science are inseparable, but the problem goes deeper. To Kagan, this tradition treats the individual as an isolated atom. He suggests replacing "the properties of an individual as the primary unit with properties in a context, awarding equal power to gene and brains, on the one hand, and to culture, historical era, social class, and the local setting, on the other."[66]

Cognitive science may be a special case among the major human sciences in its quest to become a science, but it has provoked competition and fear in the disciplines that are supposed to be its main contributors. At the heart of an interdiscipline is the nature of the relationships among the disciplines.[67]

In *Speaking Minds: Interviews with Eminent Cognitive Scientists*, Lotfi Zadeh, a professor of electrical engineering, remarks: "My perception at this point is that there is not as yet a kind of unity [in cognitive science]. You have an aggregation of disciplines" without "an identity of its own." For him, as for Fodor, "cognitive science is essentially part of psychology . . . because cognitive science is concerned with human thinking, human reasoning, human cognition. Artificial Intelligence plays a secondary role, because Artificial Intelligence has to do with the modeling of human reasoning using computers. Cognitive scientists have a more direct interest in human reasoning, whether or not it is modeled by computers." In his view, in contrast to Fodor's, the domination of Cog Sci by psychology is damning. "The Artificial Intelligence community view the cognitive science community as comprising for the most part people who are not capable of doing serious work insofar as Artificial Intelligence is concerned. . . . This kind of feeling of superiority inhibits the growth of interaction. The Artificial Intelligence people think they have nothing to learn from the others." After acknowledging that those in "the cognitive science community" do not exhibit "a similar superiority complex," he is asked, "Will these differences be overcome?" He replies in the negative.[68] With such antagonism between two of the strongest disciplines that are supposed to constitute cognitive science, its prospects for interdisciplinarity are dim indeed.

Relations with neuroscience are equally problematic. Each field's advocates seem to suspect the other of imperial designs. Despite some claims to the contrary, they compete for funding and lobby against one another for sponsors and the creation of programs and initiatives. Their professional identifies are mixed, sometimes conflicting. Most but not all, I am told by scholars in the field, identify with a discipline. Some scholars (and some campuses) identify with cognitive science but have contrasting conceptions of what that is. This uncertainty is illustrated by the relatively small size of the Cognitive Science Society, a loosely organized umbrella founded in 1979, and the existence of multiple professional organizations.

Gardner titles his essay "Will Neuroscience Devour Cognitive Science?" When competition is so intense, cooperation is out of the question. An interdiscipline cannot emerge if so many fear the influence of other core disciplines. Gardner asserts, "Researchers in the neurosciences stand out from their cognitive-scientific peers because they most closely partake of the model of the 'successful' sciences of physics and biology, because they can most readily state their questions unambiguously and monitor progress toward their solutions." Still insufficiently appreciated beyond circles of specialists is the problem of reductionism. As Gardner observes in 1987, "There are those (perhaps a majority) within the neurosciences who would maintain that cognitive scientific concepts and concerns are not relevant to a biologically oriented science. On this reductionist view, the goal of any natural science should be to explain phenomena at the most elementary level possible. . . . The neurosciences should become oriented increasingly toward the nerve cell and the chemical and electrical events that occur within." Ironically, despite his conclusion that "I think it best to regard neuroscience as one of the border disciplines of cognitive science," it has risen to the top of the octagon. Today, many observers are likely to suggest that neuroscience *is* cognitive science. Dominance is the obverse of collaboration. More recent discussions show little evidence of change from Gardner's 1987 observation about reductionistic and mechanistic neglect of human activity and culture: "From the perspective of cognitive science . . . these lines of argument are untenable."[69]

A 2010 essay in *Topics in Cognitive Science* discusses "The Troubled Marriage of Cognitive Science and Neuroscience." Layer upon layer of conflict threatens the dream of an interdisciplinary cognitive science, Richard Cooper and Tim Shallice write.

> The field risks being driven too much by the . . . possibilities that arise from new and improved technologies, rather than by scientific questions aimed at teasing apart different cognitive theories or extending our cognitive understanding of specific processes. This threat is compounded by a reductionist risk, namely that concepts and theoretical progress of the cognitive revolution are forgotten as teams with different types of empirical expertise attempt to reverse engineer the brain through increasingly sophisticated techniques. In our view, if cognitive neuroscience focuses too much on the "neuroscience" at the expense of the "cognitive" then not only will its contribution to cognitive science be marginalized, but also it will be unable to make sense of the increasing masses of brain-based data now being generated.[70]

This overload would tend to obstruct progress in comprehending the workings of the human mind.

Moreover, Cooper and Shallice call attention to the "sociological, ethical, and legal issues that need to be confronted. On the sociological front, the rise of combined methods (simultaneous fMRI and EEG, etc.) continue the push toward 'big science.' As research becomes more resource intensive, it becomes more centralized and as a consequence probably less cognitive. . . . On the ethical and legal side, questions are raised by the increasing possibility of using neuroimaging techniques to detect for business, forensic, or political purposes otherwise private mental phenomena."[71] Specialists, ethicists, activists, and some policy makers debate the seriousness of such threats. Although they are easy to exaggerate, they are nonetheless very real. It is difficult to know whether Cooper and Shallice purposefully invoke dystopian fiction and films, but the politics and potentials for abuse are stark. So, too, is the question of the extent to which cross-, multi-, and interdisciplinary efforts promote such risks and provide the grounds for necessary regulation. Genetic and biomedical research and development raise the same questions.

In response to such alarms and ambitions, sociologist of science Nikolas Rose counsels calm, suggesting that what neuroscientists can actually do falls far short of these visions, be they nightmares or dreams. He cautions scholars from the social and human sciences who aspire to contribute to this field to look closely at what neuroscientists actually do and to "be rather humble about what we can contribute. . . . Overpromising is exceptionally damaging for science."[72] Raising unrealistically high expectations is equally risky for interdisciplinary ventures.

Potential Pitfalls for the Social Sciences

Unlike the other interdisciplines examined in this book, cognitive science is having a significant impact on fields and disciplines outside its usual domain. At times there almost seems to be a "cognitive revolution" outside of cognitive science. Herein lies another key dimension of interdisciplinarity. The claims run the gamut: new knowledge, unprecedented breakthroughs, highly specialized findings, and the promise of new syntheses; the power of science to reveal the secrets of the human brain; the ubiquity of the cognitive domain; the alluring pursuit by teams of scientists; the science of the future here today; the lure of sponsorship and funding. All these make cognitive science attractive—and dangerous—to scholars in the humanities. If working, however selectively, across disciplines is so difficult, what are the pitfalls and promises of "borrowing" or "applying" theories, approaches, methods, and findings across such great distances? The appeal of what are taken to be the conclusions of cognitive science exerts a powerful influence on fields ranging from political science to literary studies, the arts, and education. Even the president of the United States holds understanding the brain to be the next frontier. The illogical line of reasoning goes: if cognitive science or neuroscience shows x, then y. This problem is exactly what worries Gardner and Kagan about research in cognitive science itself.

Let me be clear. Just as I support well-founded, serious interdisciplinarity, applaud targeted research initiatives and the encouragement of communication and collaboration—and more—across boundaries, and try to tolerate unavoidable faddishness and enthusiasms, I am no less concerned about the abuses of interdisciplinarity. We have learned at great cost and sometimes bitter disappointment the fallacies of multidisciplinary "wars" on poverty, cancer, drugs, history,

communication, the human genome, and on and on. The gains, while sometimes invaluable, are always less than promised, and probably less than more
coordinated careful problem- and question-driven interdisciplinarity efforts
would promote.

In my view, the dangers are great with cognitive science, especially given
the nature of its claims to both interdisciplinary and science. The allure of all
things cognitive, the "unlocking" of mind/brain, and of Science with a capital
S is boundless. Granting the relevance of cognitive science to significant issues
in political theory and political science, John Gunnell, in "Are We Losing Our
Minds? Cognitive Science and the Study of Politics," reviews the political and
conceptual foundations of cognitive science with attention to unacknowledged
biases; questions of consciousness, individual and collective dimensions, dualism, reductionism, mental rules, and emotion; and proclamations of a new discipline of neuropolitics. His pointed conclusions bear repeating because they
speak to concerns in other disciplines and fields of study: "The manner in
which political and social theorists have accessed and deployed this literature
[in cognitive science] . . . has been highly selective and conceptually problematic. The purpose has often been to justify prior agendas, and issues relating to
how brain processes are involved in an explanation of political phenomena have
not been satisfactorily confronted. Cognitive science is itself a highly contested
field with indigenous theoretical difficulties, and it is necessary to sort out and
analyze the salient positions in this conversation and to begin, at least tenta-
tively, to assess critically its implications for both social theory and empirical
research." With respect to interdisciplinarity, this political scientist cautions,

> The propensity of social scientists to borrow from other fields is often encouraged
> and defended under the banner of interdisciplinary studies, but this sometimes
> involves an unreflective or partisan eclecticism which does not confront issues of
> the compatibility of different theoretical domains. Although interdisciplinary
> awareness can aid in pointing up theoretical problems and differences as well as
> prompt reflection and innovation, interdisciplinary inquiry only makes sense when
> there is prior theoretical agreement on the nature of the phenomena under inves-
> tigation. It is quite another thing to pluck specific ideas from theoretically diverse
> fields of natural science and philosophy, to synthesize them at some abstract level,
> and to defend the project as interdisciplinary.[73]

In other words, it is not sufficient to borrow elements from another field and
then use them to make assertions that are not supported with evidence from
the field under study.

This problem appears to be most severe in the humanities. A cluster of disci-plines marked by insecurities, perceptions of decline, ambivalence about the epistemological foundations of knowledge and claims to it, concerns about use-fulness, a sense of inadequacy when compared to the sciences, and a perpetual quest for novelty and relevance are among the contributing factors.

Perhaps the problem is stated in its most egregious form in the 2013 book *How Literature Plays with the Brain: The Neuroscience of Reading and Art* by En-glish professor Paul B. Armstrong. The point is simple: Armstrong's selective reading of cognitive science and neuroscience and avowed quest for a "neuro-phenomenology" demonstrate much less concern with a neuroscience of read-ing, or with reading itself, than with phenomenology or, for that matter, with cognitive science. Both his reading of phenomenology and cognitive science are selective, which I suspect the author would call "interpretive." The result is that he gets the problem and the question backward. The proper question is *how the brain plays with literature*; that is what, if anything, brain scans purport to study, not how literature plays with the brain. The confusion is manifest in his con-cluding lines, which say much more than I suspect he thinks and moreover have little basis in neurological or cognitive research:

> When literature plays with the brain, linguistic forms encountered in a novel, a poem, or a play by a particular, historically situated reader activate neuronal pro-cesses that are specific to the particular text and to the unique cortical writing of the recipient but that also have transhistorical, cross-cultural, and evolutionarily longstanding properties that are related to fundamental features of neural anat-omy and basic neurobiological processes. Instead of aligning itself with one or the other party in the ever-recurring debate between historicism and formalism, neuro-aesthetics can instead demonstrate how their very conflict gives evidence of the duality of the brain as a universally occurring organ in our species that is remark-ably open to adaptation, variation, and play. To do so, however, will require giving reading its due. The question of how to read and what is involved in different ways of reading has long been central to the humanities, and it is a question with both formal and historical dimensions. Asking how the brain reads, and how literature plays with these processes, consequently calls on humanists to offer the sciences the benefit of our own core knowledge and expertise. We too have much to gain from this exchange, not least of all a renewed appreciation of what it is we know that is distinctive to our work with literature.[74]

Neuroscience does not and, indeed, cannot show any such thing. Moreover, where is the evidence for "transhistorical, cross-cultural, and evolutionarily longstanding properties that are related to fundamental features of neural anatomy and basic neurobiological processes"? This claim is really quite stunning. Yes, the sciences need to learn from the core knowledge of the humanities, and vice versa. But, in effect, subsuming the humanities and reading to an unsubstantiated interpretation of cognitive science benefits neither.

The brain science of reading is primitive at best and full of both false positives and false negatives. The oft-cited diatribe by Nicholas Carr, *The Shallows: What the Internet Is Doing to Our Brains*, has provoked many (although invalid) rebuttals about the positive neurological influence of the "right" kind of reading on cognition and attitudes.[75] One case in point is a study purportedly demonstrating that the temporary retention of "better" literature (Anton Chekhov, Alice Munro) contributes to greater empathy, which examined a small sample of paid subjects found via Amazon.com. Lost in the predictable excitement over evidence for the value of "good reading" are both the experiment itself and the evidentiary and logical leaps to the conclusions. But the excitement leads immediately to such implications as this: "The study's authors and other academic psychologists said such findings should be considered by educators designing curriculums, particularly the Common Core standards adopted by most states, which assign students more nonfiction."[76] Education becomes the dumping ground for what cognitive science purportedly shows.[77]

Is it asking too much to look before you leap into new fields? To learn enough about the approach and its foundations before venturing farther? To inquire into the relevant aspects of other fields and disciplines before borrowing, adopting, or applying? To formulate questions, problems, and relationships knowingly? To engage in relationships reciprocally? I think these are solvable problems. If the answer is no, sound interdisciplinary has no future.

Matters have not changed significantly since George Mandler wrote in 1996:

> Some 25 years after the various beginnings there still is no such thing as a core cognitive science. Depending on where one looks, which departments one queries, who one's friends are, the core of cognitive science will be asserted to be neurophysiology, psychology, artificial intelligence, linguistics, or some more vague concept like human/machine interaction or symbolic or connectionist modeling. The result may not have been cognitive science, but it has been exciting and scientifically fruitful. It has created a community of interests and increased interdisciplinary communications. But as of now there are still viable independent cognitive

sciences such as neurophysiology, linguistics, and psychology that flourish with or without the cognitive science label or affiliation. It is difficult to say at this point where this will lead.[78]

That is a great achievement, but it is not an interdiscipline.

New Histories

I begin with a misleading narrative that aims to be the standard version of the emergence of the new histories. Evoking my earlier analogy of the bat, the discourse is a cascade of disciplines, dilemmas, and dichotomies.

> A number of historians who participated in the linguistic and cultural "turns" have written their experiences. From their accounts emerges a familiar narrative of the historiographic turns that begins with the development in the 1960s of the "new social history," which challenged a traditional historiography that sanctified official sources, political elites, short-term events, and descriptive narrative. This triumphant social history was then gradually challenged by a constellation of critics associated in different ways with what became known retrospectively as the linguistic turn. By the 1980s, social history was largely displaced institutionally by various strands of work collected under the rubric of cultural history. During this period, debates across the disciplines unfolded over fundamental epistemological questions regarding the relationship between the world we confront, the categories with which we attempt to think that world, and the worldly forces in relation to which these categories emerged.

But, this account quickly acknowledges, cultural history raised more questions than it answered:

> At a certain general level, those who identified with the "turns" became increasingly mindful about the non-transparent relationship between thought and being and began to reorient historical research away from facts and explanation to meaning and interpretation. But "linguistic turn" and "cultural turn" were terms of convenience that often conflated incompatible intellectual currents. Insights about the constitutive power of language or the ways that discourses mediate subjectivity and shape social life led some historians to overturn the conventional notions of individuality, intentionality, agency, and causality upon which traditional historiography depended. But they led others to reaffirm these very concepts, often through histories of marginalized actors whose subjectivity was purportedly reconstructed and experiences valorized.[79]

While this narrative is salutary in recognizing the profound philosophical and political differences among practitioners of the new histories, it points toward a field in disarray rather than an expanding field transformed by new questions that called for the incorporation of theories and methods developed by related disciplines.

In this case study of the new histories, I tell a different story. From my vantage point as an interdisciplinary historian of literacy who has long been active in the Social Science History Association, the premier professional organization for historians interested in all sorts of interdisciplinary endeavors, I see this development as marked by interdisciplinarity, success within limits, and changes in disciplinary and interdisciplinary relationships. Its signature achievement is what I call *interdisciplinarity within disciplines*, which is not as contradictory as it seems at first blush.[80]

The development of the new histories contrasts in many respects with the other endeavors at interdisciplinarity considered in this book. To the extent that they constitute interdisciplines, as well as to the extent that they do not, such endeavors expand our understanding. Perhaps most importantly, they mandate that we consider interdisciplinarity within disciplines, which puts relationships between interdisciplines and disciplines in sharper relief. It creates possibilities as well as limits. Moreover, the new histories find a place not only in history but also in economics, political science, anthropology, and sociology, which both complicates and advances matters.[81] The multiplicity and continuing succession of new histories raise questions about changing relationships among interdisciplines. Significantly, these "turns" both favor and oppose modeling histories on science and social science; indeed, the plurality of the social sciences has contributed to the diversity of the new histories. The new histories share a revisionist urge with other interdisciplinary projects, but that urge is intensified by the recognition of the ahistorical character of the social sciences and the imperative of understanding the roots of the social order to deal more effectively with contemporary problems. Finally, perceptions of threat and resistance on both sides of the establishment/newcomer divide characterize interdisciplinarity in action.

The History of New Histories

The new histories have an intellectual and social history of their own.[82] What are the historical grounds of their origins and development? A particular set of circumstances and configurations of relationships within and outside the academy stimulated the move toward interdisciplinarity. First and foremost were perceptions of a crisis in the discipline of history, which prompted a search for new theoretical frameworks, concepts, and methodologies, as well as types of sources. At its best, social science history transformed the organization and practice of historical research by fostering collaboration, both among historians themselves and between them and researchers in related disciplines. Moreover, it has made valuable contributions to discussions of theoretical questions in the social sciences and to public discourse, as well as to history.

Like other post–World War II interdisciplines, social science history was neither as new nor as shocking as both its own manifestos and the vehement critiques directed against it suggested. Since the late nineteenth century, the professionalization of academic disciplines and their institutionalization in universities has magnified the importance of both claims for novelty and counterclaims in support of tradition. Issues of location have been particularly significant for history departments. The discipline's variable placement between the arts and humanities on the one hand and the social sciences on the other has long been a source of ambiguity and conflict. According to Dorothy Ross, "there has been a succession of 'new histories' based on alliances with the social sciences" since the early twentieth century, and after World War II, American social scientists and historians "joined again, this time around a more structural analytic model of historiography."[83] Eric Monkkonen comments, "Historians who look to the other social sciences tend to be dissatisfied with what they see as their own discipline's conceptual sloppiness, its reliance on anecdotal evidence, its happy privileging of certain stories over others"; these reformers are attracted by "the seeming 'hardness' of the other social sciences, hardness in the sense of rigor, conceptual precision, and the explicit prior stipulation of what constitutes an adequate explanation."[84]

The explosion of new histories after the mid-twentieth century stemmed from the more or less simultaneous remaking of global relationships and social orders within the Western democracies; shifting and conflicting intellectual, cultural, and ideological currents; and developments in universities, disciplines, and academic professions. British historian Eric Hobsbawm emphasizes the linkage of global social change to a "general historicization of the social sciences." Revolutions and struggles for emancipation around the world that captured the attention of governments, research organizations, and social scientists directed their attention "to what are essentially problems of historic transformations. These were subjects which had hitherto been outside, or at best on the margins of, academic orthodoxy in the social sciences and had increasingly been neglected by historians."[85]

Global transformations and domestic upheavals worked in tandem to unsettle old orthodoxies and pose new questions. "The political conflict of the 1960s created new historiographical energies and directions," Ross emphasizes. The civil rights movement, the Vietnam War, youth and women's movements, and changes in higher education shattered the 1950s' faith in the virtues of consensus. Marginalized social groups cried out for recognition of their voices and their histories. They defined themselves by race or ethnicity, class, gender, age or associations, and common historical experiences. At the same time, members of these groups were finding a place in student bodies and, increasingly, on faculties; the post–World War II democratization of higher education opened the historical profession, making it more representative of American society. From the New Left, the profession gained a wider range of radical views that embraced liberal democratic, populist, Marxist, and feminist traditions. "It produced a social-cultural history that focused on the 'inarticulate,' the working class, racial minorities, and women, those who had been marginalized in American history and left out of its historiography."[86] These new social histories "from the bottom up" were also influenced by the achievements of European historiography.[87] As befits an intellectual movement that found inspiration in social and political insurgencies, the new histories were never singular; in their subjects as well as in their methods and models, they were always plural. These were expansive, heady times; they were also tense with challenges, competition, insecurity, and what John Higham called "troubles."[88]

The New Social History

An award-winning book, *The People of Hamilton, Canada West: Family and Class in a Mid-Nineteenth-Century City*, published in 1975 as the "new social history" came of age, captures much of the spirit, aims, and approaches of that era. Its author, Michael Katz, begins: "The first objective of this book . . . is to lay out in concrete and precise terms the primary social and family patterns in one nineteenth-century city and, where possible, to compare them to those in other cities. . . . Ultimately, my interest extends beyond the history of Hamilton to the way in which the complex set of structures and organizations that make up the modern world emerged from the quite different features of traditional society. One key to understanding the process, I assume, lies in the identification and explanation of the effects of the transformation usually called industrialization," which was, in fact, part of a wider process "in which not only the technology and organization of production but institutional structures and the attitudes and behavior of ordinary human beings changed in fundamental ways."[89]

This historical social science sought answers to classic problems of both history and social science. Although the study was based on careful quantitative analysis of reams of demographic, social-structural, and economic data, its focus on the attitudes and responses of ordinary people was more historical than sociological or economic. In my view, it pointed toward the "newer" new histories that followed: the cultural, linguistic, and microhistorical turns.[90] Methodologically, Katz's approach exemplifies the use of case studies defined by place and time.

Katz explicitly addresses disciplinary relationships and matters of theory. "In a sense sociology always has tried to chart this transition," he acknowledges. As Philip Abrams recognized, "a high proportion of sociological research" is based "on myths which sociologists have invented." In his view, "the right questions remain more important than the right answers. One object of social history should be formulate questions that will guide research in ways not only theoretically fruitful but historically appropriate."[91] Katz emphasizes that sociology's lack of historical perspective meant that it makes "assumptions about the nature of earlier societies that are often vague or incorrect. . . . The past, in contrast to what much social theory appears to assume, is simply not self-evident. . . . The predominance of ungrounded assumption over hard knowledge about past societies reflects partly the traditional concerns of historians, who have been more interested in politics, great men, governmental policy, and ideas than in the patterns made by the everyday lives of people." In part, the limits of historians' traditional sources shaped their assumptions and theoretical frameworks. "For the most part those sources have been literary, descriptions by more or less knowledgeable people—politicians, social reformers, novelists, journalists—of the times and conditions in which they lived." Despite their firsthand character, these sources were written largely from an elite perspective that was profoundly ignorant of the lives most people led. Those who set out to investigate the lives and mentalities of the masses face formidable difficulties. "Discovering the composition of ordinary families in the past and learning about the typical experiences of nineteenth-century laborers over ten or twenty years are not straightforward tasks or ones which most historians have been trained to undertake. The sources always have been there. . . . But the advent of electronic data-processing equipment in the last several years has made the sources accessible as never before."[92]

The new histories' interdisciplinary reconceptualization lay in seeking to explore new questions by bringing the theories, sources, and methods of the social sciences to bear on the subjects and problems of the humanities. The Social

Science History Association (SSHA), founded in 1976, became their intellectual and professional home. Initially, these fields included social, economic, political, and economic history (or cliometrics); urban, immigration, and ethnic history; labor and working-class history; demographic and family history; and the history of women, gender, and sexuality. They engaged a whole array of different social science disciplines: sociology, economics, political science, demography, and anthropology. The new histories were especially active centers for renewed interests in gender, race and ethnicity, class, family, sexuality, and age groups, often in the context of place and space. In conceptualization, and often in practice, the relationships between disciplines that developed in pursuit of these kinds of questions generated interdisciplinarity, typically within disciplinary departments. Here is a distinctive approach to interdisciplinarity that reorients relationships between and among disciplines but does not necessarily require institutional separation.

Katz's book, like most of the first new social histories, is a geographically and temporally defined case study. His modus operandus was collaborative; I worked with his research group for four years. With tongue in cheek, he described its conclusions as resting on

> a mixture of hard data and rash speculation. . . . The data can be interpreted in different ways, but at rock bottom they do provide a solid a solid and enduring contribution, which other historians who may disagree violently with what I offer as explanation nonetheless can use. One immense value of the sort of historical inquiry on which this book rests is that it offers historians the opportunity to build upon one another's work in a systematic and cumulative fashion. History can never become a science like physics or chemistry, but historians can increase enormously the extent to which the results of their research are useful in comparative inquiry, reproducible by other scholars and cumulative in character.[93]

Comparisons could be both synchronic and diachronic, between Hamilton and other industrializing cities and between the mid-nineteenth century and earlier or later periods. Building archives and databases that other scholars can share is among the foundations for interdisciplinarity.[94]

Katz identifies both conceptual and methodological reasons for the necessity of collaborative inquiry in interdisciplinary studies. First, data never "speak for themselves." They must always be examined in the light of theoretical models and scrutinized for unanticipated patterns. "As for the speculations in this book," Katz cautions, "they are not propositions offered thematically, or absolute truths, or even, sometimes, very firmly grounded generalizations. They are interpretations which seem plausible, consistent with the data, and, I hope, useful to social theorists and historians."[95] Second, data that provide solid evidence about behavior shed little light on lived experiences and mentalities. Here is an unexplored parallel with cognitive science.[96] Although both fields were propelled by the post–World War II behavioral revolution and pursued the images, models, and methods of the sciences, cognitive science sought to emphasize cognition over behavior in order to combat what in psychology was called behaviorism, although its assumptions and methods led it to ignore the relevance of culture and history. The new social history, too, aimed to comprehend culture and cognition. Emphasizing social science history's reliance on quantitative evidence, J. Morgan Kousser dubbed it QUASSH. Joyce Appleby lamented that it "swept all before it for a decade or more," though it failed "to move from data to understanding."[97] But those who critiqued the new social history for its alleged structuralist biases often ignored the fact that such scholars as Joan W. Scott, William H. Sewell Jr., and Gareth Stedman Jones combined social and cultural histories and probed the connections between language or discourse on one hand and political economy on the other.[98]

Although they ran squarely into the complications of trying to deduce thought and values from action, they were acutely aware of the problem. According to Katz,

> One issue which the project group discussed time and again, in one form or another, is a fundamental intellectual problem that underlies contemporary studies in social history; namely, the connection among structures, behaviors, and attitudes. What connection, for example, can we assume between the structure of the family and the attitudes and emotions of the people within it? Can we assume that growing up within a nineteenth-century extended family produced in a child a set of attitudes or a personality different from those that could have developed within a nuclear family? What inference can we draw from stability in the distribution of wealth over time? . . . At times, though, we can associate structural variation with differences in behavior, and this brings us closer to attitudes and to the consequences of structural difference.[99]

Unlike many social scientists and psychologists, Katz is keenly aware of the dangers and fallacies of simple deductions.[100] "Even in these cases an inferential leap must be made in assessing the consequences and impact of any social pattern. To make that leap we sometimes draw on social theory. But that often involves an assumption that the theory, even if based on reliable contemporary data, applies equally to human beings of another era."[101]

In contrast to most cognitive scientists and recent neurologically oriented "deep" histories, Katz acknowledges the historicity of both theory and emotions. "Sociological and psychological concepts . . . do not necessarily represent formulations appropriate for all times and places; they are not frozen distillations of absolute truth or governing laws. The most elementary implication of the sociology of knowledge should lead us to expect intimate connections between the generation of social or behavioral theories and the contexts in which they arise. . . . These questions are important because they illustrate the difficulty and the danger of applying social theory uncritically while making the inferential leap from structures to their consequences."[102]

Katz's third point is central to my conception of interdisciplinarity.

> These questions point out, too, that the relationship between history and the other social sciences must not be passive. The role of the historian should not be merely to receive, applying other scholars' concepts, testing their theories, adopting their methods. Data about the past must form an integral part of any solid social scientific theory, and in the attempt to discover how the world works the historian is at least the equal—in potential—if not in practice—of any other social scientists. Unfortunately, history lost its early place in the cutting edge of social science. That largely was the fault of historians who, as Hayden White has described brilliantly, failed to shed their nineteenth-century notions of art and science and refused to join the contemporary intellectual world.[103]

Writing in 1975, Katz is optimistic. We must ask if the new histories that followed have fulfilled this promise.

The collaborative "project model" that Katz championed was crucial to the interdisciplinarity that the new histories achieved. Largely forgotten are the core centers for the organization and pursuit of the new histories. Chief among them were Robert Fogel's Economic History Workshops and large-scale projects at the University of Chicago and Harvard, which focused on railroads, slavery, population and economic growth, and Charles Tilly's Center for the Study of Social Transformation at the University of Michigan, which modeled social organization and social protest movements. Michigan harbored several other important collaborative efforts, starting with Sylvia Thrupp's Comparative Studies group and culminating in the InterUniversity Consortium for Political and Social Research at the Institute for Social Research, led by Jerry Clubb, which pioneered in the archiving of machine-readable electoral, social, and geographic data. Equally formative in different ways were projects on political and agricultural history led by Alan Bogue at the University of Wisconsin; on political history, directed by William Aydelotte and Samuel Hays at the University of Iowa; and later work on social, political, and labor history by Hays and his graduate students at the University of Pittsburgh. Lee Benson initiated quantitative and social scientific history at the University of Pennsylvania; the Philadelphia Social History Project, led by Theodore Hershberg, followed in that tradition. The 1960s also saw the founding of the InterUniversity Consortium for Political and Social Research's historical archive at the University of Michigan. In 1967 *Historical Methods Newsletter* (later *Historical Methods*) began, followed in 1970 by the *Journal of Interdisciplinary History* and then a rush of other "new history" journals.

Some of these points on a larger compass lay in or between departments of history, sociology, political science, economics, or demography/population studies. In all cases, participants came from history and other social science disciplines. They took a variety of institutional forms—from project groups to centers and institutes with relatively limited departmental or university support or more substantial external government or foundation funding. Almost none was longstanding. None enjoyed the munificence of support that the sciences, major social sciences, branches of cognitive science, or operations research secured. Disciplinary and interdisciplinary differences can be pronounced. Their durations, or half-lives, vary along with their forms and locations. When the new interdisciplinary histories institutionalized, these institutions and departments occupied a prominent place in the SSHA.[104]

In *The People of Hamilton*, Katz describes the collaborative research process. "For a few years many people worked in one capacity or another on the collection and analysis of the data. Their contributions influenced my thoughts profoundly. In particular, we tried to establish a working model of research in which a group of people exploited a common data base, each pursuing his own individual interests yet drawing on the group as a whole for support, criticism, and knowledge." He emphasizes "the way in which we found it possible to reconcile the interests and desire for autonomy of individual scholars with the need for collective wisdom and energy in the analysis of the massive data base we were assembling," which contrasts clearly with

> the classic image of the historian . . . working alone with his books or manuscripts in a library, unable to carry on very much dialogue with anyone else. . . . We, to the contrary, experienced the exhilaration of continually testing our ideas with a group which had an intimate knowledge of the same sources and techniques. Through periodic project meetings we sustained for a few years a collective and

collegial intellectual life which enrich our own thinking and gave us a new perspective on the organization of scholarly activity. In one form or another all the material in this book . . . was argued over, sometimes fiercely, and there remained differences of interpretation among us. We did share, nonetheless, a sense of excitement at the potential of our work and a pleasure in our joint endeavor. The project meetings were the best seminars that most of us had attended in a long time.[105]

The main problems the research group encountered arose from the changes in team membership that inevitably occurred a people completed their graduate work. I can attest to that collective intelligence, sharing, and searching through salutary criticism, as well as the tensions and strains it involved. This group included faculty, graduate students, and staff from history, education, geography, philosophy, and other social sciences, as well as regular visitors.

At its best, social science history enhances graduate education and the conduct of research. It can be exhilarating, both demanding and supportive. For me, this experience was formative. I became a new social historian and a quantitative social science historian. My long involvement with the historical study of literacy began in Katz's seminar.[106] The organization and conduct of social science history constituted a kind of counterculture or subculture for new historians. Among the most important signs of this emergent culture were the collective mode of social organization around the principles of sharing and egalitarian exchange; an obsession with method as a membership card; and a sharp focus on matters of conceptualization and interpretation. Specialized professional language (discourse or jargon, depending on one's point of view) bound many of us together, while it distinguished and separated us from others. And, of course, there was a preoccupation with the new. These characteristics could take on an aura of cultishness with secret signs, special kinds of behavior and appearance, in-groupiness, performative elements (e.g., distributing and reviewing statistical tables), and certain patterns of speech and intellection. Many of us were seldom seen without an armload of printout or stacks of IBM cards to feed the mainframe. While that might distinguish us from humanities grad students, that we also carried piles of books separated us from our peers in social science and science. A certain blend of historical and social science rhetoric and attempts at requisite humor characterized our talk. In this construction, the SSHA, especially its early meetings, resembled, if not a rock festival, then perhaps a teach-in (more than, say, a cockfight or a love-in).

The Social Science History Association

The SSHA drew together those researchers who were attached to collaborative projects and centers with those who were undertaking this work in a less hospitable atmosphere. To an unusual degree, it constituted an interdisciplinary organizational infrastructure for the new histories. Here we see at work the critical problems of location; relationships within, among, and across disciplines with respect to specific and persisting intellectual problems and questions; and the social and intellectual organization of research. The other problematic factor is institutionalization. Here, the new histories were more limited. Overwhelmingly, they developed within departments, primarily but not solely departments of history but on occasion in the spaces between disciplines, especially history and sociology, politics, or economics. Within the general model of interdisciplinarity developed in this book, this pattern of interdisciplinarity within disciplines is a limited but illuminating case.

At the twenty-fifth anniversary meeting, William H. Sewell Jr., a future SSHA president, declared, "I am a great fan of the SSHA because these are, as far as I am concerned, consistently the most stimulating meetings anywhere in the social sciences." He then pointed to "three distinctive features" that made its gatherings so productive. "The first is that this is not only an interdisciplinary space, but in a very real sense a nondisciplinary space. I often tell my graduate students that they do not call them disciplines for nothing. The disciplines discipline: they set standards, award degrees, have official journals, decide who gets jobs, who gets awards, et cetera, et cetera. What is special about the SSHA meetings is that the stakes at play in our discussions are only intellectual. There is no job market. There is no disciplinary pecking order, and, above all, there is no power to shape university institutions. I think it is a huge advantage that we are so weak. Our weakness is our strength." The second feature is its flexibility. Although initially the organization seemed to offer a site for the construction of a more positivist discipline of historical science, it did not develop in that direction. Instead, "SSHA meetings seem to register faithfully the changing pulse of interdisciplinary social science in general, which means that by now there is probably almost as much activity at the boundaries between history and the humanities, or social science and the humanities, as between history and the social sciences on the positivist end. Keywords like 'identity' and 'historical memory' appear as often in titles of papers or session as keywords like 'occupational structure' or 'demographic transition.'" As a result, "the third distinctive feature of the SSHA is its real intellectual diversity." While "the more positivist style of

quantitative social science that was the founding impulse for the SSHA continues to thrive," different methodologies and epistemologies coexist in a climate
of mutual tolerance, which is "is a tremendous strength."[107]

Sewell then asked, "What makes the SSHA tick?" He answered with a conception that differs profoundly from perspectives that construct interdisciplinarity out of disciplines. "I would argue that the organizational continuity and
the power have resided in the networks, not in the association per se. The networks are intellectually autonomous and are not difficult to form or to disband.
They put together the program, and they do it according to their independent intellectual agendas, which reflect the wishes of their members. This is an acepha-
lous, decentralized, rhizomatic organization. It is anarchistic, and it works."[108]
Sewell's conception of a "weak organization" goes hand in hand with one characterized not only by diversity and flexibility but also by the coherence and relative autonomy of its internal networks, which to a substantial degree organize
its collective work. The SSHA operates on the boundaries between intradiscipli-
narity and interdisciplinarity.[109]

The SSHA shows the achievements and the limits of interdisciplinary histories. The history of the association is marked by steady growth. In its first
five years, 1976 to 1980, meeting mainly on college campuses, it attracted from
214 to 341 paid registrants. In the 1990s registration ranged from 650 to 800,
and by 2010 it topped 1,000. Counting participants on the program, Richard
Steckel concluded in 2000, "Associations with a traditional disciplinary focus . . .
do not match this record of growth over the same period." He also observed a
"dramatic . . . rise in participants from abroad, many of whom were attracted by
topics in family history and historical demography. . . . The appeal of interdisciplinary history is now international, and Europeans recently formed an organization with goals and operating procedures parallel to those of SSHA."[110]

The core of the SSHA lies in its dynamic network structure, which reflects
the changing interests of the new histories (table 4.1). In 1976, there were
16 networks; the largest, with 35 to 38 sessions each, were Social Structure and
Social Mobility, Historical Demography and Economic Development, Electoral
Behavior and Political Parties, followed in descending order by Methodology,
Social Theory and Social Policy, Family History and Historical Demography,
Workers and Industrialization, and Large-Scale Societal Change. Steckel out-
lined "a pattern of ebb and flow that overlays an element of consistency. Throughout its history, four strands of research have always been found within the orga-
nization: Family/Demography, Politics, Labor, and Methodology. Four durable

TABLE 4.1
Social Science History Association networks, 1976, 2014

1976	2013
Social Structure and Social Mobility	Children and Childhood
Historical Demography and Economic Development	Criminal Justice / Legal History Network
	Culture
Electoral Behavior and Political Parties	Economics
Methodology	Education, Knowledge Production, and Science Studies
Social Theory and Social Policy	
Family History and Historical Demography	Family History / Demography
Workers and Industrialization	Health/Medicine/Body
Large-Scale Societal Change	Historical Geography
History and Epistemology of the Sciences of Man	Labor
	Macro-historical Dynamics
Elites and Societal Processes	Migration/Immigration
Legislative Behavior	Politics
Historical Comparative Bureaucracy	Race and Ethnicity
Ethnohistory	Religion
Ideas and Behavior	Rural, Agricultural, and Environmental
Community Processes	States and Societies
Religion and Society	Urban
	Women, Gender, and Sexuality

Source: Social Science History Association, Annual Meeting program (1976); "Networks," Social Science History Association (2014), www.ssha.org/networks
Note: Networks listed in order of appearance in sources

new networks joined by 1980: Economic History, Criminal Justice / Legal, Urban, and Education." Some research groups fell away or became parts of other networks, particularly those linked to sociology. By 1985, four additional networks developed: Women, Migration, Rural, and Historical Geography. New networks on Race/Ethnicity, Religion, Culture, and States/Societies, and Macrohistorical Dynamics emerged between 1990 and 1995. "But the tables make clear that the predominant research groups were established by 1990."[111] Cosponsorship of sessions by networks has increased over time. Social science history may no longer be the best descriptor for these once-novel but now established new histories. But what's in a name? Is that fluidity among the abiding lessons of the history of interdisciplinarity?

SSHA's networks have played a critical if not determinative role as sites or locations for interdisciplinarity. In addition to setting up sessions, they hold planning meetings and occasional mini-conferences. Conversations that begin outside the meeting rooms at the annual conference continue afterwards, sometimes generating edited collections of papers or even new collaborative research projects (figure 4.4).

Figure 4.4 Networks of social science history. The header illustration from the Social Science History Association Networks webpage suggests a world of interconnections among disciplinary interests. From http://www.ssha.org/networks

Reflecting on external factors that have contributed to the SSHA's success Steckel pointed to the "growing success and acceptance for interdisciplinary work. . . . I suspect that the greatest flowering of interdisciplinary work over the past quarter century has occurred within a variety of interdisciplinary research centers established within academia. These centers or institutes often target particular research problems using expertise housed in numerous traditional departments." Significantly, as Steckel recognizes, "SSHA is not the primary association of affiliation for virtually all participants. Despite this obstacle, the association has consistently been able to renew its strong leadership. Year after year, the major positions . . . have attracted a capable and committed group of leaders who have been willing to devote their time and talents to the purposes of social science history."[112] For them, and for the scholars at all levels who are active participants, the association and its networks offer opportunities for exchange that are seldom available in either their home institutions or their disciplinary organizations.

The ongoing story of the new histories blends the contradictions of organization and weak institutionalization, stability with a succession of ever-newer histories that have often announced themselves under the discourse of "turns."[113] The signposts include Lynn Hunt's *The New Cultural History* (1989); Terrence

McDonald's *The Historic Turn in the Human Sciences* (1999); James W. Cook, Lawrence B. Glickman, and Michael O'Malley's *The Cultural Turn in U.S. History* (2008); and Hunt and Victoria Bonnell's *Beyond the Cultural Turn* (1999). In this vein are Geoff Eley's *A Crooked Line: From Cultural History to the History of Society* (2005) and the 2012 *American Historical Review* "Forum on Historiographical Turns."[114] The extent to which the seeds of these "turns" lay, both constructively and critically, in the new histories is insufficiently appreciated.

The agendas announced by the new histories were often overly ambitious. Some claims were excessive and deserved criticism. Alan Bogue lamented that "once organized, SSHA drifted rapidly into the pattern of activities found in most small learned societies. Association leaders devoted their attention mainly to sponsoring an annual meeting and publishing a society journal. These functions were in no way reprehensible or trivial," but the early "élan" had disappeared.[115] What Dorothy Ross has called a "drift toward conventionality" is inherent in the process of professional institutionalization and accommodation with changing circumstances inside and outside the academy.[116]

As the SSHA networks illustrate, the new histories are plural. Their practitioners follow multiple paths and have varying, sometimes conflicting, agendas, approaches, and methods. As is always the case in the study of history, substantive differences in viewpoints often involve ideology and politics, as well as professional identities and careers. The once-new histories have been followed by a succession of newer histories, providing ample fodder for bad jokes but demonstrating the constant development of vital forms of inquiry, a pattern that is visible in the sociology of knowledge and the history of disciplines, interdisciplines, and institutions. To simplify a complicated story, the new social science historians never dominated the practice of historical research or teaching. More recent new histories never gained the degree of coherence, integration, and organization that the earlier ones achieved. Their intellectual limits are shared and overlapping. That the new histories developed into interdisciplines predominantly within disciplines underscores the limits of their interdisciplinarity.

It is revealing that recent statements on the future directions of historical research, extending from Joan Scott, Geoff Eley, and William Sewell to the contributors to the *American Historical Review*'s forum on historiographical turns, all call for interdisciplinarity. Sewell in particular is keenly aware of the drive toward interdisciplinarity that shaped the emergence of the new histories; what historians could not find in one social science discipline in pursuit of their questions, they sought in another. From this pursuit arise the distinctive development, strengths, and constraints of interdisciplinarity within disciplines as it has been manifested in history's ongoing relationships with the social sciences (in the new social history of the 1960s through the 1980s), the humanities (in the linguistic and cultural turns), and the sciences (in digital history, neuro-history, and environmental history).

Conclusion

Both cognitive science and the new histories began to develop as interdisciplines within disciplines: cognitive science in psychology and the new histories in history. Although they have evolved over their almost four decades, the new histories have shared certain integrative questions in human social and cultural history. This common inquiry has allowed them to continue, despite the manufacture of successive waves of conflicting methodological and interpretive turns that supposedly arose in reaction to the new social history. The new histories and their organizational home, the Social Science History Association, reveal the possibilities and the limits of interdisciplinarity developing within a discipline. This crucial path to interdisciplinarity is obscured, when not dismissed, by the myths of autonomous, independent interdisciplines.

In contrast, the ambitions and scope of cognitive science have obstructed its development in a genuinely interdisciplinary way because of a succession of rivalries between disciplines, first cybernetics versus computation and then neuroscience versus AI. To an impressive extent, this problem was signaled relatively early in George Miller's famous hexagon logo of cognitive science, which paid little attention to the relationships among the six sides and competing visions that position neuroscience or philosophy on the top or the bottom, respectively. The contradiction is furthered in the Cognitive Science Society's octagonal version of the diagram, with its one empty side and small size relative to the expansive field. Philosophy's place also seems to be reduced as its broader, more complicated intellectual, cultural, and historical questions speak less and less to the practices of the field(s).

Cognitive science shares several qualities with operations research, including questions of the relationships among constituent disciplines. In addition to its association with behavioral science, it also shares an anxious concern with provenance and pedigree. In other ways, cognitive science sought a convergence along the lines of biology. But it has not cohered in the ways that biology did.

Admitting my own biases and the many contradictions within the new histories, I think that history and the social sciences have been more capacious homes for interdisciplinary work than the competing sciences that hosted cognitive science. The reasons are historical, rhetorical, and ideological. They include the relationships among fields of knowledge, competing locations for cross- and inter-disciplinary efforts, and problems of organization. In history, and elsewhere in the social sciences, so much less has been at stake, especially in material terms, compared to Cog Sci and its cognates. In the end, both new histories and cognitive science rise and fall on the nexus of the relationships among the disciplines and their institutionalization. Therein lay complicated paths to locations, institutionalization, and organization.

CHAPTER FIVE

A Material World and the Making of Lifeworlds

Materials Science and Cultural Studies, 1950s–1990s

In their beautifully illustrated *No Small Matter: Science on the Nanoscale,* Felice Frankel and George Whitesides reveal the nanoworld to nonspecialists.

> Small things are *now* particularly interesting to us. Why? Why *now?* To start, we have new "eyes"—new measuring devices—to see what has always before been invisible; also new tools to sculpt matter at the scale of atoms. . . . We would like to *exploit* technologies that make the smallest things for our various ends: to fabricate the components of computer chips, to control the behavior of molecules, to manipulate cells. The ability to build very small things has the potential to generate new jobs, goods, and wealth. There is also the matter of "life." "Small" is a door to the microscopic palace we call the cell. . . . Among the most sophisticated nanomachines and nanodevices we know are the components of living cells. And the cell itself—a micron-scale object—is complex in ways we do not begin to understand, and will not be able to mimic for many decades. . . . We simply *must* know what is there, at the smallest scale.[1]

Their list of reasons for investigating what happens at the nanoscale ranges from the most fundamental science to technological, medical, and environmental applications. Interestingly, Frankel and Whitesides are much less invested in the disciplinary status of the field than many of their peers. "We will not know the ultimate impact of nanoscience and nanotechnology for many years. We *do* know that it is following its own path. . . . It's already very, very cool, and very useful."[2]

Contrast that view with the more theoretical ambitions of cultural studies. Writing about interdisciplinarity and historical practices from a position "between social history and cultural studies," Geoff Eley asked:

> So what *do* we mean—what do *I* mean—by interdisciplinarity? To me, it means many of the things that were fashioned in the originary and turbulent circumstances of the 1960s—it means transgression, it means disobeying, it means rule-

breaking, it means making trouble, it means shaking things up, it means being experimental, it means trying new thoughts, taking risks, being courageous in our relationship to new and unfamiliar knowledges and our imaging of what those might be, it means finding spaces of possibility on the other side of what we already do. At one level, this is all to do with the addressing of difference, with stepping outside our familiar regimes of intelligibility, with defamiliarizing them, in fact, with unsettling our customary conditions and habits of understanding, with the release of meaning rather than its predictable accumulation. When we go to another discipline, or another field of knowledge (because what I'm saying can apply to the crossing of cultural difference, or of historical time, and so on, as much as to the traversing of disciplinary boundaries *per se*), we're entering it as a site of difference in this way.[3]

What could be more different?

Both materials science (MSE) and cultural studies (CS) present themselves, and are accepted by others, as new and different interdisciplines. Both attempt to point their way to the future, including the future of knowledge and the future of interdisciplinarity. Yet, like other interdisciplines, both suffer from limitations and contradictions and exhibit huge gaps between their claims and their achievements. But some of their problems are more novel. Intriguingly, both fields focus on a problematic regarding connections between the natural, the artificial, the constructed, and the historical. Across very different domains and locations, both MSE and CS are driven by clear ideologies, assert great claims of contemporary significance, and proclaim their power to remake the world.

Materials Science

By all accounts, materials science is more successful than cognitive science. It represents a material product, after all. We inquire into its disciplinary and interdisciplinary relationships, location, organization, and institutionalization.

Materials science (known in the trade as MSE, for materials science and engineering), which is increasingly identified with nanotechnology even though that is only one of its branches, is about the use, transformation, and construction of matter, "natural" and human-made, visible and, increasingly, invisible to the naked eye. Although it clearly overlaps with efforts in genetic biology, operations research, and bioscience, in a fundamental way it is about "stuff," to borrow a word from Ivan Amato's evocative book title.[4] That makes it different from the other cases considered thus far. Because that "stuff" is presumed to be novel, the field makes sweeping claims for its novelty and, therefore, its ability to transform the material world. I struggle unsuccessfully against the temptation to make puns about MSE "mattering" and pose questions about MSE that "matter." The discourse of MSE invites that. It is material, after all. To the contrary, cultural studies is, usually, *not* about stuff (the study of material culture developed as a separate field). Both these interdisciplines, however, pay insufficient attention to history, including their own.[5]

MSE is the most teleological of proclaimed interdisciplines, though many share that dubious quality. It is also characterized by the clearest dichotomies and divides. MSE's teleology is twofold: both in the determinative relationship of "matter/materials" to "man" over the course of civilization and in the "natural" evolution of the discipline or interdiscipline of materials science. Stephen Sass evokes the former in *The Substance of Civilization: Materials and Human History from the Stone Age to Age of Silicon*. From David and Goliath to semiconductors, "Materials guided the course of history. . . . History is an alloy of all the materials that we have invented or discovered, manipulated, used, and abused."[6] The advance of "materials" determines the stages of civilization.

According to the standard version of its origins, MSE's roots are, not surprisingly, in engineering and traditional "empiricism" as opposed to "rational science." Romantic nostalgia for artisans and craftspeople substitutes for consideration of the complicated interrelations of art and science and the history of professionalization, institutionalization, and specialization in the sciences and engineering. The engineering-versus-science dichotomy is inseparable from those of practical application versus "pure" theoretical research and industrial versus academic location. Collateral questions concern the social organization of research and the factors that propelled the development of the field.[7]

Like other cases studied here, MSE describes itself rather indiscriminately as a discipline, a multidiscipline, and an interdiscipline. Like OR, bioscience, and, increasingly, genetics and bioengineering, research and development is located on the fluid terrain between academia and industry.[8] In attaching itself to national security, on the one hand, and the quest for human betterment, on the other, MSE positions itself as a model interdiscipline or even, remarkably, a superdiscipline for the twenty-first century.[9] At the same time, revealingly, MSE—especially nanotechnology, which often stands as a synecdoche for the larger field—stimulates an unusual debate over its (inter)disciplinary status. The discourse and promotion of interdisciplinarity in materials science and nanotechnology is distinctive. Not only is this a persistent and consistent element of the case for interdisciplinarity, but it also is tied inseparably to promotional claims made on the basis of presumptions of the field's value, from national security to economic prosperity and human well-being.

Debates over Disciplinarity

Defining materials science is simultaneously simple and tricky. On one level, MSE is no more and no less than the scientific study of matter in its physical forms. But what it consists of, what intellectual and organizational forms it takes, where it is located, and how it relates to other fields are more difficult and sometimes controversial issues. In his widely recognized insider's history, *The Coming of Materials Science*, metallurgist and MSE founder R. W. Cahn offers a map of materials science and engineering. In the conclusion of his 560-page book, he asks for the first time: "What is materials science? I have gone through my professional life almost without addressing this question explicitly; I have always believed that the right way to address it is by means of what philosophers call an 'ostensive definition,' pointing to something and saying 'This is it.'" In 1965, he responded to the question by way of an analogy to the biologist, who works from the cell to the organism; so, too, materials scientists studying "inanimate and artificial nature . . . work at several levels of organisation, each of which is underpinned by the next level. . . . The concept of *microstructure* is the most important single defining theme of MSE. To this can be added the slightly broader modern concept of *mesostructure*, a term particularly beloved of modellers and stimulators of polymers . . . the level of organisation in between the atomic/molecular and macroscopic appearance."[10]

To an unusual degree, the discourse and representation of MSE's definition and historical development pivot on its identification, location, and disciplinary status. In *Stuff: The Materials the World Is Made of*, Ivan Amato proclaims categorically that materials science is a "superdiscipline." After thousands of years of "a multitude of technical traditions" and "so many new materials . . . sprouting from such a disjointed approach . . . by the first half of the twentieth century, what might come out of a concerted effort to alloy the specific strengths of each materials tradition into a more systematic superdiscipline?"[11] His teleological story starts too late and conflates multidisciplinary with interdisciplinary endeavors. "A yet-to be-recognized multidisciplinary materials research culture" was "in the midst of forming itself," he begins.

> The seed crystals of the culture were set down in places like Los Alamos, New Mexico, during the Manhattan Project, at Bell Telephone Laboratories in Murray

Hill, New Jersey, at DuPont's polymer research group in Wilmington, Delaware, at General Electric's research labs in Schenectady, New York, and a handful of other industrial labs. There also were a few seeds of the new culture at academic venues like the Massachusetts Institute of Technology. In these places teams of researchers with different training and skills were churning out new ceramic, polymeric, and metallic materials every year. These were places where physicists, chemists, mechanical engineers, electrical engineers, and other with specialized skills discovered how badly they needed one another's technical strengths.

In Amato's view, these "pockets of interdisciplinary synergism did not carry sufficient momentum to trigger a general trend. . . . There was still no single field of research known by something like 'materials science and engineering.'" The stimulus to systemization lay in the "American future": military, space age, jet aircraft, semiconductors. They "could not be assured by masters of any one discipline. It would take collaborations. Masters of different disciplines would have to transcend their traditional difference to forge more powerful partnerships. For the sake of national security . . . a new field of materials research was more than a luxury: it was a necessity." From defense to communications, atomic energy, computers, composite metals, ceramics, and polymers, one thing led to another. "Despite these gains, materials science and engineering remains an obscure outpost of the country of science," Amato laments; no doubt his grand story is designed to remedy its seemingly undeserved marginality.[12]

The major professional organization, the Materials Research Society (MRS), founded in 1973 and now 16,700 strong, describes itself as "interdisciplinary." Its founders were "a visionary group of scientists who shared the belief that their professional interests were broader in scope than existing single-discipline societies. . . . MRS members hail from physics, chemistry, biology, mathematics and engineering—the full spectrum of materials research—and they choose MRS because it is important to their work and careers." According to its mission statement, MRS "is an organization of materials researchers from academia, industry and government that promotes communication for the advancement of interdisciplinary materials research to improve the quality of life" (June 2000). The society aims to "build a dynamic, interactive global community of materials researchers to advance technical excellence by providing a framework in which the materials disciplines can convene, collaborate, integrate and advocate" (July 2008). Interdisciplinarity is one of its core values, along with "technical expertise"; it describes itself as "visionary and dynamic," "broadly inclusive and egalitarian."[13] How does this differ from cross- or multi-disciplinarity? Is interdisciplinarity a "value"? Neither disciplinary relationships nor interdisciplinary locations are scrutinized.

Not surprisingly, Wikipedia follows suit, reflexively and confusingly defining materials science as "an interdisciplinary field applying the properties of matter to various areas of science and engineering. This relatively new scientific field investigates the relationship between the structure of materials at atomic or molecular scales and their macroscopic properties. It incorporates elements of applied physics and chemistry." This seems to me backward. I would think it that "various areas of science and engineering" are applied to "the properties of matter." Here again, why interdisciplinary? The matter is not merely "academic"; it is historical, disciplinary, institutional, and social and political-economic.

To an extent that may be unique among interdisciplines, nanotechnology has stimulated debates about its claims to interdisciplinarity among philosophers, physicists, materials scientists, historians, librarians, and information researchers. Yet their substance is seldom revealing; only rarely do they touch on the history, relationships, and locations of disciplines. A particularly bold assertion of interdisciplinarity is found in the title of an undergraduate course offered in "the 'arts and sciences' context." The description of "Materials: An Interdisciplinary Integrative Approach" attempts to assuage fears of "a veritable disciplinary Tower of Babel in trying to integrate the various 'traditional' departmental units."[14] Reminiscent of the generalist-specialist dichotomy, its approach to integration is found in laboratory work.

An entirely different defense of the field's interdisciplinarity appears under the title "Crystallizing the Nanotechnical Debate," written by Stephen Wood, a psychologist of work; Alison Geldart, a freelance researcher; and Richard Jones, a physicist at the University of Sheffield and published in *Technology Analysis and Strategic Management*. According to its abstract, "Much of the initial commentary on nanotechnology assumed, implicitly or explicitly, that nanotechnology represented a radical discontinuity from existing science and technology. The birth of the nanotechnology debate was marked by the differences of opinion as to whether the technology's outcomes would be positive or negative. . . . The authors argue that nanotechnology is erroneously treated as homogeneous and is under-analysed; it is the very diversity and transdisciplinary nature of nanotechnology that makes it distinctive and interesting to social science enquiry."[15] The authors do not explain how perceptions of its "radical discontinuity" with previous work justify their pronouncement that it is "transdisciplinary." Moreover, the proffered distinction between "nanoscience" and "nanotechnology" ignores much serious writing by specialists in the field.

Other commenters are critical of nanotechnology's claims for interdisciplinarity. Although some are general cavils about interdisciplinarity itself,[16] Ismael Rafols more usefully asks: "Why are interdisciplinary practices less widespread than expected?" Without quite saying so, he implies that expectations of the fruits of interdisciplinarity are exaggerated.

> One of the central tenets of the current discourse on innovation is that the most important scientific and technological breakthroughs are the result of interdisciplinary endeavours and, therefore, innovation policies should facilitate and foster interdisciplinary research. However, a quick look at interdisciplinarity "in practice" shows that the latter is extremely diverse: interdisciplinary research is carried out in a variety of ways. . . . The idea of interdisciplinarity as a source of creativity and innovation has become particularly relevant in those areas of science and technology (S&T) that have emerged as a result of technological convergence, such as nanotechnology or NBIC technologies (nano-, bio-, info-, and cognitive-based). . . . In both discourses and policies, interdisciplinarity is presented as the result of particular strategies of knowledge acquisition: (i) research collaboration among two or more laboratories affiliated with different disciplines; or (ii) the recruitment in one laboratory of researchers from many different backgrounds.[17]

In a study of practices in the bionanosciences, he found that "projects use various strategies to acquire knowledge: interdisciplinary practices involving deep collaborations and exchanges between distinct disciplines at either the personal or institutional level are only one strategy to acquire knowledge and, indeed, not the most common. The majority of projects combine different strategies."[18] While Rafols is correct to question whether cross-disciplinary collaboration automatically yields interdisciplinary research, he seems to pose the problem backward; I would ask whether interdisciplinarity leads to "particular strategies of knowledge acquisition," rather than the reverse. In any case, these relationships are not unilinear. In my view, researchers miss the point when they fail to criticize the assumptions about and expectations of interdisciplinarity. Finding that nanoscience, and by extension much of MSE, fails to meet certain artificial tests for interdisciplinarity tells us little or nothing about the nature of its successes and failures. If there is a divergence between discourse and practice, who is to say that the fault lies in the practice rather than the theory, or, for that matter, in both?

At the same time, I have serious concerns about the research methods that have recently been adopted to investigate these questions. An approach called "bibliometrics," which analyzes the authors, subjects, and keywords of articles found in bibliographic databases, remains imprisoned by the same kinds of assumptions that plague other studies that seek to praise or criticize the interdisciplinarity of nanoscience.[19] Relying on assumptions, expectations, and definitions that are accepted uncritically and used without regard to context, bibliometric studies present contradictory findings. Sadly, this incoherence tells us more about the research than about its object; the actual content of items counted or classified is seldom addressed. These studies' neglect of the history and scope of both interdisciplinarity and nanotechnology / materials science is also telling. Perhaps most revealing is that their questions and methods prevent these writers from actually learning very much about research in the field; instead, they deliberately distance their studies from substantive matters.

For example, Scandinavian scholars Martin Meyer and Olle Persson found "that the share of boundary-spanning publications is exceptionally high in the field of nanotechnology," although exhibiting national differences in "patterns of collaboration."[20] Given their conflation of multidisciplinary with interdisciplinary in their classification of scientific periodicals, this result is only to be expected. Other bibliometric research has reported the opposite. Joachim Schummer concluded "that current nanoscale research reveals no particular patterns and degrees of interdisciplinarity and that its apparent multidisciplinarity consists of different largely mono-disciplinary fields which are rather unrelated to each other and which hardly share more than the prefix 'nano.' "[21] These differing conclusions arise directly from their overly broad and rather stringent definitions of interdisciplinarity. Is interdisciplinarity a matter of the eye of the beholder? If so—though I argue it us not—then cloudy vision is a major obstruction.[22] Schummer argues that "nanoscale research's higher multidisciplinarity without considerably higher interdisciplinarity, but with more scattered and less selective interdisciplinary relations, suggests that it consists of an artificial composition of different research fields with little to no relation to each other."[23] This finding, like that of Meyer and Persson, is wholly a construction of his research method.

Consider the discourse of multidisciplinarity and interdisciplinarity in Schummer's analysis.

The entire field of nanoscale research shows only an average degree of interdisciplinarity, comparable to classical disciplinary research, but a high degree of multidisciplinarity. Analyzed separately, however, these "nano journals" turn out to be classical disciplinary journals of physics, chemistry, electrical engineering, mechanical engineering, and materials science, respectively. In sum, current nanoscale research is neither particularly interdisciplinary nor particularly multidisciplinary, because there is not one field of nanoscale research but several different fields of "nano-physics," "nano-chemistry," "nano-electrical engineering," etc., which are quite unrelated to each other. In other words, nanoscale research is multidisciplinary only in the same trivial sense that the whole of science and engineering is multidisciplinary. Also, despite the simultaneous push of nanoscale research in many countries and institutions, nanoscale research does not differ from the received practice in science and engineering regarding intercontinental and interinstitutional research collaborations.[24]

Interdisciplinarity cannot be understood in that way. Neither can nanotechnology and materials science. We must consider their development, organization, and institutionalization.

Robert Cahn and Merton Flemings help us to navigate the divisions and confusion over these matters. In *The Coming of Materials Science*, Cahn quotes Flemings, an MIT metallurgist, who asked in 1999, "what next for MSE departments?" Neither of these giants of materials science engineering declares the field to be interdisciplinary; they purposefully alternate between multidisciplinarity and disciplinarity. In my reading, the former designates a developmental sense and the latter an institutional one. Cahn suggests that Flemings

faces, foursquare, the issue of whether something can be both a *multidiscipline*, bringing together for use many classical disciplines, and a discipline in its own right. He is sure that MSE is both of these. The path out of the dilemma "is to view the broad engineering study of structure/property/processing/performance relations of materials, with engineering emphasis . . . as a discipline." That is, he asserts, what mainline, independent MSE departments teach. The fourfold way is depicted in . . . a little tetrahedron. . . . Flemings goes so far as to say that "our survival as a discipline and as independent academic departments within the university system depends on how well we succeed in articulating this paradigm and employing it to contribute to society."[25]

For his part, Cahn declares, "I persist in my conviction that *microstructure* is the central component that best distinguishes MSE from other disciplines." Drawing on his distinction "between emergence (of a discipline) by splitting and emergence by integration, and also my insistence that MSE is a prime example (together with geology) of emergence by integration," he argues that "nearly half a century after the emergence of the concept, we its practitioners have in materials science and engineering a clearly distinct discipline which in practice doubles up as a multidiscipline, with a substantial number of independent academic departments and research institutes spread around the world, with its own multifarious journals and textbooks, and a large number of professionals, also spread around the world, who call themselves materials scientists and engineers and communicate with each other on that basis."[26] How much richer is this analysis than the usual brief statements and their inherent dichotomies. The histories of operations research, cognitive science, and even cultural studies suggest that this type of development is not so unusual.[27]

Ironically, the history of materials science clarifies many of these confusions at the same time that it illuminates the seeds of myths and misunderstandings. Like other self-proclaimed interdisciplines, materials science has a longer history than its origin myth of mid-twentieth-century beginnings acknowledges. The standard version of the field's development is teleological and marked by a great divide between an age of empiricism and an age of rational science. A process of professionalization, institutionalization, and disciplinarization saw research and teaching about the world of matter divided between and integrated into the sciences and engineering. Cahn provides a concise outline of the "emergence of disciplines" in physical chemistry, chemical engineering, solid-state physics, continuum and atomistic mechanics of solids, and a myriad of more material-specific fields that laid the foundation for the discipline or multidiscipline of MSE. Although it took this name in the late 1950s, its practices developed over the entire century. The notion of a revolution or revolutions is the leading motif in the origin myth of MSE. Materials science, like other aspiring interdisciplines such as cognitive science, remains caught between an identity based on novelty and regular recourse to its own timelines.

As Cahn shows, materials science had many predecessors that should be understood as more than preconditions or background; they were part of the active processes that made the field. Each intersected with and was transformed by the others. No simple slogan can express those multi-, intra-, and disciplinary relationships. Much of the development of materials science can be grasped in Flemings's graphic representation of performance, properties, synthesis/processing, and structure/composition, read dynamically (figure 5.1). Cahn and the U.S. National Research Council reports point to the critical, intersecting, but not always parallel history of MSE in industry and the simultaneous contributions of national materials laboratories.[28]

The disciplinary story of materials science can be understood in terms of its contradictions (figures 5.2–5.4). It is certainly told—almost always implicitly—contradictorily. Recognizing that problem is a necessary step to resolving the

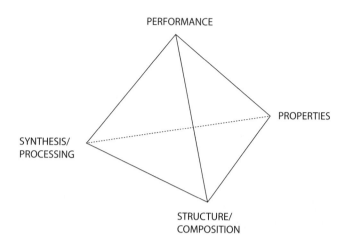

Figure 5.1 Materials science tetrahedron. Just as cognitive science has been depicted as a hexagon, materials science uses an iconic tetrahedron to represent the field graphically. Merton C. Flemings, "What's Next for Departments of Materials Science and Engineering," *Annual Review of Materials Science* 29 (1999): 2

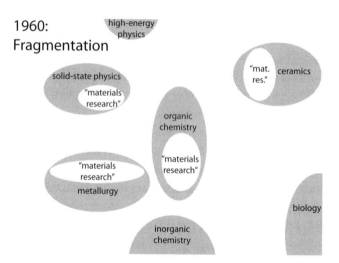

Figure 5.2 Materials science, 1960. The Dibner Institute for the History of Science and Technology at Caltech includes several diagrams of materials science's development on its website. The first represents the "fragmentation" of the field at its start: "In 1960, there was no field called materials science. Much research going in many other fields is now recognized as materials research, but at the time scientists did not think of materials research as a coherent field." From http://authors.library.caltech.edu/5456/1 /hrst.mit.edu/hrs/materials/public/changing_boundaries.htm ©2001 by the Dibner Institute for the History of Science and Technology

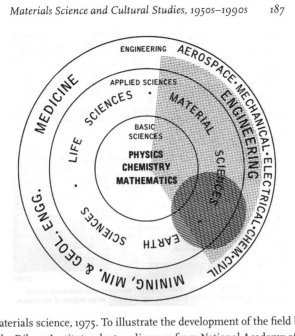

Figure 5.3 Materials science, 1975. To illustrate the development of the field by the mid-1970s, the Dibner Institute adapts a diagram from National Academy of Sciences to illustrate the "[r]elationship of subject matter of nonmetallic science and engineering to all basic and applied science and engineering. The hatched area shows qualitatively the relationship of the subject matter area considered by this Panel to the whole field of material science and engineering (dotted area) and to the traditional structures of science and technology. The important features of its location are the chemical bias, the extensiveness of the field across the basic-science-engineering boundaries, and the inter-disciplinarity nature, which is not well illustrated in this chart." Original figure from National Academy of Sciences, *Mineral Science and Technology: Non-metallic Materials* (Washington, DC, 1969), 12; text from http://authors.library.caltech.edu/5456 /1/hrst.mit.edu/hrs/materials/public/changing_boundaries.htm ©2001 by the Dibner Institute for the History of Science and Technology

debate over the interdisciplinarity of MSE and nanotechnology. Consider the representations of MSE's origin myths in the accounts of historian of science Bernadette Bensaude-Vincent and MIT materials scientist Bernhardt Wuensch, which are featured on the Caltech History of Materials Science website.

Bensaude-Vincent confuses materials with materials science, practices with organization and institutions, parts with wholes, internal with external, and operations with ideologies, creating basic conceptual problems that bedevil her account. She asks,

What can be the consistence of a field of research that that includes such diverse subjects as wood, concrete, paper, polymers, metals, semi-conductors,

2000: Would you like to draw the boundaries?

superconductivity

metastable materials

photonics

surface science

porous
materials

Materials Research

nanotechnology

nuclear waste

intercalation science

biotechnology

compound semiconductors

Figure 5.4 Materials science, 2000. The Dibner Institute brings the field to the edge of the twenty-first century by presenting an array of fields without connection and asking, "Would you like to draw the boundaries?" The caption continues: "It is no longer feasible to draw any maps of disciplines. The distinction between pure and applied is no longer seen to work, and many people work in fields that overlap. For example, some people work to apply nanotechniques to research on biocompatible materials and it might still be seen as a part of surface science. Attendees from departments with just about any conceivable name (say, from Electrical Engineering to Molecular Biology) at the annual meetings of the Materials Research Society freely borrow from each other." From http://authors.library.caltech.edu/5456/1/hrst.mit.edu/hrs/materials/public /changing_boundaries.htm ©2001 by the Dibner Institute for the History of Science and Technology

and ceramics? . . . The generic concept of materials is itself a challenge. Consequently how could materials be objects of science? . . . The notion of materials combines natural science and humanities: it combines physical and chemical properties with social needs, civilization, industrial or military interests. From this coupling of natural and human aspects embedded in the definition of materials follows one characteristic feature of materials science. Knowing and producing are never separated; the cognitive purpose and the technological interests are intertwined. . . . Here is a science made of a cluster of specialists from various disciplines (metallurgists, ceramicists, electrical engineers, chemical engineers, physicists, inorganic chemists, organic chemists, crystallographers, and so on).

What they constitute by coming together is not, she argues, a discipline similar to physics or chemistry, which remain coherent despite the diversity of their methods. Rather, "it is the product of an aggregation of several specialties already separate."[29]

Recognizing that this materials-centered view does not support the notion of MSE as an interdisciplinary field, Bensaude-Vincent continues:

> More often the emergence of materials science is described as the outcome of an internal movement of modern science towards increasing abstraction. In this view the generic notion of materials instantiates the transition from an empirically based technology to an era when the properties of materials were understood on the basis of rational sciences. The advanced materials created by MSE can be presented as a new episode of the secular process of emancipation of mankind from nature. Because they are no longer extracted from nature, new materials are supposed to testify to the increasing power of mankind to create artifacts. Man and man's needs are supposed driving force [*sic*] as indicated by a report of the National Academy of Science published in 1975 and entitled *Materials and Man's Needs*. . . . However, with such general considerations about human nature the identity of the various agencies that converged into the emergence of MSE in the USA remains obscure. Did it result from an internal evolution of the various disciplines that merged into this new entity? Was it the creature of political measures . . . ? The balance between the bottom-up and top-down constraints presumably changed over [four] decades.[30]

Universities responded to shifts in government research policies and funding. In 1972, when responsibility for the federally sponsored laboratories shifted from ARPA to the National Science Foundation, they were renamed Materials Research Laboratories. Following explicit guidelines, "thrust groups" of researchers developed multidisciplinary and "multi-investigatorial" projects. Was interdisciplinarity an artifact of external authorities and funding opportunities? Bensaude-Vincent recognizes that "cross- and multidisciplinarity became the motto of all kinds of reports on materials research all over the world," but she "prefer[s] to forge the term 'mixed-discipline.'"[31]

Bensaude-Vincent concludes with an oversimplification of the process, which betrays her misunderstanding of its history. "The emergence and evolution of MSE may be more adequately described in terms of responses to challenges than in terms of 'organic growth.' In the beginning, the generic notion of materials science has been forged in response to the Soviet challenge of Sputnik. Then in the 1980s, the Japanese challenge prompted a re-orientation towards processing and industrial competition."[32] Looking to the future, Bensaude-Vincent is equally skeptical about the prospects for "convergence." While nanotechnologies "could or should prompt the unification of the field of materials science . . . , [u]ntil now they are not really acting as converging forces nor are they creating any unified set of concepts and practices." Bensaude-Vincent's expectations seem unrealistic for either disciplinarity or interdisciplinarity. "The new perspectives opened up by the nanoscale act as diverging rather than converging forces. On the one hand, they extend the frontiers of MSE to such territories as bioengineering or artificial intelligence. Multidisciplinary cooperation is intensified. . . . As a result, if one were to map out the territory of MSE today one would get nothing like a center and a periphery or a mainstream split into various little branches. Rather, MSE appears as a booming field without clear borderlines and with dozens of streams flowing in various directions."[33] Cahn's and Flemings's less metaphorical and more complex notion of multidisciplinarity seems more persuasive.

Wuensch focuses on the historical transformation from the "empiricism" of traditional crafts that utilized "low-cost, high-volume," readily available materials to a scientific field "founded on a firm basic understanding" of materials that could only be created technologically, which "required knowing precisely what went on." While avoiding the framing discourse of interdisciplinarity, he sees a "natural" development of materials science in that direction. The change, in Wuensch's view, was partly generational, as scientists and engineers became more comfortable with collaboration across departmental, disciplinary, and professional lines. But it also derived from the Defense Advanced Research Projects Agency's initiative in founding and funding interdisciplinary laboratories. "The people in DARPA had the wisdom to realize that, in order to capitalize on the electronic properties of semiconductors, one would have to understand the chemistry of producing these materials and the way of growing single crystals of unprecedented perfection. This brought in the chemists, it brought in the crystal growers and the materials scientists. You also needed to understand the physics of these very complicated electronic structures and the way of controlling them through doping and through creation of proper interfaces." Naturally, "the only way to make any progress on this was to bring together in one place" people who could contribute "the perspective, instrumentation, and the skill and expertise of their particular discipline with a view to collaboration in a very close fashion—that is, not only formulating but also conducting the research."[34] Following the standard account, Wuensch refers to the MIT's Building 13, home to the DARPA Center for Materials Science and Engineering, where a major portion of the Department of Materials Science and Engineering was housed on the fourth and fifth floors, along with the ceramics and electronic materials group and the polymers group; the electrical engineers on the third floor; and the condensed matter physics group on the second floor.[35]

The case for interdisciplinarity in MSE is built on multidisciplinarity, first in practice and then in theory. "The charter for the Center for Materials Science and Engineering . . . was that first you will conduct materials research in a highly interactive and interdisciplinary mode—and faculty from as many as seven different departments at MIT had participated in the programs. These workers were to be grouped together in teams called Areas of Thrust in early semiconductor research, but later broadened considerably." Organization mattered, and federal as well as corporate sponsorship influenced that configuration. Wuensch identifies another element that has been instrumental in both multi- and interdisciplinary efforts and, indeed, has become one of its signature elements. "The second mandate besides creating these funded, collaborative, and interdisciplinary research teams was to establish central research facilities. . . . The next thing the sponsors did was to seek to convert young faculty to this interdisciplinary mode of operation. In order to do so they provided seed funding. It was an unabashed attempt to seduce young faculty into these interdisciplinary teams!"[36]

"The other thing that needs to be said about the program is that it evolved over time," Wuensch concludes.[37] The growth from a dozen national laboratories to labs at institutions ranging from Northwestern to MIT, Los Alamos to Oak Ridge, and Bell Labs to General Electric, all under differing auspices, demonstrates that the field's development was anything but natural; it took shape partly by decree! With materials research, both collaboration and competition were key. The social organization of research and development played a stronger and more obvious role in the manipulation of matter than in other multi- and interdisciplinary efforts. It does bear comparative study, especially with biology, cognitive science, and bioscience; so do the idea and practices of labs in the humanities and the social sciences.[38]

Amid all the ink spilled about the nature of materials science as discipline, superdiscipline, multidiscipline, or interdiscipline, prize-winning metallurgist and MSE founder Merton Flemings merits the last words. Based on his own experience and the history of material science as he understood it, he argued clearly and with reason in 1999 that "the broad field of materials science and engineering is certainly a multidiscipline," as the Committee on the Survey of Materials Science and Engineering (COSMAT) study had concluded in 1974.

The iconic tetrahedron diagram of the field (see figure 5.1) encompassed everything "from solid-state physics and fundamental chemistry at one boundary to the factory floor and societal needs at the other." The disciplines constituting that multidiscipline have changed over time. Observers like Bensaude-Vincent criticize the field's "instability" and deplore the fact that its "overall organization does not convey the image of a unified discipline." But is that not a characteristic strength of a multidiscipline? Flemings asked, if "MSE is multidisciplinary, what are the disciplines? In the 1970s . . . the fields of metallurgy and even ceramics could be viewed as disciplines, in the sense that each could claim strong professional societies, a recognition of degrees in the field by industry, and a cohesive intellectual arena sufficiently broad to merit scholarship. We could still comfortably view ourselves as metallurgists or ceramists, or polymerists, all embedded in a multidisciplinary department." At the end of the 1990s, however, MSE underwent another of its major transformations. In some graduate programs and university research centers, "the historic science and engineering disciplines" were "being brought to bear in an interdisciplinary approach to materials problems. In this instance, no one need leave his or her traditional discipline. Another answer is provided by undergraduate materials programs embedded in or allied with historic engineering disciplines. Here materials can be viewed not as a multidiscipline, but as a subdiscipline, subsumed in one or another of the historic disciplines."[39]

Flemings's concern with pedagogy is refreshing. He offers a sensible, historical and contextual, and apparently operational approach that attends to the pressing disciplinary, multidisciplinary, and interdisciplinary problems of definition, relationships, location, organization, and institutionalization. "There remains a semantic problem," he admits. "The broad field of materials science and engineering surely remains a multidiscipline. . . . I leave the appropriate terminology to others in the future, adopting herein that of simply referring to the 'discipline of MSE' as that practiced by core MSE departments, and retaining the terminology of the 'multidiscipline of materials science and engineering' as applying to the field as a whole."[40]

The fact that MSE is both a discipline and a multidiscipline and is located principally in departments of materials science and engineering but also practiced in government and industrial laboratories has implications for its organization and institutionalization. Paralleling the organization of cognitive science but with more of a center in MSE and distinct departments and seemingly less antagonism between disciplines, this differentiation is clearly reflected in the organization of the field. Cahn summarizes: "The plethora of professional societies now linked to MSE can be divided into three categories—old metallurgical societies, either unregenerate or converted to broader concerns; specialised societies, concerned with other particular categories of materials or functions; and societies devoted to MSE from the time of their foundation. Beyond this, there are some federations, umbrella organisations that link a number of societies. . . . Most of these have now changed their names because, at various times, they have sought to broaden their remit from metals to materials. . . . Some bodies have simply resolved to become broader," for example, TMS, the Minerals, Metals, and Materials Society. "The underlying idea . . . is that by changing the name, societies can bring about a broadening of interest. By and large, this has not happened."[41]

Professional and Ethical Matters

Although the largest organization, the Materials Research Society (MRS), calls itself interdisciplinary, its multidisciplinarity is reflected in a membership that is "roughly 1/3 each chemists, physicists and engineers," as well as an increasing number of mathematicians and biologists.[42] In Cahn's telling, MRS's founders chose the term "research" rather than "science" in order to "avoid specifying which kinds of scientists and engineers should be involved in the society. . . . From the start the society was to focus on research involving cooperation between different disciplines, of which MSE was to be just one—albeit a vital one." Cahn explains that the founders were also concerned about the division between academia and industry, "though that has been kept rather quiet in public. . . . Physicists and chemists working in American industry . . . were not made welcome in their professional physics and chemistry societies, which were inclined to ignore industrial concerns." They played a substantial role in bringing the MRS to life. So, did those whom Cahn calls "enlightened figures in industry, especially William O. Baker, director of research at Bell Telephone Laboratories." From the beginning, MRS welcomed industrial scientists and topics of close concern to industry.[43] While in the past up to 25 percent of its members were employed in industry, with the closing of large industrial labs that proportion fell to 15 percent. Today, scientists' paths lead more often to universities and government labs.[44]

The structure of education in MSE reflects the field's combination of disciplinarity and interdisciplinarity. As Cahn summarized the educational landscape in 2001, the number of independent departments in MSE was roughly balanced by the number of programs that were organized jointly with other disciplines or embedded within other departments.[45] According to Flemings's data, most bachelor's graduates did not move on to advanced degrees in engineering but embarked on professional careers.[46] In its academic organization, then, this is a discipline in the process of change, yet it remains much more multidisciplinary than interdisciplinary. A review of major departments accords closely with Flemings's and Cahn's views about the recent promotion of a general materials science orientation (table 5.1).[47]

Materials science and especially nanotechnology have provoked an unusual concern with matters of an ethical nature, including a federally mandated concern for the environment.[48] Unique among the case studies in this book is its aesthetic dimension. On the one hand, this dimension derives from their inescapable implications for the "natural" environment, given their double-edged commitment to new forms of manufacturing and commercial capitalism and to enhancing the quality of life. Anxieties about damage to human and nonhuman health and the exacerbation of global inequality tend to cluster around it. On the other hand, to some extent this concern derives from the legislatively mandated guidelines for the National Science Foundation and other U.S. government agencies, which stipulate that ethical matters must be addressed in educational and academic programs.[49] As a result, nanotechnology has spawned what is variously styled nanoethics, nano-ethics, and NanoEthics.

The question of the relationship of ethical issues to interdisciplinary and multidisciplinary emphases remains, to my knowledge, unexplored. This is a large topic that I can only introduce in a preliminary way. First, my sense is that ethical issues are more in the foreground with regard to materials science and nanotechnology than to other scientific fields. Bioscience, molecular biology, and genetic biology follow, perhaps fairly closely. Cognitive science seems to lag far behind. Second, the combined sense of novelty and enormous immediate significance associated with fields promoted as interdisciplinary goes some way in helping to explain this concern; some scientists promise innovations with transformative consequences for the human body. The subsidiary debate about whether or not such fields as nanotechnology stimulate new concerns parallels the debate about whether materials science and nanotechnology are disciplines, superdisciplines, multidisciplines, or interdisciplines.

For example, in an article, "Nanotechnology—A New Field of Ethical Inquiry?" Armin Grunwald comments, "Parallel to the public discussion on the benefits and risks of nanotechnology, a debate on the ethics of nanotechnology

TABLE 5.1
Materials science degree programs

University	Department	Degree/Program
Columbia	Materials Science and Engineering Program within Applied Physics and Applied Mathematics and the Henry Krum School of Mines	MS in Materials Science and Engineering; MPhil, PhD in Materials Science and Engineering, Graduate Specialty in Solid-State Science and Engineering; Doctor of Engineering Science (EngScD or DES)
Yale	Mechanical Engineering and Materials Science Department in the School of Engineering & Applied Science	MS, MPhil, PhD in Mechanical Engineering and Materials Science
Wisconsin	Materials Science and Engineering	BS in Materials Science and Engineering; MS, PhD in Materials Engineering
Michigan	Materials Science and Engineering	Bachelor of Science in Engineering (BSE) in Materials Science and Engineering; Master of Science in Engineering (MSE) in Materials Science and Engineering; PhD in Materials Science and Engineering
Berkeley	Materials Science and Engineering	Materials Science and Engineering major and minor; BS/MS in Materials Science and Engineering; Master of Engineering (MEng) in Materials Science and Engineering; MS, PhD in Materials Science and Engineering
Texas	Materials Science and Engineering	Master of Science in Engineering (MSE); MS, PhD in Materials Science and Engineering
Stanford	Materials Science and Engineering	BS, BS/MS, MS, PhD in Materials Science and Engineering
Penn	Materials Science and Engineering	BSE, MSE, PhD in Materials Science and Engineering
Cornell	Materials Science and Engineering	BS, Master of Engineering (ME), MS, PhD in Materials Science and Engineering
UMass Amherst	Polymer Science and Engineering Department	MS, PhD in Polymer Science and Engineering

(continued)

TABLE 5.1 (*continued*)

University	Department	Degree/Program
MIT	Department of Metallurgy	BS in Materials Science and Engineering; BS without specification; BS in Archaeology and Materials; Master of Science (SM), PhD, Doctor of Science in Materials Science and Engineering (ScD) in Materials Science and Engineering
Northwestern	Materials Science and Engineering	BS in Materials Science and Engineering; BA in Materials Science; BS/MS, MS, PhD in Materials Science and Engineering
Penn State	Materials Science and Engineering	Associate degree in Materials Engineering Technology; MS, PhD in Materials Science and Engineering
UC Davis	Department of Chemical Engineering and Materials Science	Materials Science and Engineering major; MS, MEngr, PhD in Materials Science and Engineering
Carnegie Mellon	Department of Materials Science and Engineering	BS in Materials Science and Engineering; BS in Materials Science; BS in Materials Science and Engineering / Biomedical Engineering, Materials Science and Engineering / Engineering and Public Policy; BS/MS, MS, PhD in Materials Science and Engineering and MS in Materials Science; MS in Engineering & Technology Innovation Management; MS in Energy Science and Technology and Policy

has begun. It has been postulated that a new 'nano-ethics' is necessary. In this debate, the—positive as well as negative—visionary and speculative innovations which are brought into connection with nanotechnology stand in the foreground." Yet after a systematic search for "new ethical aspects of nanotechnology," he finds "that there are hardly any completely new ethical aspects raised by nanotechnology. It is much rather primarily a case of gradual shifts of emphasis and of relevance in questions which, in principle, are already known and which give reason for ethical discussions on nanotechnology. In a certain manner, structurally novel ethical aspects arise through the important role played by visions in the public discourse. New questions are also posed by the fact that previously separate lines of ethical reflection converge in the field of nanotechnology. The proposal for an independent 'nano-ethics,' however, seems exaggerated."[50]

The question of interdisciplinarity in ethics joins that of interdisciplinarity in nanoscience, nanotechnology, and materials science more generally. Complication and confusion obscure clarity. These contortions lead me to propose that proclamations of interdisciplinarity may well stimulate a heightened but more diffuse and disconnected concern with matters of ethics. Is this, too, a characteristic of common discourse on interdisciplinarity?

Cultural Studies

Inside the university and to some extent beyond it, cultural studies stimulates the strongest reactions of all the fields that assert their interdisciplinarity. Nanoscience also attracts strong reactions, but responses to cultural studies are especially intense. It is also the most difficult to discuss in the terms of the comparative history of interdisciplinarity. For many commentators, it is unquestionably an interdiscipline. Wikipedia falls immediately into contradictions when it describes the field: "Characteristically interdisciplinary, cultural studies is an academic discipline. . . . Cultural Studies is not a unified theory, but a diverse field of study encompassing many different approaches, methods and academic perspectives."[51] The Cultural Studies Association states without qualification that cultural studies is a discipline.

For its proponents and participants, cultural studies is the epitome of interdisciplinarity: in its contemporary relevance, its range of disciplines and breadth, its challenge to the structure and organization of knowledge and its production as we know it, and its critical power. For many critics, cultural studies represents interdisciplinarity run amok. It is undisciplined and unscholarly, explicitly ideological and avowedly political, disrespectful of scholars in other fields, and critical of the contemporary university and its established divisions. It panders to "difference" and "identity," especially as they relate to gender, race and ethnicity, social class, popular cultures, and diverse forms of popular expression.[52] Cultural studies is a notorious subject of caricature; physicist Alan Sokal published a hoax that he intended to be a parody of cultural studies of science in the journal *Social Text* in 1996.[53]

Cultural studies is associated with a variety of "crises" in the humanities. For some, it is contributing cause, an exacerbating factor, a striking symptom, or a symbol of what ails us. But for others, cultural studies offers solutions and alternative paths. Many commentators and even a few supporters admit or otherwise demonstrate ambivalence. Some reveal an awareness of the field's longer, more complicated, histories, which include affiliations with conservative, liberal, and radical criticism, and of its relationships to specific disciplines. Fewer consider major questions of its intellectual and programmatic location and its problems of organization and limited institutionalization. Nonetheless, cultural studies is inseparably associated with the discourse of interdisciplinarity.[54]

The titles of prominent books suggest this quest for identity and internal diversity: *Culture and Power, Cultural Studies in Question, Relocating Cultural Studies, The Renewal of Cultural Studies, Cultural Studies in the Present Tense, Disciplinarity and Dissent in Cultural Studies, Life and Times of Cultural Studies, Dictionary of Cultural Theorists, Theorizing Culture, Blow Up the Humanities.* There are readers, handbooks, encyclopedias, and an endless literature preoccupied by defining, explaining, accounting, and differentiating. Cultural studies, it sometimes seems, is everywhere. But, we also ask, is it anywhere?[55]

Locating Cultural Studies

Steven Marcus locates cultural studies within the historical development of the humanities. "As cultural studies began to emerge in the 1960s and after as a broad, reshaping tendency with the humanities, the organizational model customarily pursued was that of the interdisciplinary programs of American studies. . . . Such innovations began frequently as movements within disciplines and departments. They then typically branched out into interdepartmental explorations. . . . Including literature, history, art history, law, sociology, anthropology, and whatever else has seemed appropriate, such programs have regularly been the organizational paradigm and umbrella for cultural studies." Here Marcus follows the conventional narrative in seeing cross-disciplinarity subject and area studies as interdisciplinary. He continues expansively, "The titles and interests of such program are now too numerous to list, but they include prominently African American studies, women's studies, ethnic studies, postcolonial studies, New Historicist studies, and gay and lesbian studies. They are, as the saying goes, where the action has been, and it isn't difficult to see why—they are doing something intrinsically right, however much one want to hold concretely and specifically in reserve."[56]

Like many other commentators, Marcus points to "two large influences." The first is the "untimely return of Marxism, a particularly awkward matter in a post-Marxist world." The second is "the general notion of the cultural construction of knowledge," which he regards as "a powerful and useful conception both in theory and application." Yet he finds that this concept is often not employed with "tact and urbanity. . . . For it is only one moderately short intellectual step from the measured historical relativism of this perspective to the lamentable portion of identity politics, the assertion that one's personal or group situation—class, race, or gender—determines the substance of one's thoughts and beliefs. And from this point it is merely one step again to the claims that 'everything is political.'" While many see these complications as damning, Marcus does not. "A new range of topics and themes has been legitimately started," and "new cultural and historical materials are being brought forward for discussion and analysis." By the time he was writing this piece in 2000, he thought "that the most intense moments of acrimony may be past, that some settling is taking place, and that pitched battle has given way, if not to peace, then to smaller guerilla actions and even, here and there, to armed, if exhausted truce."[57]

In Marcus's expansive hopes, I do not see interdisciplinarity. He may be read as arguing just the opposite, that cultural studies is having a diffuse, trickle-down effect on work in the humanities. "Equally cogent, however, is the sense they communicate of an awareness of intellectual and disciplinary *fragmentation* of both perspective and knowledge and of the need for new shapes of intellectual *integration*."[58] That need has not been met.

Marcus's case for cultural studies differs from those made by others. A common argument made by both critics and defenders of disciplines links cultural studies with attacks on disciplines and disciplinarity, although they are not the same thing. This theme is stated most starkly in Toby Miller's 2012 book, *Blow Up the Humanities*. Without qualification, taking on both disciplinarity and interdisciplinarity, Miller lays out an ambitious agenda: to change "the current *doxa* of the humanities in this direction, . . . enrich students' and professors' knowledge base, increase their means of intervention in cultural production, counter charges of social and cultural irrelevance, challenge the safe houses of interdisciplinarity and disciplinarity and make the field's citizenship and social movement claims more credible." How to achieve *all* this? "That would mean abandoning history and literature as core nodes of the humanities, turning instead to the study of media and culture—a necessity recognized even by lovers of literary critique who acknowledge that older forms can spring from and into emergent ones."[59]

Cultural studies is Miller's promised land.

At its best, cultural studies blends and blurs textual analysis of the popular with social theory and materialism, focusing on the margins of power rather than reproducing established lines of force and authority. In the place of concentrating on canonical works of art, government leadership, or quantitative social data, cultural studies devotes time to subcultures, popular media, music, clothing, and sport. By looking at how culture is used and transformed by "ordinary" and "marginal" social groups, cultural studies sees people not simply as consumers but as potential producers of new social values and cultural languages. This amounts to a comprehensive challenge to academic business as usual. The investment in the popular makes waves in the extramural world, too, as the humanities' historic task of criticizing entertainment is side-stepped.[60]

As Miller rushes headlong toward this imagined future, it is not clear what he is saying regarding disciplines, interdisciplines, or academic institutions. "Cultural studies is a tendency across disciplines rather than a discipline itself. This is evident in practitioners' simultaneously expressed desires to refuse definition, insist on differentiation, and sustain conventional departmental credentials (as well as pyrotechnic, polymathematical capacities for reasoning and research). Cultural studies' continuities come from shared concerns and methods." What kind of liberation lies in "refusing definition"? What are "pyrotechnic, polymathematical capacities for reasoning and research"? (Note that he confuses the adjective "polymath" with a form of mathematics!) In the place of definitions and relationships, he offers metaphors. In the place of questions, he makes pronouncements.

In Marcus's schema, duplicative lists of fields from which cultural studies takes its theory and methods substitute for any consideration of disciplines and interdisciplinarity.

> Cultural studies must be animated by subjectivity and power—how human subjects are formed and experience cultural and social space. It takes its agenda and mode of analysis from economics, politics, media, and communication studies, sociology, literature, education, the law, science and technology studies, environmentalism, anthropology and history. The focus is gender, race, class, and sexuality in everyday life, under the sign of a commitment to progressive social change. We can specify a desirable cultural studies as a mixture of economics, politics, textual analysis, gender theory, ethnography, history, postcolonial theory, material objects, and policy, animated by a desire to reveal and transform those who control the means of communication and culture and undertaken with constant vigilance over one's raison d'être and modus operandi.[61]

Cultural studies transforms all that stands before us: institutions and structures of knowledge, metaphysics and epistemology, values and ethics, ideology and politics. For a more progressive future, in other words, "blow up the humanities."

Disciplinarity and Dissent in Cultural Studies, edited by Cary Nelson and Dilip Parameshwar Gaonkar, represents a second strand in the case for cultural studies. Neither disciplines nor interdisciplines "as we know them" are banished; both intended and unintended contradictions are acknowledged. The first part of the collection is titled "Disciplinarity and Its Discontents," with a heavy accent on the discontents. These range from the alleged illegitimacy of divergent subject matter, rigid forms of publication or production required by established disciplinary departments, and fixed criteria for recognition and promotion to threats to academic freedom. While no one recommends blowing up disciplinary clusters, the contributors' agendas range from additions through subversion to transformation.

In the introduction, the editors proclaim that "cultural studies has—in both its research and its pedagogy—abandoned a narrow, circumscribed professionalism in preference for a broad, politically reflective cultivation of a cosmopolitan self." If its practitioners change the disciplines, they suggest, then perhaps they can change the world. Yet they also warn "that there are significant consequences to the intellectual commitments people make. . . . Disciplinary and transdisciplinary differences . . . often have painful bearing on people's lives and their careers." Cultural studies scholars, especially in the social sciences, find themselves "marginalized, disempowered, and sometimes actively harassed." Although "for the most part institutionalization is on hold" because of budget cuts in universities, "on two other fronts—the work of individual scholars and the conceptual struggles within existing disciplines—cultural studies is alive and well, holding its ever-changing ground." Amid these struggles, "the emerging marriage of cultural studies with area studies" offers "a way out of this impasse that is also focused on the increasingly global nature of cultural exchanges."[62] The lines between cultural studies and area studies are blurred. Some commentators view cultural studies as originating in American studies and then spreading outward, as first hyphenated racial or ethnic studies and then global and transnational studies have gained in popularity. The relationships remain unclear.

In a startling concession to the virtues of disciplinarity, Nelson and Gaonkar concede that "detailed knowledge of both an appropriate intellectual tradition and the history of at least one relatively autonomous cultural domain [is] essential to good cultural studies work. Either a traditional or more recent academic discipline in many cases can fulfill this need." Contributors from anthropology, literature, history, and communication "see potential futures of mutual criticism and transformation. Neither cultural studies nor the disciplines they would be in dialogue with would remain the same in the process. Indeed, the implication here is that, while traditional disciplines need the cultural studies difference, cultural studies also needs the critique and challenge of disciplinarity." Their final assertion betrays a striking combination of confidence and confusion: "Cultural studies is committed to the ongoing critique of disciplinarity and the redefinition and recombination of disciplines in response to new or newly recognized historical realities."[63]

Writing in 1996, the editors evince a rare openness about the possible institutional location for cultural studies, admitting that "we have no firm notions of where they belong in the university. . . . Is it the duty of the new generations of academics to move freely across the cultural field taking up any and all issues and objects in an interpretive politics with no limits? Clearly one answer within cultural studies—though not necessarily an exclusive one—is yes." Right or wrong, that answer makes organization and institutionalization very difficult. "Inherent" in the field's dissent from disciplinarity is "also a dissent from both the internal organization and the cultural positioning of the contemporary university." Nelson and Gaonkar predict that its structure will tumble like a house of cards. "As academics invade one another's turf with social and political commentary and evaluation, not only will disciplines' exclusive power to represent themselves to the public be undermined" but so will "the institution's overall ability to manage the relative hierarchization of its components."[64]

In part two, "Going Public, Going Global, Going Historical: Cultural Studies in Transition," *Disciplinarity and Dissent* speaks to a second strong claim of cultural studies: it does public work. This formulation links ethics, ideology, and academic service. It bows respectfully to the three founders of cultural studies, Raymond Williams, Richard Hoggart, and Stuart Hall of the University of Birmingham's Centre for Contemporary Cultural Studies, sometimes acknowledging the field's roots in adult and workers' education and the labor and socialist movements.

In an evocatively named collection of essays, *Cultural Studies in the Present Tense*, American communication professor Lawrence Grossberg speaks to what he identifies as the "heart" of cultural studies. For him, "the project of cultural studies . . . involves a commitment to a particular practice of intellectual-political work, and to the claims that such intellectual work matters both inside and outside of the academy. Cultural studies is a way of inhabiting the position of scholar, teacher, artist, and intellectual, one way (among many) of politicizing theory and theorizing politics." It is at once expansive and limiting, ambitious and humble.

> It constructs for itself a more limited and modest claim to authority than one is used to from the academy; it refuses any and all dreams of universal, absolute, complete, and perfect truth, and at the same time, it refuses to give up the dream of truth to the burdens of relativism. Its modesty is based in its rigorous efforts to tell the best story that can be told, about any context, within that context. It accepts that knowledge and politics, as well as the tools of their production, are always, unavoidably contextually bound. But it refuses to conclude that knowledge or judgments about competing knowledges are impossible. . . . At the same time, its modesty undermines any assumption of being a cultural studies scholar . . . makes one into an expert on everything and anything. Instead, cultural studies takes work![65]

How different a vision than Miller's. But this version of cultural studies, too, seems to be everywhere and nowhere. Grossberg does not speak to disciplinary relationships, location, organization, or institutionalization.

In *Life and Times of Cultural Studies: The Politics and Transformation of the Structures of Knowledge*, Richard Lee explores another plank in the platform of cultural studies: interdisciplinarity as collective work, which is a refrain in the discourse and, in some cases, the practice of interdisciplinarity. In "Interdisciplinary and Collective Work," Lee treats the two categories as sides of the same coin. In discussing the three founders of the field, however, he indicates the diversity of their perspectives regarding disciplinarity. Hoggart had no particular quarrel with the disciplines and disciplinary clusters, although the program he developed crossed disciplinary lines. In sharp contrast, Hall, who effectively built the Birmingham Centre, configured it in opposition to the mainstream disciplines, which treated its original projects with undisguised hostility. "Interdisciplinarity at CCCS did not mean 'a kind of coalition of colleagues from different departments,' but rather a decentering or destabilization of 'a series of interdisciplinary fields.' "[66] Lee emphasizes that Richard Johnson was acutely aware of the limitations of work done by isolated individuals, so "from the beginning, research at CCCS was conducted collectively."[67]

An expansive but oddly blinkered view of cultural studies comes from proponents of interdisciplinarity. Julie Thompson Klein describes the field as a kind of catch-all for recent intellectual movements.

"Cultural studies" is the umbrella label for a profusion of academic, social, and political interests that signal wider alternatives across national contexts. Many practices were already introduced through other interdisciplinarity fields and new approaches to the study of culture in disciplinary domains. The label is also affiliated with a number of revitalized interests, including neo-Marxism, social history, ethnomethodology, and textualism. The field's current momentum derives from overlapping structural, pedagogical, and ideological changes that have occurred in universities since the 1960s. The theory and canon wars of the 1960s and 1970s occurred when most current practitioners were cutting their intellectual and political teeth. They emerged into middle age in a time of bad job markets, postcolonial political movements, the growing influence of mass and popular culture, and a wide-spread sense of disciplinary "crisis."

In an attempt to be inclusive, her discourse proceeds by dichotomies. " 'The culture' of cultural studies is not a single entity but a cumulative reformulation of the concept of culture. . . . Culture is simultaneously the object of study and the site of critique and intervention. Like other interdisciplinary fields, cultural studies exhibits both generality and specificity. It is located within disciplines, on their margins, and in the newly cleared space of interdisciplinary studies." This account confuses disciplinary and interdisciplinary relationships and indiscriminately mixes locations. "Cultural studies is a sheltering space, a catalyst, a subfield, an alternative practice, a network of overlapping projects and comparative theory, and a generalizing problematizing force." It also conflates objects of study with approaches to them. For example, she states that "new areas," such as "popular film, popular music, pornography, and pulp literature—are appearing at different sites across disciplinary and institutional terrain."[68]

Is cultural studies a discipline, an interdiscipline, a multidiscipline, a critical interdiscipline, or a counterdiscipline? Klein obfuscates rather than clarifies: "A critical interdisciplinarity conceived in opposition to both disciplinary and past interdisciplinary practices is counterdisciplinary in stance, usually multidisciplinary in form, sometimes collaborative in its work patterns, and transdisciplinary in its creation of a broadly shared category of culture. . . . The label 'cultural studies' will continue to have a characteristic 'elasticity.' It is not so much a specific discipline or theoretical and political tradition as a 'gravitational field' in which a number of traditions and forces are finding a 'provisional rendezvous.' "[69] Indeed, evasion of these questions seems a hallmark of those who advocate cultural studies. Everywhere or nowhere, cultural studies is a cross- or multidisciplinary subfield or approach, neither a discipline nor an interdiscipline.

Critiques

The case against interdisciplinary cultural studies and interdisciplinarity through cultural studies is made just as forcefully. Critics share a few common themes. They are repeated frequently. In *The Marketplace of Ideas: Reform and Resistance in the American University*, Louis Menand deplores what he terms "the revolution in the humanities," whose epicenter is cultural studies. Like other critics, Menand equates interdisciplinarity with antidisciplinarity, arguing that what he calls "new paradigms" or fields of study "defined themselves essentially in antagonisms toward traditional disciplines" and "justified themselves as means of accommodating what the old paradigms were leaving out." He points to women's studies, gay and lesbian studies, and postcolonial studies, as well as science studies, all of which gather under the umbrella of cultural studies, as "nondepartmental by bureaucratic design" and "interdisciplinary by definition." He blames "the marriage of theoretical positions that the disciplines are limiting and factitious ways to organize knowledge with the institutional failure, initially, to integrate new areas of inquiry adequately into the traditional departments." But does it follow from the "perception of a gender bias in the disciplines . . . that . . . its spirit was, in the beginning, fundamentally anti-disciplinary"? Paradoxically, Menand goes on to contend that "interdisciplinarity is not, as a thing in itself, subversive or transformational or even new. . . . When you ask [people] why interdisciplinarity is important, they often answer by saying that it solves the problem of disciplinarity. But this is a non sequitur. Interdisciplinarity is simply disciplinarity raised to a higher power."[70]

Even odder is Menand's construction of a subsequent move toward postdisciplinarity. In his view, after the 1990s there was no "return to disciplinarity" but "a movement in two only partly related directions: toward interdisciplinarity and toward what might be called postdisciplinarity. . . . These terms are harder to define than they seem. What true interdisciplinarity might look like no one really knows. Postdisciplinarity signifies a variety of tendencies, including methodological eclecticism, boundary-crossing work (a literature professor writing on music or fashion), post-professionalism (writing for a non-academic audience), and the role of the public intellectual."[71] Menand is troubled that, by erasing the separation between the academic and the non-academic worlds, these moves are on a slippery slope.[72] As the declarations of its proponents reveal, it is easy to confuse cultural studies as a field—whether discipline, multidiscipline, interdiscipline, antidiscipline, or postdiscipline—with cultural studies as a critical, reshaping influence on the disciplines.[73]

English professor Michael Bérubé slides back and forth across this line in "What's the Matter with Cultural Studies?" In his view, the story is one of grandiose aspirations and unfulfilled promises. "Cultural studies hasn't had much of an impact at all," he declares. "In the late 1980s and early 1990s, we heard (and I believed) that cultural studies would fan out across the disciplines of the humanities and the social sciences, inducing them to become at once more self-critical and more open to public engagement. Some people even suggested, in either hope or fear, that cultural studies would become the name for the humanities and social sciences in toto." In comparing "institutional achievements" to "initial hopes," however, he is disappointed. "In most universities, cultural studies has no home at all, which means (among other things) that graduate students doing work in cultural studies have to hope they'll be hired in some congenial department that has a cultural studies component." He is pleased to find cultural studies work in various departments. But "the bad news is that the place where cultural studies has arguably had the greatest impact is in English departments," which "are just a tiny part of the university."[74]

Bérubé's most serious critique focuses on the intellectual dimension of cultural studies. In his view, cultural studies is "misunderstood" by cultural studies scholars as "coextensive with the study of popular culture. . . . It is what we get for saying . . . that cultural studies has no specific methodology or subject matter." His conclusion in this respect parallels my own. "The result is that cultural studies now means everything and nothing: it has effectively been conflated with 'cultural criticism' in general, and associated with a cheery 'Pop culture is fun!' " The field's final failing, in Bérubé view, is political: "Cultural studies has had negligible impact on the American academic left in a political sense."[75] Neither a discipline nor an interdiscipline, cultural studies nonetheless remains his only hope for a better understanding of hegemony.

Perhaps the most sweeping condemnation of cultural studies is Stanley Fish's polemical 1989 presidential address to the Modern Language Association, "Being Interdisciplinary Is So Very Hard to Do." Fish's target is what he identifies as a "recent and urgent agenda [for an] interdisciplinarity [that] seems to flow naturally from the imperatives of left culturalist theory, that is, from deconstruction, Marxism, feminism, the radical version of neopragmatism, and the new historicism." Reductionistically, Fish asserts that what unites this coterie is their hostility "to the current arrangement of things as represented by (1) the social structures by means of which the lines of political authority are maintained and (2) the institutional structure by means of which the various academic disciplines establish and extend their territorial claims." He condemns their "antiprofessionalism," which he equates with their critique of academic disciplines. Cultural studies is the link between interdisciplinarity and this attack on the academy.[76]

In 1999, John Brenkman took another tack, almost defining cultural studies away. "Cultural studies, in this its moment of ascendancy, exhibits an exuberant ignorance of itself. It takes great pride in going beyond literature, high culture, and disciplinarity. It defines itself as just this threefold transcendence. But what exactly is the practice of cultural studies?" Cultural studies, he declares, is literature. It belongs to high culture. It "requires an extraordinary level of educational attainment, the mastery of rarefied styles of discourse and argument, and, most importantly, a methodically alienated attitude toward ordinary cultural objects, practices, and experiences. It bears all the marks of the elite and specialized training on which it depends." Therefore, he concludes, cultural studies amounts to "intellectual mystification."[77]

Beyond Disciplinarity

What *is* cultural studies? The question is more relevant for this field than for most interdisciplines. And how, and to what degree, has cultural studies become institutionalized? To a surprising, but perhaps revealing, extent, the literature on cultural studies has little to say about its social organization. Only the major professional organizations—the Cultural Studies Association (CSA) in the United States, along with its namesakes in Australia, Canada, Finland, Japan, Spain, Switzerland, Taiwan, and Turkey and its counterparts in Korea, Norway, and the United Kingdom—seriously address the question.

The CSA mission is "to create and promote an effective community of cultural studies practitioners and scholars; to represent the discipline and its committed practitioners everywhere; and to advance cultural studies knowledges, projects, approaches, and methodologies throughout the world." It describes itself as "the nation's largest network of cultural studies practitioners: scholars, educators, artists, and activists." Its internal organization resembles that of the Social Science History Association, though its networks, which are called working groups, seem to lack the vigor of those in the SSHA. According to its website, "members gather to debate the latest events and theories, as well as host conference sessions, roundtables, and seminars" in these groups. As of December 2013, the working groups are

Critical Feminist Studies	Cultural Policy Studies
Culture and War	Environment, Space and Place
Globalisms	Literature

Media and Cinema   Media Interventions
Pedagogy   Racial and Ethnic Studies
Technology   Theories of Cultural Studies
Visual Culture

The CSA also publishes an online journal, *Lateral,* which is "designed to foster experimentation and collaboration. . . . It is committed to critical studies of culture that advance and extend the reach of cultural studies as a field and method of inquiry and as an intellectual/political project." The journal is organized by "research threads . . . curated" by people who disseminate calls for papers, develop "material through a dialogic peer review process," and work with a production team. After publication, "thread editors invite responses, reflections, and elaborations. . . . These co-lateral interventions may take a variety of forms— visual, aural, textual." The latest issue (as of fall 2014) includes threads on "Culture Industries—Critical Purchase in Neoliberal Times," an edited conversation among four persons; "Universities in Question," with four manifestos and three SmartActions; "Declaration of the Occupation of New York City"; "Theory—In Search of Digital Feminisms" with five contributions; and an explanatory video. There are no responses to earlier "threads."[78]

In response to my inquiries, the CSA reported that it had about 540 members, mainly academics, of whom about 80 percent are graduate students. The organization does not keep track of members' disciplinary affiliations, but the officers listed "English, Media Studies, Communication, History, Women's Studies, Gender Studies, Philosophy, and other humanities fields (as well as Cultural Studies, of course)."[79] The introduction to the program of the Eleventh Annual Meeting, "Beyond Disciplinarity: Interventions in Cultural Studies in the Arts," held at Columbia College, Chicago, in May 2013, stated:

> This year's conference focuses on the possibilities that open up when Cultural Studies moves laterally across disciplines within institutions of higher education and sectors beyond them. It showcases sessions and work that reflect on the nature, limits, and merits of interdisciplinarity and transdisciplinary practices across the humanities, social sciences, and the arts. It aims to build collaborations among scholars, artists, and activists committed to reorganizing and redistributing the sensibilities and assumptions that shape those knowledge fields and practices. At a moment when the so-called "crisis of the humanities" is proclaimed across the political spectrum both inside and outside the university, we see this focus on cross-disciplinary and cross-sectional exchanges as particularly urgent.

What instantiations of the humanities do we want to defend as we look forward? Which should we jettison? How can the long critical engagement of Cultural Studies with the humanities (and its fellow travelers) allow us to identify and invoke new publics and audiences for the artifacts we create and the claims we make about them?

The call for papers prompted over 700 submissions, and over 500 people were "expected to attend, representing more than 22 countries and 190 institutions." The index of participants lists just 443 names, a surprising number of which appear in multiple sessions.[80]

Describing the academic programs that fall under the umbrella of cultural studies seems impossible, so diffuse and all-encompassing is this field. Online searches turn up countless programs at institutions large and small, public and private, classroom and online, not-for-profit and for-profit. They appear as departments, programs, majors, and minors that offer associate's, bachelor's, and PhD degrees. The number of specializations, subspecializations, and emphases are endless. They include liberal arts, social science, and interdisciplinary studies; disciplines such as history, English, sociology, psychology, political science, geography, philosophy, cultural anthropology, media studies, and communication; ethnic studies and area studies; women, gender, and sexuality studies; and preprofessional fields such as public administration and policy, organizational management, and human services.[81] A website touting "popular career options" lists publishing, public relations, journalism, writing, editing, social work, museum administration, media comment, program development, and documentary filmmaking, as well as academia. A wide array of topics is listed under "program coursework": theories, histories, and practices of cultural studies; race theory; political and cultural representations; rhetorics of culture; political economy and culture; sexuality and gender; post-colonialism; social institutions; nation, race, and ethnicity; and visual culture and performance.[82]

Well established and coherent institutes, some with degree programs, exhibit great diversity in their focus: the Humanities Center at Harvard; the Center for Global Studies at Johns Hopkins, a fusion of the Institute for Global Studies, Power, and History with the Program in Atlantic History, Culture, and Society; the Center for Cultural Sociology and the Media and Cultural Studies Program at Wisconsin; and the Center for Arts and Cultural Policy Studies at Princeton.

Although many academic journals, especially in the humanities, publish "new cultural studies" of literature, history, media, or popular culture, only a handful focus specifically on cultural studies: *Cultural Studies* in the UK; the *International Journal of Cultural Studies*; *European Journal of Cultural Studies*; *Theory, Culture, and Society*; and U.S.–based journals such as *Social Text* and *New Formations*. The mission statement of *Cultural Studies* is representative of the field's broad reach and its confusion of subjects, methods, and goals: "*Cultural Studies* is an international journal which explores the relation between cultural practices, everyday life, material, economic, political, geographical and historical contexts. It fosters more open analytic, critical and political conversations by encouraging people to push the dialogue into fresh, uncharted territory. It also aims to intervene in the processes by which the existing techniques, institutions and structures of power are reproduced, resisted and transformed. *Cultural Studies* understands the term 'culture' inclusively rather than exclusively, and publishes essays which encourage significant intellectual and political experimentation, intervention and dialogue."[83]

Cultural studies has a strong presence in many other fields and organizations, including American studies; other area studies; women's, gender, and sexuality studies; and ethnic studies. The attribution of interdisciplinarity to these fields is a common source of confusion.[84] At most, they are multidisciplinary; at the least, they constitute a loosely connected miscellany. American studies, which is often treated as the poster child for interdisciplinary cultural studies, is primarily literary and historical, although its interests and methodologies have recently expanded. The American Studies Association website announces that the ASA "is the nation's oldest and largest association devoted to the interdisciplinary study of American culture and history," but it is only partly or occasionally interdisciplinarity, as Jerry Jacobs's *In Defense of Disciplines* shows.

American studies and other so-called hyphenated studies are generally associated with the political left, as critics and proponents alike observe. Criticism of and dissent from national and global politics, social-cultural relations, and political economy, as well as from the corporate or neoliberal university, are significant contexts for cultural studies and American studies. Indeed, they constitute both cause and consequence for these forms of asserted interdisciplinarity. American studies and, to an even greater degree, other area studies were sponsored by the federal government as intellectual tools for the international promotion of Western political, cultural, and institutional arrangements from the 1940s through the Cold War and various "alliances for progress." While the political commitments of cultural studies scholars are often remarked, the transformations in area and American studies—which remain partial, given continu-ing governmental contributions—have gone largely unnoticed. These contra-dictions call out for sustained inquiry. The place of politics and ideology and that of governmental and corporate support for interdisciplinarity lack the atten-tion they demand.[85]

Conclusion

What is the relationship of cultural studies to disciplines, area studies, and topics or subjects within them, such as women, gender, and sexuality studies or ethnic studies? Do we gain, or lose, by uncritically declaring them all in-terdisciplinarity? Cultural studies may serve as an important answer to that question.[86]

I give the last words in this chapter to John Guillory's unusually broad, yet penetrating, historical and philosophical reflections on the so-called Sokal hoax, when physicist Alan Sokal had a fake essay accepted and published in a special issue of *Social Text* on "the science wars." Guillory considers disciplinar-ity within and across the humanities and the sciences. He is concerned with relations and locations. Placing cultural studies in historical context, he argues that "the division of the disciplines cannot be reduced to the difference between positivism"—the sciences and social sciences—"and skepticism"—the humani-ties as interpretive and critical—"any more than it can be elevated to the great war of Left and Right. . . . Its relation to both sets of antagonisms is more complex, more historically ambiguous. The fact that . . . several antagonisms are confused in the spontaneous postmodernism of the literary academy suggests that it is a mistake to channel these antagonisms through the conflict of the faculties" in the humanities and the sciences.[87]

Guillory proposes a reorientation of the relationships between and within disciplinary clusters. Criticism of the sort advocated by the humanities and social sciences "might now advance by withdrawing from the conflict. If positiv-ism is a holistic or totalizing ideology that reserves the name of knowledge only for the results of the scientific method (narrowly defined), it does not follow that the critical disciplines must be based on a counterholism in which everything is interpretation, in which the very possibility of a positive knowledge is called into question."[88]

Guillory's primary concern is with the humanities, not the sciences, and particularly with the identification and criticism of what he calls "spontaneous criticism," which can be taken as roughly synonymous with cultural studies. He proposes to stop allegorizing the disciplines, a move that others might construe as reification, reductionism, or universalization.

> Let us above all acknowledge the danger of allegorizing the disciplines as representative of inherent political or philosophical positions. The cost of this allegorization has been very heavy for those who do literary and cultural studies. Having failed to settle the epistemic status of their criticism, which threatens always to fall to the level of mere opinion, the critics have embraced their abjection and turned it around into its opposite, into epistemic superiority. The division of the disciplines into sciences and humanities has been triumphantly reconceived as the distinction between *knowledge* and the *critique of knowledge*. It is by no means necessary to deny the value of critique in order to make the argument that the critique of knowledge is not the privilege of one discipline or group of disciplines.[89]

Although he addresses the relationships between different structures and organizations of knowledge across disciplines, rather than interdisciplinarity per se, Guillory speaks to two of the major issues surrounding interdisciplinarity. The first is the power of a supposedly science-based model or ideal of interdisciplinarity and its influence on other disciplines and disciplinary clusters. The second is the dichotomization and opposition between scientific and cultural views or definitions of interdisciplinary in the many forms in which we encounter them. Both are dangerous sources of confusion. Guillory continues with respect to cultural and literary studies: "To insist further upon adherence to a series of more or less formulaic and therefore spontaneous positions—antirealism, relativism, antifoundationalism, interpretive holism—is to condemn literary and cultural studies to rehearse without surpassing the conflict of cultural criticism with science."[90]

Cultural studies' complications are exceptional. In my view, it needs to deal with issues and questions involving its own multiplicity and its own histories before presuming to be interdisciplinary, multidisciplinary, or disciplinary, whether in academe or the public square. Does Guillory offer, at least in theory, a new path to interdisciplinarity? Or perhaps another way to think about intersections among disciplines, multidisciplines, and interdisciplines? Cultural studies' relations to the disciplines remain muddled and contradictory. In this respect, it may be more similar to materials science, in theory and practice, than we might otherwise expect.

Materials science and nanotechnology may well offer a salutary example in embracing multidisciplinarity, finding a location and a level of organization, and inquiring about disciplinarity interrelations, rather than engaging in an endless quest for interdisciplinarity. How it deals with the challenges of nano-ethics and nanoaesethetics—in accepting the dimensions and limits, and connecting the arts and humanities with the sciences—may prove heuristic to cultural studies and the humanities.

CHAPTER SIX

The Past and Future of Interdisciplinarity

Bioscience and Literacy Studies

How does interdisciplinarity matter? The long and complicated history reviewed in these pages supports a strong argument to limit use of the word and its associated vocabulary. Those who pronounce transdisciplinarity or, more recently with respect to bioscience, convergence to be "beyond interdisciplinarity" are seldom aware of the baggage that both those terms carry.[1] Is there more heat than light in all the fuss over interdisciplinarity? The institutionally and personally costly grandstanding on all sides of these debates has failed to make clear the advances that interdisciplinarity facilitates.[2] Is interdisciplinarity mainly a matter for groups of natural scientists in applied fields, or for metaphysicians, epistemologists, and philosophers of language?

These are very real questions in 2015, as they were in 1980, 1950, or 1910. This history shows clearly the uses and abuses, fads and achievements, and limits of interdisciplinarity. To say that there is no single answer to questions regarding interdisciplinarity is only to begin to ask better questions, which requires caution and humility, as well as precise definitions and cogent logic. Better questions affect how we understand the past and, most importantly, the present and future of research and education.

What is at stake is nothing less than the framing of efforts to make progress on major intellectual and social problems; issues of public policy; expectations and anticipations; the allocation of resources, including the time and efforts of people and institutions; the articulation of organizations and structures; and professional careers and human lives. Declared and undeclared interdisciplinary "wars" on enemies or aliens ranging from poverty and disease to genes, the brain, outer space, and offending groups or nations underscore the importance of getting it right. The history of interdisciplinarity is littered with great expectations and disappointed hopes, as well as being replete with sheer absurdity, wasteful competition, and hurtful personal invective. Willful and negligent ignorance and incomprehension may be found on all sides. Overly inflated ambitions mingle promiscuously with disciplinary divides, jealous name-calling, and images that run the gamut from mad scientists heading up large teams with huge budgets, Internet, and Skype empires to lonely humanists longing for digital connections and online databases.

The "name game" in which interdisciplinarity is construed by listing or denying disciplines is symptomatic of the severe problems that result from multiple, conflicting, and contradictory discourses in which dichotomies substitute for clarity. Definitions are often absent; transdisciplinarity is an especially egregious example. The endless typologies, classifications, and hierarchies of multi-, inter-, and transdisciplinarities are not helpful. Most important, we must recognize that interdisciplines could not exist without disciplines; mutually and reciprocally, they shape and reshape each other.

Inseparable from these complications is the conflict between interdisciplinarity as synthetic, basic, and nonspecialized and interdisciplinarity as advanced, specialized, and groundbreaking. Both kinds of initiatives claim to be novel,[3] except when they allege to be rediscovering wisdom and precedents from the past. It is possible that contradictory paths lead to interdisciplinarity, but neither the common discourse nor institutional arrangements allow or encourage that multiplicity. It is especially problematic that proclaimed interdisciplines ignore their relationships to disciplines. Throughout this history, and still today, efforts to understand interdisciplinary are marked by a signal failure to scrutinize definitions, disciplinary and interdisciplinary relationships, and the locations, organization, and institutionalization of declared or developing interdisciplines.

I am not asserting that such systematic and flexible attention would resolve all the complications, but I do think that it would be a major step forward. Recognizing differences, tightening sloppy language and thinking, and promoting respectful exchanges and strategic planning would do even more. Not to be utopian, this approach also suggests different relationships between and among the sciences, social sciences, humanities, technical and professional fields, and "pure" and applied endeavors.[4]

Of one thing there should be no doubt: interdisciplinarity is regularly and profoundly misunderstood. Yet I remain a believer, albeit with qualifications, as a result of my education; my experience as a researcher, writer, and teacher; my various university roles and responsibilities; the influence of the world in which I grew up; and my sense of the world we now inhabit and how we might make it better. More specifically, that experience includes formative activities as a historian in literacy studies; children, youth, and family studies; urban studies; and in the development of interdisciplinary programs in very different institutions and at different levels, most recently, founding and building

LiteracyStudies@OSU, a university-wide interdisciplinary initiative at Ohio State University.[5]

As we conclude, I consider two avowed interdisciplines that are very much of the moment: literacy studies and bioscience / molecular biology. Although hardly a broadly recognized area of study, literacy studies certainly identifies itself as interdisciplinary. In the popular imaginary, literacy is a sine qua non of civilization and progress for individuals, societies, and nations. It exists in dizzying numbers of varieties but also seems resistant to universal transmission. Bioscience—or, more narrowly, molecular biology—is much more readily identified, in part because of its associations with healthcare, government, and corporations.[6] It, too, is inseparable from images of progress but sometimes is feared because of its power to do harm if unregulated or uncontrolled.

Like the other pairs of case studies, bioscience and literacy studies share important elements. Both proclaim their novelty. Bioscience seems to presume its interdisciplinarity uncritically and without explication, but it remains deeply rooted in its disciplinary and multidisciplinary past; after all, biology itself developed as the convergence of separate disciplines. It also has substantial applied and commercial elements. Literacy studies, too, seems to have formed at the crux between the long tradition of reading and writing and contemporary concerns for the mobilization of disempowered social groups. Bioscience and literacy studies both campaign relentlessly for recognition, institutionalization, and funding. Both are tied to quests for national economic and cultural superiority. Both, although sometimes contradictorily, promote their commitment to making a better world.

At the same time, both fields neglect, to their detriment, the disciplinary and interdisciplinary relationships on which they are built and to which they seek to contribute. Without a critical examination of their history of internal divisions, they tend to reduplicate rather than resolve them. Literacy studies in particular is unusually riven by dichotomies, beginning with literacy/illiteracy, literacy/orality, and reading/writing. Other chronic problems arise from the confusion of parts with wholes. Bioscience resembles operations research, materials science, and cognitive science: waiting for convergence may be like waiting for Godot.

Bioscience

In his history of modern biology, Garland Allen observes that "in recent years the term 'molecular biology' has become fashionable and its uses varied. For some it has become synonymous with biochemistry practiced 'without a license,' as one writer has remarked. For others it is a shibboleth for getting onto the band-wagon of research funding; for still others it is nothing more than a branch of ultrastructural biology, carried down to the level of molecular architecture. John Kendrew, an x-ray crystallographer, has pointed out that, in fact, although the term is frequently used, many molecular biologists are not even clear on exactly what their subject is about." Like other multidisciplinary areas of research that have struggled for location, organization, and institutionalization among established disciplines, molecular biology confronted problems of both definition and relationships. According to W. T. Astbury, Allen explains, "it implies not so much a technique as an approach, an approach from the viewpoint of the so-called basic sciences with the leading idea of searching below large-scale manifestations of classical biology for the corresponding molecular plan. . . . This definition is incomplete. It only hints at the relation between molecular form and function, the keynote of the present-day conception of molecular biology."[7]

Writing in the mid-1970s, Allen essays:

> Current "molecular biology" includes not only a structural and functional element, but also an informational element. It is concerned with the structure of biologically important molecules (such as proteins or nucleic acids) in terms of how they function in the metabolism of the cell and how they carry specific biological information. The methods of physics and structural chemistry (such as x-ray diffraction of crystalline molecules, and molecular model building) have been employed to investigate molecular architecture, while biochemistry has been used to determine how large molecules interact with each other and with smaller molecules outside the cell. Historically, three lines of thinking have gone into the formation of molecular biology as we know it today.

Structural, biochemical, and informational approaches existed as relatively separate areas until the 1950s. Only with their fusion did molecular biology achieve a preeminent position.[8]

In 2009, the U.S. National Research Council (NRC) issued a report entitled *A New Biology for the 21st Century*. Its goal, which was written into the committee's title, was "Ensuring the United States Leads the Coming Biology Revolution." Two years later, MIT's *The Third Revolution: The Convergence of the Life Sciences, Physical Sciences, and Engineering* was issued by a committee headed by Nobel Prize–winning biologist Philip Sharp. These documents are signs of our times and signposts in the history of interdisciplinarity. "Integration" marks the "new biology" of the coming revolution; "convergence" heralds the "third revolution." Neither report acknowledges that these terms are not transparent, or even new.

The history of biology has been a succession of one "new biology" after another, at least in the 1910s, 1930s, 1950s, and 1980s; genetic biology, biochemistry, and molecular biology have all been hailed as "revolutionary." All have precipitated fierce battles over disciplinarization and departmentalization (often between science departments, agricultural colleges, and medical schools) and sown divisions among biologists as well as chemists and physicists. They have had problematic relationships with the established field of biology and struggled for place and position.

A New Biology begins with a familiar refrain of "revolutionary change" but does not acknowledge that the term has been used many times before: "Biological research is in the midst of a revolutionary change due to the integration of powerful technologies along with new concepts and methods derived from inclusion of physical sciences, mathematics, computational sciences, and engineering. As never before, advances in biological sciences hold tremendous promise for surmounting many of the major challenges confronting the United States and the world. Historically, major advances in science have provided solutions to economic and social challenges. . . . Scientific efforts based on meeting societal needs have laid the foundations for countless new products, industries, even entire economic sectors that were unimagined when the work began." Proclaiming "the fundamental unity of biology," proponents propose that the new biology represents a point of convergence, much as the advocates of genetic biology did in the early twentieth century.

> The essence of the New Biology is integration—re-integration of the many subdisciplines of biology, and the integration into biology of physicists, chemists, computer scientists, engineers, and mathematicians to create a research community, with the capacity to tackle a broad range of economic and societal problems. The committee chose biological approaches to solving problems in the areas of food, environment, energy, and health as the most inspiring goals to drive the development of the New Biology. But these are not the only problems that we both hope and expect a thriving New Biology to be able to address: fundamental questions in all areas of biology, from understanding the brain to carbon cycling in the ocean, will all be more tractable as the New Biology grows into a flourishing reality.[9]

A "New Biology" mandates a "New Biologist," who

> is not a scientist who knows a little bit about all disciplines, but a scientist with deep knowledge in one discipline and basic "fluency" in several. One implication of this is that not all "New Biologists" are, now, or will in the future be, biologists!

The physicists who study how the laws of physics play out in the crowded and de-cidedly non-equilibrium environment of the cell, or the mathematicians who de-rive new equations to describe the complex network interactions that characterize living systems are New Biologists as well as being physicists or mathematicians. In fact, the New Biology includes any scientist, mathematician, or engineer striv-ing to apply his or her expertise to the understanding and application of living systems.[10]

"Everyone a new biologist" traces a pathbreaking circuit through or around the disciplines. But does it lead to interdisciplinarity?

The MIT version treats convergence as a synonym for integration. *The Third Revolution* seeks to "to delineate an important new research model—convergence—which draws on an ongoing merger of life, physical, and engineer-ing sciences." Propelling the contemporary merger mania, "this new model is being adopted at many institutions in different forms. The past decade has seen the evolution of new interdisciplinary research areas—bioinformatics, synthetic biology, nanobiology, computational biology, tissue engineering, biomaterials, and systems biology are examples. These new fields share a comparable, underlying research model, convergence, and there is a need to see them as a unity in order to ensure their continued progress. The successful application of this model will require not simply collaboration between disciplines, but true disciplinary integration." Just how these allegedly interdisciplinary research fields are to be integrated is never specified, beyond the circular reasoning that leads back to the invocation of this "underlying research model, convergence." What is alter-nately called a "new paradigm" and a "dynamic and emerging field" holds the promise of producing "critical advances in a broad variety of sciences." In par-ticular, it constitutes "a blueprint for addressing the healthcare challenges of the 21st century by providing a new knowledge base, as well as a new generation of diagnostics and therapeutics." Among the challenges is that of "embedding convergence" within the programs of the major research sponsors, particularly the National Institutes of Health, the primary audience for a report addressed to "Dear Colleagues."[11]

As the "third biomedical revolution," convergence follows "the first revolu-tion: molecular and cellular biology" and the "second revolution: genomics." Recognizing, if only momentarily, that assertions do not suffice as definitions, the report asks, "What exactly is convergence?" What follows, however, is hopelessly diffuse: "the merging of distinct technologies, processing disciplines, or devices into a unified whole that creates a host of new pathways and opportunities. It involves the coming together of different fields of study—particularly engineering, physical sciences, and life sciences—through collaboration among research groups and integration of approaches that were originally viewed as distinct and potentially contradictory." In the forecasting of *The Third Revolution*, convergence is a blueprint for innovation. But it promises much more. "The convergence revolution is a paradigm shift, but not just in Thomas Kuhn's terms, a paradigm shift *within* a discipline. Convergence means a broad rethinking of how all scientific research can be conducted, so that we can capitalize on *a range* of knowledge bases, from microbiology to computer science to engineering design." Biomedicine will be "a major beneficiary . . . as interdisciplinary research enhances our existing knowledge and leads to new medical treatments." At the same time, convergence "challenges the historic structure of universities, which are organized into departments focusing on discrete disciplines," and the categories used for federal funding of research.[12] Although the political agenda of these reports is readily apparent, their hyperbolic rhetoric cannot be taken uncritically, whether the thrust is described as convergence, integration, or interdisciplinarity.[13] The excesses are revealing, for they are themselves historical products.[14]

Consider the discourse. Interestingly, the reports only occasionally employ the word "interdisciplinarity." *A New Biology* uses "integration" in place of "interdisciplinarity"; that is its most common substitute or synonym. But the rhetoric is inconsistent. "Fields of study," "subdisciplines," "disciplines," "interdisciplines," and "clusters of disciplines" all mix promiscuously in the move toward unity. It is never clear just what is being integrated or converging. It matters whether we consider subdisciplines, disciplines, or clusters such as the physical sciences, biological sciences, and engineering. The problems alluded to are "societal" or "economic," not questions around which specific research is designed. But "integration" takes place, interdisciplinary relationships develop and are practiced, and programs, centers, and institutes are built around those questions and amid those subfields. Economic leadership among nations may, or may not, result; that economic leadership may result is a great leap made for transparent and self-serving reasons.

Language shifts without acknowledgement into concept and conceptualization. "Convergence means a broad rethinking of how all scientific research can be conducted, so that we can capitalize on *a range* of knowledge bases, from microbiology to computer science to engineering design. In other words, the convergence revolution does not rest on a particular scientific advance but on a new integrated approach for achieving advances."[15] Convergence, the MIT report tells us, is a research method. But it is more metaphor than method, which disqualifies it from interdisciplinarity. This approach is dismissive of comparisons and relationships among disciplines.

Searching for unity and searching to escape unity are central both to arguments in favor of interdisciplines and to the animus against them. "Unity" itself demands explication. Some biologists are committed to the unity of the biological sciences (or is it the unity of life?), while others disavow it. Geneticists are a leading case in point. Philosophers of science, who are sometimes very distant from their subject, readily proclaim or decry the integration of biology. For example, one philosopher attacks both biologists and other philosophers and confuses integration with reductionism. "Philosophical theories about reduction and integration in science are at variance with what is happening in science. A realistic approach to science shows that possibilities for reduction and integration are limited. The classical ideal of a unified science has long since been rejected in philosophy. But the current emphasis on integration in philosophy and in science shows that it survives in a different guise. . . . Methodological analysis shows that many of the grand interdisciplinary theories involving biology represent pseudo-integration covered up by inappropriate, overgeneral concepts."[16] While this critique is overstated (though no more so than the praises of the convergence revolution), its call to pay attention to the actual work of science is salutary. The prophets of unity, integration, and convergence are not in touch with many working scientists, philosophers of science, and especially historians and science studies scholars.[17]

The question of interdisciplinarity and unity in bioscience has been the subject of long-standing debates among scientists and historians, sociologists, and philosophers of science.[18] These debates and the differences on which they are based will never be resolved to the satisfaction of all, but they deserve consideration. For example, in pursuit of relationships between and among disciplines in biological sciences, Lindley Darden and Nancy Maull have explored "interfield theories." William Bechtel, interested in "integrating scientific disciplines," has suggested that biochemistry developed from a "cross-disciplinary endeavor that discovered a distinctive domain" and (in 1986) "show[ed] all the signs of an independent discipline." This philosopher of science focuses on the "cognitive," arguing that "developments in the understanding of the subject matter of biochemistry provided a basis for its autonomous status." While others examine the practices, locations, and sociological characteristics of a discipline and often come to opposing conclusions, Bechtel saw in the 1930s a new awareness that "the subject matter is not part of either organic chemistry or of physiology, but lies between."[19] Without definition, historian of molecular biology Pnina Abir-Am calls it "a new scientific discipline" or "a highly successful and recent 'ultra-discipline.'" She describes it "as a broad transdisciplinary movement of people and ideas at the interface of biology, physics, and chemistry" that "became a sociohistorical reality in the 1930s"; however, "not until a generation later, in the 1960s, did the scientific establishment begin to register and respond to this ongoing restructuring of the scientific order away from traditional disciplinary regimes, with their monopolies over the academic reproduction of 'knowledge-power' systems and resulting social control."[20] Philosopher and M.D. Kenneth Schaffner, in contrast, challenges notions of convergence. "It would thus seem that *for the present and foreseeable future* neurobiology as well as general biology will not be fully reducible sciences."[21]

In a synoptic piece on molecular biology, historian of biology Robert Olby offers a more complex version that nonetheless exemplifies some basic problems that most accounts share. He writes, "the second half of the twentieth century witnessed a transformation in our understanding of certain key mechanisms fundamental to life. . . . More than a toolkit and manual, molecular biology represents a combination of approaches of the chemist, biochemist, geneticist, and microbiologist, and offers a unifying conceptual structure provided by the mechanism and genetic determinants of protein synthesis. It can hardly be called a discipline, however because its techniques have been absorbed by biochemists and geneticists, by embryologists, immunologists, and ecologists, and their disciplines have not blended." If so, then "why has molecular biology stirred up so much adverse comment? . . . Molecular biology is interdisciplinary to an extent biochemistry never was before biochemists faced those who were to call themselves molecular biologists." In his view, molecular biologists, unlike biochemists, attend to genetics, structural crystallography, and nucleic acids.[22]

Is it possible that bioscience, when examined with a view toward its development, disciplinary relationships, locations, organization, and institutionalization may be, selectively, a discipline, multidiscipline, and interdiscipline? In that way it would resemble operations research, cognitive studies, materials science, and communication. Other fields spend more words asserting their interdisciplinarity. This view is consistent with the discussions of interdisciplinarity in the periodical *BioScience* and accounts of the development of molecular biology, bioscience, and their foundations.[23] A common representation of bioscience shows its principal components of genetics, biochemistry, and molecular biology (figure 6.1). Without overinterpreting a simple schematic, the absence of interconnections between the components is provocative. The matter is even more telling

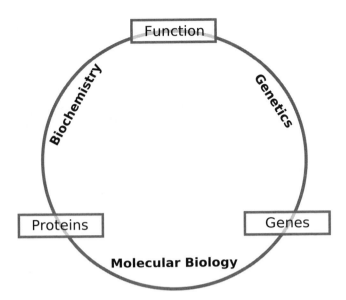

Figure 6.1 Molecular biology. The Wikipedia representation of the bioscience field shows the principal components of genetics, biochemistry, and molecular biology yet neglects to designate interconnections among them. "Schematic relationship between biochemistry, genetics and molecular biology," by OldakQuill, http://commons .wikimedia.org/wiki/File:Schematic_relationship_between_biochemistry,_genetics _and_molecular_biology.svg, CC BY 2.5

when we realize that all three of these bases struggled for intellectual recognition and are still fighting for institutional autonomy in the form of disciplinary and interdisciplinary location and organization, including departmental status. The multiple subfields and specializations in the life sciences add layers of division and difference to an emerging understanding. Despite the symmetry, this is not a picture of unification.

The history of the biosciences and molecular biology is much more interesting than a grand tableau or teleological epic of integration and convergence would suggest.[24] Biology and bioscience are deeply divided fields. Continuing conflicts over genetics, biotechnology, biohazards, and bioethics are indicative. How often is this the stuff of science fiction and apocalyptic fantasies! Convergence is a pipe dream, yet the fact that interdisciplinary is asserted within a set of multidisciplinary and intradisciplinary relationships is nonetheless important. Identifying and studying those developments could teach us a great deal. The work at the Cavendish Laboratory in Cambridge that led to modeling the structure of DNA was one critical location. So too was earlier work on genes and proteins at Caltech.[25] That those processes and connections only partly represent the nature and the workings of these sciences does not minimize their advances and contributions.

In the biological sciences the sum of the parts is greater than the whole. Bioscience is a series of fragments rather than any singular entity, as the diversity of its organizational forms and lack of major integrating organizations indicate. Understanding interdisciplinarity as part of larger historical processes of scientific practice, understanding, and development—pursuing problems and questions in context—leads us in new and different directions.

The biological sciences (a much more useful term than bioscience) often succeed without cohering. Recognizing that fact allows us to grapple with a history replete with conflict, rigidity, and rupture. And such grappling, I argue, is a very good thing for understanding interdisciplinarity in science and elsewhere. Such an approach remains dynamic and interactive. It keeps the relationships between and among disciplines, their parts, and their comings-together (long-term and short) and resulting locations (no matter how long or short in duration), organization, and institutionalization clearly in view.

When interdisciplinarity does develop, it is located quite variously among disciplines: in the sciences, agriculture, and medicine; among biologists (and within their divisions of genetics, embryology, and cytology), chemists (including physiologists and physical chemists), biochemists, who struggled for a place, and physicists (including biophysicists and crystallographers). Today, divisions and constantly changing patterns of cooperation and competition between academic and research science, academic and medical science, research and applied science, and university and corporate bioscience persist. That prophets of corruption and malignancy line up on all sides is understandable.[26] In fact, it is possible that when technology finds a home in many places and has commercial as well as medical potential, its research and development advance for the lack of institutional consolidation. This may be the case for other fields as well.

Bioscience is a revealing case among the interdisciplines. Abir-Am has been at great pains to criticize myth creation, hero worship, rhetoric, genres and orders of legitimation, deterministic sociology, and apologetics in histories of modern biology.[27] Recent works in history and science studies raise a number of important issues that impinge on interdisciplinarity in bioscience and molecular biology, and other fields as well. These issues prominently include myths, conflicts, and disciplinary relationships.

The history of molecular science and bioscience since at least the 1920s is characterized by neither unity nor convergence but by a few moments of partial integration amid many bitter conflicts. Central to this story are the conflict-ridden relationships among biologists and other scientists, including geneticists, chemists, physical chemists, and physicists, that the myths of convergence seek to erase or dismiss. We do well to keep in mind the question: What are the uses and abuses of interdisciplinarity?

Historians of biology Soraya de Chadarevian and Jean Gaudillière reflect on these tensions: "The combination of the words 'biochemistry' and 'molecular biology' evokes debates about the definition and institutional boundaries of the two disciplines." The origins of molecular biology constitutes the largest question. "Biochemists have repeatedly stressed their contributions to the making of the new 'molecular' paradigm," especially their influence in understanding the structure of macromolecules and protein synthesis. Historians insist on "the multidisciplinary origins of molecular biology and by showing the complex, broad, and heterogeneous interests that led scientists to work on proteins and other macromolecules from the 1930s onward."[28] They could also be writing about genetics or biochemistry. Physical chemists, other physicists, and crystallographers contributed to ongoing revolutions in biology. "Spokespersons for previously established 'neighboring' disciplines initially responded to the rise of molecular biology with enthusiasm or resistance, depending primarily on their disciplinary provenance and rhetorical situations." In Abir-Am's view, they did so to defend their disciplines' "boundaries and image, rather than to reflect upon molecular biology's impact on the scientific order in its entirety." This "criticism suggests that molecular biology posed a threat to a wide range of disciplines, because it was redefining, and hence appropriating, many concepts, both central and peripheral, around which the 'classical' disciplinary monopolies were constituted."[29]

Varying degrees of support for molecular biology came from cell biology, microbiology, and microbial genetics. Resistance came chiefly from organismic biology and biochemistry, "two large, philosophically divergent, and institutionally separated disciplinary establishments." The former challenged molecular biology's claims to novelty, "especially its claim to have displaced evolution as the central problem of biology, thus upsetting the prevailing unity of the biological order." Some theorists stressed what they saw as the limited biological relevance of molecular biology, which they referred to as " 'mere' chemistry." Biochemists "resist[ed] loss of authority in the biomolecular order, a loss derived from the rediscovery of nucleic acids by molecular biologists, and their transformation into new objects such as messages of biological information, messages that transcended the biochemists' traditional preoccupation with small molecules."[30]

Myths of interdisciplinarity underlie conflicting studies of biological sciences in unquestioned, undefined, and unreflective ways. They influence both general accounts and studies of particular laboratories.[31] Recent analyses of contemporary research institutes by Rogers Hollingsworth and Ellen Jane Hollingsworth and by Eric Scerri, for example, assert the centrality of interdisciplinarity, but neither article defines it nor examines it in practice.[32] The term "interdisciplinarity" is ubiquitous in both science studies and historical research, but distinctions between cross-, multi-, inter-, or transdisciplinarity are elided. The fads and fancies of the present unavoidably infect accounts of the past. Consider for example Simcha Jong's study, "How Organizational Structures in Science Shape Spin-Off Firms: The Biochemistry Departments of Berkeley, Stanford, and UCSF and the Birth of the Biotech Industry." As an organizational sociologist, Jong adopts a teleogical, ahistorical approach in which "interdisciplinary" seems more a mantra or an ideology than a practice or relationship.[33] The gradual emergence of biochemistry, one base of molecular and biological science, has been fraught with conflicts. Not the least of them surround its location, organization, and institutionalization across science departments, medical schools, and agricultural colleges. Despite their differences, general and case studies make clear that institutional and professional contexts as well as broader political economic factors matter. Robert Kohler's classic history, *From Medical Chemistry to Biochemistry: The Making of a Biomedical Discipline*, which is framed as a political economy of science, shows this clearly: "Disciplines are not homogeneous, consensual communities. They consist of diverse segments, often identified with competing styles or programs. These different programs are adapted to different institutional contexts, and, most important, they prescribe favored relationships with other disciplines." Before 1940, "there were at least three distinct styles of biochemistry: clinical, bioorganic and biophysical, and biological. One program took from biology its concern with a broad range of fundamental processes and its tolerance of tentative solutions. Another favored the narrow problems and stringent explanations that chemists prefer. A third prescribed the utilitarian problem solving of clinical science. Each defined a style by pointing to paradigms and constituencies in other disciplines."[34]

Those differences interacted with institutionalization and professional patterns. Kohler argues that

> biochemists' programmatic conceptions of their discipline were shaped by institutional contexts and relationships, such as channels of recruitment, political alliances, and service roles. In American and many European universities, the bio-

chemists' professional role was teaching medical students and training medical graduates in clinical investigations. Biochemists depended on clinicians . . . , and clinicians depended on them. . . . Quite different relations shaped the careers of those fewer biochemists employed in departments of chemistry, physiology, and biology. Physiologists valued biochemistry as an essential subdivision of their discipline. . . . In contrast, chemists saw biochemistry as an important external marker for organic or physical chemistry. Departments of chemistry almost never appointed biochemists to their staffs. . . . Traditional biologists mistrusted biochemists' reductionist views.[35]

Kohler traces these locations and relationships, attending to differing developments at specific universities. The worlds of medicine (including physiology and pathology), agriculture, and academic sciences; research and pedagogy; and "pure" and applied science became more closely connected. But conflicts and institutional, professional, and academic obstacles continued. Kohler's central story is the transition to biochemistry departments within schools of medicine, and their role in partly reshaping biology and chemistry as well as medicine. If a singular discipline emerged, its definition, location, and relationships varied, sometimes significantly, from university to university. Interdisciplinary may well have been furthered on the margins of this uneven, irregular disciplinization process. That, however, is a hypothesis to investigate rather than to postulate.

This perspective suits the stories told by recent historians of biology.[36] A prominent example is how closely the research interests of virologist Wendell Stanley's landmark "free-standing" Department of Biochemistry at Berkeley replicated the problems of the disciplines. Angela Creager explains that, on the one hand, "Stanley achieved his mission of building the first free-standing biochemistry department in the country." He brought together biochemists from medicine and agriculture, along with "bright young recruits" and virologists who came with him from the Rockefeller Institute. On the other hand, his privileging virus research over "more conventional programs" of biochemical research created a department "fraught with political infighting." Moreover, "differences in research methodology provided additional obstacles to consolidating the previously dispersed biochemists."[37] Plant biochemists and medical biochemists differed over "structural" versus "physical" chemistry. There were also inequalities in academic responsibilities among the researchers. The department fragmented into several dispersed units and multiple departments.[38] In 1958, the medical biochemists moved to the University of California at San Francisco medical school. Studies of pioneering research across disciplines, as well as within molecular biology, emphasize the advances at UCSF and Stanford and reiterate the obstacles at Berkeley.[39]

Eric Vettel's cautionary tale, *Biotech: The Countercultural Origins of an Industry*, extends the Berkeley episodes into the larger realms of bioscience and biotechnology. With respect to Stanley and his Berkeley Virology Laboratory (BVL), Vettel argues that "it was not disciplinary rupture that thwarted an otherwise worthy effort of the BVL . . . but disciplinary rigidity. In general, rather than confront and adapt to new scientific discoveries, investigators at the BVL tried to direct them, believing in a sense that they had to control the intellectual foundations that supported their work." Failure to respond programmatically to Watson and Crick's discovery of the structure of DNA contributed to "disciplinary rupture." The environments at Stanford and UCSF differed from that at Berkeley, which meant that bioscientists faced different opportunities and institutional possibilities. Vettel characterizes Berkeley as marked by "the ascent of pure research."[40] At Stanford and UCSF, in contrast, the boundaries between medical work, "pure research," and applied science were significantly lower. This development took place at a time of new emphasis on science and its support that derived from wars hot and cold; success with vaccines against polio and other infections; groundbreaking discoveries in DNA, physical biology, and chemistry; the shock of Sputnik; and visions of government and foundation support for endless "new frontiers." At UCSF and Berkeley, the State of California also contributed financial support.[41]

Institutional leaders at Stanford, especially Frederick Terman, encouraged new directions and relationships. Eminent scientists such as Arthur Kornberg, Joshua Lederberg, and Paul Berg were hired. Federal and disciplinary networks facilitated communication and exchange. The close proximity of multiple centers in the Bay Area was especially valuable.[42]

But in the deep recesses of the field lay troubling frustrations. Bioscientists could have reflected on their own discomforting internal situations—how quickly they had expanded their field; how incessant interdepartmental tanglings had disrupted their work; how their unwavering pursuit of fundamental knowledge overlooked practical needs; how the emphasis on scientific research shifted resources away from clinical care; or how they had largely built their empire on the public's money and deference—but they did not. Rather, many in the profession found certain external connections more troubling: the proliferation and testing of nuclear weapons, the pressures placed upon them by the military to contribute to weapons development, and the vigorous security checks conducted by the relentless House Committee on UnAmerican Activities (HUAC).[43]

Scientists responded differently to these conflicts and contradictions. Some became activists for commercial bioscience; others organized against it. Historian Eric Vettel, for example, tells the story of Cetus Corporation and the divisive Asilomar conference on recombinant DNA technology in *Biotech: The Countercultural Origins of an Industry*. Scientists, universities, and biomedical commerce all changed in the process, increasing the pressures and, I add, the confusions of multi- and proclaimed interdisciplinarity.

"One of the great underlying shifts of view was the development of a new appreciation for practical experimentation. . . . Beginning in the mid-1960s, the field began to move . . . away from 'pure research.'" Applied, for-profit, and entrepreneurial experiments all became points of organization and aroused opposition based on environmental and ethical concerns. "Of all the applied bioscience research projects under way in this new era, . . . one in particular stood out, both for its scientific novelty and its impact on humanity: genetic engineering."[44] Recombinant DNA and genetic engineering were touted as humankind's salvation and condemned as its nemesis. Can they be both?

That contradiction may follow from molecular biology's development as a congeries of fragments, rather than an integrated site of interdisciplinary convergence. If we take another step, we may also ask whether fields such as bioscience, operations research, cognitive science, and materials science, which find homes in a number of locations and have commercial and medical potential, are *more* effective because of their lesser degree of institutional consolidation.

Literacy Studies

While interdisciplinarity in bioscience may be characterized as fragmentary, in literacy studies it may be viewed as a fiction, although perhaps a necessary, hopeful, or even utopian gesture. The problems of synecdoche are familiar: the parts (including their disciplinary bases) may substitute for or dominate the whole. The question of knowledge and understanding an interdiscipline's major or most relevant parts, including their intellectual, social, and disciplinary histories, are closely related. The task of understanding is inseparable from the identification of central questions and problems for research and, in some cases, applications. How well interconnected is literacy studies as a presumed interdiscipline? What are the relations among its major disciplines and fields? Are conflicts and contradictions recognized, and how are they dealt with?[45]

Claims about literacies and their lack proliferate. Different observers see either an abundance of literacies forming the foundation for flowing multi-modalities or a looming crisis rooted in the presumed absence or inadequacy of appropriate literacies, which threatens the future of our civilization and polity.[46] Reflecting the historical legacies of literacy and the power of literacy narratives, Leon Lederman, former director of the Fermi National Accelerator Laboratory, recently editorialized in *Science News*: "In a world in which illiteracy is the shame of societies where it is found, science illiteracy is increasingly disastrous. And wherever it is measured, this illiteracy rate is 90 to 95 percent."[47] "Science literacy" is only one of many examples, yet its implicit significance and pre-sumed trajectory need no extended argument or explanation; in itself, it consti-tutes an interdisciplinarity narrative. In this typical formulation, literacy studies embraces two more or less opposing positions: that of "many literacies" and that of dangerously low levels of literacy, as well as their causes and consequences. When conceptualized complexly (which is not the most common practice), their contradictory relationships form part of our subject of inquiry and part of the challenge for explication and response.

The difficulties and potentialities related to literacy stimulated a field of liter-acy studies during the last quarter of the twentieth century. "The word literacy . . . has become a unifying term across a range of disciplines for changing views of reading and writing," writes sociolinguist David Barton.[48] "In many ways Liter-acy Studies grew out of a dissatisfaction with conceptions of reading and writing which were prevalent in education in all areas. . . . These were conceptions of reading and writing which were based on overly simplistic psychological mod-els. The critique has been made from a range of disciplinary vantage points and in a range of ways."[49] Literacy studies has striven to become an interdisciplinary field of study and knowledge.

Tensions between the principal disciplines and their contributions to a poten-tial interdiscipline mark the dynamics of its development. The most common, and perhaps most notorious, is the clash between the cognitive/psychological approaches used in psychology and cognitive science (and sometimes also in literature, history, linguistics, or philosophy) and the social/contextual approaches of anthropology, sociology, linguistics, and history. These differences parallel the conflicts between "strong" or "great divide" theories that emphasize autono-mous, universal, and determinative impacts of literacy, on the one hand, and contextual understandings and practice-related influences, on the other. On the practical level, a long struggle has been waged between departments of English and colleges of education over institutional ownership of literacy, as well as the necessity for good writing and proper reading. In this case, as in others, efforts at interdisciplinarity are an inseparable part of the processes of disciplinary formation, not a later or separate movement. They are commonly tied to concerns and conflicts over human conditions and their improvement, politics and policies, and the theories and assumptions on which they rest.

Alternatives that arose to counter this understanding include Barton's "New Literacy Studies" and Brian Street's "ideological model" of literacy.[50] Along with the dominant narrative of the equation of literacy with civilization and its advance, authority is claimed in part by the act of naming. Incipient interdisciplines frequently proclaim or identify themselves as "new." It is no coincidence that the earlier dominance of "strong theories," "great divides," or dichotomous understandings of literacy had no need for a nominal cover like "literacy studies." Literacy was unreflectingly incorporated into the principal narratives of the rise of the West and the triumph of democracy, modernization, and progress. Indeed, literacy was equated with those qualities, each seemingly the cause of the other.

Interdisciplinary literacy studies developed from different methods and sources, with various presuppositions and expectations. As suggested by Jens Brockmeier, Min Wang, and David Olson, "over-simplistic psychological" notions were often rooted in reductive leaps across relatively rarefied cognitive and philosophical artifacts.[51] Radical dichotomies substituted for the dynamics of social and cultural change. Unqualified generalizations were applied unhesitatingly to large numbers of persons. The dynamics of literacy itself were reduced to cartoonish images of literacy versus orality and print versus manuscript, paramount among the many damaging dichotomies that substituted for explorations of complicated and mutually constitutive relationships.

Across the sweep of the twentieth century, empirical and critical studies in oral literature, folklore, psychology, anthropology and archaeology, linguistics, philosophy, sociology, classics, and history began to tell different, more variegated, stories. They turned to more direct evidence of literacy's development, distribution, and uses via case studies, ethnographies, and histories that paid more attention to matters of practice and social context. Sources and subjects were approached and interpreted more carefully and critically. Ironically, "New Literacy Studies" scholars over the past three or four decades only slowly rediscovered the groundbreaking work earlier in the century of oral literature researchers who climbed mountains in eastern Europe to record performances, constructing "singers of tales," as Milman Parry and Albert Lord famously dubbed them, and comparing oral narratives.[52]

No less momentous, but also neglected, is the dynamic activism of the cultural-historical psychology of Lev Vygotsky, Alexander Luria, and their colleagues from the 1930s.[53] So much richer than the modernization studies of American sociologists after World War II, this Russian work seems destined for repeated rediscovery. That phenomenon may also be a stop on paths to interdisciplinarity, constituting a step forward accompanied by a constraining half-step backward. Specialized areas often competed and interfered with the periodic quests and claims for synthesis, both within and across disciplinary domains.

By and large, these approaches and their appropriation for literacy studies derived from distinct disciplines, in particular anthropology, linguistics, and cognitive psychology (now shifting toward cognitive science). Through its multiple origins, literacy studies represents a search for a different, but common or shared, place amid the disciplines, often outside the walls of colleges and departments of education or psychology. Literacy studies drew important insights from history, classics, and, most recently, cultural studies. We see parallels here with the humanities and cultural studies, just as bioscience at times paralleled operations research and cognitive and materials science. Comparisons with other efforts at interdisciplinarity, unfortunately, are typically mimetic and self-promotional. Critical comparisons are as rare as efforts to learn from the history of one's own field.

Literacy studies, like interdisciplinary studies separately and together, can be better understood by encompassing a longer chronological span of intellectual and sociocultural development and adopting a broader, more dynamic focus on its place and play among an array of disciplines and institutional locations. As we have seen repeatedly, relationships among disciplines and interdisciplinary efforts are central. Subfields that deal with literacy include reading, writing, child and human development, cognitive studies, comparative and development studies, communication or media studies, visual studies, mathematics, and science. The recent discovery or, indeed, explosion of multiple literacies has taken place largely without notice or exploration of these relationships.

Social, cultural, and political-economic factors and developments that are external to the normal workings of a discipline or field—the imperatives of wartime; consequences of global cross-cultural contacts and colonialism; "discovery" of new social problems; presumptions about the course of social, political, economic, and cultural development—combine, often contradictorily, with shifting currents within and across disciplines. They shape fields of study and relationships among disciplines as powerfully as they do their objects of study. They may then stimulate changing views that, in the context of universities and their organization of knowledge, lead to criticism, alternative assertions, and differing institutional articulations both within and outside the boundaries of departments or divisions that sometimes claim the name of interdisciplinarity. Sponsorship and funding, government and corporate interests, and perceptions of potential profits from research and development all propel or retard interdisciplinary efforts. Within and across institutions, competition and imitation become intense.

A more complete and useful approach to literacy studies, which also deepens our understanding of interdisciplinarity, begins no later than the 1920s and 1930s. It looks back to the period spanning the mid-eighteenth through the early twentieth century, or even glances as far back as the Renaissance and classical antiquity. There it locates in historical context the dynamic building blocks for our expectations, theories, policies, and institutions that culminate in modern literacies and their travails, as well as in literacy studies.

The possibilities and limits of interdisciplinary arise in the interplay within and across major disciplinary clusters. No less important is the dynamic, simultaneously critical and complementary interplay between disciplines. In this case, the key disciplines of anthropology, linguistics, and psychology provide powerful examples. Among them, orality and oral literature, everyday and privileged writing practices, the ubiquity of "reading" and "writing" across multiple media, and the search for cognitive and noncognitive implications of literacy are formative. So, too, is literacy's active presence as values, ideology, and both cultural and political capital. Destabilizing times become opportunities for disciplinary approaches to fall from favor and for interdisciplinary movements to emerge. These moments call for more sustained exploration and development of relationships and possible common locations and organization.

In literacy studies, one of the most powerful forces has long been the fear, or even the conviction, that literacy is declining or, at least, not rising, and thus families, morality, social order, progress, and socioeconomic development are also declining. This anxiety accompanied one of the most momentous transformations in the history of literacy and its study: from a "pre-modern" order, in which literacy was restricted because of its potential dangers, to a more modern order, in which illiteracy (or literacy gained outside of formal institutional controls) is feared. When heightened by international conflict or competition, social disorder and division, international migration of "aliens," declining fertility and rising mortality, the failure of "human capital" to grow, and similar circumstances, literacy levels become flashpoints for study and action to reverse the dreaded tide. Schools and popular culture attract attention, which has in turn the potential to propel disciplinary action and conflict, as well as interdisciplinary efforts. The apparently chronic "crisis" of literacy from the mid-twentieth through the early twenty-first centuries is inseparable from Cold War anxieties, global economic restructuring and collateral social and cultural change, transformations in the media of communications, and both persistent and emerging inequalities. Seemingly unprecedented "social problems" become calls for and stimulants of interdisciplinary "solutions." Literacy's role as cause or consequence is very tricky to unravel.

In the second half of the twentieth century, in conjunction with trends in other disciplines and interdisciplines, literacy studies took social, contextual, cognitive, linguistic, and historical "turns." With them came the adoption of signifying French theorists as "godfathers," ranging from Lucien Lévy-Bruhl and Claude Lévi-Strauss to Pierre Bourdieu and Bruno Latour. These developments have at times interacted with and deepened conflicts among disciplines but simultaneously promoted interest in interdisciplinary resolution. This dynamic is also visible in the histories and recent developments of most of the cases studied here.

Literacy studies' paths are revealing. Recent years have witnessed an emphasis on the everyday and the practical, including the concept of practice itself. This trend has led to the overturning of grand theories that stressed the universal importance of the written over the oral, the printed over the written, the literate over the unlettered and untutored. Practice and context, explored in a variety of contexts and traditions, replaced presumptions of the unmediated powers and advantages of literacy.[54] These recognitions demand, on the one hand, more critical and dynamic relationships between theory and practice, and, on the other hand, as a corollary, rejection of dichotomies in favor of studying and promoting relationships. Therein may lay the foundations for new levels of interdisciplinary connections. As with other fields we have examined, the lack of a dominating center may prove advantageous.

Successful construction of recognized interdisciplines is not the most common consequence of changes in the relationships among disciplines and even of deliberately interdisciplinary efforts. Literacy studies, too, continues to struggle over matters of interdisciplinarity. Some observers refuse to recognize it as interdisciplinary because of the general absence of departments of literacy studies, despite a plethora of centers and programs. Even when that criterion is disregarded, literacy studies lacks a center, stable locations, and organization or institutionalization. Typically, it is part of various disciplines, with problematic relationships within and beyond them.[55]

Interdisciplinary literacy studies continues to struggle with foundational dichotomies between oral and literate, writing and print, and printed and electronic forms. The long-standing neglect of rich research on orality and oral literature is almost as much a mark of the limits of many interdisciplinary endeavors as of the power of disciplines.[56] The persistence and importance of orality, as well as visuality, are regularly rediscovered across disciplines. The heterogeneity of constructions of the cognitive domain also plagues literacy studies. Confusion about the constitution of central problems in the field obstructs attention to the relationships among different literacies and distinct disciplines. Both issues cry out for sustained attention with respect to literacies' acquisition, practices, uses, and abuses.

We confront the antinomies of interdisciplinary studies mirrored in literacy studies. For many, interdisciplinarity represents synthetic and integrative general education in major clusters of the curriculum or the search for unification across broad realms of knowledge. Some observers and practitioners regard it as basic and foundational, while to others it is specialized and advanced. For the first group, instruction in general education takes a higher priority; to the second, sophisticated research and the interpretation of its results rules. Literacy studies at times seems to aspire to the former. One traditional narrative of (Western) civilization is logocentric, holding literacy as the engine of modernizing changes. But literacy's study and understanding tends to contribute more to the latter perspective, however ironically or contradictorily. This advanced track is more closely aligned to specialization or fragmentation of knowledge and multiple literacies than to general education or unification. Claims of interdisciplinary synthesis or integration are often asserted, yet they need to be read within specialized research areas. An analysis of their foundational knowledge, development, and intellectual and institutional contexts seems the place to begin.

Striving for recognition, literacy studies occupies ambiguous ground. This is in part a question of location, but it is also a matter of status. The rise of literacy studies, its generally successful emergence and development within limits, contributes to its presence in many academic departments and disciplines, especially education, the social sciences, and the humanities and to a lesser extent in the sciences, medicine, public health, the law, and business. This pattern is problematic in some critical respects. In the pantheon of disciplines, centers of interest in literacy studies do not usually rank highly. That the study of literacy is often seen as basic or elementary does not boost its standing; in this respect it resembles the place of composition in English and the liberal arts. By reputation, it is often viewed as inseparable from schools or colleges of education.

Literacy studies has achieved institutionalization mainly within education, in the form of departments, degree programs, or areas of concentration under the rubric of "literacy, language, and culture," sometimes complemented with a research, outreach, or service center. Both "literacy" and "interdisciplinary" serve as promotional labels: new, relevant, sexy (in academic terms), and appealing for applied and practical reasons to citizens, governments, and corporations. Publishers dream of riches through the promotion of reading.

That interdisciplinarity is often deemed best suited to "solving problems" that fall outside the domain, traditions, or intellectual resources of any given discipline is regarded as wonderful by some but as damning by others. Literacy studies engages both the practical and applied. While the field has serious interests in theory and knowledge generation about the uses and influences of literacy, social and geographic variations, and multiple literacies, research into practical problems remains its most common scholarly pursuit.

Conclusion

Likening interdisciplines to disciplines and to other interdisciplines in order to find similarities, our reflexive practice may mislead more than clarify. Interdisciplinary developments follow different paths toward a variety of institutional, intellectual, and societal ends over different timelines. They may prove influential without attaining the stable niches and continuity of disciplines. They are likely to take different forms of organization and institutionalization and have shorter half-lives. These are among their strengths, and understanding that fact may carry powerful implications for literacy studies and for interdisciplinary studies.

Doing interdisciplinary differs from "talking" interdisciplinary. Interdisciplinary efforts differ among and within disciplinary clusters. There is no single organization, form, pattern of institutionalization, or set of rules that signifies interdisciplinarity. This history warns us repeatedly of the dangers of exaggeration, excessive claims of novelty, and imitation, especially of a simplified model of scientific research. It emphasizes the centrality of humility, learning the basics and doing one's homework, and recognizing and appreciating variety and variability. Finally, the history of interdisciplinarity mandates a greater role for history and the humanities.

Book epigraph. Roberta Frank, "'Interdisciplinarity': The First Half-Century," *Words for Robert Burchfield's Sixty-Fifth Birthday*, ed. E. G. Stanley and T. F. Hoad (Cambridge: D. S. Brewer, 1988), 100–101.

Introduction • *The Problem of Interdisciplinarity in Theory and Practice over Time*

1. I will publish a critique of the literature and discourse of interdisciplinarity separately.

2. University of Michigan News Service, May 5, 2008.

3. Advertisement, *Chronicle of Higher Education* (*CHE*), May 2, 2008.

4. "Institutionalizing Interdisciplinary Study," *CHE*, Jan. 30, 2007.

5. "Study Finds That Ph.D.s Who Write Interdisciplinary Dissertations Earn Less," *Inside Higher Education*, Oct. 31, 2013. The report did not specify how "interdisciplinary" was defined or whether there was a significant difference in salaries within or across fields of employment.

6. Stephanie L. Pfirman, James P. Collins, Susan Lowes, and Anthony Michaels, "Collaborative Efforts: Promoting Interdisciplinary Scholars," *CHE*, Feb. 7, 2005. See also Bok, *Higher Education in America*, chapter 16.

7. See Jacobs, *In Defense of Disciplines*.

8. Steve Fuller, "Interdisciplinarity: The Loss of the Heroic Vision in the Marketplace of Ideas," Oct. 1, 2003, http://interdisciplines.org/interdisciplinarity/papers3, 1. See also "Nikolas Rose Interviewed by Todd Meyers," *Public Culture* 25 (2013): 435–52.

9. Pfirman et al., "Collaborative Efforts." For a perspective based on my own experiences, see Graff, "LiteracyStudies@OSU as Theory and Practice."

10. Jacobs, *In Defense of Disciplines*.

11. *CHE*, June 14, 2002.

12. There are many typologies and epistemologies of interdisciplinarity. In her numerous books (*Interdisciplinarity*; *Crossing Boundaries*; *Humanities, Culture, and Interdisciplinarity*; and *Mapping Interdisciplinary Studies*), Klein seldom defines interdisciplinarity or considers the implications of this diversity. See also Klein, *Mapping Interdisciplinary Studies*; Frodeman, Klein, and Mitcham, *Oxford Handbook of Interdisciplinarity*; Moran, *Interdisciplinarity*; and Weingart and Stehr, *Practising Interdisciplinarity*.

13. Galison, "Many Faces of Big Science."

14. See Gilman, *Fortunes of the Humanities*. For an example of the fallacies and contradictions of transdisciplinarity, see Nicolescu, *Manifesto of Transdisciplinarity* and *Transdisciplinarity*.

15. Committee on a New Biology, *New Biology for the 21st Century*.

16. Heckhausen, "Discipline and Interdisciplinarity."

17. See Abbott, *Chaos of Disciplines*, 131; Brint, "Rise of the 'Practical Arts'" and "Creating the Future"; Brint et al., "From the Liberal to the Practical Arts"; Steven Brint, Lori Turk-Bicakci, Kristopher Proctor, and Scott Patrick Murphy, "Expanding the Social Frame

of Knowledge: Interdisciplinary, Degree-Granting Fields in American Four-Year Colleges and Universities, 1975–2000," www.higher-ed2000.ucr.edu/Publications/Brint%20+%2021%(2008b).pdf.2008; and Calhoun, "Specificity of American Higher Education" and "University and the Public Good," which includes an interview and comments.

18. Tom Katsouleas, "A Convergence Science for Today's Problems," *CHE*, Aug. 14, 2011. See also Massachusetts Institute of Technology, *Third Revolution*, and Committee on a New Biology, *New Biology for the 21st Century*.

19. Frodeman, Klein, and Mitchum, *Oxford Handbook of Interdisciplinarity*, xxxii–xxxiii.

20. See Frodeman, *Sustainable Knowledge*.

21. Aronowitz, *Knowledge Factory*, 145–46.

22. Readings, *University in Ruins*, 39. See also Hunt, "Democratization and Decline?," and Newfield, *Unmaking the Public University*, 357.

23. Jacobs and Frickel, "Interdisciplinarity."

24. Brint, "Rise of the 'Practical Arts,'" 253. See also Brint, "Creating the Future"; Brint et al., "From the Liberal to the Practical Arts"; and Brint et al., "Expanding the Social Frame of Knowledge."

25. Jacobs and Frickel, "Interdisciplinarity," 52, 60.

26 Abbott, *Chaos of Disciplines*, 141, 128, 158.

27. Calhoun, "Specificity of American Higher Education," 74.

28. Jacobs and Frickel, "Interdisciplinarity."

29. Compare Jacobs and Frickel, "Interdisciplinarity," with Klein's books and with Strober, *Interdisciplinary Conversations*.

30. Jacobs and Frickel, "Interdisciplinarity," 38, 37–38. They do refer to intellectual capital, patents, and licensing agreements with respect to proprietary knowledge.

31. Peters, "Law, Literature, and the Vanishing Real," 451, 449. For interesting discussions with somewhat different emphases, see Rosaldo, "Reflections on Interdisciplinarity," and Poovey, "Interdisciplinarity at New York University." See also Modern Language Association Forum, "Perspectives from Particular Fields."

32. Abbott, *Chaos of Disciplines*, 137–39.

33. Ibid., 134.

Chapter 1 · *Sciences of Life and Society in the Making of the Research University*

1. G. Allen, *Life Science in the Twentieth Century*, 114.

2. Ross, "Changing Contours of the Social Science Disciplines," 225. In addition to the references on disciplines and interdisciplines cited in the introduction, see Lenoir, "Discipline of Nature and Nature of Disciplines"; Fuller, "Disciplinary Boundaries and the Rhetoric of the Social Sciences" and *Philosophy, Rhetoric, and the End of Knowledge*, chap. 2: "The Position: Interdisciplinarity as Interpenetration," 33–65; and Gaziano, "Ecological Metaphors as Scientific Boundary Work."

3. See listings in *American Universities and Colleges*, as well as university catalogs and registers.

4. See especially Pauly, *Biologists and the Promise of American Life* and "Appearance of Academic Biology"; Oleson and Voss, *Organization of Knowledge in Modern America*; Bannister, *Sociology and Scientism*; Haskell, *Authority of Experts*; Furner, *Advocacy and Objectivity*; and Ross, "Changing Contours of the Social Science Disciplines."

5. On the history of these fields, universities, and ways of organizing knowledge, see Oleson and Voss, *Organization of Knowledge in Modern America*; Oleson and Brown, *Pursuit of Knowledge*; D. Allen, "Amateurs and Professionals"; Pauly, *Biologists and the Promise of American Life* and "Appearance of Academic Biology"; Ross, "Changing Contours of the Social Science Disciplines"; Haskell, *Authority of Experts*; Bender, *Intellect and Public Life*; Hollinger, *In the American Province*; Reuben, *Making of the Modern University*; and Turner, "Secularization and Sacralization."

6. In addition to previous references on higher education, see Roger Geiger, *To Advance Knowledge: The Growth of American Research Universities* (New York: Oxford University Press, 1986); Robert A. McCaughey, "The Transformation of American Academic Life: Harvard University, 1821–1892." *Perspectives in American History* 8 (1974): 239–332; Ringer, *Decline of the German Mandarins* and "Intellectual Field"; Turner with Bernard, "German Model"; Roberts and Turner, *Sacred and Secular University*; and Veysey, *Emergence of the American University*.

7. D. Allen, "Amateurs and Professionals," 23–27.

8. Claiming history, heritage, and precedent is always an issue for disciplines and interdisciplines. See G. Allen, *Life Science in the Twentieth Century* and "T. H. Morgan and the Emergence of a New American Biology"; Bourdieu, *Outline of a Theory of Practice* and *Homo Academicus*; Bourdieu and Passeron, *Inheritors* and *Reproduction in Education, Society, and Culture*; Bowler and Morus, *Making Modern Science*; Calhoun, *Sociology in America* and "Sociology, Other Disciplines, and the Project of a General Understanding of Social Life"; Guillory, *Cultural Capital*; Ringer, *Decline of the German Mandarins*; and Ross, *Origins of American Social Science*.

9. Furner, *Advocacy and Objectivity*; Bannister, *Sociology and Scientism*; Haskell, *Emergence of Professional Social Science*; Ross, *Origins of American Social Science*.

10. D. Allen, "Amateurs and Professionals," 23. See also Harwood, "Universities"; G. Allen, *Life Science in the Twentieth Century* and *Thomas Hunt Morgan*; Rainger, Benson, and Maienschein, *American Development of Biology* and *Expansion of American Biology*; and Kingsland, *Evolution of American Ecology*.

11. Pauly, *Biologists and the Promise of American Life*, 5.

12. Ibid., 57, 94.

13. D. Allen, "Amateurs and Professionals," 24, 25.

14. Pauly, *Biologists and the Promise of American Life*, 126.

15. Ibid., 126, 127.

16. Pauly, "Appearance of Academic Biology," 371, 372. See also Pauly, "Summer Resort and Scientific Discipline."

17. Harwood, "Universities," 91, 90.

18. Ibid., 94.

19. Pauly, "Appearance of Academic Biology," 392.

20. G. Allen, "T. H. Morgan and the Emergence of a New American Biology." See also Bowler and Morus, *Making Modern Science*, 165–88, 189–213.

21. Brush, "How Theories Become Knowledge," 471. See also Kingsland, "Maintaining Continuity through a Scientific Revolution"; Sapp, "Struggle for Authority in the Field of Heredity" and *Genesis*. More generally, see Lorraine Daston and Elizabeth Lunbeck, eds., *Histories of Scientific Observation* (Chicago: University of Chicago Press, 2011), and Galison, *Image and Logic*. The perceived hesitations of T. H. Morgan and E. B. Wilson about

Mendelism and the challenges of evolutionary theory were overcome. Surprisingly, at least in retrospect, the research that linked mutations in chromosomes to sex determination was based on studies of only one kind of experimental organism.

22. Pauly, "Appearance of Academic Biology," 392. He mentioned Harvard, Columbia, Chicago, Penn, and Johns Hopkins. See also Maienschein, "Whitman at Chicago."

23. Pauly, "Appearance of Academic Biology," 383, 385.

24. Stanford University provides a revealing example. In 1922–23, its School of Biology, in the School of Biological Sciences, included anatomy (also in the School of Medicine); bacteriology and experimental pathology (also in medicine); biochemistry; botany; entomology; the Food Research Institute; Hopkins Marine Station; Natural History Museum; paleontology; physiology (also in medicine); experimental psychology; and zoology. "Provisions made it possible to organize courses in the fields of Biology that cut across former departmental lines, which was advantageous to faculty and students alike. Important additions were made to the faculty and advanced research was undertaken, both on the campus and in Pacific Grove. The inclusion of the Hopkins Marine Laboratory was important. It promoted the use of its facilities for undergraduates in the summer quarter and gave the faculty an opportunity to broaden their research projects by using the new laboratory, which was completed in 1928 with the aid of a gift from the Rockefeller Foundation." The "fine, well-equipped" Jacques Loeb Laboratory "was completed in 1929 and has had great teaching and research value for students, faculty, and visiting scientists. It provided for the shift in interest in Zoology and Botany from systemic and morphological studies to general physiology and particularly to the application of physics and chemistry to problems in these fields. The required facilities were provided and inspired many significant research projects for which support in the form of special grants was received." Mitchell, *Stanford University*, 78–79.

25. On genetics and especially Morgan, see, in addition to the works cited above, Elof Axel Carlson, *The Gene: A Critical History* (Philadelphia: W. B. Saunders, 1966); Erik Dopman and Daniel L. Hartl, "A Portrait of Copy-number Polymorphism in Drosophila Melanogaster," *Proceedings of the National Academy of Sciences* 104 (Dec. 11, 2007): 19920–25; Erik R. Kandel, "Thomas Hunt Morgan at Columbia University: Genes, Chromosomes, and the Origins of Modern Biology," *Columbia Magazine*, Spring 2010, www.columbia .edu/cu/alumni/Magazine/Legacies/Morgan/; Kay, *Molecular Vision of Life*, "Rethinking Institutions," "Cybernetics, Information, Life," and *Who Wrote the Book of Life?*; Keller, *Century of the Gene*; Dianna E. Kenney and Gary G. Borisy, "Thomas Hunt Morgan at the Marine Biological Laboratory: Naturalist and Experimentalist," *Genetics* 181, no. 3 (2009): 841–46; Amy Maxmen, "The Sea Spider's Contribution to T. H. Morgan's (1866–1945) Development," *Journal of Experimental Zoology Part B: Molecular and Developmental Evolution* 310B.3 (2008): 203–15; John A. Moore, "Thomas Hunt Morgan—The Geneticist," *American Zoologist* 23 (1983): 855–65; J. Schwartz, *In Pursuit of the Gene*; J. H. Schwartz, "Decisions, Decisions"; C. Kenneth Waters, "What Was Classical Genetics?" *Studies in History and Philosophy of Science* 35A.4 (2004): 783–809; Watson, *Double Helix* and *Molecular Biology of the Gene*; Watson with Berry, *DNA*; and Watson and Crick, "Molecular Structure of Nucleic Acids."

26. On Morgan, see the special issue of the *Journal of the History of Biology* 14, no. 1 (Spring 1981). See also Kohler, *Lords of the Fly*; David B. Roberts, "*Drosophila Melanogaster*:

The Model Organism," *Entomologia Experimentalis et Applicata* 121 (2006): 93–103; and Sturtevant, "Reminiscences of T. H. Morgan."

27. For a general summary, see Harwood, "Universities," 90–107.

28. Perhaps the only more romanticized scientific myth is that of Watson and Crick at Cavendish Laboratory at Cambridge University.

29. Sturtevant, "Reminiscences of T. H. Morgan," 4.

30. Kandel, "Thomas Hunt Morgan," emphasizes the importance of the democratic atmosphere and free exchange of ideas to the success of Morgan's laboratory but also acknowledges that H. J. Muller disagreed vehemently. On Morgan's "boys," see Kohler, *Lords of the Flies*, 62–65.

31. Quoted in Goodstein, *Millikan's School*, from Morgan, "New Division of Biology."

32. Goodstein, *Millikan's School*, 211–12. Kohler, *Lords of the Flies*, discusses "cross-disciplinary" "boundary crossers" and "immigrants from other disciplines." George W. Beadle, a maize geneticist, and Boris Ephrussi, an experimental embryologist, invented genetic transplantation at Caltech. On Caltech, see Kargon, "Temple to Science" and *Rise of Robert Millikan*; Kay, *Molecular Vision of Life* and "Rethinking Institutions"; and Scerri, "Interdisciplinary Research at the Caltech Beckman Institute."

33. Bannister, "Sociology," 329.

34. I would question Bannister's sense of timing and his description of the process. See Isaac, *Working Knowledge*, and Craig Calhoun and Troy Duster, "The Visions and Divisions of Sociology," *CHE*, Aug. 12, 2005.

35. Scott Jaschik, "'Two Cultures' Tension in Social Science," *Inside Higher Education*, Sept. 2, 2008; Ortolano, *Two Cultures Controversy*; Kagan, *Three Cultures*.

36. P. Abrams, "Sense of the Past and the Origins of Sociology," 20; Nisbet, *Social Change and History*.

37. Abrams, "Sense of the Past and the Origins of Sociology," 25–26.

38. Ross, "Changing Contours of the Social Science Disciplines," 212.

39. Ibid. She continues, "Still, local differences, multiple institutional locations, and limited meritocratic standards allowed for important exceptions. The radical economist Thorstein Veblen, W.E.B. DuBois and a later cadre of African-American sociologists, and several Progressive cohorts of women social scientists produced pathbreaking work by reformulating established political, racial, and gender codes or by turning them to their own advantage" (213).

40. Calhoun, "Sociology in America: An Introduction," in *Sociology in America*, 33.

41. Calhoun, *Sociology in America*, includes contributions on social work, fieldwork, criminology, and education.

42. Haskell, *Emergence of Professional Social Science*, 191. Although Haskell emphasizes the discovery of interdependence and emergence of professionalism, the story can be read toward an opposing conclusion. See, for example, Katz, *Poverty and Policy*, 174–81, and Ross, "Professionalism and the Transformation of American Social Thought" and *Origins of American Social Science*.

43. Haskell, *Emergence of Professional Social Science*, 190–91; see also 204–10.

44. Calhoun, "Sociology in America," 10–11.

45. Ross, "Changing Contours of the Social Science Disciplines," 209.

46. Ibid.

47. Ibid., 209–10. For specific examples from Chicago, see Ross, *Origins of American Social Science*, and Abbott, *Department and Discipline* and *Chaos of Disciplines*.

48. Camic and Xie, "Statistical Turn in American Social Science"; Bulmer, "Quantification and Chicago Social Science in the 1920s"; Abbott, *Department and Discipline* and *Chaos of Disciplines*.

49. Ross, "Changing Contours of the Social Science Disciplines," 219–20, 224.

50. Ibid., 225–26.

51. Abbott, *Department and Discipline*, 84–85.

52. Ibid., 86.

53. On sociology's relationships with economics, see, for example, Young, "Emergence of Sociology from Political Economy." Abbott comments that "university faculty . . . initiated the institutionalization of the discipline, but they were by no means in a stable position in their home institutions, even by the 1920s"; *Department and Discipline*, 87.

54. Quoted in Camic, "Three Departments in Search of a Discipline." Harvard developed a distinctive approach developed only in the 1930s with Talcott Parsons's goal of merging "abstraction" with empirical case studies.

55. Small, "Relation between Sociology and Other Sciences" (1906), quoted by Camic, "Three Departments in Search of a Discipline," 1020.

56. Camic, "Three Departments in Search of a Discipline," 1021. For local factors leading to differentiation, see Camic and Xie, "Statistical Turn in American Social Science."

57. Camic, "On Edge," 229.

58. Ibid., 230.

59. On biology and sociology, see also Renwick, "From Political Economy to Sociology."

60. Camic, "On Edge," 221–22, 231.

61. Ibid., 233. On departments, see Steinmetz, "American Sociology before and after World War II"; Abbott, *Department and Discipline* and *Chaos of Disciplines*; Barnes, *Introduction to the History of Sociology*; Anthony J. Blasi, "The Ph.D. and the Institutionalization of American Sociology," *American Sociologist* 35 (2004): 27–45; Bulmer, *Chicago School of Sociology*; Calhoun, *Sociology in America*; Steven J. Diner, "Department and Discipline: The Department of Sociology at the University of Chicago, 1892–1920," *Minerva* 13 (1975): 514–53; Robert E. L. Faris, *Chicago Sociology 1920–1932* (Chicago: University of Chicago Press, 1970); Roscoe C. Hinkle, *Founding Theory of American Sociology, 1881–1915* (Boston: Routledge & Kegan Paul, 1980); Anthony Oberschall, "The Institutionalization of American Sociology," in *The Establishment of Empirical Sociology*, ed. Anthony Oberschall (New York: Harper & Row, 1972), 187–251; Ross, "Changing Contours of the Social Science Disciplines," "Development of the Social Sciences," and *Origins of American Social Science*; A. Small, "Relation between Sociology and Other Sciences" and "Some Contributions to the History of Sociology"; and Young, "Emergence of Sociology from Political Economy."

62. Ross, "Changing Contours of the Social Science Disciplines," 209.

63. Young, "Emergence of Sociology from Political Economy."

64. Bond, "Ferdinand Tonnies and Academic 'Socialism,'" 23–45.

65. See Abbott, "Disciplines and the Future"; Calhoun, "Sociology, Other Disciplines, and the Project of a General Understanding of Social Life"; Camic, "Reputation and Pre-

decessor Selection" and "Reshaping the History of American Sociology"; Camic, Gross, and Lamont, *Social Knowledge in the Making*; and Heilbron, "Regime of Disciplines."

Chapter 2 · Crossing and Remaking Boundaries

1. Snow, *Two Cultures and the Scientific Revolution*. Critiques are discussed in Leavis, *Two Cultures?*, and Porter, "Two Cultures Revisited."

2. Among the relevant issues are the conception and discourse of "humanities" or "the humanities" and of "social science" or "the social sciences." There are both similarities and differences between these clusters. For example, the social sciences seldom presume a unity.

3. For example, Harpham's "Finding Ourselves" simply asserts disciplinary status. He proceeds from one dichotomy to another—amateur versus professional, subjective versus objective—without considering the resulting conflicts and contradictions. Like many other commentators, he also confuses the humanities with humanistic study.

4. Kagan, *Three Cultures*, 222.

5. See, for example, Kenneth Pomeranz's 2013–2014 address as president of the American Historical Association, "We Need More than STEM," available at www.insidehighered .com/views/2013/01/28/essay-criticizing-President-obama-and-other-politicians-who -appear-focus-only.

6. For a more knowledgeable and diplomatic critique, see Parsons, "Theory in the Humanities and Sociology." See also Ortolano, "Two Cultures, One University"; "Human Science or a Human Face?"; "F. R Leavis, Science, and the Abiding Crisis of Modern Civilization"; "Literature and Science of 'Two Cultures' Historiography"; *Two Cultures Controversy*; and "Two Cultures and Beyond."

7. Valenza, *Literature, Language*, 177.

8. Ibid., 177, 65, 128–29.

9. Ibid., 129.

10. See Jay, *Dialectical Imagination*.

11. See Guillory, "Genesis of the Media Concept," and Schiller, *Theorizing Communication*.

12. Lasswell, "Communications as an Emerging Discipline," 245.

13. Berelson, "State of Communication Research," with dissenting comments by Wilbur Schramm, David Riesman, and Raymond A. Bauer. See also E. Katz, "Why Sociology Abandoned Mass Communication Research," and Pooley and Katz, "Further Notes on Why American Sociology Abandoned Mass Communication Research."

14. Herbst, "Disciplines, Intersections," 603.

15. Ibid., 604.

16. Pfau, "Espistemological and Disciplinary Intersections," 597. Consider figure 1 on 598 and the examples on 599.

17. Cmiel, "On Cynicism, Evil, and the Discovery of Communication in the 1940s," 88, 107.

18. Grafton and Jardine, *From Humanism to the Humanities*.

19. See Menand, *Marketplace of Ideas*; Nussbaum, *Cultivating Humanity* and *Not for Profit*; M. Taylor, *Crisis on Campus*; Jacobs, *In Defense of Disciplines*; and J. Klein, *Crossing Boundaries*; *Humanities, Culture, and Interdisciplinarity*; and *Interdisciplinarity*.

20. See Eisenstein, *Printing Press as an Agent of Change*; Grafton, "Importance of Being Printed"; Baron, Lindquist, and Shevlin, *Agent of Change*; Starr, *Creation of the Media*; Kimball, *Liberal Arts Tradition*; and H. Graff, *Legacies of Literacy*. For histories of communication, see Crowley and Heyer, *Communication in History*; Heyer, *Communications and History*; McLuhan, *Gutenberg Galaxy* and *Understanding Media*; and Williams, *Communications* and *Contact*.

21. See especially Schiller, *Theorizing Communication*; McChesney, *Communication Revolution*; and Mosco, *Political Economy of Communication*.

22. At Ohio State University, there is a School of Journalism and Communication, not a department or a college; it is a unit of the Division of Social Sciences within the College of Arts and Sciences.

23. For a useful recent overview, see Hollinger, *Humanities and the Dynamics of Inclusion*.

24. See Abbott, *Chaos of Disciplines*; Guillory, "Literary Critics as Intellectuals," "Period of Literature," "Literary Study and the Modern System of the Disciplines," "Sokal Affair and the History of Criticism," "Critical Response II," "Who's Afraid of Marcel Proust?" and *Cultural Capital*; Hollinger, *Humanities and the Dynamics of Inclusion since World War II*; Scott and Keates, *Schools of Thought*; and Anderson and Valente, *Disciplinarity at the Fin de Siècle*.

25. Compare the 1980 report of the Commission on the Humanities, *Humanities in American Life*, which was commissioned by the Rockefeller Foundation, and the 2013 report of the American Academy of Arts and Sciences, *Heart of the Matter*; see also Kaufmann, *Future of the Humanities*. More generally, see Grafton and Jardine, *From Humanism to the Humanities*; Rudolph, *American College and University*; Veysey, *Emergence of the American University*; Higham, *History*; Oleson and Voss, *Organization of Knowledge*; Kuklick, "Emergence of the Humanities," *Rise of American Philosophy*, and *History of Philosophy in America*; Haskell, *Emergence of Professional Social Science*; Novick, *That Noble Dream*; Turner, *Religion Enters the Academy* and *Language, Religion, Knowledge*; Roberts and Turner, *Sacred and Secular University*; Ross, *Origins of American Social Science*; G. Graff, *Professing Literature*; Guillory, "Literary Study and the Modern System of the Disciplines"; and Hollinger, *Humanities and the Dynamics of Inclusion*.

26. See Valenza, *Literature, Language*, for the absence of such efforts in the eighteenth and nineteenth centuries.

27. Grafton and Jardine, *From Humanism*, xiii–xiv.

28. Ibid., xiv–xv.

29. Marcus, "Humanities," 17.

30. Ibid., 18, 19.

31. American Council on Education, *American Universities and Colleges* (1928, 1932, 1936). I thank Jerry Jacobs, University of Pennsylvania, for telling me about these sources, and my graduate research assistants, Julia Voss, Krista Bryson, and Cassie Patterson, for collecting the data.

32. Marcus, "Humanities," 19.

33. Ibid.

34. For viewpoints on the uses of the humanities with respect to literature, see "Uses," special issue, *New Literary History* 44 (Autumn 2013), and H. Small, *Value of the Humanities*.

35. Contrast the essays in Oleson and Voss, *Organization of Knowledge*, with the criticism expressed in Haskell's review, "Are Professors Professional?"

36. Roberts and Turner, *Sacred and Secular University*, 75. See also Guillory, "Sokal Affair and the History of Criticism."

37. Roberts and Turner, *Sacred and Secular University*, 87. Only in theory was knowledge never undivided; to think otherwise was always an act of faith.

38. Ibid., 92.

39. Ibid., 92, 93.

40. See Allardyce, "Rise and Fall of the Western Civilization Course"; Segal, "'Western Civilization' and the Staging of History in American Higher Education"; Gray, "Western Civilization and its Discontents"; and Novick, *That Noble Dream*. See also *Princeton Alumni Weekly*, Apr. 7, 2010; Rubin, *Making of Middlebrow Culture*; and Radway, *Feeling for Books*. In this history also lies also foundation of the opposition between disciplinarity construed as general *or* specialized, basic or advanced. This dichotomous misconception has been rediscovered regularly with different sides as interdisciplinary, when not multidisciplinary. See Jacobs, *In Defense of Disciplines*.

41. Roberts and Turner, *Sacred and Secular University*, 96.

42. Ibid., 97.

43. Ibid., 100, 101.

44. Ibid., 102, 104–5.

45. Ibid., 105. Although this topic does not concern us here, Roberts and Turner are explicitly interested in the place of religion in the university and the humanities. See Reuben, *Making of the Modern University*; Marsden and Longfield, *Secularization of the Academy*; and Marsden, *Soul of the American University*. Jacobs seems unaware of his connection to this tradition.

46. Roberts and Turner, *Sacred and Secular University*, 117–18, 120.

47. For English, philology, and science, see Turner, *Philology*; Warner, "Professionalism and the Rewards of Literature"; Phyllis Franklin, "English Studies in America: Reflections on the Development of a Discipline," *American Quarterly* 30 (1978): 21–38; G. Graff, *Professing Literature*; Graff and Warner, *Origins of Literary Studies in America*; Harpham, *Humanities and the Dream of America*; Parker, "Where Do English Departments Come From?"; Abrams, "Transformation of English Studies"; and the works of Guillory. For linguistics, see Aarsleff, *From Locke to Saussure*, and Aarsleff, Kelly, and Hans-Niederehe, *Papers in the History of Linguistics*. For more on philology and languages, see Andresen, *Linguistics in America*; Gurd, *Philology and Its Histories*; Martin-Nielsen, "Forgotten Social Science?"; McGann, "Philology in a New Key"; Bhambra and Holmwood, "Introduction"; and Peterson, "Art of Language Teaching."

48. H. C. G. Brandt, "How Far Should Our Teaching and Text-Books Have a Scientific Basis?" *Transactions of the Modern Language Association of America* 1 (1884–1885): 57, 58. He asserts, "I am ready to lay down and defend the following proposition: All teaching should start from a strictly scientific basis, and all aids in teaching, the text-books, reference books, etc., should be constructed upon a strictly scientific basis."

49. Ibid., 59, 60, 61.

50. See Garber, *Academic Instincts*. Discussions in the 1880s include James M. Garnett, "The Course in English and Its Value as a Discipline," *Transactions and Proceedings of the Modern Language Association of America* 2 (1886): 61–73; J. M. Hart, "The College

Course in English Literature, How It May Be Improved," *Modern Language Association of America Proceedings* 1 (Dec. 29, 1884): x–xiii; and Theodore W. Hunt, "The Place of English in the College Curriculum," *Transactions of the Modern Language Association* 1 (1884–85): 118–32.

51. Guillory, "Literary Study and the Modern System of the Disciplines," 24, 26.

52. Ibid., 27, 28; cf. Grafton and Jardine, *From Humanism to the Humanities*. Contrast James Turner and Paul Bernard, "The 'German Model' and the Graduate School: The University of Michigan and the Origin Myth of the American University," Rackham Reports, University of Michigan, 1988–89, 5–52, abridged in *History of Higher Education Annual* 13 (1993), 69–98.

53. Guillory, "Literary Study and the Modern System of the Disciplines," 28.

54. Ibid. See also Turner, *Philology*.

55. Guillory, "Literary Study and the Modern System of the Disciplines," 29.

56. Aarsleff, *From Locke to Saussure*, 32.

57. Guillory, "Literary Study and the Modern System of the Disciplines," 29. He continues: "Of course, historical discourses could maintain this claim to scientificity only insofar as they established *facts*. It was on the basis of determined facts that philology then sought to establish *laws* governing the regularity of linguistic change. . . . Philology developed an empirical mode of procedure, in which literary texts were considered to be only one kind of evidence (not necessarily the most reliable) for propositions concerning the history of language."

58. Ibid., 30.

59. Ibid., 31.

60. Ibid., 36. See Warner, "Professionalism and the Rewards of Literature," on the contradictions of professionalization in English.

61. Parker, "Where Do English Departments Come From?," 348.

62. Leland, "Recent Trends in the Humanities," 281, 282.

63. Ibid., 282, 285.

64. Green, *Meaning of the Humanities*, xiv–xv.

65. Ibid., xv, xvi. For context, see Bialas and Rabinach, *Nazi Germany and the Humanities*.

66. Perry, "Definition of the Humanities," 4. See also J. Klein, *Humanities, Culture, and Interdisciplinarity*; Newell, *Interdisciplinarity*; and Kockelmans, *Interdisciplinarity and Higher Education*.

67. Perry, "Definition of the Humanities," 4, 6, 32. He continues: "Institutions dedicated to humanism [freedom] perpetually develop agencies which thwart this purpose. There are four such dehumanizing influences that may be singled out for special mention—technique, the multiplication of accessory disciplines, departmental separations, and vocational utility. Technique tends to become a game played for its own sake. It tends to divorce expertness from significance, and thus to trivialize research and blind both student and teacher to the purposes by which technique is justified."

68. Ibid., 42.

69. Have we learned any lessons? See "Uses," *New Literary History* 44 (Autumn 2013).

70. See G. Graff, *Professing Literature*, 136.

71. Hawkes, "Curriculum Revision at Columbia College," 34. For a retrospective analysis, see Howley and Hartnett, "Columbia's Grand Narrative of Contemporary Civilization."

72. See Frickel and Gross, "General Theory of Scientific/Intellectual Movements," and Jacobs and Frickel, "Interdisciplinarity."

73. See Guillory, "Who's Afraid of Marcel Proust"; Bell, *Reforming General Education*; and Jencks and Riesman, *Academic Revolution*.

74. Quoted in Tannenbaum, "University Seminar Movement at Columbia University," 162, 163, 164.

75. Ibid., 166–67.

76. Ibid., 172.

77. Gross, "Columbia University Seminars," 45. The scale that Gross described in 1982 is a far cry from the small, contained "movement" envisioned by Miller and Tannenbaum in 1940s and early 1950s.

78. This statement barely hints at the real difficulties for faculty, graduate students, and programs. See Abbott, *Chaos of Disciplines*.

79. McGrath, "General Education Movement," 3. John Guillory, Jerry Jacobs, Bill Readings, and Stanley Aronowitz are among the many critics of this view. Most attempts at explaining interdisciplinarity in general education obfuscate more than they clarify. See also Kaufmann, *Future of the Humanities*, and Chopp, Frost, and Weiss, *Remaking College*.

80. McGrath, "General Education Movement," 5.

81. J. Klein, *Humanities, Culture, and Interdisciplinarity*, 35.

82. Stevens, "Philosophy of General Education and Its Contradictions," 174–75.

83. Guillory, "Who's Afraid of Marcel Proust," 27.

84. Ibid., 30.

85. Ibid., 30, 36. On the problems of the humanities in curricular reform, see, for example, Porwancher, "Humanism's Sisyphean Task."

86. Bell, *Reforming of General Education*, 289–90. See Guillory, "Who's Afraid of Marcel Proust?"; Committee on General Education, *General Education in a Free Society*; Belknap and Kuhns, *Tradition and Innovation*; Hutchins, *Higher Learning in America*; Jencks and Riesman, *Academic Revolution*; Grant and Riesman, *Perpetual Dream*. More generally, see Rubin, *Making of Middlebrow Culture* and "Scholar and the World"; and Radway, *Feeling for Books*.

87. See *Issues in Integrative Studies*, now *Issues in Interdisciplinary Studies*.

88. The humanities do not always benefit by borrowing from the sciences and social sciences. Consider, for one example, the argument made in Casey, "Quiet Revolution," 71: "A transformation has occurred in the humanities during the past four decades which has permitted the humanistic disciplines to reintegrate with each other and with the social sciences. The gradual absorption of Saussurean linguistics has brought about a profound change in our understanding of the relationship between language and the world. This, in turn, has resulted in an age of theory and in the production of metalanguages which reinforce the connective power of the humanistic disciplines. Linguistic models have replaced models borrowed from the natural sciences." Linguists would laugh, I fear. See also "The Future of Interdisciplinary Studies: Papers from the Association

for Integrative Studies National Meeting, Feb., 1984," *Issues in Integrative Studies* 3 (1984–1985); Kockelmans, "Interdisciplinarity and the University"; Newell, *Interdisciplinarity*; Klein and Newell, "Advancing Interdisciplinary Studies"; Saxberg and Newell, "Integration of Interdisciplinary Research"; Borrego and Newswander, "Definitions of Interdisciplinary Research"; and "Interdisciplinary Studies," special issue, *European Journal of Education* 27, no. 3 (1992).

89. J. Klein, *Humanities, Culture, and Interdisciplinarity*, 77.

90. Ibid., 78. See also J. Klein, *Creating Interdisciplinary Campus Cultures*.

91. For a display of the current faddishness amid confusion, see "Interdisciplinarity at the Crossroads," *Liberal Education* 94, no. 1 (2008), esp. "From the Editor" and Ethan Kleinberg, "Interdisciplinary Studies at a Crossroad," 6–11. For more confusion about interdisciplinarity but also a sense of chronology, see G. Graff, *Professing Literature*, chap. 13: "Promise of American Literature Studies." See also Greenblatt and Gunn, *Redrawing the Boundaries*; "The Second Book Project," *American Literary History* 25, no. 1 (Spring 2013); Smithson and Ruff, *English Studies / Culture Studies*.

92. They include departments of Journalism and Mass Communication; English, Theatre, and Communications; Communication Sciences and Disorders; Communication; Communications; Communication, Mass Media, and Theatre; Communication and Journalism; Journalism, Public Relations, and New Media; Communication Studies; Journalism and Technical Communications; Strategic Communications; Media Arts and Entertainment; Communication Science; Interactive Media; Communication Arts; Mass Communication; Journalism, Media Studies, and Public Relations; Communications and Rhetoric Studies; Speech Communication; Communication and Art; Communication and Fine Arts; Communication and the Arts; Journalism and Public Communications; Communication Sciences and Speech Disorders; Communication and Sociology; Cinema and Interactive Media; Journalism and Media Management; Contemporary Media and Journalism; Communication Studies and Theater Arts, in various schools, colleges, and divisions including Arts and Sciences, Social Sciences, Arts, Education, and professional schools. There are schools and colleges and graduate schools (many named and endowed for famous journalists, media moguls, or corporations) of Communication; Communications; Graduate School of Journalism and Mass Communication; School of Journalism and Graphic Communication; Journalism and Communications; Mass Communication; Journalism and Media Studies; Public Communications; Communication and Information; Communication Science; Journalism and Telecommunications; Communication and Information; and Journalism and Broadcasting. My thanks to graduate research assistant Krista Bryson for compiling this list.

93. The field is dominated by American Communication Association, International Communication Association, Speech Communication Association, and especially the National Communication Association. A longer list includes the Association for Education in Journalism and Mass Communication, Association for Educational Communications and Technology, Canadian Communication Association, Center for Global Communication, Center for the Study of Communication and Culture, Communication Arena, Conference on College Composition and Communication, International Association for Intercultural Communication Studies, International Association of Business Communicators, International Telecommunication Union, National Association of Broadcasters,

Public Relations Society of America, Religious Communication Association, Rhetoric Society of America, and Society of Technical Communications, World Communication Association, and various regional associations including Southern States Communication Association, Eastern Communication Association, Central States Communication Association, and Western States Communication Association, as well as international associations. The American Library Association's Association of College and Research Librarians Collection Development Toolkit roster of Associations and Organizations in Communication includes 46 separate groups; see http://wikis.ala.org/acrl/index.php /Associations_&_Organizations.

94. See Carey, *Communication as Culture*; Schiller, *Theorizing Communication*; Park and Pooley, *History of Media and Communication Research*; Barton, "Paul Lazarsfeld and Applied Social Research" and "Paul Lazarsfeld and the Invention of the University Institute for Applied Social Research"; Glickman, "Consumer and the Citizen"; Sproule, "Communication"; Pooley, "Fifteen Pages That Shook the Field"; Beniger, "Toward an Old New Paradigm" and "Who Are the Most Important Theorists of Communication?"; Glander, "Wilbur Schramm and the Founding of Communication Studies"; Igo, "Gold Mine and Tool for Democracy"; Jowett, "Propaganda and Communication"; Lasswell, "Communications as an Emerging Discipline"; and Peters and Simonson, *Mass Communication and American Social Thought*.

95. Rogers, *History of Communication Study*, which includes Darwin, Freud, and Marx (in that order); Dennis and Wartella, *American Communication Research*; Park and Pooley, *History of Media and Communication Research*.

96. Robinson, "Constructing a Historiography for North American Communication Studies," 157, 159. My review of the literature shows that communication is ill served by its histories. History was not among the subjects of the 2008 special issue of *Journal of Communication*.

97. Robinson, "Constructing a Historiography for North American Communication Studies," 161. Compare her periodization with Hardt, "Return of the 'Critical' and the Challenge of Radical Dissent."

98. Dennis and Wartella, *American Communication Research*, 171. More generally, see Czitrom, *Media and the American Mind*; Pooley, "Daniel Czitrom, James W. Carey, and the Chicago School"; Wahl-Jorgensen, "How Not to Found a Field" and "Rebellion and Ritual"; Gitlin, "Media Sociology"; Pietila, "Perspectives on Our Past"; Sproule, "Propaganda Studies in American Social Science."

99. Schiller, *Theorizing Communication*, 55–56. Although Schiller overemphasizes ideas and does not make grounded connections, his is one of the most incisive works on communication.

100. Ibid., 56–57.

101. Ibid., 58–59, 63.

102. For one view see Cmiel, "On Cynicism, Evil, and the Discovery of Communication in the 1940s."

103. Wahl-Jorgensen, "How Not to Found a Field," 561.

104. Lasswell, "Communications as an Emerging Discipline," 253.

105. E. Katz, "Why Sociology Abandoned Mass Communication Research"; see also Pooley and Katz, "Further Notes on Why American Sociology Abandoned Mass Communication Research."

106. "Who abandoned whom?" is the wrong question. Katz's answer, too, is teleological: "It is likely that these pioneers of communication research saw sociology as only one of the ingredients of an interdisciplinary enterprise; it is also possible that they perceived such an amalgamation becoming increasingly fashionable as modernity proceeded. Perhaps the sociologists among them just jumped ship." E. Katz, "Why Sociology Abandoned Mass Communication Research," 173.

107. Pooley, "New History of Mass Communication Research," 59, 60.

108. For recent examples, see "Humanities Scholars Grapple with Their Pitch to the Public," *CHE*, May 12, 2014; "At MIT, the Humanities Are Just as Important as STEM," *Boston Globe*, Apr. 30, 2014; David Hollinger, "The Wedge Driving Academe's Two Families Apart: Can STEM and the Humanities Get Along?" *CHE*, Oct. 14, 2013.

Chapter 3 · *In Search of Unification for War and Peace*

1. Isaac, *Working Knowledge*, 8, 9.

2. For examples, compare Crowther-Heyck, "Patrons of the Revolution" and *Herbert A. Simon*, and Agar, *Lively Science*.

3. Isaac neglects other visions of human science and different notions of science itself, especially in Europe. On "forgetting" Soc Rel, see Calhoun, *Sociology in America*. Soc Rel was both a vision of behavioral science and critique of normative empiricist versions—a problem in theory and practice over which wrangling continues.

4. Isaac, *Working Knowledge*, 8, 9.

5. "Operations Research," *Wikipedia* (modified Oct. 25, 2014), http://en.wikipedia.org/wiki/Operations_research.

6. Soc Rel stimulated criticisms from the beginning, particularly from OR and the founders of cognitive science, such as Jerome Bruner.

7. The duration of the Department of Social Relations, 1946–1970, is not as much an issue here as its integrity as a department. Soc Rel is briefly mentioned several times in Calhoun, *Sociology in America*. But it is not listed in its index or in the index of Backhouse and Fontaine, *History of the Social Sciences since 1945*. Roger Smith does not discuss it in his lengthy *Norton History of the Human Sciences*, although he does mention Parsons once. It does not appear at all in Porter and Ross, *Modern Social Sciences*.

8. See Isaac, "Human Sciences and Cold War America" and "Human Sciences in Cold War America"; Crowther-Heyck, "Patrons of the Revolution" and *Herbert A. Simon*; Solovey and Cravens, *Cold War Social Science*; Engerman, "Rethinking Cold War Universities," "Rise and Fall of Wartime Social Science," "Ironies of the Iron Curtain," and *Know Your Enemy*; Gleason, "World War II and the Development of American Studies"; Engerman et al., *Staging Growth*; Brick, *Transcending Capitalism*; Leslie, *Cold War and American Science*; Lecuyer, *Making Silicon Valley*; Mindell, *Between Man and Machine*; Mirowski, *Machine Dreams*; and Erickson et al., *How Reason Almost Lost Its Mind*.

9. Isaac, *Working Knowledge*, 16, 23.

10. See also Camic, "Making of a Method," "*Structure* after 50 Years," and "Reputation and Predecessor Selection." Cf. Brick, "Talcott Parsons's 'Shift Away from Economics'" and "Reformist Dimension of Talcott Parsons's Early Social Theory." This point is missed in Nichols, "Social Relations Undone" and "Establishment of Sociology at Harvard," and Johnston, "Sorokin and Parsons at Harvard."

11. Isaac lists the Royce Club, Pareto circle, Society of Fellows, Alfred North White-head's Cambridge salon, the Science of Science Discussion Group, and the Institute for the Unity of Science in Boston, as well as the Department of Social Relations and the general education program of James Bryant Conant.

12. Isaac, *Working Knowledge*, 23–24.

13. The movement had other failings and fallacies; it neither institutionalized nor integrated.

14. Morris, "Unity of Science Movements and the United States"; "Unity of Science Forum," chartered by the Board of Regents, State of New York, July 31, 1947. See Isaac, *Working Knowledge*; Hollinger, "Science as a Weapon in *Kulturkampfe*" and "Unity of Knowledge and Diversity of Knowers"; Galison, "Americanization of Unity"; and Galison and Stump, *Disunity of Science*. See also C. Taylor, "Interpretation and the Sciences of Man," and Choi, "Defending Anti-Naturalism after the Interpretive Turn."

15. On the notion of a "movement," see Frickel, "Building an Interdiscipline," and Frickel and Gross, "General Theory of Scientific / Intellectual Movements."

16. Most approaches to Soc Rel are overly concerned with its singularity and miss the fact that it was part of important general currents and more concrete efforts that took a variety of forms in theory and practice. For related movements, some with associated programs, see J. Miller, "Toward a General Theory for the Behavioral Sciences"; Fontaine, "Stabilizing American Society"; Morawski, "Organizing Knowledge and Behavior"; and Ralph W. Tyler, "Study Center for Behavioral Scientists," *Science* 123 (Mar. 9, 1956): 405–8. For the relationships of OR to concerns about unity and general theory, see the work of Herbert Simon and his University of Chicago connections, as explained in Crowther-Heyck, *Herbert A. Simon*.

17. For Parsons's introductions to theory, see Parsons, "Prospects of Sociological Theory," "Clyde Kluckhohn and the Integration of Social Science," and "Theory in the Humanities and Sociology." On Parsons and the Department of Social Relations, see Camic, "Making of a Method," "*Structure* after 50 Years," and "Reputation and Predecessor Selection"; Eisenstadt, "Social Evolution and Modernity"; Homans, *Coming to My Senses*; Johnston, "Sorokin and Parsons at Harvard"; Isaac, "Tangled Loops," "Tool Shock," "Theorist at Work," and "Epistemic Design"; Owens, "Producing Parsons' Reputation"; Powers, "Harvard Study of Values"; Triplet, "Harvard Psychology, the Psychological Clinic, and Henry Murray"; Vidich, "Department of Social Relations and 'Systems Theory'"; Johnson and Johnson, "Integrating of Social Sciences"; and Fox, "Talcott Parsons, My Teacher." For criticisms of Parsons, see Brick, "Optimism of the Mind," "Reformist Dimension of Talcott Parsons's Early Social Theory," "Talcott Parsons's 'Shift Away from Economics,'" and *Transcending Capitalism*; Engerman, "Rise and Fall of Wartime Social Science"; N. Gilman, *Mandarins of the Future*; and Robin, *Making the Cold War Enemy*.

18. Kuper, *Culture*, 53, 52.

19. Vidich, "Department of Social Relations and 'Systems Theory,'" 615.

20. Camic, "Three Departments in Search of a Discipline," 1008.

21. Ibid., 1011, 1016–17, 1025.

22. Camic, "*Structure* after 50 Years," 94.

23. Allport and Boring, "Psychology and Social Relations," 119–20; see also M. Bentley, "The Harvard Case for Psychology," *American Journal of Psychology* 61 (1948): 275–82.

24. Isaac, *Working Knowledge*, 177.

25. Steinmetz, "American Sociology before and after World War II," 350, 351. See also Buck, *Social Sciences at Harvard*.

26. Camic, "*Structure* after 50 Years," 94-95. He continues: "instead of interpreting *Structure* . . . as the 'ideology' of an already established socioeconomic or religious group, we may approach it as a charter, a charter for the still 'emerging science that was the domain of the sociologist.'"

27. Quoted in Isaac, *Working Knowledge*, 176. The comparison with biology is not accidental.

28. Ibid.

29. Ibid., 177, quoting Johnson and Johnson, "Integrating the Social Sciences."

30. Isaac, *Working Knowledge*, 178.

31. See Parsons, "Clyde Kluckhohn and the Integration of Social Science."

32. Isaac, *Working Knowledge*, 178. Space is a common concern with regard to the institutionalization of interdisciplinarity; see, for example, Strober, *Interdisciplinary Conversations*, and Lattuca, *Creating Interdisciplinarity*.

33. Isaac, *Working Knowledge*, 178.

34. Ibid., 178–79.

35. Homans, *Coming to My Senses*, 301–2.

36. Ibid.

37. Ibid., 302–3.

38. Vidich, "Department of Social Relations and 'Systems Theory,'" 617, 618, 620–21. Vidich illustrates the gap between "an idealized image of research methods and research in action." The student report he excerpts is "a hodge-podge of terms and definitions, a free borrowing of definitions from psychology that had little or no relation to each other. The enterprise, in short, was a distillation of definitions taken from the extant psychological literature. . . . [making] a statement which seems to have very little meaning, if any" (627).

39. Homans, *Coming to My Senses*, 304.

40. Isaac, *Working Knowledge*, 184–90. Social psychologists who had sought freedom from experimental and physiological psychology in Soc Rel soon found themselves outside the bounds of Parsons's program. By 1959, they were considering rejoining the other psychologists. With George Miller of the psychology department, Jerome Bruner established the Center for Cognitive Studies. He later reflected on fissures in both psychology and Social Relations. Psychology was divided between B. F. Skinner's "operant conditioning" and S. S. Stevens's psychophysics, while "my department, Social Relations, was moving further and further away from psychological concerns." Bruner, *In Search of Mind*, 122.

41. Isaac, *Working Knowledge*, 190–91. On the department's decline in the 1950s and 1960s, see Nichols, "Social Relations Undone." Engerman, *Know Your Enemy*, chap. 7, discusses offshoots of Soc Rel in area studies, especially Harvard's Russian Research Center. World War II experiences and fears, postwar concerns about conflict and consensus, liberalism and conservatism, and political economy and international affairs are all part of this history.

42. Mirowski, *Machine Dreams*, 177.

43. See Mirowski, *Machine Dreams*; Augier and March, *Roots, Rituals, and Rhetorics of Change*; and Aaronson, "Serving America's Business?"

44. See Crowther-Heyck, *Herbert A. Simon*, and Mirowski, *Machine Dreams*. See also Edwards, *Closed World*; Heims, *Cybernetics Group*; and Mindell, *Between Man and Machine*.

45. Waring, *Taylorism Transformed*; Shenhav, "From Chaos to Systems."

46. Important (though flawed) works on the history of OR include Aaronson, "Serving America's Business?"; Assad and Gass, *Profiles in Operations Research*; Augier and March, *Roots, Rituals, and Rhetorics of Change*; Braverman, *Labor and Monopoly Capital*; Crowther-Heyck, *Herbert A. Simon*; Dawson et al., "Operations Research at Bell Laboratories"; Dyson, *Turing's Cathedral*; Edwards, *Closed World*; Galison, "Ontology of the Enemy"; Gass and Assad, *Annotated Timeline of Operations Research*; Gertner, *Idea Factory*; Heims, *Cybernetics Group*; Heukelom, "Measurement and Decision Making"; Hounshell, "Cold War, RAND"; S. Johnson, "Three Approaches to Big Technology"; Kirby, "Operations Research Trajectories," "Paradigm Change in Operations Research," "Intellectual Journey of Russell Ackoff," and "Spreading the Gospel of Management Science"; Kirby and Capey, "Origins and Diffusion of Operational Research in the UK"; Kirby and Godwin, "Invisible Science"; McCloskey, "Beginnings of Operations Research," "Training for Operations Research," "British Operations Research in World War II," and "U.S. Operations Research in World War II"; Mindell, *Between Man and Machine*; Mirowski, *Machine Dreams* and "When Games Grow Deadly Serious"; Noble, *America by Design* and *Forces of Production*; Shenhav, "From Chaos to Systems"; J. Smith, *Idea Brokers*; Solovey and Cravens, *Cold War Social Science*; Thomas, "Selling Operations Research," "Heuristics of War," and "Operations Research vis-à-vis Management"; Thomas and Williams, "The Epistemologies of Non-Forecasting Simulations," parts 1 and 2; Waring, "Cold War Calculus" and *Taylorism Transformed*; and Zuckerman, *Beyond the Ivory Tower, Monkeys, Men, and Missiles*, and *Scientists and War*.

See also Atsushi Akera, *Calculating a Natural World: Scientists, Engineers, and Computers during the Rise of US Cold War Research* (Cambridge, MA: MIT Press, 2007); Derman Christopherson and E. C. Baughan, "Reminiscences of Operational Research in World War II by Some of Its Practitioners," *Journal of the Operational Research Society* 43, no. 6 (1992): 569–77; James R. Beniger, *The Control Revolution: Technological and Economic Origins of the Information Society* (Cambridge, MA: Harvard University Press, 1986); Alfred D. Chandler Jr. *The Visible Hand: The Managerial Revolution in American Business* (Cambridge, MA: Harvard University Press, 1977); M. Fortun and S. S. Schweber, "Scientists and the Legacy of World War II: The Case of Operations Research," *Social Studies of Science* 23 (1993): 595–642; Saul I. Gass and Carl M. Harris, *Encyclopedia of Operations Research and Management Science* (Boston: Kluwer Academic, 2000); Agatha C. Hughes and Thomas P. Hughes, eds., *Systems, Experts, and Computers: The Systems Approach in Management and Engineering, World War II and After* (Cambridge, MA: MIT Press, 2000); Daniel J. Kevles, *The Physicists: The History of a Scientific Community in Modern America* (New York: Vintage, 1979); Michael E. Latham, "Ideology, Social Science, and Destiny: Modernization and the Kennedy-Era Alliance for Progress," *Diplomatic History* 22 (1998): 199–229; Jennifer Light, "Taking Games Seriously," *Technology and Culture* 49 (2008): 347–75; Hugh J. Miser, "The Scientist as Adviser: The Relevance of the Early Operations Research Experience," *Minerva* 11 (1973): 95–108; Theodore M. Porter, *Trust in Numbers:*

The Pursuit of Objectivity in Science and Public Life (Princeton, NJ: Princeton University Press, 1995); Erik P. Rau, "Combat Scientists: The Emergence of Operations Research in the United States during World War II" (PhD diss., University of Pennsylvania, 1999); S. Schweber, "The Mutual Embrace of Science and the Military: ONR and the Growth of Physics in the United States after World War II," *Science, Technology, and the Military* 12 (1988): 1–456; Peter Temin, ed., *Inside the Business Enterprise: Historical Perspectives on the Use of Information* (Chicago: University of Chicago Press, 1991); and JoAnne Yates, *Control through Communication: The Rise of System in American Management* (Baltimore, MD: Johns Hopkins University Press, 1989).

For an overview of the field's development, see the professional journals, especially "Milestones in OR," *Journal of the Operational Research Society* 60, suppl 1 (May 2009): s1–s179; "The Foundation, Development and Current Practice of OR," *Journal of the Operational Research Society* 49, no. 4 (April 1998): i–443; "Special Issue on New Directions in Operations Management," *Operations Research* 44, no. 1 (Jan.–Feb. 1996); Russell L. Ackoff, "A Reply to the Comments of Keith Chesterton, Robert Goodsman, Jonathan Rosenhead, and Colin Thurnhurst," *Operational Research Quarterly* 26 (1975): 96–99; "The Future of Operational Research Is Past," *Journal of the Operational Research Society* 30 (1979): 93–104; and "Resurrecting the Future of Operational Research," *Journal of the Operational Research Society* 30 (1979): 189–95; Kenneth J. Arrow, "Decision Theory and Operations Research," *Operations Research* 5, no. 6 (1957): 765–74; C. W. Churchman, "OR as a Profession," *Management Science* 17 (1970): B3–53; Charles J. Corbett and Luk N. van Wassenhove, "The Natural Drift: What Happened to Operations Research?" *Operations Research* 41 (1993), 625–40; A. S. Douglas, "New Opportunities for O.R.," *Journal of the Operational Research Society* 32 (1981): 251–54; R. G. Dyson, "Editorial: The 50th Anniversary of the Founding of the OR Society," *Journal of the Operational Research Society* 49 (1998), 303; John S. Edwards, B. Ababneh, M. Hall, and Duncan Shaw, "Knowledge Management: A Review of the Field and of OR's Contribution," *Journal of the Operational Research Society* 60, S1 (2009): s114–25; Charles D. Flagle, "Some Origins of Operations Research in the Health Services," *Operations Research* 50 (2002): 52–60; Elizabeth Galloway Rubbo, "ORSA Turns 40," *OR/MS* 19 (1992): 50–52; Herbert Holt and Melvin E. Salveson, "Psychoanalytic Contributions to an Operational Research Study of Marketing," *OR* 11 (1960); Peter R. Horner, "TIMS Turns 40," *OR/MS Today* 20, no. 2 (1993): 40–43; Michael C. Jackson, "Fifty Years of Systems Thinking for Management," *Journal of the Operational Research Society* 60, S1 (2009): S24–32; Murat Koksalan, Jyrki Wallenius, and Stanley Zionts, *Multiple Criteria Decision Making: From Early History to the 21st Century* (Hackensack, NJ: World Scientific, 2011); Luiz Fernando Loureiro Legey and Saul Fuks, "Critique of a Materialist Analysis of Operational Research," *Journal of the Operations Research Society* 39 (1988): 1095–100; John D. C. Little, "Philip M. Morse and the Beginnings," *Operations Research* 50 (2002); Magee, "Operations Research at Arthur D. Little"; Thomas W. Malone and Kevin Crowston, "The Interdisciplinary Study of Coordination," *ACM Computing Surveys* 26 (1994): 87–119; Jeffrey Pfeffer and Robert I. Sutton, *The Knowing-Doing Gap: How Smart Companies Turn Knowledge into Action* (Cambridge, MA: Harvard Business School Press, 2000); Robin R. Rider, "Operations Research and Game Theory: Early Connections," in *Toward a History of Game Theory*, ed. E. Roy Weintraub, *History of Political Economy Annual Supplement* 24 (1992): 225–39; G. Royston, "One Hundred Years of Operational Research in Health—UK 1948–2048," *Journal of the*

Operational Research Society 60 (2009): S169–79; Melvin E. Salveson, "The Founding Fathers of TIMS: Historical Re-Examination of Humanity Inspired the Development of the Management Sciences," *OR/MS Today* 30 (2003), and "The Institute of Management Sciences: A Prehistory and Commentary on the Occasion of TIMS' 40th Anniversary," *Interfaces* 27 (1997): 74–85; Donald Schoen, *The Reflective Practitioner: How Professionals Think in Action* (New York: Basic Books, 1984); Mark Tadajewski, "The Politics of the Behavioural Revolution in Organization Studies," *Organization* 16 (2009): 733–54; Florence N. Trefethen, "A History of Operations Research," in *Operations Research for Management*, ed. Joseph F. McCloskey and Florence N. Trefethen (Baltimore, MD: Johns Hopkins University Press, 1954), 3–35; Mike Trick, "OR: Past, Present and Future (President's Desk)," *OR/MS Today* 29, no.5 (2002); and Andrew Vazsonyi, "Milestone Manifesto (Celebrating 50 Years of Operations Research)," *OR/MS Today* 29, no. 5 (2002).

47. Horner, "History in the Making"; J. Hall, "Issue-Oriented History of TIMS."

48. The early definitions and compendiums reflect a dominance of matters of practice, including mathematical methods. See, for example, Operations Research Center, Massachusetts Institute of Technology, *Notes on Operations Research* (Cambridge, MA: MIT Press, 1959); Russell L. Ackoff and Maurice W. Saieni, *Fundamentals of Operations Research* (New York: John Wiley, 1968); Irwin D. J. Bross, *Design for Decision* (New York: Macmillan, 1953); Herman Chernoff and Lincoln E. Moses, *Elementary Decision Theory* (New York: Wiley, 1959); Walter W. Garvin, *Introduction to Linear Programming* (New York: McGraw-Hill, 1960); Charles Goodeve, "Operations Research," *Nature* 161 (Mar. 13, 1948): 377–84; David Bendel Hertz, *The Theory and Practice of Industrial Research* (New York: McGraw-Hill, 1950); William J. Horvath, "Operations Research—A Scientific Basis for Executive Decisions," *American Statistician* 2 (1948): 6–8; Ellis A. Johnson, "Operations Research in the World Crisis in Science and Technology," in *Operations Research and Systems Engineering*, ed. Charles D. Fagle, William H. Huggins, and Robert H. Roy (Baltimore, MD: Johns Hopkins University Press, 1960), 28–57; Albert Lepawsky, *Administration: The Art and Science of Organization and Management* (New York: A. A. Knopf, 1949); P. Stewart Macaulay, "The Market Place and the Ivory Tower," in *Operations Research and Systems Engineering*, ed. Charles D. Fagle, William H. Huggins, and Robert H. Roy (Baltimore, MD: Johns Hopkins University Press, 1960), 3–7; Morse and Kimball, *Methods of Operations Research*; Robert H. Roy, "The Development and Future of Operations Research and Systems Engineering," in Fagle, Huggins, and Roy, *Operations Research and Systems Engineering*, 8–27; Melvin E. Salveson, *Dynamic Organization Planning* (New Canaan, CT: Center for Advanced Management, 1959); Melvin E. Salveson, *Mathematical Methods in Management Programming* (Los Angeles: University of California Press, 1954), *The Modern Entrepreneur* (New Canaan, CT: CAM Press, 1958), and *Organization Planning for Integrated Decision Making* (New Canaan, CT: CAM Press, 1957); Society for the Advancement of Management, *Managing Progress through Operations Research* (New York, 1959); Herbert Solow, "Operations Research," *Fortune*, Apr. 1951, 105–12; John von Neumann and Oskar Morgenstern, *Theory of Games and Economic Behavior* (Princeton, NJ: Princeton University Press, 1953).

49. I am sympathetic to many of the criticisms of the field's uses to support corporate growth, monopoly capitalism, and globalization. Those are different issues from the concerns of this book. Some critical perspectives are immature, derivative, and very late in coming.

50. Waring, "Cold War Calculus," 28. See also Waring, *Taylorism Transformed*.

51. Isaac, "Human Sciences in Cold War America," 739.

52. Ibid. See also Crowther-Heyck, "Patrons of the Revolution" and *Herbert A. Simon*.

53. Mirowski, *Machine Dreams*, 182.

54. In addition to Steven Waring, other leftist critics include Harry Braverman and David Noble.

55. Mirowski, *Machine Dreams*, 117–18.

56. The editor notes that Gass stated that "some items may be missing, and the inclusion of some items may be debatable" (n.p.).

57. Gass and Assad, *Annotated Timeline of Operations Research*, ix.

58. Ibid., ix–x.

59. Ibid., x.

60. Mirowski, *Machine Dreams*, 178–79.

61. Ibid., 180.

62. Ibid., 182.

63. Mirowski argues that the United States was more receptive to OR than Great Britain was because of its culture, ideology, and state policies toward science, but I am not persuaded by these assertions. One example of his prose suffices: "Just as gun control was transubstantiated into cybernetics, OR became subsequently transmuted into systems analysis; and the drive to subsume organizational reform under the umbrella of quantification and computer expertise led inexorably to another search for a Theory of Everything every bit as ambitious as the holy grail of a unified field theory" (184).

64. McCloskey, "Beginnings of Operations Research," 143.

65. In addition to McCloskey, "Beginnings of Operations Research," see Thomas, "Heuristics of War."

66. McCloskey, "Beginnings of Operations Research," 147.

67. Charles Kittel's 1947 paper in *Science*, "The Nature and Development of Operations Research," was among the first to bring the ideas of OR to the U.S. scientific community. Kittel stated: "It is hoped that the publication of this paper will serve to stimulate the establishment of operations research groups in the United States for the advancement of peaceful objectives. This powerful new tool should find a place in government and industry." Most important, Kittel formulated a clear definition of OR: "Operations Research is a scientific method for providing executive departments with a *quantitative basis for decisions*." This definition was modified by Charles Goodeve (1948) to read: "Operational Research is a scientific method of providing executive departments with a quantitative basis for decisions regarding the operations under their control." This definition was popularized by Morse and Kimball's *Methods of Operations Research* (1951). Kittel, a physicist, served as an operations analyst with the U.S. fleet from 1943 to 1945 and then on the faculty of the University of California, Berkeley. See also Morse, "Of Men and Machines," and McCloskey, "Beginnings of Operations Research."

68. Thomas, "Heuristics of War," 253.

69. Ibid., 251, 272, 273. See also Thomas, "Selling Operations Research"; Thomas and Williams, "Epistemologies," parts 1 and 2.

70. Contrast this view with Mirowski, of whom Thomas is critical but not always convincingly so. Cf. Dyson, *Turing's Cathedral*, and Gertner, *Idea Factory*. Mirowski's

"cyborg" history also differs from Williams and Thomas's view of management training at MIT. See Thomas and Williams, "Epistemologies of Non-Forecasting Simulations," part 2.

71. Crowther-Heyck, "Herbert Simon and the GSIA," 313; see also Crowther-Heyck, *Herbert A. Simon.*

72. Mirowski, *Machine Dreams,* 117.

73. Thomas, "Selling Operations Research," 1. See also Augier and March, *Roots, Rituals, and Rhetorics of Change;* Aaronson, "Serving America's Business?"; Foucade, *Economists and Societies;* and table 3.1 in this volume.

74. Morse, "Of Men and Machines"; 60.

75. Ibid. Morse acknowledges the limits of OR: "Final decisions on alternative measures of value must be decided by the administrator; but the operations analyst can investigate the various possibilities and report on the quantitative implications of each. In any administrative decision there enter a great number of considerations which cannot be put into quantitative form. Knowledge of these qualitative aspects and ability to handle them are the proper functions of the administrator and are not the prerogative of operations research." See also Kittel, "Nature and Development of Operations Research."

76. J. Smith, *Idea Brokers,* 115–16.

77. Hounshell, "Cold War, RAND," 242. Hounshell, "Medium is the Message, or How Context Matters," deals with the economics of innovation. See also Gene H. Fisher and Warren E. Waler, "Operations Research and the RAND Corporation," *Encyclopedia of Operations Research and Management Science,* ed. Saul J. Gass and Carl M. Harris (Boston: Kluwer Academic, 1996), 566–71.

78. Hounshell, "Cold War, RAND," 242.

79. AT&T was another important site for OR research; see Gertner, *Idea Factory.* On Bell Labs, see Dawson et al., "Operations Research at Bell Laboratories." If accounts like Gertner's are indicative, not all major innovations strictly followed OR paths, and problems often arose in the process of translation and application. On consulting, see Thomas, "Operations Research vis-à-vis Management," and Magee, "Operations Research at Arthur D. Little, Inc." For critiques, see Galison, "Ontology of the Enemy"; Reintjes, *Numerical Control;* and Waring, "Cold War Calculus" and *Taylorism Transformed.* Important criticisms also come from popular culture, such as *Dr. Strangelove.* Politics, ideology, and culture are inherent in the use of interdisciplinarity in OR, although that is not our subject.

80. Thomas, "Selling Operations Research," 3.

81. Thomas, "Operations Research vis-à-vis Management"; Thomas and Williams, "Epistemologies of Non-Forecasting Simulations," parts 1 and 2. See also Morse, "Of Men and Machines" and *In at the Beginning.*

82. Thomas, "Selling Operations Research," 3.

83. Ibid., 3, 5.

84. Quoted in Thomas, "Selling Operations Research," 5. See also Thomas, "Operations Research vis-à-vis Management," and Dawson et al., "Operations Research at Bell Laboratories."

85. Horner, "History in the Making," available at www.lionhrtpub.com/orms/orms-10-02/history.html.

86. Ibid., 1, 2.

87. Ibid., 2–3.

88. Hall, "Issue-Oriented History of TIMS," 9, 11, 19.

89. Thomas, "Operations Research vis-à-vis Management." 101; Heukelom, "Measure and Decision-Making"; Augier and March, *Roots, Rituals, and Rhetorics*; Aaronson, "Serving America's Business?"; Issac, *Working Knowledge*; Crowther-Heyck, *Herbert A. Simon*.

90. Augier and March, *Roots, Rituals, and Rhetorics of Change*, 92–93.

91. Ibid., 137 and chapter 7.

92. Crowther-Heyck, "Herbert Simon and the GSIA," 143, and *Herbert A. Simon*.

93. Augier and March, *Roots, Rituals, and Rhetorics*, 307. See also Aaronson, "Serving America's Business?" and Foucade, *Economists and Societies*.

94. Thomas, "Operations Research vis-à-vis Management," 101—although this is an overstatement. See also Magee, "Operations Research at Arthur D. Little, Inc."

95. Thomas, "Operations Research vis-à-vis Management," 103.

96. Ibid., 105, 107, 109. Thomas presents the arguments of Cyril C. Herrmann and John F. Magee, " 'Operations Research' for Management," *Harvard Business Review* 31 (1953): 107.

97. Operations Evaluation Group memorandum, "A Course on Operations Research," Morse Papers, box 9, "NRC-Comm on OR" folder, MIT Archives, quoted in Thomas, "Operations Research vis-à-vis Management," 110.

98. Ibid., 112.

99. Ibid., 115, 118. Morse remained director until his retirement in 1968 and then passed the office to his first OR doctoral student, John D. Little.

100. Ibid., 119.

101. Splits continue to mark the field. See, for example, Kirby, "Paradigm Change in Operations Research" and "Intellectual Journey of Russell Ackoff"; the debates between Ackoff and his critics in *Operations Research Quarterly* 26 (1975) and *Journal of the Operational Research Society* 30 (1979); and West Churchman, "OR as a Profession," *Management Science* 17 (1970): B37–53. See also Randall S. Robinson, "The Operations Research Profession: Westward, Look, the Land is Bright," in *Perspectives in Operations Research: Papers in Honor of Saul Gass' 80th Birthday*, ed. Frank B. Alt, Michael C. Fu, and Bruce L. Golden (New York: Springer, 2006), 135–49; J. Rosenhead, "Reflections on Fifty Years of Operational Research," *Journal of the Operational Research Society* 60 (2009): S5–15; and Robert H. Roy, "The Development and Future of Operations Research and Systems Engineering," in *Operations Research and Systems Engineering*, ed. Charles D. Fagle, William H. Huggins, and Robert H. Roy (Baltimore, MD: Johns Hopkins University Press, 1960), 8–27. This work is often pretentious, showing that what passes for science is never far from politics and ideology. See Jonathan Rosenhead and Colin Thunhurst, "A Materialist Analysis of Operational Research," *Journal of Operations Research* 33 (1982): 111–22, with comments, 757–68; Michael C. Jackson, "Social Systems Theory and Practice: The Need for a Critical Approach," *International Journal of General Systems* 10 (1985): 135–51; and Jackson and Keys, *New Directions in Management Science*. In the 1980s, the critics discovered Foucault. Some were self-styled Maoists: e.g., Rosenhead, "From Management Science to Workers' Science." See also Patrick Rivett, "Thoughts on Post Graduate OR Programmes," *Journal of the Operational Research Society* 45 (1994): 970–71; Sam Eilon, "Thoughts on Post Graduate OR Programmes: Response," *Journal of the Operational*

Research Society 45 (1994): 972–73; and Sam Eilon and Patrick Rivett, "OR—Past, Present and Future," *Journal of the Operational Research Society* 45 (1994): 969–70.

Chapter 4 · Between Mind and Mentality

1. Ulric Neisser, *Cognitive Psychology* (New York: Appleton-Century-Crofts, 1967), 4 (emphasis added), quoted in Boden, *Mind as Machine*, 358. See the interesting review of Boden by Vincent C. Müller in *Minds and Machines* 18 (2008): 121–25, which underscores cognitive science's fragmentation.

2. Varela, Thompson, and Rosch, *Embodied Mind*, 5. See the review by Daniel Dennett, *Journal of Psychology* 106 (1993): 121–26. For a confusing introduction to the challenge of an interdisciplinary curriculum, see Elisabeth Zimmerman, Markus F. Peschl, and Brigitte Rommer-Nossek, "Constructivist Curriculum Design for the Interdisciplinary Study Program MEi—A Case Study," *Constructivist Foundations* 5 (2010): 144–57.

3. I am very critical of the assumptions as well as the pretensions of cognitive science and particularly skeptical of the uninformed uses to which it is put in the humanities, social sciences, and education. But my task in this book is not to criticize the endeavor itself, which can be extremely important.

4. "Cognitive Science," Wikipedia, http://en.wikipedia.org/wiki/Cognitive_science, quoting Paul Thagard, "Cognitive Science," *Stanford Encyclopedia of Philosophy* (fall 2008 ed.), http://plato.stanford.edu/archives/fall2008/entries/cognitive-science/.

5. Paul Thagard, "Cognitive Science," *Stanford Encyclopedia of Philosophy* (summer 2010 ed.), http://plato.stanford.edu/archives/sum2010/entries/cognitive-science/. For an unintentionally revealing and surprisingly inaccurate view, see De Mey, "Cognitive Science as an Interdisciplinary Endeavour." In 2000, in the introduction to a new edition of his 1982 *Cognitive Paradigm*, he refers to cognitive science as "still fashionable."

6. Fodor, "How the Mind Works," 94.

7. Burke, *New Perspectives on Historical Writing*, 1.

8. For the new "deep history," see Marc Perry, "The Shape of History: Ian Morris, Historians on a Grand Scale," *CHE*, Feb. 25, 2013; Roth, "Scientific History and Experimental History"; Shryock and Smail, *Deep History*; and Smail, *On Deep History and the Brain*. This recent "new history" presumes the status of a science without grappling seriously with the limits of "deep science" and its implications for human history. It is, perhaps, a new history for the twenty-first century and a confirmation of the incoherence and fragmentation of other recent new histories. Deep history shares the reductionism of some cognitive science, along with its neglect of history, society, and culture.

9. That is, science in the empiricist Anglo-American sense, not the French or continental tradition of systematic scholarship. Compare the journals of the Social Science History Association, the U.S.–based Economic History Association, and the Economic History Society in the UK with France's *Annales*. In the UK, a Social History Society began later, its focus more cultural and diffuse.

10. G. Miller, "Cognitive Revolution," 143. For the opposite view, see Leahey, "Mythical Revolutions of American Psychology." In between is Mandler, "Origins of the Cognitive Revolution."

11. Lakoff and Johnson, "Metaphorical Structure of the Human Cognitive System," 195. See also Lakoff and Johnson, *Metaphors We Live By*.

12. "Cognitive Science," Wikipedia.

13. "Celebrities in Cognitive Science," http://carbon.ucdenver.edu/~mryder/itc/cogsci .html.

14. S. J. Keyser, G. A. Miller, and E. Walker, *Cognitive Science in 1978* (unpublished report submitted to the Alfred P. Sloan Foundation, New York).

15. G. Miller, "Cognitive Revolution," 143.

16. A line between disciplines does not reflect or represent tools or relations built on questions and problems. Relationships are problematic. See Gardner, *Mind's New Science*; Boden, *Mind as Machine*; Cohen-Cole, "Reflexivity of Cognitive Science," "Instituting the Science of Mind," "Creative American," and *Open Mind*; Crowther-Heyck, *Herbert A. Simon*, "Herbert Simon and the GSIA," "Patrons of the Revolution," "George A. Miller, Language, and the Computer Metaphor of Mind," and "Producing Reason"; and Isaac, *Working Knowledge*.

17. It is not clear how work in the field and the literature in cognitive science reflect that distinction. Consider, for example, philosophers on artificial intelligence, neuroscience, and anthropology—and vice versa.

18. Wikipedia is at great pains regarding graphic standards. It is hard to see how the addition of the Greek letters *psi* and *phi* for psychology and philosophy or the clichéd icons for linguistics, artificial intelligence, anthropology, and neuroscience "more accurately reflect[s] the image."

19. Gardner, *Mind's New Science*, 38.

20. Miller, "Cognitive Revolution," 141–44. See also Baumgartner and Payr, *Speaking Minds*; Baars, *Cognitive Revolution in Psychology*; Harnish, *Minds, Brains, Computers*; Meyering, *Historical Roots of Cognitive Science*; Brook, *Prehistory of Cognitive Science*; Hirst, *Making of Cognitive Science*; R. Smith, *Between Mind and Nature*; and Cooper and Shallice, "Cognitive Neuroscience."

21. Mandler, "Origins of the Cognitive Revolution," 339.

22. Geoffrey Pullum, "Is the Cognitive Revolution Here Yet?" *CHE*, Sept. 30, 2013.

23. See John D. Greenwood, "Understanding the 'Cognitive Revolution' in Psychology," *Journal of the History of the Behavioral Sciences* 35 (1999): 1–22.

24. Harnish, *Minds, Brains, Computers*, 1. In 2013, the Cognitive Science Society had 1,918 members; Susan Trickett, Executive Director, to author, Oct. 14, 2013.

25. Harnish, *Minds, Brains, Computers*, 1. He continues, "Philosophy's analytical methodology is useful in sophisticating thinking in these areas" (3). Lest it be said that I am unfair to a textbook, Harnish's book presents itself as more than a beginner's guide or introduction and purports to be "historical."

26. Gardner, *Mind's New Science*, 5.

27. Crowther-Heyck, "George A. Miller, Language, and the Computer Metaphor of Mind," 38.

28. Boden, *Mind as Machine*, 90, 123.

29. For philosophy following science, see Klaus Mainzer, "The Emergence of Mind and Brain: An Evolutionary, Computational, and Philosophical Approach," *Progress in Brain Research*, ed. R. Banerjee and B. K. Chakrabarti, 168 (2008): 115–32. This piece takes assertions about evolution and brain science at face value without criticism or evidence in order to reach its conclusion, which seems backward. Writing three years later, Aarre Laakso offers a more balanced and limited (if sympathetic) conclusion, "Embodiment and Development in Cognitive Science," *Cognition, Brain, Behavior: An Interdisci-*

plinary Journal 15 (2011): 409–25. See also De Mey, *Cognitive Paradigm* and "Cognitive Science as an Interdisciplinary Endeavour," and William Bechtel, ed., *Integrating Scientific Disciplines* (Dordrecht: Martinus Nijhoff, 1986).

30. Boden, *Mind as Machine*, 183, 184. The field was called "meta-epistemology" by John McCarthy, quoted in ibid., 191. See also Tara H. Abraham, "(Physio)logical Circuits: The Intellectual Origins of the McCulloch-Pitts Neural Networks," *Journal of the History of the Behavioral Sciences* 38 (2002): 3–25.

31. Boden, *Mind as Machine*, 200, 210. See also Mandler, "Origins of the Cognitive Revolution," and Gardner, *Mind's New Science*. For the role of the Macy Foundation, see Steve Joshua Heims, *The Cybernetics Group* (Cambridge, MA: MIT Press, 1991), and Mirowski, *Machine Dreams*.

32. Boden, *Mind as Machine*, 232, 231. The "mind-brain" conflict, of course, is a very old divide. Boden is aligned with the computationists; see, for example, Müller's review.

33. Boden, *Mind as Machine*, 282–83. Boden adds, "A note about nomenclature: This chapter is about what cognitive scientists were doing in the 1950s and early 1960s, and how they saw themselves at the time. As for what they *called* themselves, that varied—but it wasn't 'cognitive scientists.' The term 'Cognitive Studies' was coined in 1960, and 'cognitive science/s' had to await the early 1970s. Even 'cognitive psychology' wasn't named until 1967."

34. Ibid., 282, 5, 328–29, 330. See also Mandler, "Origins of the Cognitive Revolution," and Gardner, *Mind's New Science*. "Face-to-face" interaction does not make an interdiscipline. Conferences are useful symbols and signposts.

35. Susan Trickett, Executive Director, Cognitive Science Society, to author, Oct. 14, 2013. In response to my question, she replied: "I do not have more information about how the different disciplines are represented by our members, or about where they are employed."

36. A convenient but even less complete "list of institutions granting degrees in cognitive science," of unknown provenance, appears at "Cognitive Science," Wikipedia.

37. Gardner, *Mind's New Science*, 5–6.

38. Ibid., 7.

39. Cohen-Cole, "Instituting the Science of Mind," 368, 568. On the Center for Cognitive Studies, see also Hirst, *Making of Cognitive Science*, and Boden, *Mind as Machine*.

40. Cohen-Cole, "Instituting the Science of Mind," 579–80.

41. Ibid., 589.

42. See, esp., Crowther-Heyck, "Patrons of the Revolution."

43. Crowther-Heyck, "Herbert Simon and the GSIA," 325.

44. Ibid.

45. Ibid., 326, 327.

46. Ibid., 327, 328, 329. See also Crowther-Heyck, *Herbert A. Simon*.

47. Crowther-Heyck, "Herbert Simon and the GSIA," *Herbert A. Simon*, and "Patrons of the Revolution."

48. Baumgartner and Payr, *Speaking Minds*. Those interviewed include Patricia Smith Churchland, Paul M. Churchland, Aaron V. Ciourel, Daniel C. Dennett, Hubert L. Dreyfus, Jerry A. Fodor, John Haugeland, George Lakoff, James L. McClelland, Allan Newell, Stephen E. Palmer, Hilary Putnam, David E. Rumpelhart, John R. Searle, Terrence J. Sejnowski, Herbert A. Simon, Josephen Weitzenbaum, Robert Wilensky, Terry A. Winograd, and

Lotfi A. Zadeh. The balance of disciplines would differ today. See also Baars, *Cognitive Revolution in Psychology*, which has a greater representation of cognitive psychologists and a lesser representation of philosophers.

49. Baumgartner and Payr, introduction, *Speaking Minds*, 11–12.

50. Ibid., 12–13. Speculation underlies questions asked of the subjects and sometimes elicits very unhelpful responses. See, for example, Allen Newell interview, ibid., 147–48.

51. Baumgartner and Payr, *Speaking Minds*, 26, 25–26, 39, 72.

52. Ibid., 51.

53. Ibid., 203–4.

54. Ibid., 85; "If you are a cognitive psychologist but know nothing about these fields, you are a cognitive psychologist but not a cognitive scientist," states Fodor.

55. Ibid., 267.

56. Ibid., 143.

57. Ibid., 234.

58. Ibid., 167; see also Robert Wilensky, "Why Play the Philosophy Game?" in ibid., 265–82.

59. Baumgartner and Payr, *Speaking Minds*, 35.

60. Gardner, *Mind's New Science*, 291, 293.

61. Ibid., 294. Note Gardner's use of the phrase "cognitive scientific" and his references to the natural sciences.

62. Ibid.

63. Ibid., 390.

64. Ibid. There are implications here for the foundational elements he describes for cognitive science.

65. Ibid., 390, 391.

66. Kagan, "Missing Contexts," chapter 1 of *Psychology's Ghosts*, and "Psychology's Missing Contexts." On concerns about the reporting of experimental results, human subject research review and approval, and documented fraud, see Tom Bartlett, "Is Psychology about to Come Undone," *CHE*, Apr. 18, 2010.

67. See special issue, "The Role of Linguistics in Cognitive Science," *Linguistics Review* 24, no. 4 (2007).

68. Baumgartner and Payr, *Speaking Minds*, 302, 306.

69. Gardner, *Mind's New Science*, 285, 286, 287.

70. Cooper and Shallice, "Cognitive Neuroscience," 403.

71. Ibid. See also Crofts, "Challenges of Interdisciplinary Epistemology in Neuroaesthetics"; Emil C. Toescu, "Integration and interdisciplinarity in contemporary neurosciences," *Journal of Cellular Molecular Medicine* 9 (2005): 529–30; Martyn Pickersgill, "The Social Life of the Brain: Neuroscience in Society," *Current Sociology* 61 (2013): 322–40; Rose and Abi-Rached, *Neuro*; and "Nikolas Rose Interviewed by Todd Meyers," *Public Culture* 25 (2013): 435–52. See also Fodor, "How the Mind Works," and Lakoff and Johnson, "Metaphorical Structure of the Human Cognitive System" and *Metaphors We Live By*.

72. "Nikolas Rose Interviewed by Todd Meyers."

73. Gunnell, "Are We Losing Our Minds?" 704, 722. For an example of uncritical response in sociology, see the special issue introduced by Douglas D. Heckathorn, "Cog-

nitive Science, Sociology, and the Theoretic Analysis of Computer Systems," *Journal of Mathematical Sociology* 14, nos. 2–3 (1989): 139–69.

74. Armstrong, *How Literature Plays with the Brain*, 182.

75. Carr, *Shallows*.

76. *New York Times*, Oct. 4, 2013. The study is David Comer Kidde and Emanuele Castano, "Reading Literary Fiction Improves Theory of Mind," *Science*, Oct. 3, 2013, 377–80.

77. Terms like "theory of mind" are deeply misleading. As a historian of literacy, I am engaged with the act of reading. Another case in point, which reads like a caricature, is Natalie Philips, "The Neuroscience of Narrative: An fMRI Study of Literary Attention in Jane Austen" (presented to Project Narrative, Ohio State University, Sept. 23, 2013). For similar criticisms, see Donald Beecher, "Will the Cognitive Sciences Take on the Renaissance? Or, Will Renaissance Studies Admit the Cognitive Sciences?" *Sixteenth Century Journal* 40 (2009): 233–36; Angus Fletcher, "Another Literary Darwinism," *Critical Inquiry* 40 (2014): 450–69; Jonathan Kramnick, "Against Literary Darwinism," *Critical Inquiry* 37 (2011): 315–47; Tony E. Jackson, "Questioning Interdisciplinarity: Cognitive Science, Evolutionary Psychology, and Literary Criticism," *Poetics Today* 21 (2000): 319–47; Crofts, "Challenges of Interdisciplinary Epistemology in Neuroaesthetics"; Ruth Denkhau and Mathias Bos, "How Cultural Is 'Cultural Neuroscience'? Some Comments on an Emerging Research Paradigm," *BioSocieties* 7 (2012): 433–58; Jennifer Ashton, "Two Problems with a Neuroaesthetic Theory of Interpretation," *NONsite.org*, issue 2 (June 12, 2011); and Alissa Quart, "Adventures in Neurohumanities," *The Nation*, May 27, 2013, 18–22. For another example of oversimplification, see Carol Tavris, "History Gets into Bed with Psychology, and It's a Happy Match," *History News Network*, Nov. 11, 2013, which has nothing to do with cognitive science, cognitive psychology, or history.

78. George Mandler, "The Situation of Psychology: Landmarks and Choicepoints," *American Journal of Psychology* 109 (1996), 23, quoted in Boden, *Mind as Machine*, 1445.

79. Gary Wilder, "*AHR* Forum: From Optic to Topic: The Foreclosure Effect of Historic Turns," *American Historical Review* 117 (2012): 724–26.

80. This section is based in part on H. Graff, "Shock of the 'New (Histories).'" See also Immanuel Wallerstein, *Open the Social Sciences: Report of the Gulbenkian Commission on the Restructuring of the Social Sciences* (Stanford: Stanford University Press, 1996); Immanuel Wallerstein, *The Uncertainties of Knowledge* (Philadelphia: Temple University Press, 2004) and "Anthropology, Sociology, and Other Dubious Disciplines," Sidney W. Mintz Lecture for 2003 with Comments and Response, *Current Anthropology* 44 (2003): 453–65; Novick, *That Noble Dream*; Eley, "Between Social History and Cultural Studies," "Is All the World a Text?" and *Crooked Line*; *AHR* Forum: Eley's *Crooked Line*; H. Klein, "Old Social History and New Social Sciences"; Burke, *New Perspectives on Historical Writing*; McDonald, *Historic Turn in the Human Sciences*; Hunt, *New Cultural History*; Hunt and Bonnell, *Beyond the Cultural Turn*; Sewell, *Logics of History*; and George Steinmetz, Dylan Riley, and David Pedersen in "Special Section: *Logics of History*," *Social Science History* 32, no. 4 (2008). See also Jean-Pierre V. M. Hérubel, "Situating Clio's Influence in Humanities and Social Science Monographs: Disciplinary Affiliations and Historical Scholarship," *Journal of Scholarly Publishing* 40 (2009): 55–66.

81. For a useful approach to these matters, see Abbott, "History and Sociology." See also Sewell, *Logics of History* and "Three Temporalities," and McDonald, *Historic Turn in the Human Sciences.*

82. Among the seminal works on the new histories are Aydelotte, Bogue, and Fogel, *Dimensions of Quantitative Research in History*; Bogue, *Emerging Theoretical Models in Social and Political History, Clio and the Bitch Goddess*, "Systematic Revisionism," and "Great Expectations and Secular Depreciation"; Bogue and Clubb, "History and the Social Sciences" and "History, Quantification, and the Social Sciences"; Hobsbawm, "From Social History to the History of Society" and "Social Function of the Past"; Monkkonen, "Lessons of Social Science History"; and C. Tilly, *Vendée, As Sociology Meets History*, and *Big Structures, Large Processes, Huge Comparisons.* Major criticisms, some sympathetic and others not, include Eley, "Is All the World a Text?" and *Crooked Line*; Fox-Genovese and Lasch-Quinn, *Reconstructing History*; Ginzburg, "Microhistory"; Hamerow, *Reflections on History*, 3–38; Higham, *History*; Sigurður Gylfi Magnússon, *Wasteland with Words: A Social History of Iceland* (London: Reaktion Books, 2010); Novick, *That Noble Dream*; Ross, "Grand Narrative in American Historical Writing" and "New and Newer Histories"; Sewell, *Logics of History*, "Concept(s) of Culture," and "Three Temporalities"; Sewell, Steinmetz, and Maynes, "Narrative Analysis in Social Science"; Biernacki, "Method and Metaphor"; and Steinmetz, *"Logics of History* as a Framework." For an intemperate and inaccurate critique, see Richard Pells, "The Obsession with Social History," *CHE*, Jan. 28, 2013, and the response by James Grossman and Elaine Carey, "An Undisciplined Report on the Teaching of History," CHE, Feb. 1, 2013.

83. Ross, "New and Newer Histories," 85, 89.

84. Monkkonen, "Lessons of Social Science History," 4. See also Bogue, "Systematic Revisionism," 137; Katz, Doucet, and Stern, *Social Organization of Early Industrial Capitalism*, ix–xiii.

85. Hobsbawm, "From Social History to the History of Society," 4.

86. Ross, "New and Newer Histories," 91.

87. A notable example is C. Tilly, *Vendée*. See the illuminating essays in the special section on the book in *French Historical Studies* 33, no. 2 (Spring 2010), especially William H. Sewell, Jr., "Charles Tilly's *Vendée* as a Model for Social History," 307–15; Mark Traugott, "Charles Tilly, Sociologist and Historian," 318–24; and Mary Jo Maynes, "Charles Tilly's Legacy: The License to Think Big," 199–306. Other exemplary and influential works include Scott, *Gender and the Politics of History* and *Glassworkers of Carmaux*; Sewell, *Work and Revolution in France* and *Logics of History*; Stedman Jones, *Outcast London*; and Maynes, *Taking the Hard Road.*

88. Higham, *History.*

89. M. Katz, *People of Hamilton*, 7–9. See also Katz, Doucet, and Stern, *Social Organization of Early Industrial Capitalism.*

90. See Ginzburg, "Microhistory"; Sigurður Magnússon and István Szijártó, *What Is Microhistory? Theory and Practice* (London: Routledge, 2013).

91. M. Katz, *People of Hamilton*, 8–9, discussing P. Abrams, "Sense of the Past." Those myths included for example, the size and structure of families, and the extent of migration and social mobility over time.

92. M. Katz, *People of Hamilton*, 7–8.

93. Ibid., 10.

94. The premier example of social history database building is Theodore Hershberg's University of Pennsylvania–based Philadelphia Social History Project. For a distorted example of the criticism such efforts could stimulate, see Stone, "History and the Social Sciences," "Revival of Narrative," and *Past and Present Revisited*. Stone's attack on Charles Tilly is especially egregious.

95. Katz, *People of Hamilton*, 10.

96. See also Biernacki, "Method and Metaphor after the New Cultural History"; *AHR* Forum: Eley's *Crooked Line*; Sewell, *Logics of History*; and Cook, Glickman, and O'Malley, *Cultural Turn in U.S. History*.

97. Kousser, "History QUASSHED"; Appleby, "Power of History," 5, 6.

98. Scott, *Gender and the Politics of History*; Sewell, *Work and Revolution in France* and *Logics of History*; Stedman Jones, *Outcast London*; Maynes, *Taking the Hard Road*.

99. M. Katz, *People of Hamilton*, 12–13.

100. See Katz's critical review of Michael Anderson, *Family Structure in Nineteenth-Century Lancashire* (Cambridge: Cambridge University Press, 1971), in *Journal of Social History* 7 (1973): 86–92.

101. M. Katz, *People of Hamilton*, 10.

102. Ibid., 13. The new histories were criticized about this issue, but later new cultural historians often fell short as well. Ibid., 14; see also Sewell, *Logics of History*, and Biernacki, "Method and Metaphor."

103. M. Katz, *People of Hamilton*, 13–14; Hayden White, "The Burden of History," *History and Theory* 5 (1966): 111–34.

104. Steckel, "Evolution of SSHA Meetings," 102–5.

105. M. Katz, *People of Hamilton*, 11, 12.

106. See H. Graff, *Literacy Myth*, *Legacies of Literacy*, *Labyrinths of Literacy*, and *Literacy Myths, Legacies, and Lessons*.

107. William H. Sewell Jr., contribution to "Social Science History at 2000: Critical Perspectives," in Graff, Moch, and McMichael, *Looking Backward and Looking Forward*, 77. See also Sewell, *Logics of History*; Hunt and Bonnell, *Beyond the Cultural Turn*; McDonald, *Historic Turn in the Human Sciences*; and Abbott, "History and Sociology."

108. Sewell, *Logics of History*, 78.

109. For relevant reflections, see Abbott, "History and Sociology"; Sewell, *Logics of History* and "Three Temporalities"; and Calhoun, "Rise and Domestication of Historical Sociology." There are very real problems and limits to interdisciplinarity in the new histories. On conflicts, see Eley, *Crooked Line*, "Between Social History and Cultural Studies," and "Is All the World a Text?"; *AHR* Forum: Eley's *Crooked Line*; and L. Tilly, "Problems in Social History." There is much misunderstanding, often self-serving. See Stedman Jones, "From Historical Sociology to Theoretical History"; Judt, "A Clown in Royal Purple"; and Fox-Genovese and Genovese, "Political Crisis of Social History." Cf. Schafer, "Still Turning"; and Scott, "Wishful Thinking," "History-writing as Critique," "Evidence of Experience," and *Gender and the Politics of History*.

110. Steckel, "Evolution of SSHA Meetings," 102, 103. Of course, attendance always exceeds paid registration; William Block, Executive Director, to author, Oct. 14, 2013.

111. Steckel, "Evolution of SHA Meetings," 106.

112. Ibid., 110, 112. See also Block to author, Oct. 14, 2013.

113. See Sewell, Steinmetz, and Maynes, "Narrative Analysis in Social Science." Sewell mentions social science historians turning to narrative, literary theory, poststructuralism, cultural anthropology, feminist theory, and other currents as early as the 1960s and 1970s.

114. See also "The Future of the Discipline," *AHA Perspectives on History* 50 (Dec. 2012); Eustace et al., "*AHA* Conversation"; Bynum, "Perspectives, Connections, and Objects"; Hunt and Bonnell, *Beyond the Cultural Turn*; Cook, Glickman, and O'Malley, *Cultural Turn in U.S. History*; Eley, *Crooked Line*; Antony Grafton, "History under Attack," *AHA Perspectives* 49 (Jan. 2011), "History's Postmodern Fates," and "In Clio's American Atelier"; Hunt, *New Cultural History*; Joyce, *Social in Question*; McMahon and Moyn, *Rethinking Modern European Intellectual History*; Allan Megill and Zupeng Zhang, "Questions on the History of Ideas and Its Neighbors," *Rethinking History* 17 (2013): 333–53; Teichgraebner, "Beyond 'Academicization.'"

115. Bogue, "Systematic Revisionism," 338, 333. See also Monkkonen, "Lessons of Social Science Histories."

116. Ross, "New and Newer Histories," 93.

Chapter 5 · A Material World and the Making of Lifeworlds

1. Frankel and Whitesides, *No Small Matter*, 2. "Two words are often associated with small things: *nano* and *micro*. Each is a unit of size; both are invisibly small. A nanometer is a billionth of a meter, or the size of a small molecule, which is five times the size of the smallest atom, hydrogen. A micron, or micrometer, is much larger—a millionth of a meter, or a little less than the diameter of a red blood cell. Still, it is invisible to the unaided eye. The smallest objects we can see without a microscope—a hair, for example—are about a hundred times larger, or about 100 microns in diameter."

2. Ibid., 9. See also Spector, "Nanoaesthetics." For "over the top" expressions, see Drexler, *Engines of Creation* and *Nanosystems*. See also Diane Ackerman, "Nanotechnology Shock Waves," *New York Times*, May 6, 2012; Tom Saisouleas, "A Convergence Science for Today's Problems," *Chronicle of Higher Education Review*, Aug. 14, 2011; David H. Freedman, "Exploiting the Nanotechnology of Life," *Science* 254, no. 5036 (Nov. 29, 1991): 1308–10; and the debate on nanotechnology between Eric Drexler and Richard Smalley in *Scientific American*, 2001–2003, starting with Smalley, "Of Chemistry, Love and Nanobots." For institutional statements, see Committee on the Survey of Materials Science and Engineering, (COSMAT), *Materials and Man's Needs* and Committee on Materials Science and Engineering, *Materials for Science and Engineering in the 1990s*.

3. Eley, "Between Social History and Cultural Studies," 99.

4. Amato, *Stuff*.

5. "But *matter* is not the same as *material*. . . . The science part of MSE seeks to discover, analyze, and understand the nature of materials, to provide coherent explanations of the origin of the properties that are used, whereas the engineering aspect takes this basic knowledge and whatever else is necessary . . . to develop, prepare, and apply materials for specified needs, often the advanced objectives of the times." Kranzberg and Smith, "Materials in History and Society," 91.

6. Stephen Sass, *The Substance of Civilization: Materials and Human History from the Stone Age to Age of Silicon* (New York: Arcade, 1998), 5, 6. According to Kranzberg and

Smith, "The transitions from, say, stone to bronze and from bronze to iron were revolutionary in fact, but they were relatively slow in terms of the time scale. Changes in materials innovation and application within the last half century, however, have occurred in a time span which was revolutionary rather than evolutionary. The materials revolution of our times is qualitative as well as quantitative. It breeds the attitude of purposeful creativity rather than modification of natural materials, and also a new approach—an innovative organization of science and technology" ("Materials in History and Society," 88.) See also COSMAT, *Materials and Man's Needs*, and M. S. Dresselhaus, "Materials Science and Cultural Change," *New Literary History* 23 (1992): 839–44.

7. For evidence on both sides of the coin, see Cahn, *Coming of Materials Science*.

8. There are relationships with bioscience and OR that bear investigation. On universities and industry, see Mirowski, *Science-Mart*, and Zuckerman, *Beyond the Ivory Tower*. See also Elizabeth Popp Berman, "Why Did Universities Start Patenting?: Institution-Building and the Road to the Bayh-Dole Act," *Social Studies of Science* 38 (2008): 835–71; "Explaining the Move toward the Market in U.S. Academic Science: How Institutional Logics Can Change without Institutional Entrepreneurs," *Theory and Society* 41 (2012): 261–99; and *Creating the Market University: How Academic Science Became an Economic Engine* (Princeton, NJ: Princeton University Press, 2013); Robert Bud, "Framed in the Public Sphere: Tools for the Conceptual History of 'Applied Science'—A Review Paper," *History of Science* 51 (2013): 413–33; Ronald E. Doel, *Solar System Astronomy in America: Community, Patronage, and Interdisciplinary Science, 1920–1960* (Cambridge: Cambridge University Press, 1996); Jeffrey L Furman and Megan MacGarvie, "When the Pill Peddlers Met the Scientists: The Antecedents and Implications of Early Collaborations between U.S. Pharmaceutical Firms and Universities," *Essays in Economic and Business History* 26 (2008): 133–46; Roger Geiger, "Organized Research Units—Their Role in the Development of University Research," *Journal of Higher Education* 61 (1990): 1–19; Daniel S. Greenberg, *Science for Sale: The Perils, Rewards, and Delusions of Campus Capitalism* (Chicago: University of Chicago Press, 2007); R. E. Marshak, "Basic Research in the University and Industrial Laboratory," *Science* 154 (Dec. 23, 1966): 1521–24; Michael D. Reagan, "Basic and Applied Research," *Science* 155 (Mar. 17, 1967): 1383–86; Maria Rentetzi, "The U.S. Radium Industry: Industrial In-house Research and the Commercialization of Science," *Minerva* 46 (2008): 437–62; Schrum, "Administering American Modernity"; Paula E. Stephan and Ronald G. Ehrenberg, eds., *Science and the University* (Madison: University of Wisconsin Press, 2007); and David Tyfield, "A Cultural Political Economy of Research and Innovation in the Age of Crisis," *Minerva* 50 (2012): 149–67.

9. On interdisciplinarity in materials science, see Amato, *Stuff*; Bensaude-Vincent, "Construction of a Discipline" and "Materials Science and Engineering"; Cahn, *Coming of Materials Science*; M. C. Flemings and R. W. Cahn, "Organization and Trends in Materials Science and Engineering Education in the US and Europe," *Acta Metallurgica* 48 (2000): 371–83; Drexler, *Engines of Creation, Nanosystems*, and "Nanotechnology"; K. Kadowaki, "21st Century COE Program 'Promotion of Creative Interdisciplinary Materials Science for Novel Functions," *Science and Technology of Advanced Materials* 6 (2005): 549–50; COSMAT, *Materials and Man's Needs*; Smalley, "Of Chemistry, Love, and Nanobots"; and Wuensch, "Bernhardt Wuensch: An Interview."

10. Cahn, *Coming of Materials Science*, 539.

11. Amato, *Stuff,* 87–88. This is purple prose in an era of green energy!

12. Ibid., 87–89, 101. Amato proceeds by lumping and listing. His table/timeline is instructive. So is the book's perspective on history: "Mark Eberhart, a materials researcher at the Colorado School of Mines, where most work focuses on ways of harvesting the rawest of ingredients from the world, characterizes the emergence of materials design this way: 'I consider what is going on in materials by design as comparable in scope and importance to the beginnings of the scientific method. Now we are at a point where we can do computer simulations and use these as hypotheses in materials development.' . . . This is akin to the evolutionary leap in which brains simulated the consequences of potential actions before hazarding the action itself" (259).

13. See www.mrs.org.

14. Robert I. Boughton, "Materials: An Interdisciplinary Integrative Approach," *American Journal of Physics* 69 (2001): 902.

15. Wood, Geldart, and Jones, "Crystallizing the Nanotechnology Debate," 13.

16. Jan C. Schmidt, "Tracing Interdisciplinarity of Converging Technologies at the Nanoscale: A Critical Analysis of Recent Nanotechnosciences," *Technology Analysis and Strategic Management* 20 (2008): 45.

17. Rafols, "Strategies for Knowledge Acquisition," 395–96. He defines interdisciplinarity "to represent all types of research crossing knowledge boundaries, including multi-, trans- and cross-disciplinarity."

18. Ibid., 395.

19. Application of numerical methods to databases of one kind or another has become a major growth area in interdisciplinarity, often under the rubric of digital humanities or "big data." One critical area is how the key sources—often journals or research articles—are classified. Surprisingly little attention is directed to that issue, with the exception of Jacobs, *Defense of Disciplines.* For some of the limits of bibliometrics, see Mirowski, *Science-Mart,* chap. 6.

20. Meyer and Persson, "Nanotechnology," 195.

21. Schummer, "Multidisciplinarity, Interdisciplinarity, and Patterns of Research Collaboration," 425.

22. I can say this as a recipient, so far, of four cornea transplants in my right eye.

23. Schummer, "Multidisciplinarity, Interdisciplinarity, and Patterns of Research Collaboration," 448.

24. Ibid., 461.

25. Cahn, *Coming of Materials Science,* 539–40. "Others prefer to make this little diagram more complicated."

26. Ibid., 541.

27. On the history of materials science, see, for example, Beaver, *Metallurgy and Materials Science Engineering,* 91–100; Bensaude-Vincent, "Construction of a Discipline" and "Materials Science and Engineering"; Emanuel Bertrand and Bernadette Bensaude-Vincent, "Materials Research in France: A Short-lived National Initiative (1982–1994)," *Minerva* 49 (2011): 191–214; Cahn, *Coming of Materials Science;* COSMAT, *Materials and Man's Needs;* Hyungsub Choi and Cyrus C. M. Mody, "The Long History of Molecular Electronics: Microelectronics Origins of Nanotechnology," *Social Studies of Science* 39 (2009): 11–50; Flemings, "What Next for Departments of Materials Science and Engineering?"; Forester, *Materials Revolution;* Yasu Fukukawa, "Polymer Science: From Organic

Chemistry to an Interdisciplinary Science," in *Chemical Sciences in the 20th Century: Bridging Boundaries*, ed. C. Reinhardt (Weinheim: Wiley-VCH, 2001), 228–45; Gertner, *Idea Factory*; Hounshell and Smith, *Science and Corporate Strategy*; Leonard V. Interrante, L. A. Casper, and Arthur B. Ellis, "Materials Chemistry: An Emerging Discipline" (Washington, DC: American Chemical Society, 1995); Eun-Sung Kim, "Directed Evolution: A Historical Exploration into an Evolutionary Experimental System of Nanotechnology, 1965–2006," *Minerva* 46 (2008): 463–84; Leslie, *Cold War and American Science*; Lecuyer, "Making of a Science-Based Technological University"; Cyrus C. M. Mody, "Small, but Determined: Technological Determination in Nanoscience," *HYLE—International Journal for Philosophy of Chemistry* 10 (2004): 99–128, and *Instrumental Community: Probe Microscopy and the Path to Nanotechnology* (Cambridge, MA: MIT Press, 2011); L. Schwartz, "Materials Research Laboratories"; Servos, "Industrial Relations of Science"; C. Smith, "Development of Ideas on the Structure of Metals"; Spencer R. Weart, "The Solid Community," in *Out of the Crystal Maze: Chapters from the History of Solid State Physics*, ed. Lillian Hoddeson, Ernest Braun, Jürgen Teichman, and Spencer Weart (New York: Oxford University Press, 1992), 617–69; and Wuensch, "Bernhardt Wuensch: An Interview."

28. See for example Gertner, *Idea Factory*, and Cahn, *Coming of Materials Science*.

29. Bensuade-Vincent, "Materials Science and Engineering." I cite the website version because, despite lack of proofing or correction of the text, it is fuller. Compare with Bensaude-Vincent, "The Construction of a Discipline: Materials Science in the United States," *History Studies in the Physical and Biological Sciences* 31 (2001): 223–48.

30. Bensaude-Vincent, "Materials Science and Engineering."

31. Ibid. See her "Aristotelian" gloss on "mixt."

32. See Forester, *Materials Revolution*.

33. Ibid.

34. Wuensch, "Bernhardt Wuensch: An Interview."

35. One wonders what Cohen-Cole would make of this discussion of physical space. This was the second major interdisciplinary laboratory at MIT. The first was an outgrowth of the Radiation Lab, called the Research Laboratory of Electronics after World War II. See Beaver, *Metallurgy and Materials Science Engineering*; Lecuyer, "Making of a Science-Based Technological University"; and Leslie, *Cold War and American Science*.

36. Wuensch, "Bernhardt Wuensch: An Interview."

37. Ibid.

38. See COSMAT, *Materials and Man's Needs*; L. Schwartz, "Materials Research Laboratories"; Cahn, *Coming of Materials Science*; and Gertner, *Idea Factory*. We need a good study of relationships between locations and modes of organization, movement and circulation between universities, government labs, and corporate-industrial labs. "Interdisciplinary" is used especially indiscriminately in references to industrial labs.

39. Flemings, "What Next for Departments of Materials Science and Engineering?" 17.

40. Ibid., 19. For interesting institutional histories, see Beaver, *Metallurgy and Materials Science Engineering*; Cahn, *Coming of Materials Science*; Lecuyer, "Making of a Science-Based Technological University"; Leslie, *Cold War and American Science*; and Servos, "Industrial Relations of Science."

41. Cahn, *Coming of Materials Science*, 508.

42. Todd Osman, Executive Director, MRS, to author, Nov. 27 and Dec. 2, 2013.

43. Cahn, *Coming of Materials Science*, 510.

44. See, for example, G. Pascal Zachary, "Bell Labs Is Gone; Academia Steps In," *New York Times*, Dec. 16, 2007.

45. Cahn, *Coming of Materials Science*, 503. For details, see Flemings, "What Next for Departments of Materials Science and Engineering?"; Flemings and Cahn, "Organization and Trends in Materials Science"; and Peter Groenewegen and Lois Peters, "The Emergence and Change of Materials Science and Engineering in the United States," *Science, Technology, and Human Values* 27 (2002): 112–33.

46. Cahn, *Coming of Materials Science*, 505; Flemings, "What Next for Departments of Materials Science and Engineering?"

47. Thanks to graduate research assistant Nora McCook for summarizing the data; see also the statements of the following programs on their websites. The 18 schools with materials science departments offer the following degrees: BS (12), BS/MS (5), MS or MSE (16), MA (1), PhD (18). Harvard and Johns Hopkins offer mechanical engineering degrees with materials sciences emphases/tracks.

48. On ethics in nanotechnology, see John Balbus, Richard Denison, Karen Florindi, and Scott Walsh, "Getting Nanotechnology Right the First Time," *Issues in Science and Technology* 21 (2005): 65–71; Robert W. S. Dunkley, "Nanotechnology: Social Consequences and Future Implications," *Futures* 36 (2004): 1129–32; Edna F. Einsiedel and Linda Goldenberg, "Dwarfing the Social? Nanotechnology Lessons from the Biotechnology Front," *Bulletin of Science, Technology, and Society* 24 (2004): 28–33; Helen Gavaghan, "Governments Prime Basic Nanotech Research, Applied Activity Yet to Soar," *Nature* 408 (Nov. 2000): 619–20; Grunwald, "Nanotechnology"; Andrew Jamison, "On Nanotechnology and Society," *EASST Review* 21 (2005): 3–6; Matthew Kearnes and Phil MacNaghten, "Introduction: (Re)Imagining Nanotechnology," *Science as Culture* 15 (2006): 279–90; Kristen Kulinowski, "Nanotechnology: From 'Wow' to 'Yuck'?" *Bulletin of Science, Technology, and Society* 24 (2004): 13–20; Patrick Lin, "Nanotechnology's Dilemmas," *Scientist* 19 (2005): 10; José Lopez, "Compiling the Ethical, Legal and Social Implications of Nanotechnology," *Health Law Review* 12 (2005): 24–27; Chris MacDonald, "Nanotechnology, Privacy and Shifting Social Conventions," *Health Law Review* 12 (2005): 27–40; Phil MacNaghten, Matthew B. Kearnes, and Brian Wynne, "Nanotechnology, Governance, and Public Deliberation: What Role for the Social Sciences?" *Science Communication* 27 (2005): 268–91; Elise McCarthy and Christopher Kelty, "Responsibility and Nanotechnology," *Social Studies of Science* 40 (2010): 405–32; Alfred Nordmann, "If and Then: A Critique of Speculative NanoEthics," *Nanoethics* 1 (2007): 31–46; Douglas Parr, "Will Nanotechnology Make the World a Better Place?" *Trends in Biotechnology* 23 (2005): 395–98; Ruben Rodriques, "The Implications of High-Rate Nanomanufacturing on Society and Personal Privacy," *Bulletin of Science, Technology, and Society* 26 (2006): 38–45; Spector, "Nanoaesthetics"; and Stephen Wilson, *Information Arts: Intersections of Art, Science, and Technology* (Cambridge, MA: MIT Press, 2002).

49. See the websites of the National Science Foundation and National Institutes of Health. This issue has also arisen in other countries.

50. Grunwald, "Nanotechnology," 187.

51. "Cultural Studies," Wikipedia, http://en.wikipedia.org/wiki/Cultural_studies.

52. The body of scholarship that considers cultural studies seems unusually large, perhaps an index of the controversies it has aroused. See "Cultural Theory and its Fu-

tures," *Theory, Culture and Society* 24, no. 3 (2007): 49–110; "Special Issue on the Centre for Cultural Studies," *Cultural Studies* 27, no. 5 (2013); Bennett, "Making Culture, Changing Society," "Cultural Studies," and "Putting Policy into Cultural Studies"; Blundell, Shepherd, and Taylor, *Relocating Cultural Studies*; Brantlinger, *Bread and Circuses* and *Crusoe's Footprints*; Brenkman, "Extreme Criticism"; Crane, "Cultural Sociology and Other Disciplines"; Eley, *Crooked Line* and "Between Social History and Cultural Studies"; Grossberg, "Formation of Cultural Studies," "Toward a Genealogy of the State of Cultural Studies," *Cultural Studies in the Future Tense*, and *Bringing It All Back Home*; Grossberg, Nelson, and Treichler, *Cultural Studies*; Guillory, "Sokal Affair," "Name of Science," and "Literary Study and the Modern System of the Disciplines"; S. Hall, "Emergence of Cultural Studies," "Cultural Studies and Its Theoretical Legacies," and *Representation*; Hall et al., *Culture, Media, Language*; Hall and du Gay, *Questions of Cultural Identity*; Higgins, *Raymond Williams* and *Raymond Williams Reader*; Hoggart, *On Culture and Communication*, *Uses of Literacy*, and "Schools of English and Contemporary Society"; Inglis, *Culture, Cultural Studies*, and *Raymond Williams*; R. Johnson, "Historical Returns"; Johnson et al., *Making Histories*; Kellner, *Media Culture*; Klein, *Crossing Boundaries* and *Humanities, Culture, and Interdisciplinarity*; Krabbendam and Verheul, *Through the Looking Glass*; Kuper, *Culture*; Lee, *Life and Times of Cultural Studies*; Marcus, "Humanities from Classics to Cultural Studies"; T. Miller, *Blow Up the Humanities*; Moran, *Interdisciplinarity*; Morley, *Television, Audiences, and Cultural Studies*; Morley and Chen, *Stuart Hall*; Morley and Robins, *British Cultural Studies*; Nelson and Gaonkar, *Disciplinarity and Dissent in Cultural Studies*; Nelson and Grossberg, *Marxism and the Interpretation of Culture*; and Williams, *Communications, Contact, Culture, Marxism and Literature, Materialism and Culture, Politics of Modernism, Sociology of Culture, Writing in Society*, and *Year 2000*. See also Jeffrey C. Alexander and Philip Smith, "The Discourse of American Civil Society: A New Proposal for Cultural Studies," *Theory and Society* 22 (1993): 151–207; Benedict Anderson, *Imagined Communities: Reflections on the Origin and Spread of Nationalism* (London: Verso, 1983); Sean Johnson Andrews, "What We Should Want with History: A Meditation on Cultural Studies, Methodology, and Politics," *Journal of Historical Sociology* 26 (2013): 442–78; Nancy Armstrong, "Who's Afraid of the Cultural Turn?" *Differences* 12 (2001): 17–49; Jan Baetens, "Cultural Studies after the Cultural Studies Paradigm," *Cultural Studies* 19 (2006): 1–13; Mieke Bal, ed., *The Practice of Cultural Analysis: Exposing Interdisciplinary Interpretation* (Stanford, CA: Stanford University Press, 1999); Iain Chambers, *Popular Culture: The Metropolitan Experience* (London: Methuen, 1986); Rey Chow, *Writing Diaspora: Tactics of Intervention in Cultural Studies* (Bloomington: Indiana University Press, 1993); Michael Denning, *Culture in the Age of Three Worlds* (London: Verso 2004); Norman K. Denzin, *Symbolic Interactionism and Cultural Studies* (Oxford: Blackwell, 1992); Jane Desmond, *Meaning in Motion: New Cultural Studies of Dance* (London: Routledge, 1996); Nicholas B. Dirks, ed., *In Near Ruins: Cultural Theory at the End of the Century* (Minneapolis: University of Minnesota Press, 1998); Meenakshi Gigi Durham and Douglas M. Kellner, ed., *Media and Cultural Studies: Keyworks*, rev. ed. (Oxford: Blackwell, 2006); Simon During, ed., *The Cultural Studies Reader* (London: Routledge, 1993); Terry Eagleton, ed., *Raymond Williams: Critical Perspectives* (Cambridge: Polity, 1989); Sara Friedrichsmeyer, "Cultural Studies and the Future of Doctoral Education," *PMLA* 115 (2000): 1268–66; John Frow, *Cultural Studies and Cultural Value* (Oxford: Oxford University Press, 1995); Patrick Fuery and Nick Mansfield, *Cultural Studies and the New*

Humanities: Concepts and Controversies (Oxford: Oxford University Press, 1997); Marjorie B. Garber, Paul B. Franklin, and Rebecca L. Walkowitz, *Field Work: Sites in Literary and Cultural Studies* (New York: Routledge, 1996); Nicholas Garnham, "Political Economy and Cultural Studies: Reconciliation or Divorce?" *Critical Studies in Mass Communication* 12 (1995): 62–71; Mark Gibson, *Culture and Power: A History of Cultural Studies* (Oxford: Berg, 2007); Paul Gilroy, Lawrence Grossberg, and Angela McRobbie, eds., *Without Guarantees: In Honour of Stuart Hall* (London: Verso, 2000); Henry Giroux, David Shumway, Paul Smith, and James Sosnoski, "The Need for Cultural Studies: Resisting Intellectuals and Oppositional Public Spheres," *Dalhousie Review* 64 (1985): 472–86; Larry J. Griffen and Robert A. Gross, "American Studies' Two Cultures: Social Science, Humanities, and the Study of America," in Krabbendam and Verheul, *Through the Looking Glass,* 116–132; Shane Gunster, *Capitalizing on Culture: Critical Theory for Cultural Studies* (Toronto: University of Toronto Press, 2004); Michael Gurevitch, Tony Bennett, James Curran, and Janet Woollacott, ed., *Culture, Society, and the Media* (London: Methuen, 1982); Scott Lash, "Power after Hegemony: Cultural Studies in Mutation?" *Theory, Culture, and Society* 24 (2007): 55–78; Paul Lauter, "Reconfiguring American Disciplines: The Emergence of American Studies," in Krabbendam and Verheul, *Through the Looking Glass,* 229–43; Elizabeth Long, *From Sociology to Cultural Studies: New Perspectives* (Malden, MA: Blackwell Publishers, 1997); Chandra Mukerji and Michael Schudson, eds., *Rethinking Popular Culture: Contemporary Perspectives in Cultural Studies* (Berkeley: University of California Press, 1991); Alan O'Connor, *Raymond Williams: Writing, Culture, Politics* (Oxford: Blackwell, 1989); Christopher Prendergast, ed., *On Raymond Williams: Cultural Materialism* (Minneapolis: University of Minnesota Press, 1995); Michael R. Real, *Super Media: A Cultural Studies Approach* (Newbury Park, CA: Sage, 1989); Barry D. Riccio, "Popular Culture and High Culture: Dwight McDonald, His Critics and the Ideal of Cultural Hierarchy in Modern America," *Journal of American Culture* 16 (1993): 7–18; Andrew Ross, *Strange Weather: Culture, Science, and Technology in the Age of Limits* (London: Verso, 1991); Andrew Ross, *No Respect: Intellectuals and Popular Culture* (New York: Routledge, 1989); José David Saldívar, *Border Matters: Remapping American Cultural Studies* (Berkeley: University of California Press, 1997); James Seaton, *Cultural Conservatism, Political Liberalism: From Criticism to Cultural Studies* (Ann Arbor: University of Michigan Press, 1996); Steven Jay Sherwood, Philip Smith, and Jeffrey C. Alexander, "The British Are Coming . . . Again! The Hidden Agenda of 'Cultural Studies,'" *Contemporary Sociology* 22 (1993): 370–75; Paul Smith, ed., *The Renewal of Cultural Studies* (Philadelphia: Temple University Press, 2011); Gayatri Chakravorty Spivak, *Death of a Discipline* (New York: Columbia University Press, 2003); Carolyn Steedman, "Culture, Cultural Studies, and the Historians," in Grossberg, Nelson, and Treichler, *Cultural Studies,* 613–22; Kenneth Thompson, "Cultural Studies, Critical Theory, and Cultural Governance," *International Sociology* 16 (2001): 593–605; Jaap Verheul, "The Ideological Origins of American Studies," in Krabbendam and Verheul, *Through the Looking Glass,* 91–103.

53. See Guillory, "Sokal Affair," with critical responses and his reply, "Name of Science." The major texts are collected in *The Sokal Hoax: The Sham That Shook the Academy,* ed. the editors of *Lingua Franca* (Lincoln, NE: Lingua Franca, 2000). In his criticism of interdisciplinarity, *In Defense of Disciplines,* Jacobs takes American studies as an example of cultural studies.

54. For perhaps unintended illustrations of ambiguities, see Nelson and Gaonkar's introduction to *Disciplinarity and Dissent in Cultural Studies*.

55. There are many comments on differences in cultural studies between the UK and the United States, and more recently global cultural studies. See especially Brantlinger, *Crusoe's Footprints*; Inglis, *Cultural Studies*; Grossberg, "Formation of Cultural Studies," "Toward a Genealogy of the State of Cultural Studies" and *Bringing It All Back Home*; Grossberg, Nelson, and Treichler, *Cultural Studies*; and Lee, *Life and Times of Cultural Studies*.

56. Marcus, "Humanities from Classics to Cultural Studies," 19. In *Crusoe's Footprints*, Brantlinger wants to add Victorian studies, his own field.

57. Marcus, "Humanities from Classics to Cultural Studies," 20, 21.

58. Ibid., 21.

59. T. Miller, *Blow Up the Humanities*, 107.

60. Ibid., 107–8.

61. Ibid., 108.

62. Nelson and Gaonkar, *Disciplinarity and Dissent in Cultural Studies*, 2, 5.

63. Ibid., 8, 6, 14.

64. Ibid., 17, 18. For amplification, see Appadurai, "Diversity and Disciplinarity as Cultural Artifacts," 23–36.

65. Grossberg, *Cultural Studies in the Future Tense*, 9–10.

66. Lee, *Life and Times of Cultural Studies*, 106–7. After rereadings, I do not know what that means.

67. Ibid., 107. See Hoggart, "Schools of English and Contemporary Society"; Hall, "Emergence of Cultural Studies"; Johnson et al., *Making Histories*.

68. Klein, *Crossing Boundaries*, 123–24, 129.

69. Ibid., 129–30, quoting Bennett, "Putting Policy into Cultural Studies." She addresses "institutionalization" no more clearly; see 131–32. See also Moran, *Interdisciplinarity*, and Bennett, "Putting Policy into Cultural Studies," 23–34. For a moderate view, see Crane, "Cultural Sociology and Other Disciplines." Klein continues: "The familiar call to 'prod' the disciplines becomes a strategy of transgression that faults disciplines for their 'blindness.' Interdisciplinary keywords are entwined with keywords of disciplinary redescription—'negotiation,' 'intervention,' and 'transgression.' Epithets of restructuring signify an interdisciplinarity that irritates and disturbs, disrupts and destabilizes. 'Bricolage,' the ultimate postmodern cross-court word, is not just a trendy of stating an old idea. Loosely translated as 'odds and ends,' bricolage signifies the character of critical interdisciplinarities. The older interdisciplinary move from part to whole becomes a recursive movement from part to whole and back again as new interests arise and rearticulations are made." Is Klein writing a parody of cultural studies?

70. Menand, *Marketplace of Ideas*, 85, 96.

71. Ibid., 87.

72. Ibid., esp. 56, 158. For an unusually offensive slap at interdisciplinary studies, see Camille Paglia, "Scholars in Bondage: Dogma Dominates Studies of Kink," *CHE*, May 20, 2013.

73. English professor David Mikics compares this view with Menand on "interdisciplinarity and anxiety" in "Cultural Studies: Bane of the Humanities," *CHE*, Oct. 7, 2013,

in support of his book, *Slow Reading in a Hurried Age* (Cambridge, MA: Harvard University Press, 2013).

74. Michael Bérubé, "What's the Matter with Cultural Studies? The Popular Discipline Has Lost Its Bearings," *CHE*, Sept. 14, 2009.

75. Ibid.

76. Fish, "Being Interdisciplinary Is So Very Hard to Do," 15.

77. Brenkman, "Extreme Criticism," 109–10.

78. The journal is available online at http://lateral.culturalstudiesassociation.org/.

79. Jaafar Aksikas and Robert W. Gehl to author, Jan. 29, 2014.

80. Program for the Eleventh Annual Meeting of the CSA, Chicago, IL, May 23–26, 2014. The program itself was so hard to follow that relationships among sessions, presentations, and presenters were not clear.

81. All these subjects appear on searches for cultural studies programs conducted by research assistants, especially Nora McCook.

82. See http://educationportal.com/cultural_studies_Graduate.html.

83. "Publications | Cultural Studies @ UNC," http://culturalstudies.web.unc.edu /resources-2/publications/.

84. Wikipedia's article on cultural studies includes a note: "In a separate usage, the phrase cultural studies, as a general term referring to the academic study of particular cultures in departments and programs such as Islamic studies, Asian studies, African American studies, et al. However, strictly speaking, cultural studies programs are not concerned with specific areas of the world so much as specific cultural practices"; http://en .wikipedia.org/wiki/Cultural_studies.

85. On American studies and area studies, see Engerman, "Ironies of the Iron Curtain" and *Know Your Enemy*; Gleason, "World War II and the Development of American Studies"; Jacobs, *In Defense of Disciplines*; McCaughey, *International Studies and Academic Enterprise*; and Solovey and Cravens, *Cold War Social Science*. See also Ali Behdad, "What Can American Studies and Comparative Literature Learn from Each Other?" *American Literary History* 24 (2012): 608–17; Joshua Kjerulf Dubrow, "Sociology and American Studies: A Case Study in the Limits of Interdisciplinarity," *American Sociologist* 42 (Dec. 2011): 303–15; Larry J. Griffin and Maria Tempenis, "Class, Multiculturalism, and the *American Quarterly*," *American Quarterly* 54 (2002): 67–99; Linda K. Kerber, "Diversity and the Transformation of American Studies," *American Quarterly* 41 (1989): 415–31; Christopher Lasch, *The Agony of the American Left* (New York: Knopf, 1968); Richard S. Lowry, "American Studies, Cultural History, and the Critique of Culture," *Journal of the Gilded Age and Progressive Era* 8 (2009): 301–40; Lucy Maddox, ed., *Locating American Studies: The Evolution of a Discipline* (Baltimore, MD: Johns Hopkins University Press, 1999); Lucian W. Pye, ed., *Political Science and Area Studies: Rivals or Partners?* (Bloomington: Indiana University Press, 1975); David L. Szanton, "The Origin, Nature, and Challenges of Area Studies in the United States," in *The Politics of Knowledge: Area Studies and the Disciplines* (Berkeley: University of California Press, 2004), 1–33.

86. For African American Studies, see Esperanza Brizuela-Garcia, "Towards a Critical Interdisciplinarity: African History and the Reconstruction of Universal Narratives," *Rethinking History* 12 (2008): 299–316; Fabio Rojas, *From Black Power to Black Studies: How a Radical Social Movement Became an Academic Discipline* (Baltimore, MD: Johns

Hopkins University Press, 2007); Olzak and Kangas, "Ethnic, Women's, and African American Studies Majors"; and Mario L. Small, "Departmental Conditions and the Emergence of New Disciplines: Two Cases in the Legitimation of African-American Studies," *Theory and Society* 28 (1999): 659–707. For women's studies, see Marilyn Boxer, *When Women Ask the Questions: Creating Women's Studies in America* (Baltimore, MD: Johns Hopkins University Press, 1998); Sue-Ellen Case, "Feminism and Performance: A Post-Disciplinary Couple," *Theatre Research International* 26 (2001): 145–52; Alice E. Ginsberg, ed., *The Evolution of American Women's Studies: Reflections on Triumphs, Controversies, and Change* (New York: Palgrave Macmillan, 2008); Elizabeth Lapovsky Kennedy and Agatha Beins, eds., *Women's Studies for the Future: Foundations, Interrogations, Politics* (New Brunswick, NJ: Rutgers University Press, 2005); Olzak and Kangas, "Ethnic, Women's, and African American Studies Majors"; and Scott, *Gender and the Politics of History*.

87. Guillory, "Sokal Affair," 504.

88. Ibid. See also Guillory's response to Newfield in "Nature of Science."

89. Guillory, "Sokal Affair," 505.

90. Ibid., 506. Guillory urges, "Without question, the disciplinary bridge over this gap is history, which has intermittently grounded literary and cultural studies.... It is certainly within our power to move in the direction of a complementarity of methodologies, in which the claims of different kinds of science, and also of different kinds of historical interpretation, can be assigned to appropriate objects and registers, and conflicting claims in the human sciences reconciled by negotiation rather than conflicts" (507).

Chapter 6 • The Past and Future of Interdisciplinarity

1. "Convergence" as it relates to new biology is discussed in more detail below. The term is used in MIT, *Third Revolution*, which is based on National Research Council, *New Biology*. On questions of the location of interdisciplines and multidisciplines, see Bok, *Higher Education in America*, chapter 16.

2. See Jacobs, *In Defense of Disciplines*, and cf. Frodeman, Klein, and Mitcham, *Oxford Handbook of Interdisciplinarity*.

3. See Michael North, *Novelty: History of the New* (Chicago: University of Chicago Press, 2013).

4. Important features include the hierarchies and relationships among disciplines and disciplinary clusters; see Kagan, *Three Cultures*.

5. I have commented on literacy studies in my essays "Literacy Studies and Interdisciplinary Studies" and "LiteracyStudies@OSU as Theory and Practice." In retrospect, I believe that I was too sanguine in my arguments in support of interdisciplinarity in literacy studies in those pieces. I took a more critical view in my final comments in "Literacy Studies and Interdisciplinary Studies with Notes on the Place of Deborah Brandt."

6. "Molecular biology" and "bioscience" are not synonymous, but so much of contemporary bioscience develops from molecular biology, and molecular biology is so much a product of genetics and biochemistry, that I use these terms interchangeably.

7. G. Allen, *Life Science*, 189.

8. Ibid., 189–90. On interdisciplinarity in bioscience, see Appel, *Shaping Biology*; Berman, *Creating the Market University*; Etzkowitz, "Entrepreneurial Scientists and Entrepreneurial Universities" and *MIT and the Rise of Entrepreneurial Science*; Frickel and

Gross, "General Theory of Scientific/Intellectual Movements"; Furman and Stern, "Climbing atop the Shoulders of Giants"; Hollingsworth and Hollingsworth, "Major Discoveries and Biomedical Research Organizations"; Kleinman, *Politics on the Endless Frontier*; Kleinman and Vallas, "Science, Capitalism, and the Rise of the 'Knowledge Worker' "; Lam, "From 'Ivory Tower Traditionalists' to 'Entrepreneurial Scientists'?"; Mirowski, *Science-Mart*; Powell and Owen-Smith, "New World of Knowledge Production"; Powell and Snellman, "Knowledge Economy"; Powell et al., "Network Dynamics and Field Evolution"; Powell, Owen-Smith, and Colyvas, "Innovation and Emulation"; Scerri, "Interdisciplinary Research"; Schrum, "Administering American Modernity"; Vallas and Kleinman, "Contradiction, Convergence"; and Zuckerman, *Beyond the Ivory Tower*. See also Robert Bud, "Framed in the Public Sphere: Tools for the Conceptual History of 'Applied Science'—A Review Paper," *History of Science* 51 (2013): 413–33; Daryle E. Chubin, "The Conceptualization of Scientific Specialties: State of the Field," *Sociological Quarterly* 17 (1976): 448–76; Jeanette A. Colyvas and Walter W. Powell, "From Vulnerable to Venerated: The Institutionalization of Academic Entrepreneurship in the Life Sciences," *The Sociology of Entrepreneurship, Research in the Sociology of Organizations* 25 (2007): 219–59; Jeffrey L. Furman and Megan MacGarvie, "When the Pill Peddlers Met the Scientists: The Antecedents and Implications of Early Collaborations between US Pharmaceutical Firms and Universities," *Essays in Economic and Business History* 26 (2008): 133–46; Roger Geiger, "Organized Research Units—Their Role in the Development of University Research," *Journal of Higher Education* 61 (1990): 1–19; Martin Kenney, *Biotechnology: The University-Industrial Complex* (New Haven, CT: Yale University Press, 1986); Karin Knorr-Cetina, *Epistemic Cultures: How the Sciences Make Knowledge* (Cambridge, MA: Harvard University Press, 1999); Monica Konrad, "Placebo Politics: On Comparability, Interdisciplinarity, and International Collaborative Research," *Monash Bioethics Review* 25 (2007): 67–84; Rebecca Lowen, *Creating the Cold War University: The Transformation of Stanford* (Berkeley: University of California Press, 1997); Martina Newell-McGloughlin and Edward Re, *The Evolution of Biotechnology: From Natufians to Nanotechnology* (Dordrecht: Springer Netherlands, 2006); Harold Orlans, *The Nonprofit Research Institute: Its Origin, Operation, Problems, and Prospects,* Carnegie Commission on Higher Education (New York: McGraw-Hill, 1972); Paula E. Stephan and Ronald G. Ehrenberg, eds., *Science and the University* (Madison: University of Wisconsin Press, 2007); Toby E. Stuart and Waverly W. Ding, "When Do Scientists Become Entrepreneurs? The Social Structural Antecedents of Commercial Activity in the Academic Life Sciences," *American Journal of Sociology* 112 (2006): 97–144; David Tyfield, "A Cultural Political Economy of Research and Innovation in the Age of Crisis," *Minerva* 50 (2012): 149–67; and G. Pascal Zachary, "Bell Labs Is Gone, Academia Steps In," *New York Times*, Dec. 16, 2007.

9. National Research Council, *New Biology*, vii–viii. "The New Biology relies on integrating knowledge from many disciplines to derive deeper understanding of biological systems [that] both allows the development of biology-based solutions for societal problems and also feeds back to enrich the individual scientific disciplines that contributed to the new insights" (17). See figure 2.1, p. 18.

10. Ibid., 20.

11. "Letter to Our Colleagues," in MIT, *Third Revolution*.

12. Ibid., 4–5.

13. For caution about "unity," see, for example, Karl J. Niklas, Thomas G. Owens, and Randy O. Wayne, "Unity and Disunity in Biology," *BioScience* 63 (2013): 811–16. Many of these reports espouse reforming the peer-review processes to encourage cross-disciplinary grants.

14. On Jan. 14, 2014, with a full-page color advertisement in the *New York Times*, the University of Southern California announced, "A historic $50 million gift establishes the USC Michelson Center for Convergence Bioscience. . . . Building upon USC's unique strengths at the intersections of engineering, the biomedical sciences and medicine, the University of Southern California is rapidly accelerating journeys into greater understanding of living systems and advances in lifesaving biomedical breakthroughs. . . . The USC Michelson Center will help USC transform the biological sciences into quantitative and predictive sciences, fast-tracking the detection and cure of diseases."

15. MIT, *Third Revolution.*

16. Van der Steen, "Interdisciplinary Integration in Biology?" 23; see also van der Steen, "Towards Disciplinary Disintegration in Biology," 259–75. Compare this view to others in biology and in philosophy. They are no more balanced than the prophets of convergence. "Unity" is a keynote in biology, but so is "diversity." The history and usage of that language merits notice by those who adopt it, and needs to be communicated to nonspecialists. My friends, biologists Susan Fisher and Steve Rissing, remind me of this point.

17. See Bechtel, "Biochemistry"; Schaffner, "Theory Structure, Reduction, and Disciplinary Integration"; and van der Steen, "Interdisciplinary Integration in Biology?" and "Towards Disciplinary Disintegration in Biology."

18. See Bechtel, *Integrating Scientific Disciplines,* "Nature of Scientific Integration," and "Biochemistry"; Lenoir, "Discipline of Nature and the Nature of Disciplines"; Wolf Lepenies, "Toward an Interdisciplinary History of Science," *International Journal of Sociology* 8 (1978): 45–69; and Schaffner, "Theory Structure, Reduction, and Disciplinary Integration."

19. Lindley Darden and Nancy Maull, "Interfield Theories," *Philosophy of Science* 44 (1977): 43–64; Bechtel, "Biochemistry."

20. Abir-Am, "Themes, Genres, and Orders of Legitimation," 73; "Politics of Macromolecules," 164; "Molecular Revolution." In her 1985 paper, "Themes, Genres, and Orders of Legitimation," Abir-Am promised an exploration of the science establishment in the 1960s and a definition of "ultradiscipline." But, to the best of my knowledge and despite the efforts of the excellent librarians at the NHC, she never published the paper, listed as forthcoming. Abir-Am has criticized many others working in the area, not always fairly.

21. Schaffner, "Theory Structure, Reduction, and Disciplinary Integration in Biology."

22. Olby, "Molecular Biology."

23. *BioScience* "is a peer-reviewed monthly sometimes daily scientific journal that is published by the American Institute of Biological Sciences (AIBS). The content is written and edited for accessibility to researchers, educators, and students alike." Discussions of interdisciplinarity, which are not well informed, include Mary L. Cadenasso et al., "An Interdisciplinary and Synthetic Approach to Ecological Boundaries," *BioScience* 53 (2003): 717–22; James R. Collins, "May You Live in Interesting Times: Using Multidisciplinary and Interdisciplinary Programs to Cope with Change in the Life Sciences," *Bioscience*

52 (2002): 76–83; Ronald N Kostoff, "Overcoming Specialization," *BioScience* 52 (2002): 937–41; and Sharachchandra Lélé and Richard B. Norgaard, "Practicing Interdisciplinarity," *BioScience* 55 (2005): 967–75. See also John McCarthy, "Tackling the Challenges of Interdisciplinary Bioscience," *Nature Reviews: Cell Biology* 5 (2004): 933–37.

24. On the history and practice of bioscience, see Frederick Thomas Attenborough, " 'To Rid Oneself of the Uninvited Guest': Robert Koch, Sergei Winogradsky, and Competing Styles of Practice in Medical Microbiology," *Journal of Historical Sociology* 25 (2012): 50–82; George A. Beadle, "Biochemical Genetics: Some Recollections," in *Phage and the Origins of Molecular Biology*, ed. C. Carins, G. S. Stent, and J. D. Watson (Cold Spring Harbor, NY: Cold Spring Harbor Laboratory Press, 1992), 23–32; Bud, *Uses of Life*; Richard M. Burian, " 'The Tools of the Discipline: Biochemists and Molecular Biologists': A Comment," *Journal of the History of Biology* 29 (1996): 461–62; Seymour S. Cohen, "The Origins of Molecular Biology. Book Review," *Science* 187 (1975): 827–30, and "A Guide to the History of Biochemistry," *Isis* 91 (2000): 120–24; Creager, "Wendell Stanley's Dream"; de Chadarevian, *Designs for Life*; de Chadarevian and Gaudillière, "Tools of the Discipline"; Max Delbruck, "A Physicist Looks at Biology," in *Phage and the Origins of Molecular Biology*, ed. C. Carins, G. S. Stent, and J. D. Watson (Cold Spring Harbor, NY: Cold Spring Harbor Laboratory Press, 1992), 9–22; Gaudillière, "Molecular Biologists, Biochemists, and Messenger RNA" and "New Wine in Old Bottles?"; Gaudillière and Rheinberger, *From Molecular Genetics to Genomics*; Hagan, "Naturalists, Molecular Biologists"; Hess, "Origins of Molecular Biology"; Jong, "How Organizational Structures in Science Shape Spin-off Firms"; Kay, *Molecular Vision of Life*; Kohler, *From Medical Chemistry to Biochemistry*; Latour and Woolgar, *Laboratory Life*; Morange, *History of Molecular Biology* and "Transformation of Molecular Biology"; Rabinow, *Making PCR*; Nicolas Rasmussen, *Gene Jockeys: Life Science and the Rise of Biotech Enterprise* (Baltimore, MD: Johns Hopkins University Press, 2014); Smith Hughes, *Genentech*; van Helvoort, "Institutionalizing Biochemistry"; Vettel, *Biotech*; Watson, *Double Helix* and *Molecular Biology of the Gene*; Watson and Crick, "Molecular Structure of Nucleic Acids"; Yoxen, "Giving Life a New Meaning."

25. See G. Allen, *Life Science*; Creager, "Wendell Stanley's Dream"; de Chadarevian, *Designs for Life*; Kohler, *From Medical Chemistry to Biochemistry*; Morange, *History of Molecular Biology*; Smith Hughes, *Genentech*; and Vettel, *Biotech*.

26. On cooperation, see Furman and Stern, "Climbing atop the Shoulders of Giants; Kleinman and Vallas, "Science, Capitalism, and the Rise of the 'Knowledge Worker' "; Lam, "From 'Ivory Tower Traditionalists' to 'Entrepreneurial Scientists'?"; Powell and Owen-Smith, "New World of Knowledge Production"; Powell and Snellman, "The Knowledge Economy." More critical are Berman, *Creating the Market University*; Etzkowitz, *MIT*, and Mirowski, *Science-Mart*.

27. See Abir-Am, "From Biochemistry to Molecular Biology," "How Scientists View Their Heroes," "Beyond Deterministic Sociology and Apologetic History," "Biotheoretical Gathering," "Assessment of Interdisciplinary Research," " 'New' Trends in the History of Molecular Biology," and "Molecular Biology and Its Recent Historiography." See also Mercedes Guzman-Casado and Antonio Parody-Morreale, "Notes on the Early History of the Interaction between Physical Chemistry and Biochemistry: The Development of Physical Biochemistry," *Journal of Chemical Education* 79 (2002): 327–31.

28. de Chadarevian and Gaudillière, "Tools of the Discipline," 327.

29. Abir-Am, "Politics of Macromolecules," 164, 166.

30. Ibid., 165–66. On the famous clashes among the structural, biochemical, and informational traditions, see Scott F. Gilbert, "Intellectual Traditions in the Life Sciences: Molecular Biology and Biochemistry," *Perspectives in Biology and Medicine* 26 (1982): 151–62; and Allen, *Life Science*. Morange, "Transformation of Molecular Biology," focuses on "an epistemological crisis" in biology.

31. For general accounts, see Allen, *Life Science*; Morange, *History of Molecular Biology*; and Olby, "Molecular Biology." On particular laboratories, see Latour and Woolgar, *Laboratory Life*; Rabinow, *Making PRC*; de Chadarevian, *Designs for Life*; Creager, "Wendell Stanley's Dream," Smith Hughes, *Genentech*; and Vettel, *Biotech*.

32. See Scerri, "Interdisciplinary Research," and Hollingsworth and Hollingsworth, "Major Discoveries and Biomedical Research Organizations." Despite the emphasis on interdisciplinarity in earlier work, in the Hollingsworths' newer book, written with the assistance of David M. Gear, *Major Discoveries, Creativity, and the Dynamics of Science*, Complexity Design Series, vol. 15 (Vienna: Edition Echoraum, 2011), the term does not appear in the index. Here I also simply note the rise of newly popular ethnographies of science and the issues that they raise.

33. Jong is given to expressions like "unified interdisciplinary research community"; see "How Organizational Structures in Science Shape Spin-off Firms," 268, 269, 274. Her story differs greatly from Smith Hughes, *Genentech*, and Vettel, *Biotech*. The complication is not only one of researchers' own disciplinary practices, as van Helvoort, "Institutionalizing Biochemistry," shows. This confusing account also sprinkles in a language of "unified," "integration," and interdisciplinary without definition or investigation of practice or relationships. He italicizes *inter*, as in "The [Rockefeller Foundation] report recommended taking up the mechanisms of action of enzymes as a suitable subject for *inter*disciplinary study" (456). "Group action" is another mantra. Yet the tale that he tells is perhaps most interesting with respect to biochemistry's efforts to gain respect, recognition, autonomy, and establish a location for itself vis-à-vis chemistry, biology, and the sciences more generally (460–64). Revealingly, in the end, van Helvoort is unsure if biochemistry is a "multidisciplinary specialty or singular branch of science" (477). He is also confusing on the role of location, at Wisconsin and elsewhere.

34. Kohler, *From Medical Chemistry to Biochemistry*, 7–8.

35. Ibid.

36. That is, the history, if not always the interpretation.

37. Creager, "Wendell Stanley's Dream," 352, 353.

38. The medical biochemists in 1952 renamed their group "Physiological Chemistry" and in 1958 moved across San Francisco Bay to the UCSF medical school. Stanley's group in the Virus Laboratory became the Department of Virology and established stronger connections with the Department of Bacteriology. By the 1960s, a separate Department of Molecular Biology was created. "The falling-out with the Berkeley biochemists was rapidly followed by the establishment of a Department of Molecular Biology, attesting to the economic and institutional possibilities for an authoritative 'general biology' (or two, for that matter) to take hold" (Creager, "Wendell Stanley's Dream," 360).

39. Creager's study of Wendell Stanley at Berkeley provides a case in point well into 1950s, 1960s, and beyond.

40. Vettel, *Biotech*, 47; see also his chap. 4.

41. This is reimagined in National Research Council, *New Biology*; see Appel, *Life Science*; Kleinman, *Politics on the Endless Frontier*; and Schrum, "Administering American Modernity."

42. Compare to earlier developments at Rockefeller University and Cambridge University. See de Chadarevian, *Designs for Life*; Vettel, *Biotech*; Smith Hughes, *Genentech*; and Jong, "How Organizational Structures in Science Shape Spin-off Firms."

43. Vettel, *Biotech*, 101.

44. Ibid., 176. 177. This continuing battle is too important, too expensive, and too political to be left to scientists. For early history of Cetus and the Asilomar conference in California in 1975. For Genentech, see Smith Hughes, *Genentech*, who describes that company's culture as "recombinant" (132). See also Bud, *Uses of Life*.

45. These questions are the subject of my next book, *Searching for Literacy: The Intellectual and Social Origins of Literacy Studies*. For examples, see H. Graff, "Assessing the History of Literacy," *Literacy Myth*, and "*Literacy Myth* at 30"; and Graff and Duffy, "Literacy Myth."

46. D. Barton, "Directions for Literacy Research" and *Literacy*; Barton and Hamilton, *Local Literacies*; Barton et al., *Literacy, Lives, and Learning*; Brandt and Clinton, "Limits of the Local"; Brockmeier, Wang, and Olson, *Literacy, Narrative, and Culture*; Michael Clanchy, *From Memory to Written Record: England, 1066–1307* (Oxford: Blackwell, 1979); Cole, *Cultural Psychology*; James Collins and Richard K. Blot, *Literacy and Literacies: Texts, Power, and Identity* (Cambridge: Cambridge University Press, 2003); James Gee, "The New Literacy Studies and the 'Social Turn'" (2007), www.schools.ash.org.au/litweb/page 300.html; Jack Goody, *The Domestication of the Savage Mind* (Cambridge: Cambridge University Press, 1977), *The Logic of Writing and the Organization of Society* (Cambridge: Cambridge University Press, 1986), *The Interface Between the Written and the Oral* (Cambridge: Cambridge University Press, 1987), and *Literacy in Traditional Societies*; Jack Goody and Ian Watt, "The Consequences of Literacy," in Goody, *Literacy in Traditional Societies*, 27–68; H. Graff, "Assessing the History of Literacy"; Graff, *Labyrinths of Literacy*, *Legacies of Literacy*, *Literacy Myth*, "*Literacy Myth* at Thirty," *Literacy Myths, Legacies, and Lessons*, "LiteracyStudies@OSU as Theory and Practice," "Literacy Studies and Interdisciplinary Studies," and "Literacy Studies and Interdisciplinary Studies with notes on the place of Deborah Brandt"; Graff and Duffy, "Literacy Myths"; John Halverson, "Olson on Literacy," *Language and Society* 20 (1991): 619–40, and "Goody and the Implosion of the Literacy Thesis," *Man* 27 (1992): 301–17; William V. Harris, *Ancient Literacy* (Cambridge, MA: Harvard University Press, 1989); Eric Havelock, *Preface to Plato* (Cambridge, MA: Harvard University Press, 1963, 1976), *The Origins of Western Literacy* (Toronto: Ontario Institute for Studies in Education, 1976), and *The Literate Revolution in Greece and Its Consequences* (Princeton, NJ: Princeton University Press, 1982); Heath, *Ways with Words*; Alex Inkeles and David Horton Smith, *Becoming Modern: Individual Change in Six Developing Countries* (Cambridge, MA: Harvard University Press, 1974); Carl F. Kaestle, Helen Damon-Moore, Lawrence C. Stedman, Katherine Tinsley, and William Vance Trollinger Jr., *Literacy in the United States: Readers and Reading since 1880* (New Haven, CT: Yale University Press, 1991); Leon Lederman, editorial, *Science News* 173 (May 10, 2008): 36; Daniel Lerner, *The Passing of Traditional Society: Modernizing the Middle East* (New York: Free Press, 1965); Lord, *Singer of Tales*; David R. Olson, "Mind and Media: The Epistemic Functions of Literacy," *Journal of Communication* 38 (1988): 27–36, and *The World on*

Paper: The Conceptual and Cognitive Implications of Reading and Writing (Cambridge: Cambridge University Press, 1994); Parry, *Making of Homeric Verse*; Sylvia Scribner and Michael Cole, *The Psychology of Literacy* (Cambridge, MA: Harvard University Press. 1981); Street, *Literacy in Theory and Practice*, "Introduction: The New Literacy Studies," and "New Literacies in Theory and Practice"; Wertsch, *Vygotsky*.

47. Lederman, editorial, 36.

48. D. Barton, *Literacy*, 23.

49. D. Barton, "Directions for Literacy Research," 93.

50. Street, *Literacy in Theory and Practice*.

51. Brockmeier, Wang, and Olson, *Literacy, Narrative and Culture*, 6–7.

52. Lord, *Singer of Tales*; Parry, *Making of Homeric Verse*.

53. See Wertsch, *Vygotsky*, and Cole, *Cultural Psychology*.

54. For the controversy over local literacy and its limits, see Street, "Introduction: New Literacy Studies," and Brandt and Clinton, "Limits of the Local."

55. See Graff, "LiteracyStudies@OSU as Theory and Practice." For LiteracyStudies @OSU, visit http://literacystudies.osu.edu/.

56. See, for example, Heath, *Ways with Words*, and Ruth Finnegan, "Literacy versus Non-Literacy: The Great Divide," in *Modes of Thought*, ed. Robin Horton and Ruth Finnegan (Faber and Faber, 1973), 112–44.

Sources cited only once appear only in the notes.

Aaronson, Susan Ariel. Serving America's Business? Graduate Business Schools and American Business, 1945–60. *Business History* 34 (1992): 60–182.

Aarsleff, Hans. *From Locke to Saussure: Essays on the Study of Language and Intellectual History.* Minneapolis: University of Minnesota Press, 1982.

Aarsleff, Hans, Louis G. Kelly, and Hans-Josef Niederehe, eds. *Papers in the History of Linguistics: Proceedings of the Third International Conference on the History of the Language Sciences, Princeton, 19–23 August 1984.* Philadelphia: J. Benjamins, 1987.

Abbott, Andrew. *Chaos of Disciplines.* Chicago: University of Chicago Press, 2001.

———. *Department and Discipline: Chicago Sociology at One Hundred.* Chicago: University of Chicago Press, 1999.

———. The Disciplines and the Future. In Brint, *Future of the City of Intellect,* 205–30.

———. History and Sociology: The Lost Synthesis. *Social Science History* 15 (1991): 201–38.

Abir-Am, Pnina G. The Assessment of Interdisciplinary Research in the 1930s: The Rockefeller Foundation and Physico-chemical Morphology. *Minerva* 26 (1988): 153–76.

———. Beyond Deterministic Sociology and Apologetic History: Reassessing the Impact of Research Policy upon New Scientific Disciplines (Reply to Fuerst, Bartels, Olby, and Yoxen). *Social Studies of Science* 14 (1984): 252–63.

———. The Biotheoretical Gathering, Trans-Disciplinary Authority and the Incipient Legitimation of Molecular Biology in the 1930s: New Perspective on the Historical Sociology of Science. *History of Science* 25 (1987): 1–70.

———. From Biochemistry to Molecular Biology: DNA and the Acculturated Journey of the Critic of Science Erwin Chargaff. *History and Philosophy of the Life Sciences* 2 (1980): 3–60.

———. How Scientists View Their Heroes: Some Remarks on the Mechanism of Myth Construction. *Journal of the History of Biology* 15 (1982): 281–315.

———. Molecular Biology and Its Recent Historiography: A Transnational Quest for the "Big Picture." *History of Science* 44 (2006): 95–118.

———. The Molecular Revolution in Twentieth-Century Biology. In *Science in the Twentieth Century,* ed. John Krige and Dominique Pestre, 495–520. Amsterdam: Harwood Academic, 1997.

———. "New" Trends in the History of Molecular Biology. *Historical Studies in the Physical and Biological Sciences* 26 (1995): 167–95.

———. The Politics of Macromolecules: Molecular Biologists, Biochemists, and Rhetoric. *Osiris* 7 (1992): 164–91.

———. Themes, Genres, and Orders of Legitimation in the Consolidation of New Scientific Disciplines: Deconstructing the Historiography of Molecular Biology. *History of Science* 59 (1985): 73–117.

Abrams, M. H. The Transformation of English Studies, 1930–1995. *Daedalus* 126 (1997): 105–31.

Abrams, Philip. The Sense of the Past and the Origins of Sociology. *Past and Present*, no. 55 (May 1972): 18–32.

Agar, Michael. *The Lively Science: Remodeling Human Social Research.* Minneapolis, MN: Mill City Press, 2013.

AHR Forum: Geoff Eley's *A Crooked Line. American Historical Review* 113 (2008): 391–437.

AHR Forum: Historiographic "Turns" in Critical Perspective. *American Historical Review* 117 (2012): 698–813.

Allardyce, Gilbert. The Rise and Fall of the Western Civilization Course. *American Historical Review* 87 (1982): 695–72.

Allen, David E. Amateurs and Professionals. In *The Cambridge History of Science*, vol. 6: *The Modern Biological and Earth Sciences*, ed. Peter J. Bowler and John V. Pickstone, 13–33. Cambridge: Cambridge University Press, 2009.

Allen, Garland E. *Life Science in the Twentieth Century.* Cambridge: Cambridge University Press, 1975.

———. T. H. Morgan and the Emergence of a New American Biology. *Quarterly Review of Biology* 44 (1969): 168–88.

———. *Thomas Hunt Morgan: The Man and His Science.* Princeton, NJ: Princeton University Press, 1978.

Allport, Gordon W., and Edwin G. Boring. Psychology and Social Relations at Harvard University. *American Psychologist*, April 1946, 119–22.

Amato, Ivan. *Stuff: The Materials the World Is Made Of.* New York: Basic Books, 1997.

American Academy of Arts and Sciences (AAAS). *The Heart of the Matter: The Humanities and Social Sciences for a Vibrant, Competitive, and Secure Nation.* Cambridge, MA: AAAS, 2013.

American Council on Education. *American Universities and Colleges*, ed. David Allan Robertson. New York: Charles Scribner's Sons, 1928.

———. *American Universities and Colleges*, ed. John Henry McCracken. 2nd revised and enlarged edition. Baltimore, MD: Williams & Wilkins, 1932.

———. *American Universities and Colleges*, ed. Clarence Stephens Marsh. 3rd ed. Washington, DC: American Council on Education, 1936.

Anderson, Amanda, and Joseph Valente, eds. *Disciplinarity at the Fin de Siècle.* Princeton, NJ: Princeton University Press, 2002.

Andresen, Julie Tetel. *Linguistics in America, 1769–1924: A Critical History.* London: Routledge, 1990.

Appadurai, Arjun. Diversity and Disciplinarity as Cultural Artifacts. In *Diversity and Dissent in Cultural Studies*, ed. Cary Nelson and Dilip Parameshwar Gaonkar, 22–36. New York: Routledge, 1996.

Appel, Toby A. *Shaping Biology: The National Science Foundation and American Biological Research 1945–1975.* Baltimore, MD: Johns Hopkins University Press, 2000.

Appleby, Joyce. The Power of History. Presidential Address to the American Historical Association. *American Historical Review* 103 (1998): 1–17.

Armstrong, Paul B. *How Literature Plays with the Brain: The Neuroscience of Reading and Art.* Baltimore, MD: Johns Hopkins University Press, 2013.

Aronowitz, Stanley. *The Knowledge Factory: Dismantling the Corporate University and Creating True Higher Learning*. Boston: Beacon, 2000.

Assad, Arjang A., and Saul I. Gass, eds. *Profiles in Operations Research: Pioneers and Innovators*. New York: Springer, 2011.

Augier, Mie, and James G. March. *The Roots, Rituals, and Rhetorics of Change: North American Business Schools after the Second World War*. Stanford, CA: Stanford University Press, 2011.

Aydelotte, William A., Alan Bogue, and Robert W. Fogel, eds. *The Dimensions of Quantitative Research in History*. Princeton, NJ: Princeton University Press, 1972.

Baars, Bernard J. *The Cognitive Revolution in Psychology*. New York: Guilford, 1986.

Backhouse, Roger E., and Philippe Fontaine, eds. *The History of the Social Sciences since 1945*. Cambridge: Cambridge University Press, 2010.

Bannister, Robert C. Sociology. In Porter and Ross, *Modern Social Sciences*, 329–53.

———. *Sociology and Scientism: The American Quest for Objectivity, 1880–1940*. Chapel Hill: University of North Carolina Press, 1987.

Barnes, Harry Elmer. *An Introduction to the History of Sociology*. Chicago: University of Chicago Press, 1948.

Baron, Sabrina Alcorn, Eric N. Lindquist, and Eleanor F. Shevlin, eds. *Agent of Change: Print Culture Studies after Elizabeth L. Eisenstein*. Amherst: University of Massachusetts Press, 2007.

Barton, Allen H. Paul Lazarsfeld and Applied Social Research. *Social Science History* 3 (1979): 4–44.

———. Paul Lazarsfeld and the Invention of the University Institute for Applied Social Research. In *Organizing for Social Research*, ed. Burkart Holzner and Jirir Nehnevaysa, 17–83. Cambridge, MA: Schenkman, 1982.

Barton, David. Directions for Literacy Research: Analysing Language and Social Practices in a Textually Mediated World. *Language and Education* 15 (2001): 92–104.

———. *Literacy: An Introduction to the Ecology of Written Language*. 2nd ed. Oxford: Blackwell, 2007.

Barton, David, and Mary Hamilton, *Local Literacies: Reading and Writing in One Community*. London: Routledge, 1998.

Barton, David, Roz Ivanic, Yvon Appleby, Rachel Hodge, and Karin Tusting. *Literacy, Lives, and Learning*. London: Routledge, 2007.

Baumgartner, Peter, and Sabine Payr, eds. *Speaking Minds: Interviews with Twenty Eminent Cognitive Scientists*. Princeton, NJ: Princeton University Press, 1995.

Beaver, Michael B. *Metallurgy and Materials Science Engineering at MIT, 1965–1988*. Cambridge, MA: MIT Press, 1988.

Bechtel, William. Biochemistry: A Cross-Disciplinary Endeavor That Discovered a Distinctive Domain. In Bechtel, *Integrating Scientific Disciplines*, 77–100.

———, ed. *Integrating Scientific Disciplines*. Dordrecht: Martinus Nijhoff, 1986.

———. The Nature of Scientific Integration. In Bechtel, *Integrating Scientific Disciplines*, 3–52.

Belknap, Robert L., and Richard Kuhns. *Tradition and Innovation: General Education and the Reintegration of the University*. New York: Columbia University Press, 1977.

Bell, Daniel. *The Reforming of General Education: The Columbia College Experience in Its National Setting*. New York: Columbia University Press, 1966.

Bender, Thomas. *Intellect and Public Life*. Baltimore, MD: Johns Hopkins University Press, 1993.

Beniger, James R. Toward an Old New Paradigm: The Half-Century Flirtation with Mass Society. *Public Opinion Quarterly* 51 (1987): S546–66.

———. Who Are the Most Important Theorists of Communication? *Communication Research* 17 (1990): 698–715.

Bennett, Tony. Cultural Studies: A Reluctant Discipline. *Cultural Studies* 12 (1998): 528–45.

———. Making Culture, Changing Society: The Perspective of "Cultural Studies." *Cultural Studies* 21 (2007): 610–29.

———. Putting Policy into Cultural Studies. In Grossberg, Nelson, and Treichler, *Cultural Studies*, 23–34.

Bensaude-Vincent, Bernadette. The Construction of a Discipline: Materials Science in the United States. *History Studies in the Physical and Biological Sciences* 31 (2001): 223–48.

———. Materials Science and Engineering: An Artificial Discipline about to Explode? *History of Materials Research*. Dibner Institute for the History of Science and Technology, California Institute of Technology, 2001. http://authors.library.caltech.edu/5456 /1/hrst.mit.edu/hrs/materials/public/Bernadettespaperforhrst_files/intro(bbv histMSE).htm.

Bentley, M. The Harvard Case for Psychology. *American Journal of Psychology* 61 (1948): 275–82.

Berelson, Bernard. The State of Communication Research, with dissenting comments by Wilbur Schramm, David Riesman, and Raymond A. Bauer. *Public Opinion Quarterly* 23 (1959): 1–6.

Berman, Elizabeth Popp. *Creating the Market University: How Academic Science Became an Economic Engine*. Princeton, NJ: Princeton University Press, 2013.

Bhambra, Gurminder K., and John Holmwood. Introduction: Translation and the Challenge of Interdisciplinarity. *Journal of Historical Sociology* 24, no. 1 (2011): 1–8.

Bialas, Wolfgang, and Anson Rabinach, eds. *Nazi Germany and the Humanities*. Oxford: Oneworld, 2007.

Biernacki, Richard. Method and Metaphor after the New Cultural History. In *Beyond the Cultural Turn*, ed. Lynn Hunt and Victoria Bonnell, 61–92. Berkeley: University of California Press, 1999.

Blundell, Valda, John Shepherd, and Ian Taylor, eds. *Relocating Cultural Studies: Developments in Theory and Research*. London: Routledge 1993.

Boden, Margaret A. *Mind as Machine: A History of Cognitive Science*. Vol. 1. Oxford: Oxford University Press, 2006.

Bogue, Alan G. *Clio and the Bitch Goddess: Quantification in American Political History*. Beverly Hills, CA: Sage, 1983.

———, ed. *Emerging Theoretical Models in Social and Political History*. Beverly Hills, CA: Sage, 1973.

———. Great Expectations and Secular Depreciation: The First Ten Years of the Social Science History Association. *Social Science History* 11 (1987): 329–42.

———. Systematic Revisionism and a Generation of Ferment in American History. *Journal of Contemporary History* 21 (1986): 135–62.

Bogue, Alan G., and Jerome M. Clubb. History and the Social Sciences: Progress and Prospects [introduction to special issue]. *American Behavioral Scientist* 21 (Nov. 1977): 165–66.

———. History, Quantification, and the Social Sciences *American Behavioral Scientist* 21 (Nov. 1977): 167–85.

Bok, *Derek. Higher Education in America.* Princeton, NJ: Princeton University Press, 2013.

Bond, Niall. Ferdinand Tönnies and Academic "Socialism." *History of the Human Sciences* 24 (2011): 23–45.

Borrego, Maura, and Lynita K. Newswander. Definitions of Interdisciplinary Research: Toward Graduate-Level Interdisciplinary Learning Outcomes. *Review of Higher Education* 34 (2010): 61–84.

Bourdieu, Pierre. *Homo Academicus.* 1984. Trans. Peter Collier. Cambridge: Polity, 1990.

———. *Outline of a Theory of Practice.* 1972. Trans. Richard Nice. Cambridge: Cambridge University Press, 1977.

Bourdieu, Pierre, and Jean-Claude Passeron. *The Inheritors: French Students and Their Relations to Culture.* 1964. Trans. Richard Nice. Chicago: University of Chicago Press, 1979.

———. *Reproduction in Education, Society, and Culture.* 1970. Trans. Richard Nice. Beverly Hills, CA: Sage, 1990.

Bowler, Peter J., and Iwan Rhys Morus. *Making Modern Science.* Chicago: University of Chicago Press, 2005.

Brandt, Deborah, and Katie Clinton. Limits of the Local: Expanding Perspectives on Literacy as a Social Practice. *Journal of Literacy Research* 34 (2002): 337–56.

Brantlinger, Patrick. *Bread and Circuses: Theories of Mass Culture and Social Decay.* Ithaca, NY: Cornell University Press, 1983.

———. *Crusoe's Footprints: Cultural Studies in Britain and America.* New York: Routledge, 1990.

Braverman, Harry. *Labor and Monopoly Capital: The Degradation of Work in the Twentieth Century.* New York: Monthly Review Press, 1974.

Brenkman, John. Extreme Criticism. *Critical Inquiry* 26 (1999): 109–27.

Brick, Howard. Optimism of the Mind: Imagining Postindustrial Society in the 1960s and 1970s. *American Quarterly* 44 (1992): 348–80.

———. The Reformist Dimension of Talcott Parsons's Early Social Theory. In *The Culture of the Market: Historical Dimensions,* ed. Thomas Haskell and Richard F. Teichgraeber III, 357–96. Cambridge: Cambridge University Press, 1993.

———. Talcott Parsons's "Shift Away from Economics," 1937–1946. *Journal of American History* 87 (2000): 490–514.

———. *Transcending Capitalism: Visions of a New Society in Modern American Thought.* Ithaca, NY: Cornell University Press, 2006.

Brint, Steven. Creating the Future: "New Directions" in American Research Universities. *Minerva* 43 (2005): 23–50.

———, ed. *The Future of the City of Intellect: The Changing American University.* Stanford, CA: Stanford University Press, 2002.

———. The Rise of the "Practical Arts." In Brint, *Future of the City of Intellect,* 61–89.

Brint, Steven, Mark Riddle, Lori-Turk-Bicakci, and Charles S. Levy. From the Liberal to the Practical Arts in American Colleges and Universities: Organizational Analysis and Curricular Change. *Journal of Higher Education* 76 (2005): 151–80.

Brockmeier, Jens, Min Wang, and David R. Olson, eds. *Literacy, Narrative, and Culture.* Richmond, UK: Curzon, 2002.

Brook, Andrew, ed. *The Prehistory of Cognitive Science.* Hampshire: Palgrave Macmillan, 2007.

Bruner, Jerome. *In Search of Mind: Essays in Autobiography.* New York: Harper & Row, 1983.

Brush, Stephen G. How Theories Become Knowledge: Morgan's Chromosome Theory of Heredity in America and Britain. *Journal of the History of Biology* 35 (2002): 471–535.

Buck, Paul, ed. *The Social Sciences at Harvard, 1860–1920: From Inculcation to the Open Mind.* Cambridge, MA: Harvard University Press, 1965.

Bud, Robert. *The Uses of Life: History of Biotechnology.* Cambridge: Cambridge University Press, 1993.

Bulmer, Martin. *The Chicago School of Sociology: Institutionalization, Diversity, and the Rise of Sociological Research.* Chicago: University of Chicago Press, 1984.

———. Quantification and Chicago Social Science in the 1920s: A Neglected Tradition. *Journal of the History of the Behavioral Sciences* 17 (1981): 312–31.

Burke, Peter. *New Perspectives on Historical Writing.* University Park: Pennsylvania State University Press, 1992.

Bynum, Caroline W. Perspectives, Connections, and Objects: What's Happening in History Now? *Daedalus* 128 (2009): 71–86.

Cahn, R. W. *The Coming of Materials Science.* Amsterdam: Pergamon, 2001.

Calhoun, Craig. The Rise and Domestication of Historical Sociology. In McDonald, *Historic Turn in the Social Sciences,* 305–38.

———, ed. *Sociology in America: A History.* ASA Centennial Publication. Chicago: University of Chicago Press, 2007.

———. Sociology, Other Disciplines, and the Project of a General Understanding of Social Life. In *Sociology and Its Publics: The Forms and Fates of Disciplinary Organization,* ed. Terence C. Halliday and Morris Janowitz, 137–95. Chicago: University of Chicago Press, 1992.

———. The Specificity of American Higher Education. *Comparative Social Research* 19 (2000): 48–81.

———. The University and the Public Good. *Thesis Eleven,* no. 84 (2006): 7–43.

Camic, Charles. The Making of a Method: A Historical Reinterpretation of the Early Parsons. *American Sociological Review* 52 (1987): 421–39.

———. On Edge: Sociology during the Great Depression and the New Deal. In Calhoun, *Sociology in America,* 225–80.

———. Reputation and Predecessor Selection: Parsons and the Institutionalists. *American Sociological Review* 57 (1992): 421–45.

———. Reshaping the History of American Sociology. *Social Epistemology* 8 (1994): 9–18.

———. *Structure* after 50 Years: The Anatomy of a Charter. *American Journal of Sociology* 95 (1989): 38–107.

————. Three Departments in Search of a Discipline: Localism and Interdisciplinary Interaction in American Sociology, 1890–1940. *Social Research* 62 (1995): 1003–33.

Camic, Charles, Neil Gross, and Michele Lamont, eds. *Social Knowledge in the Making.* Chicago: University of Chicago Press, 2011.

Camic, Charles, and Yu Xie. The Statistical Turn in American Social Science: Columbia University, 1890 to 1915. *American Sociological Review* 59 (1994): 773–805.

Carey, James W. *Communication as Culture: Essays on Media and Society.* New York: Routledge, 1989.

Carr, Nicholas. *The Shallows: What the Internet Is Doing to Our Brains.* New York: W. W. Norton, 2010.

Casey, Beth A. The Quiet Revolution: The Transformation and Reintegration of the Humanities. *Issues in Integrative Studies* 4 (1986): 71–91.

Choi, Naomi. Defending Anti-Naturalism after the Interpretive Turn: Charles Taylor and the Human Sciences. *History of Political Thought* 30 (2009): 693–718.

Chopp, Rebecca, Susan Frost, and Daniel H. Weiss, eds. *Remaking College: Innovation and the Liberal Arts.* Baltimore, MD: Johns Hopkins University Press, 2013.

Christopherson, Derman, and E. C. Baughan. Reminiscences of Operational Research in World War II by Some of Its Practitioners: II. *Journal of the Operational Research Society* 43 (1992): 569–77.

Cmiel, Kenneth. On Cynicism, Evil, and the Discovery of Communication in the 1940s. *Journal of Communication* 46 (1996): 88–107.

Cohen-Cole, Jamie. The Creative American: Cold War Salons, Social Science, and the Cure for Modern Society. *Isis* 100 (2009): 219–62.

————. Instituting the Science of Mind: Intellectual Economies and Disciplinary Exchange at Harvard's Center for Cognitive Studies. *British Journal for the History of Science* 40 (2007): 567–97.

————. *The Open Mind: Cold War Politics and the Sciences of Human Nature.* Chicago: University of Chicago Press, 2014.

————. The Reflexivity of Cognitive Science: The Scientist as Model of Human Nature. *History of the Human Sciences* 18 (2005): 107–39.

Cole, Michael. *Cultural Psychology: A Once and Future Discipline.* Cambridge, MA: Harvard University Press, 1996.

Commission on the Humanities. *The Humanities in American Life.* Berkeley: University of California Press, 1980.

Committee on General Education in a Free Society, Harvard University. *General Education in a Free Society* [Harvard Red Book]. Cambridge, MA: Harvard University Press, 1945.

Committee on Materials Science and Engineering (COSMAT), Solid State Sciences Committee, Board on Physics and Astronomy, Commission on Physical Sciences, Mathematics, and Resources and National Materials Advisory Board, Commission on Engineering and Technical Systems, National Research Council. *Materials for Science and Engineering in the 1990s: Maintaining Competitiveness in the Age of Materials.* Washington, DC: National Academy Press, 1989.

Committee on a New Biology for the 21st Century, Ensuring the United States Leads the Coming Biology Revolution, Board on Life Sciences, Division on Earth and Life

Studies, National Research Council. *A New Biology for the 21st Century*. Washington, DC: National Academies Press, 2009.

Committee on the Survey of Materials Science and Engineering (COSMAT), National Research Council. *Materials and Man's Needs: Materials Science and Engineering*. Washington, DC: National Academy of Sciences, 1974.

Cook, James W., Lawrence B. Glickman, and Michael O'Malley, eds. *The Cultural Turn in U.S. History: Past, Present, and Future*. Chicago: University of Chicago Press, 2008.

Cooper, Richard P., and Tim Shallice. Cognitive Neuroscience: The Troubled Marriage of Cognitive Science and Neuroscience. *Topics in Cognitive Science* 2 (2010): 398–406.

Crane, Diana. Cultural Sociology and Other Disciplines: Interdisciplinarity in the Cultural Sciences. *Sociology Compass* 4, no. 3 (2010): 169–79.

Creager, Angela N. H. Wendell Stanley's Dream of a Free-Standing Biochemistry Department at the University of California, Berkeley. *Journal of the History of Biology* 29 (1996): 331–60.

Crofts, James. The Challenges of Interdisciplinary Epistemology in Neuroaesthetics. *Mind, Brain, and Education* 5 (2011): 5–11.

Crowley, David, and Paul Heyer, eds. *Communication in History: Technology, Culture, Society*. 6th ed. New York: Pearson, 2010.

Crowther-Heyck, Hunter. George A. Miller, Language, and the Computer Metaphor of Mind. *History of Psychology* 2 (1999): 37–64.

———. *Herbert A. Simon: The Bounds of Reason in Modern America*. Baltimore, MD: Johns Hopkins University Press, 2005.

———. Herbert Simon and the GSIA: Building an Interdisciplinary Community. *Journal of the History of the Behavioral Sciences* 42 (2006): 311–34.

———. Patrons of the Revolution: Ideals and Institutions in Postwar Behavioral Science. *Isis* 97 (2006): 420–46.

———. Producing Reason. In Solovey and Hamilton, *Cold War Social Science*, 99–116.

Czitrom, Daniel J. *Media and the American Mind: From Morse to McLuhan*. Chapel Hill: University of North Carolina Press, 1989.

Dawson, Cree S., Charles J. McCallum, R. B. Murphy, and Eric Wolman. Operations Research at Bell Laboratories through the 1970s: Parts 1–3. *Operations Research* 48, nos. 2, 3, 4 (2000): 205–15, 251–61, 512–25.

de Chadarevian, Soraya. *Designs for Life: Molecular Biology after World War II*. Cambridge: Cambridge University Press, 2002.

de Chadarevian, Soraya, and Jean-Paul Gaudillière. The Tools of the Discipline: Biochemists and Molecular Biologists. *Journal of the History of Biology* 29 (1995): 327–30.

De Mey, Marc. *The Cognitive Paradigm: Cognitive Science, a Newly Explored Approach to the Study of Cognition Applied in an Analysis of Science and Scientific Knowledge*. 1982. Reprinted with new introduction, Dordrecht: D. Reidel, 2000.

———. Cognitive Science as an Interdisciplinary Endeavour. In Weingart and Stehr, *Practising Interdisciplinarity*, 154–72.

Dennis, Everette E., and Ellen Wartella, eds. *American Communication Research: The Remembered History*. Mahwah, NJ: Lawrence Erlbaum Associates, 1996.

Drexler, K. Eric. *Engines of Creation*. New York: Doubleday Anchor, 1986.

———. *Nanosystems: Molecular Machinery, Manufacturing, and Computation*. New York: Wiley Interscience, 1992.

Dyson, George. *Turing's Cathedral: The Origins of the Digital Universe*. New York: Pantheon, 2012.

Edwards, Paul N. *The Closed World: Computers and the Politics of Discourse in Cold War America*. Cambridge, MA: MIT Press, 1996.

Eisenstadt, S. N. Social Evolution and Modernity: Some Observations on Parsons's Comparative and Evolutionary Analysis: Parsons's Analysis from the Perspective of Multiple Modernities. *American Sociologist* 35 (2004): 5–24.

Eisenstein, Elizabeth L. *The Printing Press as an Agent of Change*. Cambridge: Cambridge University Press, 1979.

Eley, Geoff. Between Social History and Cultural Studies: Interdisciplinarity and the Practice of the Historian at the End of the Twentieth Century. In *Historians and Social Values*, ed. Joep Leerssen and Ann Rigney, 93–109. Amsterdam: Amsterdam University Press, 2000.

———. *A Crooked Line: From Cultural History to the History of Society*. Ann Arbor: University of Michigan Press, 2005.

———. Is All the World a Text? From Social History to the History of Society Two Decades Later. In McDonald, *Historical Turn in the Human Sciences*, 193–244.

Engerman, David C. The Ironies of the Iron Curtain: The Cold War and the Rise of Russian Studies in the United States. *Cahiers du Monde Russe* 45 (2004): 465–95.

———. *Know Your Enemy: The Rise and Fall of America's Soviet Experts*. New York: Oxford University Press, 2009.

———. Rethinking Cold War Universities: Some Recent Histories. *Journal of Cold War Studies* 5 (2003): 80–95.

———. The Rise and Fall of Wartime Social Science: Harvard's Refugee Interview Project, 1950–1954. In Solovey and Hamilton, *Cold War Social Science*, 25–44.

Engerman, David C., Nils Gilman, Mark H. Haefele, and Michael E. Latham, eds. *Staging Growth: Modernization, Development, and the Cold War*. Amherst: University of Massachusetts Press, 2003.

Erickson, Paul, Judy L. Klein, Lorraine Daston, Rebecca Lemov, Thomas Sturn, and Michael D. Gordin. *How Reason Almost Lost Its Mind: The Strange Career of Cold War Rationality*. Chicago: University of Chicago Press, 2014.

Etzkowitz, Henry. Entrepreneurial Scientists and Entrepreneurial Universities in American Academic Science. *Minerva* 21 (1983): 198–233.

———. *MIT and the Rise of Entrepreneurial Science*. London: Routledge, 2002.

Eustace, Nicole, Eugenia Lean, Julie Livingston, Jan Plamper, William M. Reddy, and Barbara H. Rosenwein. AHR Conversation: The Historical Study of Emotions. *American Historical Review* 117 (2012): 1487–531.

Fish, Stanley. Being Interdisciplinary Is So Very Hard to Do. Presidential Forum, Modern Language Association, 1989. *Profession* 89 (1989): 15–22.

Flemings, Merton C. What Next for Departments of Materials Science and Engineering? *Annual Review of Materials Science* 29, no. 1 (1999): 1–23.

Flemings, Merton C., and R. W. Cahn. Organization and Trends in Materials Science and Engineering Education in the U.S. and Europe. *Acta Materialis*, 48, no. 1 (2000): 371–83.

Fodor, Jerry A. How the Mind Works: What We Still Don't Know. *Daedalus* 135 (2006): 86–94.

Fontaine, Phillippe. Stabilizing American Society: Kenneth Boulding and the Integration of the Social Sciences, 1943–1980. *Science in Context* 23 (2010): 221–60.

Forester, Tom, ed. *The Materials Revolution: Superconductors, New Materials, and the Japanese Challenge.* Cambridge, MA: MIT Press, 1988.

Foucade, Marion. *Economists and Societies: Discipline and Profession in the United States, Britain, and France, 1890s to 1990s.* Princeton, NJ: Princeton University Press, 2009.

Fox, Renee C. Talcott Parsons, My Teacher. *American Scholar*, June 1997, 395–410.

Fox-Genovese, Elizabeth, and Eugene Genovese. The Political Crisis of Social History. *Journal of Social History* 10 (1976): 205–21.

Fox-Genovese, Elizabeth, and Elizabeth Lasch-Quinn, eds. *Reconstructing History: The Emergence of a New Historical Society.* New York: Routledge, 1999.

Frankel, Felice C., and George M. Whitesides. *No Small Matter: Science on the Nanoscale.* Cambridge, MA: Harvard University Press, 2009.

Frickel, Scott. Building an Interdiscipline: Collective Action Framing and the Rise of Genetic Toxicology. *Social Problems* 51 (2004): 269–87.

Frickel, Scott, and Neil Gross. A General Theory of Scientific/Intellectual Movements. *American Sociological Review* 70 (2005): 204–32.

Frodeman, Robert. *Sustainable Knowledge: A Theory of Interdisciplinarity.* New York: Palgrave Macmillan, 2013.

Frodeman, Robert, Julie Thompson Klein, and Carl Mitcham. *The Oxford Handbook of Interdisciplinarity.* New York: Oxford University Press, 2010.

Fuller, Steve. Disciplinary Boundaries and the Rhetoric of the Social Sciences. *Poetics Today* 12 (1991): 301–25.

———. *Philosophy, Rhetoric, and the End of Knowledge: The Coming of Science and Technology Studies.* Madison: University of Wisconsin Press, 1993.

Furman, Jeffrey L., and Scott Stern. Climbing atop the Shoulders of Giants: The Impact of Institutions on Cumulative Research. *American Economic Review* 104 (2011): 1933–63.

Furner, Mary O. *Advocacy and Objectivity: A Crisis in the Professionalization of American Social Science, 1865–1905.* Lexington: University Press of Kentucky, 1975.

Galison, Peter. The Americanization of Unity. *Daedalus* 127 (1998): 45–71.

———. *Image and Logic: A Material Culture of Microphysics.* Chicago: University of Chicago Press, 1997.

———. The Many Faces of Big Science. In *Big Science: The Growth of Large Scale Research,* ed. Peter Galison and Bruce Hevly, 12–17. Stanford, CA: Stanford University Press, 1992.

———. The Ontology of the Enemy: Norbert Wiener and the Cybernetic Vision. *Critical Inquiry* 21 (1994): 228–66.

Galison, Peter, and David J. Stump, eds. *The Disunity of Science: Boundaries, Contexts, and Power.* Stanford, CA: Stanford University Press, 1996.

Garber, Marjorie. *Academic Instincts.* Princeton: Princeton University Press, 2001.

Gardner, Howard. *The Mind's New Science: A History of the Cognitive Revolution.* New York: Basic Books, 1987.

Gass, Saul I., and A. Assad. *An Annotated Timeline of Operations Research: An Informal History.* New York: Kluwer Academic, 2005.

Gaudillière, Jean-Paul. Molecular Biologists, Biochemists, and Messenger RNA: The Birth of a Scientific Network. *Journal of the History of Biology* 29 (1996): 417–45.

———. New Wine in Old Bottles? The Biotechnology Problem in the History of Molecular Biology. *Studies in the History of Biological and Biomedical Sciences* 40 (2009): 20–28.

Gaudillière, Jean-Paul, and Hans-Jorg Rheinberger, eds. *From Molecular Genetics to Genomics: The Mapping Cultures of Twentieth-Century Genetics.* London: Routledge, 2004.

Gaziano, Emanuel. Ecological Metaphors as Scientific Boundary Work: Innovation and Authority in Interwar Sociology and Biology. *American Journal of Sociology* 101 (1996): 874–907.

Gertner, Jon. *The Idea Factory: Bell Labs and the Great Age of American Innovation.* New York: Penguin, 2012.

Gilman, Nils. *Mandarins of the Future: Modernization Theory in Cold War America.* Baltimore, MD: Johns Hopkins University Press, 2003.

Gilman, Sander L. *The Fortunes of the Humanities: Thoughts for after the Year 2000.* Stanford, CA: Stanford University Press, 2000.

Ginzburg, Carlo. Microhistory: Two or Three Things That I Know about It. Trans. John Tedeschi and Anne E. Tedeschi. *Critical Inquiry* 20 (Autumn 1993): 10–35.

Gitlin, Todd. Media Sociology: The Dominant Paradigm. *Theory and Society* 6 (1978): 205–53.

Glander, Timothy. Wilbur Schramm and the Founding of Communication Studies. *Educational Theory* 46 (1996): 273–91.

Gleason, Philip. World War II and the Development of American Studies. *American Quarterly* 36 (1984): 343–58.

Glickman, Lawrence B. The Consumer and the Citizen in Personal Influence. *Annals of the American Academy of Political and Social Science* 608 (2006): 205–12.

Goodeve, Charles. Operational Research as a Science. *Journal of the Operations Research Society of America* 1 (1953): 166–80.

———. Thirtieth Anniversary of the Use of the Term Operational Research: Conversazione—December 1967. The Growth of Operational Research in the Civil Sector in the United Kingdom. *Journal of the Operational Research Society* 19 (1968): 113–16.

Goodstein, Judith R. *Millikan's School: A History of the California Institute of Technology.* New York: W. W. Norton, 1991.

Goody, Jack, ed. *Literacy in Traditional Societies.* Cambridge: Cambridge University Press, 1968.

Graff, Gerald. *Professing Literature: An Institutional History.* Chicago: University of Chicago Press, 1987.

Graff, Gerald, and Michael Warner, eds. *The Origins of Literary Studies in America: A Documentary Anthology.* London: Routledge, 1989.

Graff, Harvey J. Assessing the History of Literacy in the 1990s: Themes and Questions. In *Escribir y leer en Occidente*, ed. Armando Petrucci and M. Gimeno Blay, 5–46. Valencia, Spain: Universitat de València, 1995.

———. *The Labyrinths of Literacy: Reflections on Literacy Past and Present*, rev. ed. Pittsburgh: University of Pittsburgh Press, 1995.

————. *The Legacies of Literacy: Continuities and Contradictions in Western Society and Culture.* Bloomington: Indiana University Press, 1987.

————. *The Literacy Myth: Literacy and Social Structure in the Nineteenth-Century City.* New York: Academic Press, 1979.

————. *The Literacy Myth at Thirty. Journal of Social History* 43 (2010): 635–61.

————. *Literacy Myths, Legacies, and Lessons: New Studies.* New Brunswick, NJ: Transaction, 2011.

————. Literacy Studies and Interdisciplinary Studies: Reflections on History and Theory. In *Valences of Interdisciplinarity: Theory, Practice, Pedagogy,* ed. Raphael Foshay, 273–307. Edmonton, AB: Alberta University / Athabasca University Press, 2012.

————. Literacy Studies and Interdisciplinary Studies, with Notes on the Place of Deborah Brandt. In *Literacy, Economy, and Power: New Directions in Literacy Research,* ed. Julie Nelson Christoph, John Duffy, Eli Goldblatt, Nelson Graff, Rebecca Nowacek, and Bryan Trabold, 203–26. Carbondale: Southern Illinois University Press, 2014.

————. LiteracyStudies@OSU as Theory and Practice. In *Literacy Myths, Legacies, and Lessons,* 141–78.

————. The Shock of the "New (Histories)": Social Science Histories and Historical Literacies. *Social Science History* 25 (2001): 483–84. Reprinted in Graff, Moch, and McMichael, *Looking Backward and Looking Forward:,* 13–56.

Graff, Harvey J., and John Duffy. Literacy Myths. In *Encyclopedia of Language and Education,* 2nd ed., vol. 2: *Literacy,* ed. Brian V. Street and Nancy Hornberger, 42–52. Berlin: Springer, 2007. Reprinted as The Literacy Myth, in Graff, *Literacy Myths, Legacies, and Lessons,* 35–48.

Graff, Harvey J., Leslie P. Moch, and Phillip McMichael, eds. *Looking Backward and Looking Forward: Perspectives on Social Science History.* Madison: University of Wisconsin Press, 2005.

Grafton, Anthony. History's Postmodern Fates. *Daedalus* 135 (2006): 54–69.

————. The Importance of Being Printed. *Journal of Interdisciplinary History* 11 (1980): 265–86.

————. In Clio's American Atelier. In *Social Knowledge in the Making,* ed. Charles Camic, Neil Gross, and Michele Lamont, 89–117. Chicago: University of Chicago Press, 2011.

Grafton, Anthony, and Lisa Jardine. *From Humanism to the Humanities: Education and the Liberal Arts in Fifteenth- and Sixteenth-Century Europe.* Cambridge, MA: Harvard University Press, 1986.

Grant, Gerald, and David Riesman. *The Perpetual Dream: Reform and Experiment in the American College.* Chicago: University of Chicago Press, 1978.

Gray, Hanna H. Western Civilization and its Discontents. *Historically Speaking* 7 (2005): 41–42.

Green, Theodore Meyer, ed. *The Meaning of the Humanities: Five Essays by Ralph Barton Perry, August Charles Krey, Erwin Panofsky, Robert Lowry Calhoun, and Gilbert Chinard.* Princeton, NJ: Princeton University Press, 1938.

Greenblatt, Stephen, and Giles Gunn, eds. *Redrawing the Boundaries: The Transformation of English and American Studies.* New York: Modern Language Association, 1992.

Gross, Ronald. Columbia University Seminars—Creating a "Community of Scholars." *Change* 14 (1982): 43–45.

Grossberg, Lawrence. *Bringing It All Back Home: Essays on Cultural Studies*. Durham, NC: Duke University Press, 1997.

———. *Cultural Studies in the Future Tense*. Durham, NC: Duke University Press, 2010.

———. The Formation of Cultural Studies: An American in Birmingham. In *Relocating Cultural Studies: Developments in Theory and Research*, ed. Valda Blundell, John Shepherd, and Ian Taylor, 21–66. London: Routledge 1993.

———. Toward a Genealogy of the State of Cultural Studies: The Discipline of Communication and the Reception of Cultural Studies in the United States. In *Disciplinarity and Dissent in Cultural Studies*, ed. Cary Nelson and Dilip Parameshwar Gaonkar, 131–47. New York: Routledge, 1996.

Grossberg, Lawrence, Cary Nelson, and Paula A. Treichler, eds. *Cultural Studies*. New York: Routledge, 1992.

Grunwald, Armin. Nanotechnology—A New Field of Ethical Inquiry? *Science and Engineering Ethics* 11 (2005): 187–201.

Guillory, John. Critical Response II: The Name of Science, the Nature of Politics. *Critical Inquiry* 29 (2003): 526–41.

———. *Cultural Capital: The Problem of Literary Canon Formation*. Chicago: University of Chicago Press, 1993.

———. Genesis of the Media Concept. *Critical Inquiry* 36 (2010): 321–62.

———. Literary Critics as Intellectuals: Class Analysis and the Crisis of the Humanities. In *Rethinking Class: Literary Studies and Social Formations*, ed. Wai Cee Dimock and Michael T. Gilmore, 107–49. New York: Columbia University Press, 1994.

———. Literary Study and the Modern System of the Disciplines. In *Disciplinarity at the Fin-de-Siècle*, ed. Amanda Anderson and Joseph Valente, 19–43. Princeton, NJ: Princeton University Press, 2002.

———. The Name of Science, the Nature of Politics. *Critical Inquiry* 29 (2003): 526–41.

———. The Period of Literature. *PMLA* 115, no. 7, Special Millennium Issue (2000): 1972–74.

———. The Sokal Affair and the History of Criticism. *Critical Inquiry* 28 (2002): 470–508.

———. Who's Afraid of Marcel Proust? The Failure of General Education in the American University. In Hollinger, *Humanities and the Dynamics of Inclusion*, 25–49.

Gunnell, John. Are We Losing Our Minds? Cognitive Science and the Study of Politics. *Political Theory* 35 (2007): 704–31.

Gurd, Sean, ed. *Philology and Its Histories*. Columbus: Ohio State University Press, 2010.

Hagan, John B. Naturalists, Molecular Biologists, and the Challenges of Molecular Evolution. *Journal of the History of Biology* 32 (1999): 321–41.

Hall, John R., Jr. An Issue-Oriented History of TIMS. *Interfaces* 13 (1983): 9–19.

Hall, Stuart. Cultural Studies and Its Theoretical Legacies. In Grossberg, Nelson, and Treichler, *Cultural Studies*, 277–94.

———. The Emergence of Cultural Studies and the Crisis of the Humanities. *October* 53 (1990): 11–23.

———, ed. *Representation: Cultural Representations and Signifying Practices*. Beverly Hills, CA: Sage, 1997.

Hall, Stuart, and Paul du Gay, ed. *Questions of Cultural Identity*. Beverly Hills, CA: Sage, 1996.

Hall, Stuart, Dorothy Hobson, Andrew Lowe, and Paul Willis, eds. *Culture, Media, Language*. London: Hutchinson, 1980.

Hamerow, Theodore. *Reflections on History*. Madison: University of Wisconsin Press, 1995.

Hardt, Hanno. The Return of the "Critical" and the Challenge of Radical Dissent: Critical Theory, Cultural Studies, and American Mass Communication Research. *Communication Yearbook* 12 (1989): 558–600.

Harnish, Robert M. *Minds, Brains, Computers: An Historical Introduction to the Foundations of Cognitive Science*. Oxford: Blackwell, 2002.

Harpham, Geoffrey Galt. Finding Ourselves: The Humanities as a Discipline. *American Literary History* 25 (2013): 509–34.

———. *The Humanities and the Dream of America*. Chicago: University of Chicago Press, 2011.

Harwood, Jonathan. Universities. In *The Cambridge History of Science*, vol. 6: *Modern Life and Earth Sciences*, ed. Peter J. Bowler and John V. Pickstone, 90–107. Cambridge: Cambridge University Press, 2009.

Haskell, Thomas L. Are Professors Professional? A Review of *The Organization of Knowledge in Modern America*, ed. Alexandra Oleson and John Voss. *Journal of Social History* 14 (Spring 1981): 485–93.

———, ed. *The Authority of Experts*. Bloomington: Indiana University Press, 1984.

———. *The Emergence of Professional Social Science: The American Social Science Association and the Nineteenth-Century Crisis of Authority*. Baltimore, MD: Johns Hopkins University Press, 1977.

Hawkes, Herbert E. Curriculum Revision at Columbia College. *Educational Record* 10 (1929): 29–39.

Heath, Shirley Brice. *Ways with Words: Language, Life, and Work in Communities and Classrooms*. Cambridge: Cambridge University Press, 1983.

Heckhausen, Heinz. Discipline and Interdisciplinarity. In Center for Educational Research and Innovation (CERI), Organization for Economic Co-operation and Development (OECD), *Interdisciplinarity: Problems of Teaching and Research in Universities*, 83–89. Paris: CERI/OECD, 1972.

Heilbron, Johan. A Regime of Disciplines: Toward a Historical Sociology of Disciplinary Knowledge. In *The Dialogical Turn: New Roles for Sociology in the Postdisciplinary Age*, ed. Charles Camic and Hans Joas, 23–42. Lanham, MD: Rowman & Littlefield, 2004.

Heims, Steve Joshua. *The Cybernetics Group*. Cambridge, MA: MIT Press, 1991.

Herbst, Susan. Disciplines, Intersections, and the Future of Communication Research. *Journal of Communication* 58 (2008): 603–14.

Hess, Eugene L. Origins of Molecular Biology. *Science* 168 (1970): 664–69.

Heukelom, F. Measurement and Decision Making at the University of Michigan in the 1950s and 1960s. *Journal of the History of the Behavioral Sciences* 46 (2010): 189–207.

Heyer, Paul. *Communications and History: Theories of Media, Knowledge, and Civilization*. New York: Greenwood Press, 1988.

Higgins, John. *Raymond Williams: Literature, Marxism, and Cultural Materialism*. London: Routledge, 1999.

———, ed. *The Raymond Williams Reader*. Oxford: Blackwell, 2001.

Higham, John. *History: Professional Scholarship in America.* Rev. ed. Baltimore, MD: Johns Hopkins University Press, 1989.

Hirst, William, ed. *The Making of Cognitive Science: Essays in Honor of George A. Miller.* Cambridge: Cambridge University Press, 1988.

Hobsbawm, Eric. From Social History to the History of Society. In *Historical Studies Today,* ed. Felix Gilbert and Stephen Graubard, 1–26. New York: W. W. Norton, 1972.

———. The Social Function of the Past: Some Questions. *Past and Present* 55 (1972): 3–17.

Hoggart, Richard. *On Culture and Communication.* Oxford: Oxford University Press, 1972.

———. Schools of English and Contemporary Society. In *About Literature, Speaking to Each Other: Essays by Richard Hoggart,* 2:246–49. Oxford: Oxford University Press, 1970.

———. *The Uses of Literacy.* London: Chatto & Windus, 1957.

Hollinger, David A., ed. *The Humanities and the Dynamics of Inclusion since World War II.* Baltimore, MD: Johns Hopkins University Press, 2006.

———. *In the American Province.* Bloomington: Indiana University Press, 1985.

———. Science as a Weapon in *Kulturkampfe* in the United States during and after World War II. *Isis* 86 (1995): 440–54.

———. The Unity of Knowledge and the Diversity of Knowers: Science as an Agent of Cultural Integration in the United States between the Two Wars. *Pacific Historical Review* 80 (2011): 211–30.

Hollingsworth, Rogers, and Ellen Jane Hollingsworth. Major Discoveries and Biomedical Research Organizations: Perspectives on Interdisciplinarity, Nurturing Leadership, and Integrated Structure and Culture. In Weingart and Stehr, *Practising Interdisciplinarity,* 215–44.

Homans, George Casper. *Coming to My Senses: The Autobiography of a Sociologist.* New Brunswick, NJ: Transaction, 1984.

Horner, Peter. History in the Making. *OR/MS Today* 29, no. 5 (2002).

Hounshell, David. The Cold War, RAND, and the Generation of Knowledge, 1946–1962. *Historical Studies in the Physical and Biological Sciences* 27 (1997): 237–67.

———. The Medium Is the Message, or How Context Matters: The RAND Corporation Builds an Economics of Innovation, 1946–1962. In *Systems, Experts, and Computers,* ed. Agatha C. Hughes and Thomas Parke Hughes, 255–310. Cambridge, MA: MIT Press, 2000.

Hounshell, David, and John Kenly Smith Jr. *Science and Corporate Strategy: DuPont R&D, 1902–1980.* Cambridge: Cambridge University Press, 1988.

Howley, Aimee, and Richard Hartnett. Columbia's Grand Narrative of Contemporary Civilization. *Journal of General Education* 46 (1997): 18–38.

Hunt, Lynn. Democratization and Decline? The Consequences of Democratic Change in the Humanities. In *What's Happened to the Humanities?,* ed. Alvin Kerman, 17–31. Princeton, NJ: Princeton University Press, 1997.

———. *The New Cultural History.* Berkeley: University of California Press, 1989.

Hunt, Lynn, and Victoria Bonnell, eds. *Beyond the Cultural Turn.* Berkeley: University of California Press, 1999.

Hutchins, Robert Maynard. *The Higher Learning in America*. New Haven, CT: Yale University Press, 1936.

Igo, Sarah E. "A Gold Mine and a Tool for Democracy": George Gallup, Elmo Roper, and the Business of Scientific Polling, 1935–1955. *Journal of the History of the Behavioral Sciences* 42 (2006): 109–34.

Inglis, Fred. *Cultural Studies*. Oxford: Blackwell, 1993.

———. *Culture*. Cambridge: Polity, 2004.

———. *Raymond Williams*. London: Routledge, 1995.

Isaac, Joel. Epistemic Design: Theory and Data in Harvard's Department of Social Relations. In Solovey and Hamilton, *Cold War Social Science*, 79–95.

———. The Human Sciences and Cold War America. *Journal of the History of the Behavioral Sciences* 47, no. 3 (2011): 225–31.

———. The Human Sciences in Cold War America. *Historical Journal* 50 (2007): 725–46.

———. Tangled Loops: Theory, History, and the Human Sciences in Modern America. *Modern Intellectual History* 5 (2009): 397–424.

———. Theorist at Work: Talcott Parsons and the Carnegie Project on Theory, 1949–1951. *Journal of the History of Ideas* 71 (2010): 287–311.

———. Tool Shock: Technique and Epistemology in the Postwar Social Sciences. *History of Political Economy* 42 (2010): S133–64.

———. *Working Knowledge: Making the Human Sciences from Parsons to Kuhn*. Cambridge, MA: Harvard University Press, 2012.

Jackson, Michael C., and Paul Keys, eds. *New Directions in Management Science*. Aldershot: Gower, 1987.

Jacobs, Jerry A. *In Defense of Disciplines: Interdisciplinarity and Specialization in the Research University*. Chicago: University of Chicago Press, 2013.

Jacobs, Jerry A., and Scott Frickel. Interdisciplinarity: A Critical Assessment. *Annual Review of Sociology* 35 (2009): 43–65.

Jay, Martin. *The Dialectical Imagination: A History of the Frankfurt School and the Institute of Social Research, 1923–1950*. Boston: Little, Brown, 1973.

Jencks, Christopher, and David Riesman. *The Academic Revolution*. Garden City, NY: Doubleday, 1968.

Johnson, Benton, and Miriam M. Johnson. The Integrating of the Social Sciences: Theoretical and Empirical Research and Training in the Department of Social Relations at Harvard. In *The Nationalization of the Social Sciences*, ed. Samuel Z. Klausner and Victor M. Lidz, 131–39. Philadelphia: University of Pennsylvania Press, 1986.

Johnson, Richard. Historical Returns: Transdisciplinarity, Cultural Studies and History. *European Journal of Cultural Studies* 4 (2001): 261–88.

Johnson, Richard, Gregor McLennan, Bill Schwarz, and David Sutton, eds. *Making Histories: Studies in History-Writing and Politics*. London: Hutchinson, 1982.

Johnson, Stephen B. Three Approaches to Big Technology: Operations Research, Systems Engineering, and Project Management. *Technology and Culture* 38 (1997): 891–919.

Johnston, Barry. Sorokin and Parsons at Harvard: Institutional Conflict and the Origin of a Hegemonic Tradition. *Journal of the History of the Behavioral Sciences* 22 (1986): 107–27.

Jong, Simcha. How Organizational Structures in Science Shape Spin-off Firms: The Biochemistry Departments of Berkeley, Stanford, and UCSF and the Birth of the Biotech Industry. *Industrial and Corporate Change* 15 (2006): 251–83.

Jowett, Garth S. Propaganda and Communication: The Re-emergence of a Research Tradition. *Journal of Communication* 37 (1987): 97–114.

Joyce, Patrick, ed. *The Social in Question: New Bearings in History and the Social Sciences.* London: Routledge, 2002.

Judt, Tony. A Clown in Royal Purple: Social History and the Historians. *History Workshop Journal* 7 (Spring 1979): 66–94.

Kagan, Jerome. *Psychology's Ghosts: The Crisis in the Profession and the Way Back.* New Haven, CT: Yale University Press, 2012.

———. Psychology's Missing Contexts. *Chronicle of Higher Education*, Apr. 13, 2012.

———. *The Three Cultures: Natural Sciences, Social Sciences, and the Humanities in the Twenty-First Century.* Cambridge: Cambridge University Press, 2009.

Kargon, Robert H. *The Rise of Robert Millikan: Portrait of a Life in American Science.* Ithaca, NY: Cornell University Press, 1982.

———. Temple to Science: Cooperative Research and the Birth of the California Institute of Technology. *Historical Studies in the Physical Sciences* 8 (1978): 3–32.

Katz, Elihu. Why Sociology Abandoned Mass Communication Research. *American Sociologist*, 40 (2009): 167–74.

Katz, Michael B. *The People of Hamilton, Canada West: Family and Class in a Mid-Nineteenth-Century City.* Cambridge, MA: Harvard University Press, 1975.

———. *Poverty and Policy.* New York: Academic Press, 1983.

Katz, Michael B., Michael Doucet, and Mark Stern. *The Social Organization of Early Industrial Capitalism.* Cambridge, MA: Harvard University Press, 1982.

Kaufmann, Walter. *The Future of the Humanities.* New York: Reader's Digest Press, 1977.

Kay, Lily E. Cybernetics, Information, Life: The Emergence of Scriptural Representation of Heredity. *Configurations* 5 (1997): 23–91.

———. *The Molecular Vision of Life: Caltech, the Rockefeller Foundation, and the Rise of the New Biology.* New York: Oxford University Press, 1993.

———. Rethinking Institutions: Philanthropy as an Historiographic Problem of Knowledge and Power. *Minerva* 35 (1997): 283–93.

———. *Who Wrote the Book of Life? A History of the Genetic Code.* Stanford, CA: Stanford University Press, 2000.

Keller, Evelyn Fox. *The Century of the Gene.* Cambridge, MA: Harvard University Press, 2000.

Kellner, Douglas M. *Media Culture: Cultural Studies, Identity and Politics between the Modern and the Postmodern.* New York: Routledge, 1995.

Kimball, Bruce A., ed. *The Liberal Arts Tradition: A Documentary History.* Lanham, MD: University Press of America, 2010.

Kingsland, Sharon E. *The Evolution of American Ecology, 1890–2000.* Baltimore, MD: Johns Hopkins University Press, 2005.

———. Maintaining Continuity through a Scientific Revolution: A Rereading of E. B. Wilson and T. H. Morgan on Sex Determinism and Mendelism. *Isis* 98 (2007): 468–88.

Kirby, Maurice W. The Intellectual Journey of Russell Ackoff: From OR Apostle to OR Apostate. *Journal of the Operations Research Society* 54 (2003): 1127–40.

———. Operations Research Trajectories: The Anglo-American Experience from the 1940s to the 1990s. *Operations Research* 48 (2000): 661–70.

———. Paradigm Change in Operations Research: Thirty Years of Debate. *Operations Research* 55 (2007): 1–13.

———. Spreading the Gospel of Management Science: Operational Research in Iron and Steel, 1950–1970. *Journal of the Operational Research Society* 51 (2000): 1020–28.

Kirby, Maurice W., and R. Capey. The Origins and Diffusion of Operational Research in the UK. *Journal of the Operational Research Society* 49 (1998): 307–26.

Kirby, Maurice W., and M. T. Godwin. The Invisible Science: Operational Research for the British Armed Forces after 1945. *Journal of the Operational Research Society* 61 (2010): 68–81.

Kittel, Charles. The Nature and Development of Operations Research. *Science* 105 (Feb. 7, 1947): 150–53.

Klein, Herbert S. The Old Social History and the New Social Sciences. *Journal of Social History* 39 (2006): 935–49.

Klein, Julie Thompson. *Creating Interdisciplinary Campus Cultures: A Model for Strength and Sustainability.* San Francisco: Jossey-Bass for the Association of American Colleges and Universities, 2010.

———. *Crossing Boundaries: Knowledge, Disciplinarities, and Interdisciplinarities.* Charlottesville: University Press of Virginia, 1996.

———. *Humanities, Culture, and Interdisciplinarity: The Changing American Academy.* Albany: State University of New York Press, 2005.

———. *Interdisciplinarity: History, Theory, and Practice.* Detroit: Wayne State University Press, 1990.

———. *Mapping Interdisciplinary Studies: The Academy in Transition.* Washington, DC: Association of American Colleges and Universities, 1999.

Klein, Julie Thomson, and William H. Newell. Advancing Interdisciplinary Studies. In *Handbook of the Undergraduate Curriculum: A Comprehensive Guide to Purposes, Structures, Practices, and Change,* ed. Jerry G. Gaff and James L. Ratcliff, 393–415. San Francisco: Jossey-Bass, 1977.

Kleinman, Daniel Lee. *Politics on the Endless Frontier: Postwar Research Policy in the United States.* Durham, NC: Duke University Press, 1995.

Kleinman, Daniel Lee, and Steve P. Vallas. Science, Capitalism, and the Rise of the "Knowledge Worker": The Changing Structure of Knowledge Production in the United States. *Theory and Society* 30 (2001): 451–92.

Kockelmans, Joseph J., ed. *Interdisciplinarity and Higher Education.* College Station: Penn State University Press, 1979.

———. Interdisciplinarity and the University: The Dream and the Reality. *Issues in Integrative Studies* 4 (1986): 1–16.

Kohler, Robert E. *From Medical Chemistry to Biochemistry: The Making of a Biomedical Discipline.* Cambridge: Cambridge University Press, 1982.

———. *Lords of the Fly: Drosophila Genetics and the Experimental Life.* Chicago: University of Chicago Press, 1994.

Kousser, J. Morgan. History QUASSHED: Quantitative Social Science History in Perspective. *American Behavioral Scientist* 23 (1980): 885–904.

Krabbendam, Johannes Leendert, and Jaap Verheul, with Hans Bak. *Through the Looking Glass: American Studies in Transcultural Perspective.* Amsterdam: VU University Press, 1999.

Kranzberg, Melvin, and Cyril Stanley Smith. Materials in History and Society. 1979. Reprinted in Forester, *Materials Revolution*, 85–118.

Kuklick, Bruce. The Emergence of the Humanities. *South Atlantic Quarterly* 89 (1990): 195–206.

———. *A History of Philosophy in America, 1720–2000.* New York: Oxford University Press, 2003.

———. *The Rise of American Philosophy: Cambridge, Massachusetts, 1860–1930.* New Haven, CT: Yale University Press, 1979.

Kuper, Adam. *Culture: The Anthropologists' Account.* Cambridge, MA: Harvard University Press, 1999.

Lakoff, Geroge, and Mark Johnson. The Metaphorical Structure of the Human Cognitive System. *Cognitive Science* 4 (1980): 195–208.

———. *Metaphors We Live By.* Chicago: University of Chicago Press, 1980.

Lam, Alice. From "Ivory Tower Traditionalists" to "Entrepreneurial Scientists"? Academic Scientists in Fuzzy University-Industry Boundaries. *Social Studies of Science* 40 (2010): 307–40.

Lasswell, Harold D. Communications as an Emerging Discipline. *Audio Visual Communication Review* 9 (1958): 245–54.

Latour, Bruno, and Steve Woolgar. *Laboratory Life: The Social Construction of Scientific Facts.* Princeton, NJ: Princeton University Press, 1979.

Lattuca, Lisa R. *Creating Interdisciplinarity: Interdisciplinary Research and Teaching among College and University Faculty.* Nashville, TN: Vanderbilt University Press, 2001.

Leahey, Thomas. The Mythical Revolutions of American Psychology. In *Evolving Perspectives on the History of Psychology*, ed. Wade E. Pickren and Donald A. Dewsbury, 191–216. Washington, DC: American Psychological Association, 2002.

Leavis, F. R. *Two Cultures? The Significance of C. P. Snow.* London: Chatto & Windus, 1962.

Lecuyer, Christophe. The Making of a Science-Based Technological University: Karl Compton, James Killian, and the Reform of MIT, 1930–1957. *Historical Studies in the Physical and Biological Sciences* 23 (1992): 153–80.

———. *Making Silicon Valley: Innovations and the Growth of High Tech, 1930–1970.* Cambridge, MA: MIT Press, 2006.

Lee, Richard E. *Life and Times of Cultural Studies: The Politics and Transformation of the Structures of Knowledge.* Durham, NC: Duke University Press, 2003.

Leland, Waldo G. Recent Trends in the Humanities. *Science* 79, no. 2048 (Mar. 30, 1934): 281–85.

Lenoir, Timothy. The Discipline of Nature and the Nature of Disciplines. In *Instituting Science: The Cultural Production of Scientific Disciplines*, 45–74. Stanford, CA: Stanford University Press, 1997.

Leslie, Stuart W. *The Cold War and American Science: The Military-Industrial-Academic Complex at MIT and Stanford.* New York: Columbia University Press, 1993.

Lord, Albert B. *The Singer of Tales.* 1960. 2nd ed., Cambridge, MA: Harvard University Press, 1980.

Magee, John F. Operations Research at Arthur D. Little, Inc.: The Early Years. *Operations Research* 50 (2002): 149–53.

Maienschein, Jane. Whitman at Chicago: Establishing a Chicago Style of Biology. In Rainger, Benson, and Maienschein, *American Development of Biology*, 151–82.

Mandler, George. Origins of the Cognitive Revolution. *Journal of the History of the Behavioral Sciences* 38 (2002): 339–53.

Marcus, Steven. Humanities from Classics to Cultural Studies: Notes toward the History of an Idea. *Daedalus* 135 (2006): 15–21.

Marsden, George M. *The Soul of the American University: From Protestant Establishment to Established Nonbelief.* New York: Oxford University Press, 1994.

Marsden, George M., and Bradley J. Longfield, eds. *The Secularization of the Academy.* New York: Oxford University Press, 1992.

Martin-Nielsen, Janet. A Forgotten Social Science? Creating a Place for Linguistics in the Historical Dialogue. *Journal of the History of the Behavioral Sciences* 47 (2011): 147–72.

Massachusetts Institute of Technology (MIT). *The Third Revolution: The Convergence of the Life Sciences, Physical Sciences, and Engineering.* Washington, DC: MIT, 2011.

Maynes, Mary Jo. *Taking the Hard Road: Life Course and Class Identity in French and German Workers' Autobiographies of the Industrial Era.* Chapel Hill: University of North Carolina Press, 1995.

McCaughey, Robert A. *International Studies and Academic Enterprise: A Chapter in the Enclosure of American Learning.* New York: Columbia University Press, 1984.

McChesney, Robert W. *Communication Revolution.* New York: New Press, 2007.

McCloskey, Joseph F. The Beginnings of Operations Research, 1934–1941. *Operations Research* 35 (1987): 143–52.

———. British Operations Research in World War II. *Operations Research* 35 (1987): 453–70.

———. Training for Operations Research. *Journal of the Operations Research Society of America* 2 (1954): 386–92.

———. U.S. Operations Research in World War II. *Operations Research* 35 (1987): 910–25.

McDonald, Terrence, ed. *The Historic Turn in the Human Sciences.* Ann Arbor: University of Michigan Press, 1996.

McGann, Jerome. Philology in a New Key. *Critical Inquiry* 39 (2012): 327–46.

McGrath, Earl James. The General Education Movement (an Editorial). *Journal of General Education* 1 (1946): 3.

McLuhan, Marshall. *The Gutenberg Galaxy: The Making of Typographic Man.* Toronto: University of Toronto Press, 1962.

———. *Understanding Media: The Extensions of Man.* New York: New American Library, 1964.

McMahon, Darrin M., and Samuel Moyn, eds. *Rethinking Modern European Intellectual History.* New York: Oxford University Press, 2014.

Menand, Louis. *The Marketplace of Ideas: Reform and Resistance in the American University.* New York: W. W. Norton, 2010.

Meyer, M., and O. Persson. Nanotechnology—Interdisciplinarity, Patterns of Collaboration and Differences in Applications. *Scientometrics* 42 (1998): 195–205.

Meyering, Theo C. *Historical Roots of Cognitive Science: The Rise of a Cognitive Theory
of Perception from Antiquity to the Nineteenth Century.* Dordrecht: Kluwer Academic,
1989.

Miller, George. The Cognitive Revolution: A Historical Perspective. *TRENDS in Cognitive Sciences* 7 (2003): 141–44.

Miller, James G. Toward a General Theory for the Behavioral Sciences. *American Psychologist* 10 (1955): 513–51.

Miller, Toby. *Blow Up the Humanities.* Philadelphia: Temple University Press, 2012.

Mindell, David A. *Between Man and Machine: Feedback, Control, and Computing before
Cybernetics.* Baltimore, MD: Johns Hopkins University Press, 2002.

Mirowski, Philip. *Machine Dreams: Economics Becomes a Cyborg Science.* Cambridge:
Cambridge University Press, 2002.

———. *Science-Mart: Privatizing American Science.* Cambridge, MA: Harvard University Press, 2011.

———. When Games Grow Deadly Serious: The Military Influence on the Evolution of
Game Theory. In "Economics and National Security: A History of their Interaction,"
Annual Supplement, *History of Political Economy* 23 (1991): S227–56.

Mitchell, J. Pearce. *Stanford University 1916–1941.* Stanford, CA: Stanford University Press,
1958.

Modern Language Association (MLA) Forum. Perspectives from Particular Fields. *PMLA*
111 (1996): 298–311.

Monkkonen, Eric. Lessons of Social Science History. *Social Science History* 18 (1994):
161–68.

Moran, Joe. *Interdisciplinarity.* London: Routledge, 2001.

Morange, Michel. *A History of Molecular Biology,* trans. Matthew Cobb. Cambridge, MA:
Harvard University Press, 1998.

———. The Transformation of Molecular Biology on Contact with Higher Organisms,
1960–1980: From a Molecular Description to the Molecular Explanation. *History and
Philosophy of the Life Sciences* 19 (1997): 369–93.

Morawski, J. G. Organizing Knowledge and Behavior at Yale's Institute of Human Relations. *Isis* 77 (1986): 219–42.

Morgan, T. H. The New Division of Biology. *Bulletin of the California Institute of Technology* 36 (1927): 86–87.

Morley, David. *Television, Audiences, and Cultural Studies.* New York: Routledge, 1992.

Morley, David, and Kuan-Hsing Chen, eds. *Stuart Hall: Critical Dialogues in Cultural
Studies.* London: Routledge, 1996.

Morley, David, and Kevin Robins. *British Cultural Studies: Geography, Nationality, and
Identity.* New York: Oxford University Press, 2001.

Morris, Charles W. The Unity of Science Movements and the United States. *Synthese* 3
(1938): 25–26.

Morse, Philip M. *In at the Beginning: A Physicist's Life.* Cambridge, MA: MIT Press, 1977.

———. Of Men and Machines: Airplane Attacks on Submarines Have Little in Common with Better Automobile Traffic Systems. Yet, Their Common Element Promises
Clearer Insight into Man's Behavior. *Technology Review* 49 (1946): 30–33.

Morse, Philip M., and George E. Kimball. *Methods of Operations Research*. 1st rev. ed. Cambridge, MA: Technology Press of Massachusetts Institute of Technology; New York: John Wiley & Sons, 1951.

Mosco, Vincent. *The Political Economy of Communication*. Beverly Hills, CA: Sage, 2009.

National Research Council. *A New Biology for the Twenty-First Century*. Washington, DC: National Academies Press, 2009.

Nelson, Cary, and Dilip Parameshwar Gaonkar. *Disciplinarity and Dissent in Cultural Studies*. New York: Routledge, 1996.

Nelson, Cary, and Lawrence Grossberg, eds. *Marxism and the Interpretation of Culture*. Urbana: University of Illinois Press, 1988.

Newell, William H., ed. *Interdisciplinarity: Essays from the Literature*. New York: College Board, 1998.

Newfield, Christopher. *Unmaking the Public University: The Forty-Year Assault on the Middle Class*. Cambridge, MA: Harvard University Press, 2009.

Nichols, Lawrence T. The Establishment of Sociology at Harvard: A Case of Organizational Ambivalence and Scientific Vulnerability. In *Science at Harvard University: Historical Perspectives*, ed. Clark A. Ellliot and Margaret W. Rossiter, 191–222. Bethlehem, PA: Lehigh University Press, 1992.

———. Social Relations Undone: Disciplinary Divergence and Departmental Politics at Harvard, 1946–1970. *American Sociologist* 29 (1998): 83–107.

Nicolescu, Basarab. *Manifesto of Transdisciplinarity*, ed. Karen-Claire Voss. Albany: State University of New York Press, 2002.

———, ed. *Transdisciplinarity—Theory and Practice*. Cresskill, NJ: Hampton Press, 2008.

Nisbet, Robert A. *Social Change and History: Aspects of the Western Theory of Development*. New York: Oxford University Press, 1969.

Noble, David F. *America by Design: Science, Technology, and the Rise of Corporate Capitalism*. New York: Oxford University Press, 1979.

———. *Forces of Production: A Social History of Industrial Automation*. New York: Oxford University Press, 1984.

Novick, Peter. *That Noble Dream: The "Objectivity Question" and the American Historical Profession*. Cambridge: Cambridge University Press, 1988.

Nussbaum, Martha. *Cultivating Humanity: A Classical Defense of Reform in Liberal Education*. Cambridge, MA: Harvard University Press, 1997.

———. *Not for Profit: Why Democracy Needs the Humanities*. Princeton, NJ: Princeton University Press, 2010.

Olby, Robert. Molecular Biology. In *The Oxford Companion to the History of Modern Science*, ed. J. L. Heilbron. Oxford: Oxford University Press, 2003. Oxford Reference Online, www.oxfordreference.com/views/ENTRY.html?entry=t124.e0486.

Oleson, Alexandra, and Sanborn C. Brown, eds. *The Pursuit of Knowledge in the Early American Republic: American Scientific and Learned Societies from Colonial Times to the Civil War*. Baltimore, MD: Johns Hopkins University Press, 1976.

Oleson, Alexandra, and John Voss, eds. *The Organization of Knowledge in Modern America*, Baltimore, MD: Johns Hopkins University Press, 1979.

Olzak, Susan, and Nicole Kangas. Ethnic, Women's, and African American Studies Majors in U.S. Institutions of Higher Education. *Sociology of Education* 81 (2008): 163–88.

Ortolano, Guy. F. R Leavis, Science, and the Abiding Crisis of Modern Civilization. *History of Science* 43 (2005): 1–25.

———. Human Science or a Human Face? Social History and the "Two Cultures" Controversy. *Journal of British Studies* 43 (2004): 482–505.

———. The Literature and Science of "Two Cultures" Historiography. *Studies in History and Philosophy of Science* 39 (2008): 143–50.

———. *The Two Cultures Controversy: Science, Literature, and Cultural Politics in Postwar Britain.* Cambridge: Cambridge University Press, 2009.

———. Two Cultures and Beyond: Interview with Guy Ortolano. *Journal of Cambridge Studies* 4 (2009): 47–54.

———. Two Cultures, One University: The Institutional Origins of the "Two Cultures" Controversy. *Albion* 34 (2003): 606–24.

Owens, B. Robert. Producing Parsons' Reputation: Early Critiques of Talcott Parsons' Social Theory and the Making of a Caricature. *Journal of the History of the Behavioral Sciences* 46 (2010): 165–88.

Park, David W., and Jefferson Pooley, eds. *The History of Media and Communication Research: Contested Memories.* New York: Peter Lang, 2008.

Parker, William Riley. Where Do English Departments Come From? *College English* 5 (1967): 339–51.

Parry, Adam, ed. *The Making of Homeric Verse: The Collected Papers of Milman Parry.* Oxford: Oxford University Press, 1971.

Parsons, Talcott. Clyde Kluckhohn and the Integration of Social Science. In *Culture and Life: Essays in Memory of Clyde Kluckhohn*, ed. Walter W. Taylor, John L. Fisher, and Evon Z. Vogt, 30–57. Carbondale: Southern Illinois University Press, 1973.

———. The Prospects of Sociological Theory. ASA Presidential Address, 1949. *American Sociological Review* 15 (1950): 3–16.

———. Theory in the Humanities and Sociology. *Daedalus* 99 (1970): 495–523.

Pauly, Philip J. The Appearance of Academic Biology in Late Nineteenth-Century America. *Journal of the History of Biology* 17 (1984): 369–97.

———. *Biologists and the Promise of American Life: From Meriwether Lewis to Alfred Kinsey.* Princeton, NJ: Princeton University Press, 2000.

———. Summer Resort and Scientific Discipline: Woods Hole and the Structure of American Biology, 1882–1925. In Rainger, Benson, and Maienschein, *American Development of Biology*, 121–50.

Perry, Ralph Barton. A Definition of the Humanities. In Green, *Meaning of the Humanities*, 1–42.

Peters, John Durham, and Peter Simonson, eds. *Mass Communication and American Social Thought: Key Texts, 1919–1968.* Lanham, MD: Rowman & Littlefield, 2004.

Peters, Julie Stone. Law, Literature, and the Vanishing Real: On the Future of an Interdisciplinary Illusion. *PMLA* 120 (2005): 442–53.

Peterson, Thomas Erling. The Art of Language Teaching as Interdisciplinary Paradigm. *Educational Philosophy and Theory* 40 (2008): 900–918.

Pfau, Michael. Epistemological and Disciplinary Intersections. *Journal of Communication* 58, no. 4 (2008): 597–602.

Pietila, Veikko. Perspectives on Our Past: Charting the Histories of Mass Communication Studies. *Critical Studies in Mass Communication* 11 (1994): 346–61.

Pooley, Jefferson. Daniel Czitrom, James W. Carey, and the Chicago School. *Critical Studies in Mass Communication* 24 (2007): 469–72.

———. Fifteen Pages That Shook the Field: *Personal Influence*, Edward Shils, and the Remembered History of Mass Communication Research. *Annals of the American Association of Political and Social Science* 608 (2006): 130–56.

———The New History of Mass Communication Research. In *The History of Media and Communication Research: Contested Memories*, ed. David W. Park and Jefferson Pooley, 43–70. New York: Peter Lang, 2008.

Pooley, Jefferson, and Elihu Katz. Further Notes on Why American Sociology Abandoned Mass Communication Research. *Journal of Communication* 58 (2008): 767–86.

Poovey, Mary. Interdisciplinarity at New York University. In Scott and Keates, *Schools of Thought*, 288–312.

Porter, Roy. The Two Cultures Revisited. *Cambridge Review*, Nov. 1994, 74–80.

Porter, Theodore M., and Dorothy Ross, eds. *The Cambridge History of Science*, vol. 7: *The Modern Social Sciences*. Cambridge: Cambridge University Press, 2003.

Porwancher, Andrew. Humanism's Sisyphean Task: Curricular Reform at Brown University during the Second World War. *History of Education* 40 (2011): 481–99.

Powell, Walter W., and Jason Owen-Smith. The New World of Knowledge Production in the Life Sciences. In Brint, *Future of the City of Intellect*, 107–30.

Powell, Walter W., Jason Owen-Smith, and Jeannette A. Colyvas. Innovation and Emulation: Lessons from American Universities in Selling Private Rights to Public Knowledge. *Minerva* 45 (2007): 121–41.

Powell, Walter W., and Kaisa Snellman. The Knowledge Economy. *Annual Review of Sociology* 30 (2004): 199–220.

Powell, Walter W., Douglas R. White, Kenneth W. Koput, and Jason Owen-Smith. Network Dynamics and Field Evolution: The Growth of Interorganizational Collaboration in the Life Sciences. *American Journal of Sociology* 110 (2005): 1132–205.

Powers, Willow Roberts. The Harvard Study of Values: Mirror for Postwar Anthropology. *Journal of the History of the Behavioral Sciences* 36 (2000): 15–29.

Rabinow, Paul. *Making PCR: A Story of Biotechnology*. Chicago: University of Chicago Press, 1997.

Radway, Janice A. *A Feeling for Books: The Book-of-the-Month Club, Literary Taste, and Middle-Class Desire*. Chapel Hill: University of North Carolina Press, 1997.

Rainger, Ronald, Keith R. Benson, and Jane Maienhschein, eds. *American Development of Biology*. New Brunswick, NJ: Rutgers University Press, 1991.

———, eds. *The Expansion of American Biology*. New Brunswick, NJ: Rutgers University Press, 1991.

Rafols, Ismael. Strategies for Knowledge Acquisition in Bionanotechnology: Why Are Interdisciplinary Practices Less Widespread than Expected? *Innovation* 20 (2007): 395–410.

Readings, Bill. *The University in Ruins*. Cambridge, MA: Harvard University Press, 1996.

Reintjes, J. Francis. *Numerical Control: Making a New Technology*. Oxford: Oxford University Press, 1991.

Renwick, Chris. From Political Economy to Sociology: Francis Galton and the Social-Scientific Origins of Eugenics. *British Journal of the History of Science* 44 (2011): 343–69.

Reuben, Julie A. *The Making of the Modern University: Intellectual Transformation and the Marginalization of Morality*. Chicago: University of Chicago Press, 1996.

Ringer, Fritz. *The Decline of the German Mandarins: The German Academic Community, 1890–1933*. Cambridge, MA: Harvard University Press, 1969.

———. The Intellectual Field, Intellectual History, and the Sociology of Knowledge. *Theory and Society* 19 (1990): 269–94.

Roberts, Jon H., and James Turner. *The Sacred and the Secular University*. Princeton, NJ: Princeton University Press, 2000.

Robin, Ron. *The Making of the Cold War Enemy: Culture and Politics in the Military-Industrial Complex*. Princeton, NJ: Princeton University Press, 2001.

Robinson, Gertrude J. Constructing a Historiography for North American Communication Studies. In Dennis and Wartella, *American Communication Research*, 157–68.

Rogers, Everett M. *A History of Communication Study: A Biographical Approach*. New York: Free Press, 1994.

Rosaldo, Renato. Reflections on Interdisciplinarity. In Scott and Keates, *Schools of Thought*, 67-82.

Rose, Nikolas, and Joelle M. Abi-Rached. *Neuro: The New Brain Sciences and the Management of the Mind*. Princeton, NJ: Princeton University Press, 2013.

Rosenhead, Jonathan V. From Management Science to Workers' Science. In *New Directions in Management Science*, ed. M. C. Jackson and P. Keys, 109–31. Aldershot, UK: Gower, 1987.

Ross, Dorothy. Changing Contours of the Social Science Disciplines. In Porter and Ross, *Modern Social Sciences*, 205–37.

———. The Development of the Social Sciences. In *Discipline and History: Political Science in the United States*, ed. James Farr and Raymond Seidelman, 81–104. Ann Arbor: University of Michigan Press, 1993.

———. Grand Narrative in American Historical Writing: From Romance to Uncertainty. *American Historical Review* 100 (1995): 651–77.

———. The New and Newer Histories: Social Theory and Historiography in an American Key. In *Imagined Histories: American Historians Interpret the Past*, ed. Anthony Mohlo and Gordon S. Wood, 85–106. Princeton, NJ: Princeton University Press, 1998.

———. *Origins of American Social Science*. Cambridge: Cambridge University Press, 1991.

———. Professionalism and the Transformation of American Social Thought. *Journal of Economic History* 38 (1978): 494–99.

Roth, Randolph. Scientific History and Experimental History. *Journal of Interdisciplinary History* 40 (2013): 443–58.

Rubin, Joan Shelley. *The Making of Middlebrow Culture*. Chapel Hill: University of North Carolina Press, 1991.

———. The Scholar and the World: Academic Humanists and General Readers in Postwar America. In Hollinger, *Humanities and the Dynamics of Inclusion*, 73–103.

Rudolph, Frederick. *The American College and University*. New York: Vintage, 1962.

Sapp, Jan. *Genesis: The Evolution of Biology*. Oxford: Oxford University Press, 2003.

———. The Struggle for Authority in the Field of Heredity, 1900–1932: New Perspectives on the Rise of Genetics. *Journal of the History of Biology* 16 (1983): 311–42.

Saxberg, Bjore O., and William T. Newell. The Integration of Interdisciplinary Research with the Organization of the University. In *Interdisciplinary Research Groups: Their Management and Organization*, ed. Richard T. Barth and Rudy Steck, 224–43. Proceedings of the First International Conference on Interdisciplinary Research Groups, held at Schloss Reisensburg, Federal Republic of Germany, 22–28 April 1979.

Scerri, Eric R. Interdisciplinary Research at the Caltech Beckman Institute. In Weingart and Stehr, *Practising Interdisciplinarity*, 194–214.

Schafer, Sylvia. Still Turning: Language, "Theory," and History's Fascination with the New. *Differences* 23 (2012): 165–74.

Schaffner, Kenneth F. Theory Structure, Reduction, and Disciplinary Integration in Biology. *Biology and Philosophy* 8 (1993): 319–47.

Schiller, Dan. *Theorizing Communication: A History*. New York: Oxford University Press, 1996.

Schrum, Ethan. Administering American Modernity: The Instrumental University in the Postwar United States. PhD diss., University of Pennsylvania, 2009.

Schummer, J. Multidisciplinarity, Interdisciplinarity, and Patterns of Research Collaboration in Nanoscience and Nanotechnology. *Scientometrics* 59 (2004): 425–65. Condensed as Interdisciplinary Issues in Nanoscale Research. In *Discovering the Nanoscale*, ed. D. Baird, A. Nordman, and J. Schummer, 9–20. Amsterdam: IOS Press, 2004.

Schwartz, James. *In Pursuit of the Gene: From Darwin to DNA*. Cambridge, MA: Harvard University Press, 2008.

Schwartz, Jeffrey H. Decisions, Decisions: Why Thomas Hunt Morgan Was Not the "Father" of Evo-Devo. *Philosophy of Science* 73 (2006): 918–29.

Schwartz, Lyle H. Materials Research Laboratories: Reviewing the First Twenty-Five Years. In *Advancing Materials Research*, ed. Peter A. Psaras and Dale A. Landlord, 35–48. Washington, DC: National Academy Press, 1987.

Scott, Joan Wallach. The Evidence of Experience. *Critical Inquiry* 17 (1991): 773–91.

———. *Gender and the Politics of History*. New York: Columbia University Press, 1988.

———. *The Glassworkers of Carmaux*. Cambridge, MA: Harvard University Press, 1980.

———. History-writing as Critique. In *Manifestos for History*, ed. Keith Jenkins, Sue Morgan, and Alun Munslow, 19–38. London: Routledge, 2007.

———. Wishful Thinking. "The Future of the Discipline," *AHA Perspectives* 50 (Dec. 2012): 57–59.

Scott, Joan Wallach, and Debra Keates, eds. *Schools of Thought: Twenty-Five Years of Interpretive Social Science*. Princeton, NJ: Princeton University Press, 2001.

Segal, Daniel A. "Western Civilization" and the Staging of History in American Higher Education. *American Historical Review* 105 (2000): 770–805.

Servos, John W. The Industrial Relations of Science: Chemical Engineering at MIT, 1900–1939. *Isis* 71 (1980): 531–49.

Sewell, William H., Jr. The Concept(s) of Culture. In *Beyond the Cultural Turn*, ed. Lynn Hunt and Victoria Bonnell, 35–61. Berkeley: University of California Press, 1999.

———. *Logics of History: Social Theory and Social Transformation*. Chicago: University of Chicago Press, 2005.

———. Three Temporalities: Toward an Eventful Sociology. In McDonald, *Historic Turn in the Human Sciences*, 245–80.

———. *Work and Revolution in France: The Language of Labor from the Old Regime to 1848*. Cambridge: Cambridge University Press, 1980.

Sewell, William H., Jr., George Steinmetz, and M. J. Maynes, eds. Special section: Narrative Analysis in Social Science. *Social Science History* 16 (1992): 479–553.

Shenhav, Yehouda. From Chaos to Systems: The Engineering Foundations of Organization Theory, 1879–1932. *Administrative Science Quarterly* 40 (1995): 567–85.

Shryock, Andrew, and Daniel Lord Smail, eds. *Deep History: The Architecture of Past and Present*. Berkeley: University of California Press, 2011.

Smail, Daniel Lord. *On Deep History and the Brain*. Berkeley: University of California Press, 2008.

Small, Albion W. The Relation between Sociology and Other Sciences. *American Journal of Sociology* 12 (1906): 11–31.

———. Some Contributions to the History of Sociology. Section I: Introduction. *American Journal of Sociology* 28 (1923): 385–418.

———. Some Contributions to the History of Sociology. Section XIV: Later Phases of the Conflict between the Historical and the Austrian Schools. *American Journal of Sociology* 29 (1924): 571–98.

Small, Helen. *The Value of the Humanities*. Oxford: Oxford University Press, 2013.

Smalley, Richard E. Of Chemistry, Love, and Nanobots. *Scientific American* 285, no. 3 (2001): 76–77.

Smith, Cyril Sandley. The Development of Ideas on the Structure of Metals. In *Critical Problems in the History of Science*, ed. Marshall Clagett, 467–98. Madison: University of Wisconsin Press, 1959.

Smith, James Allen. *The Idea Brokers: Think Tanks and the Rise of the New Policy Elite*. New York: Free Press, 1991.

Smith, Roger. *Between Mind and Nature: A History of Psychology*. London: Reaktion Books, 2013.

———. *The Norton History of the Human Sciences*. New York: W. W. Norton, 1997.

Smith Hughes, Sally. *Genentech: The Beginnings of Biotech*. Chicago: University of Chicago Press, 2011.

Smithson, Isaiah, and Nancy Ruff, eds. *English Studies / Culture Studies: Institutionalizing Dissent*. Urbana: University of Illinois Press, 1994.

Snow, C. P. *The Two Cultures and the Scientific Revolution*. Cambridge: Cambridge University Press, 1959.

Solovey, Mark, and Hamilton Cravens, eds. *Cold War Social Science: Knowledge Production, Liberal Democracy, and Human Nature*. New York: Palgrave Macmillan, 2012.

Spector, Tami I. Nanoaesthetics: From the Molecular to the Machine. *Representations* 117 (2012): 1–30.

Sproule, J. Michael. Communication: From Concept to Field to Discipline. In Park and Pooley, *History of Media and Communication Research*, 163–78.

———. Propaganda Studies in American Social Science: The Rise and Fall of the Critical Paradigm. *Quarterly Journal of Speech* 73 (1987): 60–78.

Starr, Paul. *The Creation of the Media: Political Origins of Modern Communications*. New York: Basic Books, 2004.

Steckel, Richard. The Evolution of the Social Science History Association Meetings, 1976–1999. In *Looking Backward and Looking Forward*, ed. Harvey J. Graff, Leslie P. Moch, and Phillip McMichael, 101–13. Madison: University of Wisconsin Press, 2005.

Stedman Jones, Gareth. From Historical Sociology to Theoretical History. *British Journal of Sociology* 27 (Sept. 1976): 395–405.

———. *Outcast London: A Study in the Relationship between Classes in Victorian London.* Oxford: Oxford University Press, 1971.

Steinmetz, George. American Sociology before and after World War II: The (Temporary) Selling of a Disciplinary Field. In Calhoun, *Sociology in America*, 314–66.

———. *Logics of History* as a Framework for an Integrated Social Science. *Social Science History* 32 (2008): 534–53.

Stevens, Anne H. The Philosophy of General Education and Its Contradictions: The Influence of Hutchins. *Journal of General Education* 50 (2001): 165–91.

Stone, Lawrence. History and the Social Sciences in the Twentieth Century. In *The Future of History*, ed. Charles Detzell, 3–42. Nashville, TN: Vanderbilt University Press, 1977.

———. *The Past and the Present Revisited.* London: Routledge, 1987.

———. The Revival of Narrative: Reflections on a New Old History. *Past and Present* 85 (1979): 3–24.

Street, Brian V. Introduction: The New Literacy Studies. In *Cross-Cultural Approaches to Literacy*, ed. Brian Street, 1–21. Cambridge: Cambridge University Press, 1993.

———. *Literacy in Theory and Practice.* Cambridge: Cambridge University Press, 1984.

———. New Literacies in Theory and Practice: What Are the Implications for Language in Education? Inaugural professorial lecture, King's College London, 1998.

Strober, Myra H. *Interdisciplinary Conversations: Challenging Habits of Thought.* Stanford, CA: Stanford University Press, 2010.

Sturtevant, A. H. Reminiscences of T. H. Morgan. *Genetics* 159 (2001): 1–5.

Tannenbaum, Frank. The University Seminar Movement at Columbia University. *Political Science Quarterly* 68 (1953): 161–80.

Taylor, Charles. Interpretation and the Sciences of Man. *Philosophical Papers*, 3–51. Cambridge: Cambridge University Press, 1985.

Taylor, Mark C. *Crisis on Campus: A Bold Plan for Reforming Our Colleges and Universities.* New York: Knopf, 2010.

Teichgraebner, Richard, III. Beyond "Academicization": The Postwar American University and Intellectual History. *Modern Intellectual History* 8 (2011): 127–46.

Thomas, William. The Heuristics of War: Scientific Method and the Founders of Operations Research. *British Journal of the History of Science* 40 (2007): 251–74.

———. Operations Research vis-à-vis Management at Arthur D. Little and the Massachusetts Institute of Technology in the 1950s. *Business History Review* 86 (2012): 99–122.

———. Selling Operations Research: An Historical Perspective. *OR/MS Today* (October 2004): 1–7.

Thomas, William, and Lambert Williams. The Epistemologies of Non-Forecasting Simulations: Part I. Industrial Dynamics and Management Pedagogy at MIT. *Science in Context* 22 (2009): 245–70.

————. The Epistemologies of Non-Forecasting Simulations, Part II: Climate, Chaos, Computing Styles, and the Contextual Plasticity of Error. *Science in Context* 22 (2009): 271–310.

Tilly, Charles. *As Sociology Meets History.* New York: Academic Press, 1981.

————. *Big Structures, Large Processes, Huge Comparisons.* New York: Russell Sage Foundation, 1984.

————. *The Vendée: A Sociological Analysis of the Counter-Revolution of 1793.* Cambridge, MA: Harvard University Press, 1964.

Tilly, Louise A., ed. Problems in Social History: A Symposium. *Theory and Society* 9 (1980): 667–82.

Triplet, Rodney G. Harvard Psychology, the Psychological Clinic and Henry Murray: A Case in the Establishment of Disciplinary Boundaries. In *Science at Harvard University: Historical Perspectives,* ed. Clark A. Elliott and Margaret Rossiter, 223–250. Bethlehem, PA: Lehigh University Press, 1992.

Turner, James. *Language, Religion, Knowledge, Past and Present.* Notre Dame, IN: University of Notre Dame Press, 2003.

————. *Philology: The Forgotten Origins of the Modern Humanities.* Princeton, NJ: Princeton University Press, 2014.

————. *Religion Enters the Academy: The Origins of the Scholarly Study of Religion in America.* George H. Shriver Lecture Series in Religion in American History. Athens: University of Georgia Press, 2011.

————. Secularization and Sacralization: Speculations on Some Religious Origins of the Secular Humanities Curriculum, 1850–1880. In Marsden and Longfield, *Secularization of the Academy,* 74–106.

Turner, James, and Paul Bernard. The "German Model" and the Graduate School: The University of Michigan and the Origin Myth of the American University. *Rackham Reports* (1988–89), 5–52. Abridged in *History of Higher Education Annual* 13 (1993): 69–98.

Valenza, Robin. *Literature, Language, and the Rise of the Intellectual Disciplines in Britain, 1680–1820.* Cambridge: Cambridge University Press, 2009.

Vallas, Steven Peter, and Daniel Lee Kleinman. Contradiction, Convergence and the Knowledge Economy: The Confluence of Academic and Commercial Biotechnology." *Socio-Economic Review* 6 (2008): 283–311.

van der Steen, Wim J. Interdisciplinary Integration in Biology? An Overview. *Acta Biotheoretica* 38 (1990): 23–36.

————. Towards Disciplinary Disintegration in Biology. *Biology and Philosophy* 8 (1993): 259–75.

van Helvoort, Ton. Institutionalizing Biochemistry: The Enzyme Institute at the University of Wisconsin. *Journal of the History of Medicine and Allied Sciences* 57 (2002): 449–79.

Varela, Francisco J., Evan Thompson, and Eleanor Rosch. *The Embodied Mind: Cognitive Science and Human Experience.* Cambridge, MA: MIT Press, 1991.

Vettel, Eric J. *Biotech: The Countercultural Origins of an Industry.* Philadelphia: University of Pennsylvania Press, 2006.

Veysey, Laurence. *The Emergence of the American University.* Chicago: University of Chicago Press, 1965.

Vidich, Arthur J. The Department of Social Relations and "Systems Theory" at Harvard: 1948–50. *International Journal of Politics, Culture, and Society* 15 (2000): 607–8.

Wahl-Jorgensen, Karin. How Not to Found a Field: New Evidence on the Origins of Mass Communication Research. *Journal of Communication* 54 (2004): 547–664.

——. Rebellion and Ritual in Disciplinary Histories of U.S. Mass Communication Study: Looking for the "Reflexive Turn." *Mass Communication and Society* 3 (2000): 87–115.

Waring, Stephen P. Cold War Calculus: The Cold War and Operations Research. *Radical History Review* 63 (1995): 28–51.

——. *Taylorism Transformed: Scientific Management Theory since 1945*. Chapel Hill: University of North Carolina Press, 1991.

Warner, Michael. Professionalism and the Rewards of Literature. *Criticism* 26 (1985): 1–28.

Watson, James D. *The Double Helix: A Personal Account of the Discovery of the Structure of DNA*. New York: Atheneum, 1960.

——. *The Molecular Biology of the Gene*. New York: W. A. Benjamin, 1970.

Watson, James D., with Andrew Berry. *DNA: The Secret of Life*. New York: Knopf, 2003.

Watson, J. D., and F. H. C. Crick. Molecular Structure of Nucleic Acids. *Nature* 171, no. 4356 (Apr. 25, 1953): 737–38.

Weingart, Peter, and Nico Stehr, eds. *Practising Interdisciplinarity*. Toronto: University of Toronto Press, 2000.

Wertsch, James V. *Vygotsky and the Social Formation of Mind*. Cambridge, MA: Harvard University Press, 1985.

Williams, Raymond. *Communications*. London: Penguin, 1962.

——, ed. *Contact: Human Communication and Its History*. London: Thames & Hudson, 1981.

——. *Culture*. London: Fontana, 1981.

——. *Marxism and Literature*. Oxford: Oxford University Press, 1977.

——. *Materialism and Culture*. London: Verso, 1980.

——. *The Politics of Modernism: Against the New Conformists*. London: Verso, 1989.

——. *The Sociology of Culture*. New York: Shocken, 1981.

——. *Writing in Society*. London: Verso, 1983.

——. *The Year 2000*. New York: Pantheon 1983.

Wood, Stephen, Alison Geldart, and Richard Jones. Crystallizing the Nanotechnology Debate. *Technology Analysis and Strategic Management* 20 (2008): 13–27.

Wuensch, Bernhardt. Bernhardt Wuensch: An Interview Conducted at the Dibner Institute, 9 January 2001. *History of Materials Research*. Dibner Institute for the History of Science and Technology, California Institute of Technology, 2001. http://authors.library .caltech.edu/5456/1/hrst.mit.edu/hrs/materials/public/Wuensch_interview.htm.

Young, Christobal. The Emergence of Sociology from Political Economy in the United States, 1890 to 1940. *Journal of the History of the Behavioral Sciences* 45 (2009): 91–116.

Yoxen, Edward. Giving Life a New Meaning: The Rise of the Molecular Biology Establishment. *Sociology of the Sciences* 6 (1982): 123–43.

Zalta, Edward N., ed. *The Stanford Encyclopedia of Philosophy*. Stanford, CA: Metaphysics Research Lab, Center for the Study of Language and Information, Stanford University. http://plato.stanford.edu/.

Zuckerman, Solly. *Beyond the Ivory Tower: The Frontiers of Public and Private Science.* New York: Taplinger, 1971.

———. *Monkeys, Men, and Missiles: An Autobiography, 1946–88.* London: Collins, 1988.

———. *Scientists and War: The Impact of Science on Military and Civil Affairs.* New York: Harper & Row, 1967.

INDEX

Page numbers in italics indicate figures and tables.